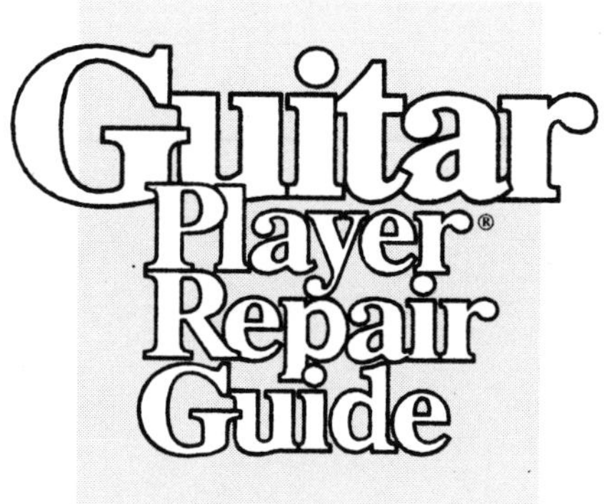
Guitar
Player®
Repair
Guide

Guitar Player® Repair Guide

How to set up, maintain, and repair electrics and acoustics

by Dan Erlewine

GPI Books
San Francisco, Cupertino, Atlanta, Boston, Chicago, New York, Brussels

GPI Books

Miller Freeman Publications,
500 Howard Street, San
Francisco, CA 94105

ISBN: 0-87930-188-0
Library of Congress Catalog
Card Number: 90-83120
Printed in the United States of
America

95 94 93 92 91 90
5 4 3 2 1

Dedication

Dedicated to Ken O'Boyle and Ralph Erlewine,
and with my thanks to Joan, Meredith, and Kate—with love.
Also thanks to:
Tom and Teresa of Tom Erlewine Design—because of you the book looks great!
David Vinopal and Jon Loomis—for helping me over my writing hurdles.
Jas Obrecht, the greatest editor a guy ever had and a patient amigo.
Bryan Galloup's Guitar Hospital in Big Rapids, Michigan, where many of the photos were taken. And to all my customers: thanks for breaking your guitars!

Editor
Jas Obrecht
Design/Illustration
Tom Erlewine
Production Supervision
Teresa Hogenson

Photo Credits

Page 37–39: Brian Blauser, Athens, OH
Page 116: Al Blixt, Ann Arbor, MI
All other photos by Tom Erlewine.
Thanks to the following companies for providing the instruments shown at the start of each chapter:
Page 1: Klein Custom Guitars
Page 3: Robert Steinegger
Page 17: ESP Guitars
Page 45: Santa Cruz Guitars
Page 59: Paul Reed Smith Guitars
Page 67: Fender Musical Instruments
Page 91: Gretsch Guitars
Page 113: Gibson Guitars/Elderly Instruments
Page 115: MV Pedulla Guitars
Page 135: CF Martin Guitars
Page 147: Rickenbacker Guitars
Page 175: Fender Musical Instruments
Page 189: Erlewine Instruments
Cover: Les Paul courtesy of Pat Edwards

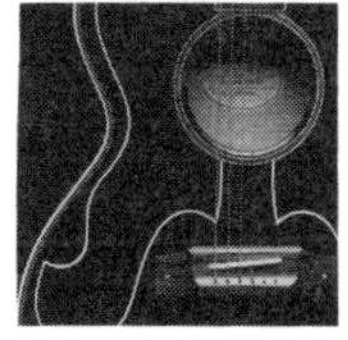

PART 1 SET-UP AND MAINTENANCE

GETTING STARTED

ELECTRIC ADJUSTMENTS

ACOUSTIC ADJUSTMENTS

NUT WORK

FRET WORK

TUNERS AND TREMOLOS

more...

PART 2
ACOUSTIC AND ELECTRIC GUITAR REPAIR

FINISHES

ACOUSTIC REPAIRS

GUITAR ELECTRONICS

MISCELLANEOUS REPAIRS

TOOLS AND SUPPLIES

Foreword

Among material objects on this earth, few possess the mysterioso voodoo of the guitar. From the moment we first pick it up, there's something about its feel, its look, its heft, that whispers—or screams—to us. Before long this intriguing stranger becomes a friend, even an extension of ourselves, and we feel the urge to nurture it, to take care of it, to caress it. Or maybe to rip out its pickups, bolt a whammy bar on there, and spray it with metalflake green enamel.

We can't keep our hands off the guitar. If we're not playing it, we're polishing it, adjusting it, altering it, or wondering about it. Why does it buzz when I bend a string? Would it get more sustain with a brass nut? How come it doesn't play in tune anymore?

Whether you want simply to maintain your guitar in performance-ready shape or hot-rod it into a radical new incarnation, Dan Erlewine is the ideal guide, guru, and godfather. He's a player, he's an extraordinary repairman, and he gets to the point.

Erlewine's credentials run deep. He was co-founder of Erlewine Instruments and proprietor of Dan Erlewine's Guitar Hospital in Big Rapids, Michigan, and is currently the author of *Guitar Player*'s popular Repairs & Modifications column, as well as Director of Technical Operations for Stewart-MacDonald's Guitar Shop Supply in Athens, Ohio. He's also produced several acclaimed how-to videos.

This is a collection of his *Guitar Player* columns, and far more than that, too. It's the product of thousands of hours spent hunkered over wounded guitars, a smoking soldering iron in hand. It's the product of experimentation and improvisation, endless hours poring over books and manuals, consultations with top repairmen, and countless weekend seminars, trade shows, and lutherie conventions. In short, it's the life work of a talented craftsman who loves his work. You'll find the good advice that all guitar owners need to know, plus loads of up-to-minute tips on new-generation whammies, finishes, acoustic pickups, and a whole lot more.

Over the years Dan's clients have included gifted, demanding players like Mike Bloomfield, Clarence White, Otis Rush, Johnny Shines, and Ted Nugent. Jerry Garcia owns one of his Strat-style electrics, and Albert King was pictured on the cover of *Guitar Player* with Lucy, the V-shaped electric blues machine that Dan custom-built for him.

Dan Erlewine has helped all these players and many more to get the most out of their guitars. Now it's your turn.

Tom Wheeler

Tom Wheeler
Editor
Guitar Player Magazine

Introduction

Every guitarist wants an axe that plays easily, stays in tune, looks and sounds good, and is set-up correctly, right? And when things go wrong, important repair decisions must be made. Who'll fix *your* guitar? Should you get a second opinion? Since 1985, my *Guitar Player* column Repairs & Modifications has looked at guitar repair and set-up from many angles. This book updates those columns for the '90s, condensing and organizing them into a manual for guitar players and repairmen. It teaches do-it-yourselfers to fix guitars, helps players keep their axes sharp, and gives advice that will help you choose a good repair shop when the chips are down.

The Set-Up and Maintenance section is for players of all levels. Beginners suspect that learning to play is easier on a well-set-up guitar, and they're right. Professionals discover that by personally setting up their own guitars, they finally realize every inch of its potential–but only after making such fine adjustments as "intonation" and "action." The Acoustic and Electric Guitar Repair section is for everyone—take what you need. Fellow repairmen are sure to find new tricks of the trade, and players: just *knowing* about guitar repair may keep you from the heartbreak of seeing your guitar ruined by inexperienced hands.

PART 1
SETUP AND MAINTENANCE

Install strings correctly, and they'll stay in tune

Learning to tune a guitar or electric bass isn't easy—especially if you're starting out. It's hard enough, in fact, that you'll want to know for sure that your guitar isn't working against you and causing tuning hassles that could be avoided. Outside of your ear, training, and playing experience, several factors determine whether or not your guitar can get in tune and stay there: the shape of the nut and bridge saddle(s), the quality and condition of the tuning keys, and how the strings are installed. Here are several tips that could help you out.

Many tuning woes are psychological. You *think* you're out of tune when you're not (I know because I suffered from this for years). At some point you must quit worrying about it and have *fun* playing. Once you get your guitar right, have confidence in your ear!

First off, the nut's string slots must not be too deep, and the slots shouldn't pinch the strings: This could cause a string to return flat after a string bend, and may produce a catchy, "chinking" sound as you tune. And attention to detail must be given to any notches or grooves in an electric guitar's bridge saddles, as well. Be sure they're well-defined (but not too deep), smoothly rounded, and gradually tapered to the saddle's peak. In other words, each end of the string's "speaking length" must have a clean, neat contact point. Adding a tiny drop of lubricant such as Tef-lube, Vaseline, or powdered graphite at each of these points makes good sense, too.

Although I'm a firm believer in keeping vintage instruments stock, I also know that replacing the tuning keys may be necessary. Your local music store can help you find exact tuner replacements (some retrofits have all the same hole spacings, but better gears and a finer gear ratio). Be sure to save the original parts!

If "vintage" isn't an issue with you, installation of replacement tuners with locking string-posts will eliminate a great

Some string brands sound better and tune easier than others, but you have to make the choice. Try all the major brands, using your favorite string-guage set, and expect to take a year or so finding what's best for you.

deal of tuning hassles. In some cases, the stock tuners' mounting holes will show after installing replacements—however, a good repairman can make these almost invisible. In fact, if you're not particularly skilled in guitar work, you'd be wise to have most tuners installed by a pro, unless the tuners are exact retrofits. Locking tuners are available from Schaller, Sperzel, and Gotoh. Ask your dealer about them.

With stock, non-locking tuners, how you install the strings may be the key to tuning troubles. With unwound strings (and sometimes a light, wound *G*), I run the string through the slot, pull it toward headstock center, loop it back underneath the string, and then up against the post, thus wrapping it against itself as seen below. This "locking tie" is more difficult with the thicker wound strings. Some people do it, although it can cause kinks, slipping, and string breakage in the heavier wound strings. Try it and find out.

For many wound strings, especially the lighter *D*, *A*, and some low-*E* gauges, make the first wrap *over* the string as it comes through the post, and the other wraps *under* as shown here. With heavier gauge *A* and low-*E* strings—especially on acoustic sets—just run the string through the post and make all the winds downward. We'll leave the number of string winds on each post up to you, but make them tight and neat.

If you have locking tuners, run the string through the post hole with the string in a natural, straight line. Hold it taut, not tight, while you tighten the string-clamp. Then, in less than a turn, you'll be at pitch. Locking tuners make sense, and I won't be surprised to find them as standard equipment on many guitars before too long.

ONE FINAL TRICK...

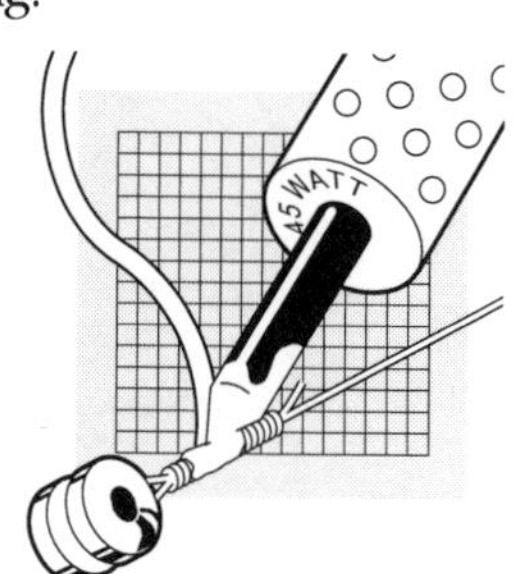

Here's one final trick that's a bit of work if you change strings often (and a labor of love if your repairman does it for you). Using a hot soldering iron with 60/40 resin-core solder, tin each string's wrapping at the ball end. This keeps it from slipping or tightening like a hangman's noose at the tailpiece. "Tinning" is the process of lightly pre-coating an electrical lead with solder and letting it cool before making the final solder joint. Well-tinned string wraps should shine like silver, and never be gloppy or heavy with solder. The use of a 40–45-watt iron will enable you to get on and off the string in a flash, without overheating it. The low-wattage (15–25-watt) hardware store soldering irons will not work as well.

Note: Don't do any soldering on, over, or near your guitar! Molten solder drips,

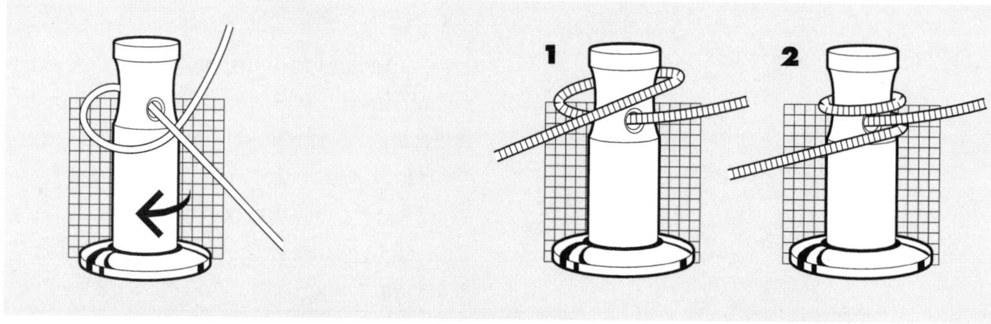

Installing an unwound string (left):

1 Pass string through slot in post.
2 Loop it toward center.
3 Bring the string end back up under the string and begin winding. String will be held tightly against post.

For wound strings:

1 The first turn wraps the string over itself.
2 Second turn wraps underneath.

splatters, and spits—and can make a beautiful finish look horrible. It's not good for your eyes, either, so wear safety glasses!

Cleaning the finish

Cleaning and polishing a guitar is the most basic maintenance task of all, and every player should know how to go about it. Maintaining a new instrument's clean good looks is simple if you keep it up from the beginning. But the lucky player who "discovers" a vintage piece that's perfect except for a finish that's been dulled by years of sweat, dirt, and exposure to bar-room smoke and the elements may need the helpful information in these pages.

Guitar finishes become dirty and hazy because dirt particles come to rest on the finish, which always has a thin film of oil on it no matter how often you clean it. Some of these oils come from your body, while others become suspended in the air from cooking, manufacturing, pollution, etc. The oil and dirt creates a "build" on the finish, which hardens in time and is quite tough to remove. When you remove the dirt, because of its abrasive qualities, you could be removing the finish too! That's why using the right cleaning technique is important.

The tools needed for cleaning and polishing new or used guitars are few, simple, inexpensive, and easy to use: Clean soft rags are the most important tool, and depending upon the situation you may also need any of the following: naphtha, liquid guitar polish, "swirl-mark remover," liquid abrasive cleaner, warm water, and elbow grease. First, I'll describe each cleaner and explain why it's used, and then follow with a few cleaning tips. As you'll see, lemon oil and silicone products are to be avoided.

EVERYTHING YOU'LL NEED...

■ Clean, soft rags head the list. With several rags and plenty of time, you can clean the dirtiest guitar without polishes or cleaners, although polishes and cleaners help you do a faster, better job. The three best cleaning rags are: used, well-cleaned baby diapers, cotton T-shirts, and 100% cotton flannel. The soft rags that many manufacturers imprint with their company logo and include with a new instrument are made from flannel. You can also buy a yard of flannel at any fabric store for $3.00. Most other rags and fabrics are too coarse for delicate guitar finishes.

■ Naphtha (lighter fluid) is a great, all-around guitar cleaner. It's a de-greaser for finishes, pickguards, fingerboards, bridges, tailpieces, and metal parts of all kinds. Used lightly on a rag, it won't harm a delicate lacquer finish, and certainly not polyurethane or polyester finishes. Naphtha leaves a flat, dry haze on a finish, but it's generally used first in the cleaning process, so guitar polish or a dry rag brings the sheen right back.

■ Guitar polish. The creamy stuff in the little plastic spritz jars is a *cleaner* because it's a liquid with an extremely fine abrasive. The liquid washes, and the abrasive lifts dirt. It's a *polish* because there's wax in it that protects as well as shines. The right polish won't scratch a finish. Martin makes a good polish/cleaner, and you can trust them to recommend something safe for high-quality guitar finishes, especially lacquer.

■ Swirl-mark remover is similar to liquid polish, but without the wax; it's actually a cleaner with an extremely mild abrasive. Swirl-mark remover is used in the auto industry for the final polish of newly-sprayed finishes. A good brand is Mirror Glaze #9—it's a delicate, excellent cleaner that even without wax leaves a nice shine.

■ Liquid cleaners are light-duty buffing compounds that are made with a mild

If you would rather not use chemicals to clean your guitar, try the moist-breath trick or use a saliva-moistened rag wrapped around your fingertip.

Remember: Don't rub your guitar down too much, even with just a rag. Polishes are more gentle than cleaners, and be very careful when working on old finishes!

abrasive, but no wax. Cleaners are best for dirtier finishes, since the absence of wax allows unlimited cleaning time without the wax drying (along with the dirt) at every polish-stroke. The abrasive is coarser than swirl-mark remover or guitar polish, so it does a good job of removing heavy dirt build-up. Cleaners won't leave scratches, but as soon as the dirt lifts, switch to a milder polish or swirl-mark remover—you don't want to rub away more finish than needed! Two good cleaner brands are Mirror Glaze #7 and Martin Seynour's Buff-eez #6355.

■ Lemon oil, while not on the list, is highly touted by some as a polish for guitar finishes, but I avoid it because it feels as though I'm wiping kerosene onto the finish. I believe that lemon oil works its way into and under the finish, especially on older vintage instruments with a lovely checked patina; this could cause the finish to lift and the wood to become saturated with oil—possibly dampening tone. Lemon Pledge should not be used on guitars!

■ Silicone is definitely not on the list, but it's added to some polishes and cleaners. Polishes or cleaners with silicone should be avoided! ArmorAll, which has silicone, is used by many music stores to keep guitar cases looking spiffy, and they shouldn't use it. Lacquer, glue, stain, and all sorts of guitar repair items just don't get along with the slippery aftermath of silicone, and subsequent repairs to an instrument exposed to silicone will be a hassle.

■ Warm water and elbow grease need no introduction, so on with the work.

Polishing is what you do to a guitar that isn't really dirty, and the process doesn't have to involve *polish* at all. A clean, dry rag may be all you need to keep a new guitar's finish in shape by wiping off sweat and oil before they get a chance to build up and oxidize. Occasionally use the liquid guitar polish for its protective wax coating. Be sure to wipe, vacuum, or blow off any *gritty* particles from your finish; otherwise you'll drag them around on the surface, causing scratches you'll never get out!

Polishing an extremely dirty guitar doesn't make sense. You don't polish dirty instruments; you clean them first and *then* polish. Since guitar polish is also a cleaner, it takes care of both jobs at once if the finish isn't too bad. But cream polish also puts a nice shiny film on top of the dirt if you're not careful. And with polish *or* cleaners, it's easy to get in a situation where you just move the dirt around without transferring it to your rag. Remember, getting dirt off the surface of the finish and onto your rag is the object! There's a knack to getting dirt to transfer,

especially on older guitars where it's heavily oxidized. Here's how you do it:

CLEANING

Take a 4" x 6" section of a clean, dry rag, fold the corners into the center, and grab the rag like a "knuckle-ball" (bunch the corners and loose parts into your palm, so that the fingers and thumb are pinching the rag into a ball shape–see photo). In the finishing world this ball of cloth is known as a tampon, and it's used for French polishing, which is the art of applying a shellac finish by hand-rubbing. This ball of cloth is a good tool for cleaning and polishing your finish. Use it with polish, naphtha, or cleaner, or use it clean and dry.

There are no strict rules for cleaning, but I generally start out with a rag dipped lightly in naphtha, since it breaks down grease and sticky residues. What naphtha won't remove, a polish or cleaner will. *Note: Naphtha is a petroleum product, and you should wear plastic gloves and safety glasses when using it. Work in a well-ventilated area and keep away from sparks, electric heating coils, or open flame.* Give the whole instrument (or any area to be cleaned) a light wiping with naphtha before switching to a polish or cleaner.

After the naphtha-wash, use polish or cleaner (depending on the situation) and work small (4" to 6") areas at time. As the dirt starts to loosen or "move," pick it up onto the face of your tampon with a quick upward twist of the wrist. When one side of the rag gets loaded, switch to a clean part; otherwise you'll put the dirt right back onto the finish. Remember, the finish, rag, *and* dirt are all warm from the friction of rubbing, which allows the dirt to lift away from or return to the finish. Another cleaning trick is to move the dirt off to an edge, where you can pick it up easier.

Let's look at a typical cleaning job. Let's say the top edge of your Les Paul is sticky and showing some dirt where you rest your arm or picking hand. This type of hazy build-up can usually be removed without polish, using only a clean dry rag, so always try the dry rag first! Rub lightly in either a straight or circular pattern (circular motions blend in best). If you're not getting the dirt onto your dry rag, pour a dab of polish onto the rag's face or directly onto the finish, and continue rubbing following the directions on the bottle (some polishes are wiped on and left to dry, some are rubbed off immediately). Or try this hi-tech method for getting normal haze and dirt to lift from a finish: Get very close and blow your warm, moist breath on the area until it fogs up, then quickly polish off the dirt; it'll transfer to your rag.

Vintage guitars must be given special consideration. Often the "moist breath fog" is the best technique for extremely thin finishes that are riddled with finish-checks, since you don't want to work polish or cleaner down into these crevices. A *light* naphtha wiping is okay—"light" meaning that you tamp off the wetness onto another rag and wait until the naphtha starts to evaporate before wiping.

Warm water has its place in cleaning vintage instruments. If I use water, it's only to *dampen* the rag, which is wrapped tightly in one thin layer around my index finger. Sometimes a barely damp rag can be a big help in removing dirt or haze from a vintage piece where you're afraid of working any petroleum-based chemicals onto a checked finish. You must be cautious of working water into a crazed finish, so it's a judgment call. Use the same light French polishing motions that you used with the tampon, just barely hitting the surface to pick up the dirt. And I hope this won't gross you out, but when nothing else works, saliva (spit!) can often dissolve the weird globs or specks fused to a finish! Of course, I'd never use spit on a customer's guitar—only on my own instruments.

Beware of soft finishes! This rare phenomenon occurs with lacquer, varnish, or the shellac-based French polish, which was used on most instruments made before the 1930s. It's still used today on many of the world's finest classical guitars. Have you ever sat in a nice wooden-armed chair and felt that sticky gummy surface that wants to stick to your skin? When you *know* that if you dragged your fingernails along the finish they'd be loaded with a sticky, grimy sludge, that's a soft finish.

Finishes get this way because there are natural plasticizers (triglycerides) in your body that transfer through the skin—especially your hands. Lacquer "breathes," allowing moisture and certain chemicals such as polishes, cleaners, and plasticizers to migrate through it. The plasticizers go right through the finish and make the wood their home. Once a finish is softened this way, there's no cure except letting it totally air-dry, and even then it may never be truly hard. The most common area of a guitar to suffer from this is the part of the body where you rest your arm when playing, although you may also see it on the neck or other areas. It's most common on dirty guitars that weren't cared for, since the oxidized dirt acts as a lid, holding the plasticizers down in the finish so that they can't migrate. If your axe suffers from these symptoms, I'm sorry, but don't try to rub, clean, or polish it away—you'll just make it worse.

POLISHING SCHEDULE

How often should you clean and polish? When should you use a liquid cleaner or guitar polish rather than just the dry rag? I haven't seen your guitar, so I can't tell you. I can only offer you some ideas:

Polyurethane or polyester (catalyzed) finishes seem impervious to anything; I suppose you can clean and polish them until the cat comes home. New guitars with lacquer finishes (ask your dealer what type of finish is on the instrument) can stand up to cleaning or polishing quite well, since the finish surface is smooth and unchecked. Remember that lacquer breathes, so when you rub polish onto your finish, you're rubbing it *into* the finish as well. This regular polishing helps keep the finish new-looking, and makes it less prone to checking.

I always clean a used guitar right after I buy it, since I haven't found a clean one yet, and I don't like someone else's dirt on my guitar. When possible I clean with naphtha and a dry rag, but usually liquid cleaner is necessary. I don't use guitar polish, because I'm afraid of the wax penetrating a thin vintage finish (but that *may* be good—I've never been sure). After that, I may not use polish or cleaner on a used guitar for up to three years—sometimes longer. But I will use a dry rag every few months or whenever it gets sticky. I really can't get too excited about rubbing any sort of liquid *on* to—or *in* to—a thin vintage guitar finish, since I don't want to do anything that might change them. Polishes are for new guitars.

Polishes and cleaners are formulated to penetrate a finish and rejuvenate it to a certain extent, adding essential nutrients that keep it softer, more flexible, and shinier. Polishes and liquid cleaners therefore help to avoid a dried-out finish that may become overly brittle and perhaps flake or chip. However, I happen to *like* a dried-out finish on a 1930s Martin. And I *like* a dried-out finish on a 1940 Gibson J-45!

I believe that dryness and brittleness are part of the reason old guitars have killer tone, so if you clean and polish a new guitar regularly, after 30 years the finish is less likely to be dry and brittle. It will look better, but maybe not sound as good as a guitar that was dry-polished somewhat regularly but liquid-polished or cleaned only occasionally.

You now know enough about finish cleaners and techniques to handle anything. Keeping the strings and fingerboard clean after playing is important, too—that's what's coming up next, and it's not nearly so complicated!

Cleaning your fingerboard

The condition of a guitar's fingerboard is essential to the quality of music that the instrument can produce. Although a warped neck or bad frets are often best left to your repairman, there is one job that any player can perform—cleaning the fingerboard. A clean fingerboard produces clean-sounding music; dirt, however, hampers smooth slides and fast playing. Dirt can also destroy, slowly rotting the wood and eventually causing the frets to work loose. Whenever I change strings, I always give the fingerboard at least a quick cleaning. Here's how to do it:

KEEPING YOUR STRINGS CLEAN

When grime and dirt have built up along the edges and between the frets and the wood itself, the board requires a thorough going over. However, if you wipe your strings clean after playing, there will be less chance for dirt to build up. Years ago, when I was playing six nights a week alongside a pedal steeler, I noticed that he would clean each string at the night's end, using a special rag called a Blitz cloth, which was commonly used by the Army to polish brass. I started using one, too, and found it to be the greatest string cleaner I'd ever seen. An Army surplus store was the only place I could find them. Now, however, they're available in music stores as String Care by Blitz.

When cleaning strings after playing, be sure to lift each one out of the nut slot and off the bridge insert (saddle), wiping that part of the string with your Blitz cloth, too. You may have to tune down slightly to do this. Once the strings are wiped and still a little slack, get in between them with a soft rag (not the Blitz cloth) and wipe down as much of the fingerboard as you can reach to get rid of the sweat. Use your thumbnail to press the rag into the crevice along the fret/fingerboard joint. This is where the wood can rot, since the fret slot (the groove that a fret is set into) has exposed end-grain and will soak up any sweat and dirt that works its way under the fret. If you clean your strings faithfully—especially after a night's playing in a club or a long time practicing—your fingerboard should only require an occasional polish with a soft, dry rag.

A Blitz cloth is great for cleaning the strings after a night's playing. Look for *String Care by Blitz.*

REMOVING HARDENED DIRT

Cleaning a filthy fingerboard is a different story. *(Note: If you own a guitar with a maple fingerboard, read the caution below before proceeding.)* If the grime has accumulated for a long time, it may have hardened, and steel wool alone won't remove it. In this case, you'll have to scrape it off carefully. Be sure to use a scraper that won't cut into the wood and leave marks. I generally rely on my trusty 6" stainless steel ruler. Use its sharp corner to get next to the fret and the long edge to scrape dirt off the fingerboard (left). You can buy these rulers at most hardware stores for a dollar or two. Follow the scraping with 0000 steel wool to remove any dirt missed by the scraper (below).

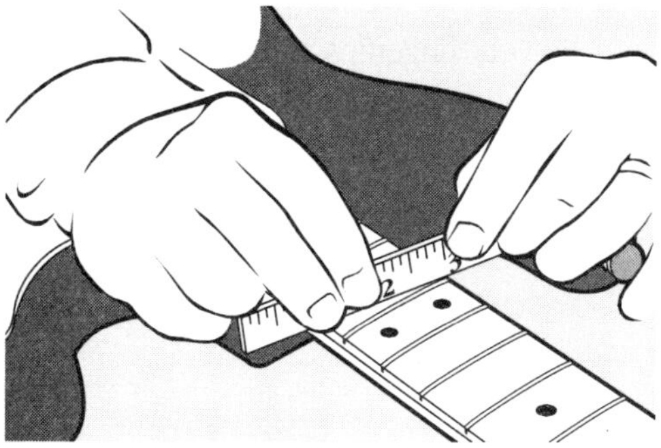

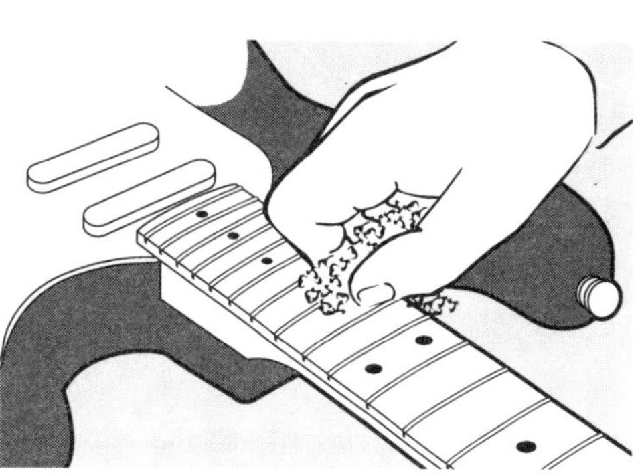

POLISHING WITH STEEL WOOL

Pinching a ball of steel wool the size of a golf ball between your thumb and index finger, push down with your thumbnail against the fret/fingerboard joint. This will clean right into that corner and smooth and polish the fret edges. Then use the steel wool to polish the wood between the frets by rubbing back and forth in a lengthwise direction with the grain. Since you've already steel-wooled the fret/fingerboard joint, the fret is partially polished. To finish the job, press your index finger on the steel wool again and rub back and forth on top of the fret to bring it to a good shine. This fret polishing is done along the fret's length (crosswise to the fingerboard).

With this task completed, you may have a burnish mark that goes in two different directions. If this bothers you, use a fresh ball of wool to rub the entire fingerboard—wood and frets—in one direction, going with the grain along the entire fingerboard's length. Now the fingerboard should have a smooth, satiny look. Remember: Use only 0000 steel wool; nothing else is fine enough.

Don't get carried away with polishing to the point where you wear out your fingerboard and frets. Be reasonable, and just don't be a total slob.

CONDITIONING THE FINGERBOARD WITH OIL

After the cleaning operation, I occasionally apply a dab of lemon oil to the fingerboard, using a soft rag. I'm not advising you to use the oil every time you change strings; use it only when the board is in need of it—several times a year for the average player. If the wood seems exceptionally dry after cleaning, it needs the lemon oil. Likewise, don't use steel wool each time you clean. Don't overdo it. I change strings every week when I'm playing on the weekends, but since I always clean my strings after the last set, I need to steel-wool the board only every month or so.

Caution: If you own a guitar with a maple neck—i.e., a maple fingerboard with a clear finish—don't use steel wool or a scraper on the finish! Use only a soft rag. For hardened dirt, dip the rag in a little lighter fluid if necessary; mostly, you will need a lot of elbow grease. Tape off the lacquered wood with masking tape while cleaning the fret/fingerboard edge or polishing the fret tops. You may use steel wool on the finish, but it will remove the gloss and leave a dull, satiny finish. Some customers ask me to "degloss" their fingerboards, since they feel it leaves the surfaces more comfortable to play.

Here's a tip for tool lovers. Take a rubber squeegee (a 3M product used to remove water when wet-sanding cars, available at auto supply stores), and cut out a piece $1\frac{1}{2}$" by $2\frac{1}{2}$". With a small round file, make a slight groove on the long edge. Wrap the steel wool pad around your new homemade fret polisher, and use it as you would your finger (left). This tool saves a lot of wear on your fingertips and thumbnail when working the steel wool.

Neck evaluation and truss rod adjustment

When customers arrive at my shop wanting a guitar neck adjustment, it's usually for one of the following reasons: the strings buzz on the frets, the "action" is too high (that is, the strings are too far from the fingerboard), or the strings buzz on the upper frets along the "tongue"—the part of the neck that overlaps the body. Sometimes the notes aren't playing clean, or the instrument has intonation problems despite having a perfectly calibrated bridge. All of these are symptoms of a neck that needs adjustment. With an understanding of the basics of neck rod adjustment, action evaluation, and fingerboard relief, you're on your way to getting your instrument to play its best.

First, "sight" the neck. Place your nose close to the headstock and look along the fingerboard edge from the nut toward the body. You're looking for straightness, humps, bow, high frets, and back-bow. Check the bass and treble sides separately; I wear safety glasses in case a string breaks. Neck sighting gives you the first of two views that are important to proper neck rod adjustment. The other view is from the side, using a 12" steel straightedge (try using a 12" combination square from a hardware store; the handle slides off, leaving only the blade). Bass players need a longer straightedge, so in this case try a rafter square, which has two edges—the shortest edge is 16" long and perfect for a bass. Always use your favorite gauge of strings, tuned to pitch, for these adjustments.

Most neck rod adjusting nuts are located at the end of the headstock or recessed into the body at the very end of the fingerboard. Some acoustic guitars are adjustable under the fingerboard, accessible through the soundhole. Find the adjusting nut and choose the proper tool for turning it; this will usually be an Allen wrench, socket/nut driver, or a Phillips or flat-bladed screwdriver.

Set the guitar on a workbench or tabletop with the neck unsupported. I let the neck hang off the table edge and weigh down the body with a padded, heavy counterbalance; a large beanbag is great. You'll need a light source in the background for the straightedge test. Set the edge of your straightedge on the fingerboard between the third and fourth strings. It should run from the 1st fret past the 12th, covering the major portion of the fingerboard. If your table is of

Some necks say "steel-reinforced," but have no adjustment. You can often straighten these by using heat to soften the glue joint before bending the neck into the desired position. Commercial neck heaters are available.

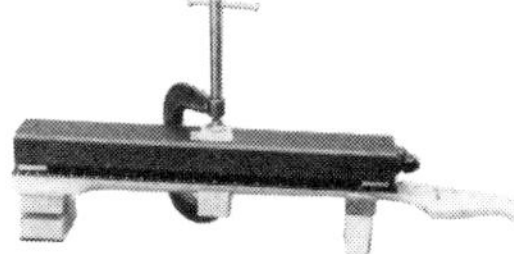

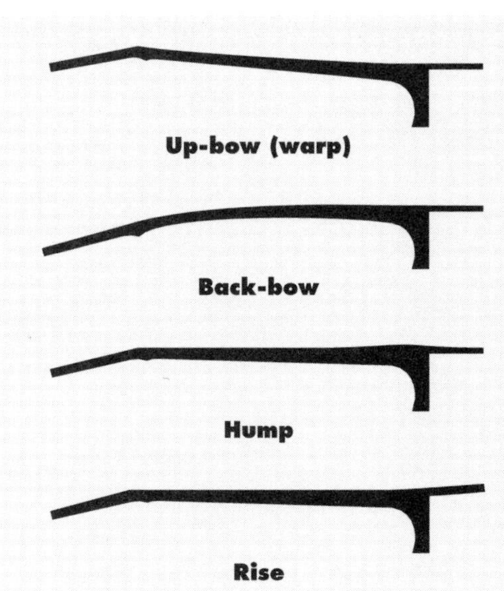

Up-bow (warp)

Back-bow

Hump

Rise

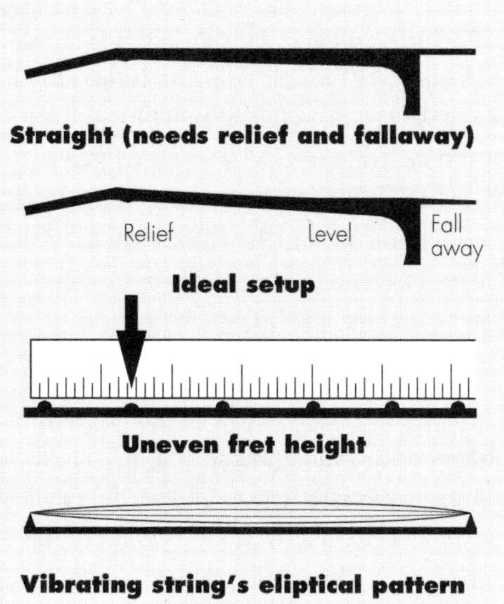

Straight (needs relief and fallaway)

Ideal setup

Uneven fret height

Vibrating string's eliptical pattern

average height, get down on one knee as you compare the fingerboard to the rule. Hold the rule with one hand and, while adjusting the rod with the other, watch the light under the rule.

If the rule "rocks" on the fingerboard due to back-bowing, loosen the nut counterclockwise, watching for the fingerboard to come into level contact with the rule. If the strings are pulling the neck up in a slight curve, slowly tighten the nut clockwise until the rule rests flat on the first 12 frets. If you loosen it now, the curve or bow will return to the fingerboard. This slight, controlled bow is called "relief." Remember how relief looks. When tightening a nut, it's best to first loosen it completely, then slowly tighten until it begins to grab and feel snug without exerting any real pressure. From this point, a quarter- to a half-turn usually straightens a neck against string pull. It would be rare to take a full turn. A telltale squeak is a sign that you are at the limit—stop there! Over-tightening can strip the nut, neck rod threads, or both.

Some necks adjust more easily than others. If you sense trouble or have doubts, find a trained person and pay the small cost for an adjustment. Ask if you might look on. A trained hand knows immediately if the rod is working properly.

Some electric basses (due to the necks' extreme length), certain Japanese imports, inexpensive guitars, and yardsale specials can be a struggle to adjust. With the strings tuned down slack, completely loosen the truss rod by turning counter-clockwise, and force a slight back-bow into the neck. Now tighten the adjusting nut and then tune back to pitch. There is a good chance that the neck will remain straight, and by loosening the rod slightly, you can gain relief.

Relief is the key to low string height, few buzzes, and comfortable action. If you pluck a string, especially a wound one, the greatest movement occurs toward the center of the string length. The string moves in a long, elliptical pattern. By loosening the rod, the fingerboard gains relief, allowing a greater clearance for the vibrating portion of the string between the fretted note and the bridge. This is helpful on open strings near the nut and the first few frets, where the strings are lowest. Different amounts of relief are necessary for different players' styles. Experiment with adjusting the rod and raising or lowering the bridge to see what happens.

After gaining a bit of relief (1/32" from the 1st to the 12th frets is often plenty), rest the rule on the 1st through 12th frets, and then slide it one fret at a time toward the body. The rule should drop from fret to fret as it moves, indicating that each fret is slightly higher than the one following it. I look for relief to run from the 1st fret to the 12th. As you slide the rule, it should level out around the 10th fret, remaining flat until the 15th. It's good when the remaining frets (from the 15th on up) fall slightly away from the rule. I call this "fall away," and it ensures clean notes in the upper register. You must have relief, leveling-out, and fall away. A hump at the neck/body joint or a rising (instead of a falling) tongue can be corrected later when we level the frets prior to dressing. Right now, you're learning to evaluate your own fingerboard and look for problems. You should be proud of yourself! You're now able to adjust your own truss rod—no small task.

Setting intonation and compensating the bridge saddle on electrics or acoustics

Repairmen are often asked: What is the reason for the different saddle positions on tunable bridges? Why are some bridge saddles closer to—or further from—the nut? These questions bring up the subject of string-length compensation (most players refer to this as "setting the intonation"). This is an essential part of setting up both acoustics and electrics.

To begin with, accept the fact that fretted string instruments are accurate to a point, but they are not perfect and never will be. With its fixed frets, the guitar is known as an even-tempered instrument. The fret scales are compromised so that a guitar plays closely in tune in all keys but, alas, never perfectly in any. Many players can hear the out-of-tune notes in the even-tempered scale, and it drives them (and their repairmen) crazy.

At best, proper intonation is a compromise among many factors, and at a certain point guitarists must accept some degree of out-of-tuneness or give up the guitar. Too often the repairman doing the set-up is blamed for not getting a guitar "perfect," and that's not fair.

Setting the intonation on guitars with adjustable bridges (which even some acoustics have) is simple. All that's needed is a small Phillips or flat-bladed screwdriver or an Allen wrench. If a string sounds sharp at the 12th fret, you move the saddle back—away from the nut—to increase the string length. If a string sounds flat at the 12th fret, you move the saddle forward—towards the nut.

Understanding the compensation factors that determine the need for intonation adjustment is a different story, and here experience is the best teacher. Your repairman is doing a lot more than turning a couple of screws. He's checking to be sure that all other important adjustments—such as truss rod, action height, fret dressing, nut and bridge saddle shape, string gauge, etc.—have been made before setting the intonation. That's important!

Many factors contribute to the need for compensation, and most are confusing to the layman (and occasionally to repairmen, as well!). I like things simple, so here are some basic facts regarding string-length compensation as I understand it. Any combination of these factors can cause a need for compensation, so try to look at the whole picture.

When we discuss a string length, or scale, we're referring to the distance from the nut to the center of the saddle when measured in a direct line down the center of the fingerboard and body. A Strat, for example, has a scale length of 25 1/2". But the bridge saddles may actually measure as much as 1/8" to 3/16" more than that, depending on string height, string gauge, etc. This addition to the string's length at the saddle is known as compensation. A basic understanding of compensation is necessary before the guitar's intonation can be properly set. Compensation is the adjustment that adds to the mathematical (measured) scale of a guitar by altering the string length at the bridge saddle when setting the intonation, thus making a guitar note properly. Compensation has been accounted for at the factory on most non-adjustable acoustic guitars and is seldom a serious problem. Most acoustic guitars with problems suffer from *sharpness* and need to be compensated by adding to the string length. Occasionally, though, flatness caused by over-compensation is found on acoustics on which the bridge has been installed out of position.

Pressing a string down into the fingerboard too hard can cause a sharping problem, especially with tall frets. This can be corrected by changing your playing style.

Although acoustic guitars are compensated at the factory, do not expect them to play in perfect tune, intonation-wise. This job must be completed after the sale to suit the individual player's needs, and it's governed by the many factors listed here.

When setting intonation, we try to get a string to play the same note when fretted at the 12th fret as when played open, only an octave higher. In theory, the distance from the nut to the 12th fret is the same as the 12th fret to the saddle, since the 12th fret is the octave and halfway point of the scale (scale length equals the measurement from the nut to the 12th fret, times two). In practice, the string length must be increased to offset the sharpness that results when the string is pressed down during playing (remember—the mathematical distance of the scale runs in a straight line from the front edge of the nut to the saddle's center). The string, however, runs up and away at an angle to this line. When pressed to the frets during playing, it becomes stretched, which causes it to go sharp. This is the basic, and the most easily understood, explanation of the need for compensation. Add it to the factors below, and you'll see why the seemingly simple job of setting the intonation can cause you to tear your hair out before you finally take the guitar to your repair shop, so they can tear their hair out!

STRING-LENGTH COMPENSATION

The closer the strings are to the fingerboard, the less compensation is needed, since the strings go sharp less when pressed. However, guitars with lighter strings generally need more compensation than heavier ones, since as string tension decreases (going from heavier-gauge strings to lighter), the compensation need increases. Therefore, the lighter the strings and the lower the tension, the more need for compensation. So, perhaps one cancels out the other. Confusing, but you can prove it for yourself by trying this test:

Using an electronic tuner, check your guitar's intonation on the low-*E* string at concert pitch. Retune the string to *D*. It will intonate sharper, which indicates the need for more compensation, or added string length. That's why the modern electric player who uses .010 strings or lighter often searches far and wide to find a repairman to set the intonation.

Wound strings need more compensation than plain ones. Because of their extra weight and slower, low-pitched vibrations, wound strings need more clearance from the fingerboard to avoid buzzing. The extra clearance is gained by raising the string height from the fingerboard for wound strings. This increase in height causes the strings to go sharp more than the unwounds when depressed. This is why bridge saddles slant toward the bass side on steel-string acoustics or electrics.

I like the term "speaking length" of a string. Franz Jahnel's comprehensive *Manual Of Guitar Technology* refers to the mathematical string length as the "true" length (the measured distance from nut to bridge saddle), and the actual vibrating length as the "playing," or speaking, length. A string, especially a wound one, doesn't actually start vibrating, or speaking, until it gets a certain distance from the nut or the saddle. So, part of the string's "length" (in terms of sound) is always lost—yet another reason for compensation.

Notice that classical guitars have saddles with no slant (see illustration at right). Why? The wound strings have a stranded core rather than a solid one, and sharp out at a rate similar to that of the solid nylon treble strings. Classical strings have a more even tension across the fingerboard than steel strings. Therefore, they require close to the same amount of compensation per string, and in general are more uniformly spaced from the fingerboard in terms of height. You may find saddles that have been slightly filed off-center (compensated) under the *B* and *G* strings on some classicals.

Instruments with longer scales need less compensation than shorter-scaled ones because the longer string must be tighter in order to reach the same pitch as a shorter string. Thus the longer string is less apt to be sharp when fretted and needs less compensation (the higher the tension, the less a string goes sharp). The two most common scales are long and short. Long scales are 25½" or thereabouts (these include Strats, all their clones, and many Gibsons; Martin uses a 25.4" and Guild a 25⅝", but we lump them all together as long scale); short scales are 24¾" or thereabouts (Gibson Les Pauls, ES-335s, smaller Martins at 24.9", etc.). Classical guitars have long scales.

Acoustic guitars have a tendency to shrink over the years because they're made of wood. Add to this the effect of the string's pressure pulling the nut and saddle toward each other, and you lose a bit of string length—measured in thousandths of an inch, perhaps, but it all adds up. Even solidbody electric guitars suffer from string tension compression on the neck and lose some string length over the years.

Differences in a string's gauge, quality, and physical makeup drastically affect intonation. As a string's cross section

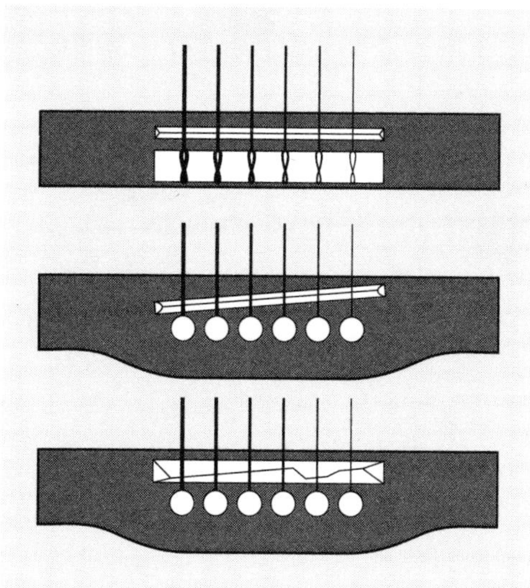

(diameter) increases, so does the need for compensation, hence the saddle slanting toward the bass side on steel-string guitars. A string's elasticity, or ability to return to its original position after being deflected, is also a compensation factor, and stiffer strings go sharp more when depressed. You'll have to try many brands and gauges before settling on the right strings for you. The sad thing is that by the time you find the set you like, your playing style may have evolved to a new level, requiring that you start all over again! (*Frets* magazine published in-depth string articles in the Nov. '84 and Aug. '87 issues; check your library for back issues.)

The standard factory-installed slant saddle on acoustic guitars is usually sufficient compensation to please most players. The saddle slants approximately ⅛" in a 3" length, toward the bass side (middle drawing at left). If the intonation doesn't please you, ask your repairman about a compensated saddle (where a wider saddle blank is inserted and then filed to staggered peaks under the different strings, as in the bottom drawing at left). If you're interested in compensating your own saddle, study the books listed at the end of this section—in particular those written by Don Teeter.

All of these are factors when it comes to setting your guitar's intonation by compensating. Their interrelation is complex, and the slightest change in any factor (especially string height) can throw the whole deal out of whack. Be sure that the important adjustments described earlier have been made before setting the intonation. An electronic tuner is a big help, also. The following approximate compensation is usually added to the scale length of any guitar:

Most electrics and steel-string acoustics—from ⅛" to $^{3}/_{16}$".
Classical saddles—from $^{1}/_{16}$" to $^{7}/_{64}$".
Electric bass—from ⅛" to ¼".

I hope this information helps you to understand how even a top-quality guitar can play out of tune, and why it's sometimes such a tough job getting it right. Support your local repairman.

Special thanks to William Cumpiano and Dick Boak from Martin Guitar's Woodworker's Dream—two expert luthiers who were very helpful with technical information. Woodworker's Dream has a great selection of rare hardwoods and guitar parts, and their catalog is a must for aspiring luthiers.

More information on this subject may be found in Don Teeter's *The Acoustic Guitar, Vols. 1 and 2,* Hideo Kamimoto's *Complete Guitar Repair,* Franz Jahnel's *Manual Of Guitar Technology,* the Guild of American Luthiers' *Data Sheets,* and *Guitar Making: Tradition And Technology,* by William Cumpiano and Jon Natelson. A list of suppliers for these books, and more, is given at the end of this book.

Bridge saddles

What's the major cause of buzzes found on guitars with low action and light-gauge strings?

Your professional guitar repairman causes those buzzes—at least that's what many players seem to think. After trying home remedies and untrained "witch-doctor" repairmen, frustrated customers often show up in a repair shop as a last resort, laying the blame at the repairman's feet for problems caused by low action, light strings, and often less-than-perfect fretwork. Guitarists may hate fret buzz, but not as much as the professional who's expected to get rid of it.

Before taking our vows, we repairmen have learned from experience that a certain amount of buzzing comes with the job—metal strings on metal frets buzz a little. Proper neck adjustment and fret-leveling removes 90% of most buzzes. The remaining 10% should be accepted as normal, and will play themselves out in time. Of course, any buzz can be eliminated by raising the action high enough, but this won't satisfy most players.

One cause of string buzz that's often overlooked, however, is the improper matching of the shape of the bridge saddle's curve to that of the fingerboard. Most steel-string guitars have curved (arched, or radiused) fingerboards, although the amount of radius differs between manufacturers (Martin and Gretsch seem to have the flattest fingerboards). If the bridge saddle curve is significantly flatter than the fingerboard's radius, the middle strings will be closer to the frets than the outer ones, causing buzzes. Correcting this poor saddle adjustment often immediately eliminates buzz, as well as the need for fret-leveling. You'll also find that a properly set-up bridge makes for a more comfortable axe, especially when you play chords. Here's how to make and use a simple tool—a radius gauge—for setting your bridge saddles correctly.

It's not much trouble to make a radius gauge, so if you're unsure about which size you need, make them all and see which fits. The most popular fingerboard radii are: 7¼"—vintage Fender; 9½"—some current Fenders; 10"—Kramer and many replacement necks; 12"—Gibson; and the 16" to 20" range for Jackson, Martin, Gretsch, and others with a flatter fingerboard. I made my radius gauges from Plexiglas, so that they'd last through years of use. Cardboard or thin wood work fine if you're only occasionally setting up your own guitar.

Start with a piece of stiff cardboard or thin wood about 24" long and 1" wide. Draw a center line on this piece and make a mark 1" in from one end—this is your starting point, axis, or center. From your axis mark, measure the correct distance for the radius you want (7", 9", 12", etc.), and make marks accordingly. Next, lay the marked-out strip on a large piece of stiff posterboard (smooth-faced cardboard) and press a sharp pin through the center, pinning the strip to the posterboard below. Now if you poke a second pin through any of the measured

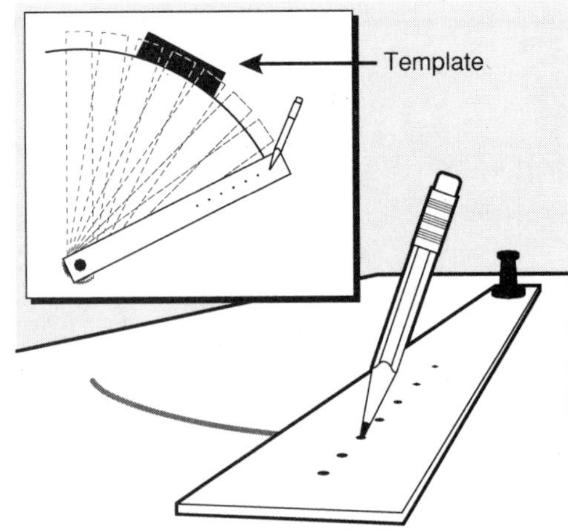

"radius" marks, you can scribe the different radii onto the posterboard as shown above.

The gauges should be 4" in length—or long enough to lay out an acoustic or electric guitar saddle. Cut out the templates with a sharp blade in the shape illustrated by the shaded area in the drawing. Thin wood or cardboard can be hard to sand or shape, so make your first cut accurate. If you do need to custom-fit your gauge to the fingerboard, reinforce the wood or cardboard gauge by saturating it with Hot Stuff original formula super glue. Once it's dried, you'll find that you can carve, file, or sand the thin material much more effectively. *Note: Always wear safety glasses when working with Hot Stuff or any super glue!*

If making a radius gauge is too much trouble, try Stewart-MacDonald's inexpensive two-piece set. Each has four radii: 7¼", 9½", 10", 12", 14", 16", 18", and 20".

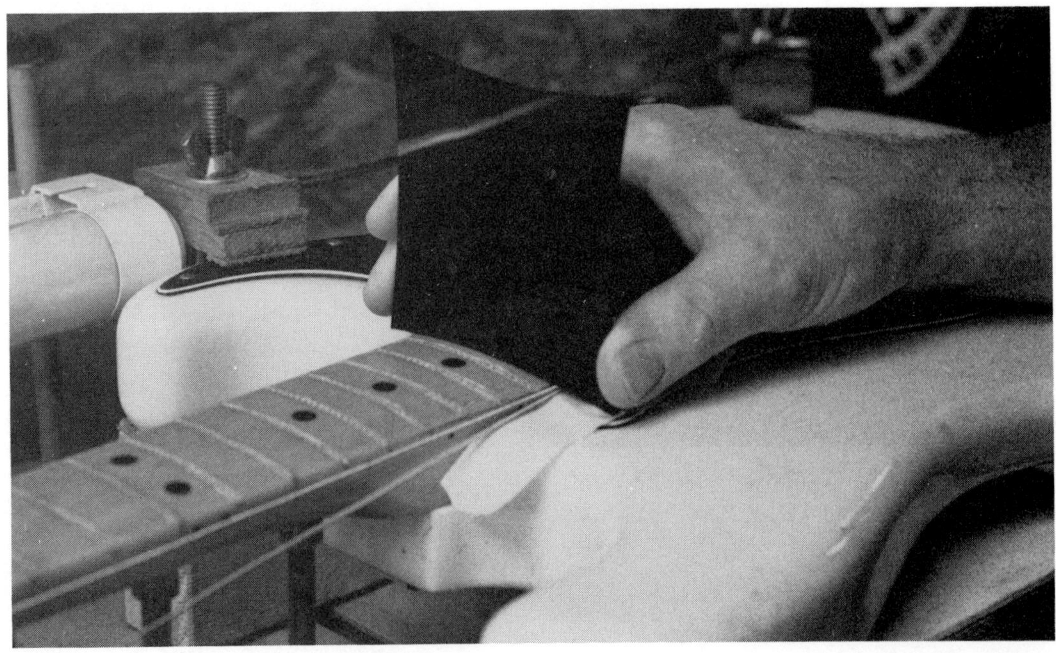

To use the gauge, first sight across your guitar's bridge saddles, lengthwise from *E* to *E*. On most electrics or acoustics, you should see a gentle rise through the *A* and *D* strings, going back down through the *G* and *B* to the *E*. This curve should approximate the fingerboard's curve. Some guitars have a curve built into the bridge (a la Gibson Tune-O-Matic and "Nashville" bridges, etc.), rather than using up/down adjustable saddles. With this Gibson type of bridge, variations on the saddle curve can be controlled by the depth of the saddle slot in each bridge insert, while overall string height is tailored by raising or lowering the bridge's treble and bass sides by adjusting the thumbscrews on either end (see the section on Gibson Tune-O-Matics coming up next). Most Fenders and many of their clones, on the other hand, have saddles that easily move up or down. Take advantage of the adjustment to set your strings exactly to the fingerboard.

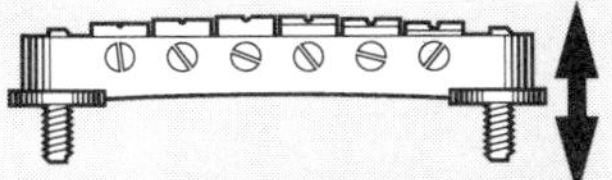

Set the outside *E* strings to the action height that you like (I suggest 5/64" for the treble-*E* string and 7/64" for the bass-*E* string). Using a dial caliper, feeler gauge, or 6" steel rule, measure the gap between the bottom of the strings and the top of the highest fret. Now place your radius gauge on the two outer *E* strings just in front of the bridge saddles, and raise or lower the four middle strings (*A D G B*) until they, too, just touch the gauge—it's really simple. Your bridge saddle curve will now match the fingerboard curve. It may not feel exactly like you want it, but it's the correct starting point from which to personalize your action, and it's much more accurate than relying on your eye.

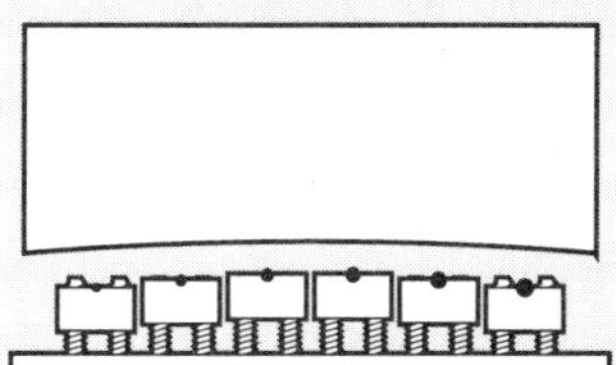

When you sight across the bridge by eye, the curve may look right even when it's not. Often the middle strings are on too flat a curve and close to the fingerboard, causing buzzes. Also, when the saddle curve matches that of the fingerboard, you'll like the feel of the action, especially for chords. Best of all, you'll usually find that you've eliminated that final 10% of annoying string buzz.

Acoustic players may use the radius gauge as a guide for laying out the proper shape onto a poorly shaped saddle, and then filing or sanding the saddle to the correct shape. Saddle making is covered in the Acoustic Adjustments chapter, but I don't mean to sound too casual about the ease with which this saddle shaping can be done—don't screw up your guitar! Take care when removing and replacing the saddle into its slot, and if you lack experience, have the saddle reshaped by a professional.

Whether on acoustic or electric, most saddles are shaped so that the strings gradually rise higher on the bass side. This compensates for the extra thickness of the wound strings and their lower, floppier vibration when struck. For this reason, I consider the perfect matching of the bridge curve as a starting point. Once the proper curve is reached with a low to medium-low action, expect to slightly raise the three lowest strings to get perfect results.

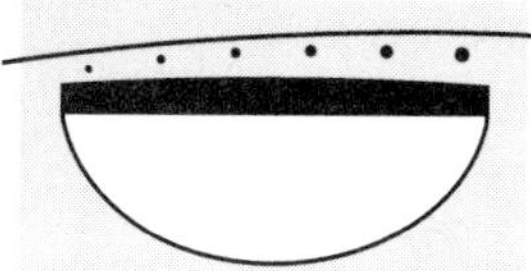

Fitting and replacing Gibson Tune-O-Matic saddles

An electric guitar's adjustable bridge occasionally needs cleaning, lubricating, de-rusting, dusting, fine tuning, and calibrating. The cleaning techniques used on the Strat bridge in the previous section apply to all electric guitar and bass bridges, and not just those made by Fender. Gibson's Tune-O-

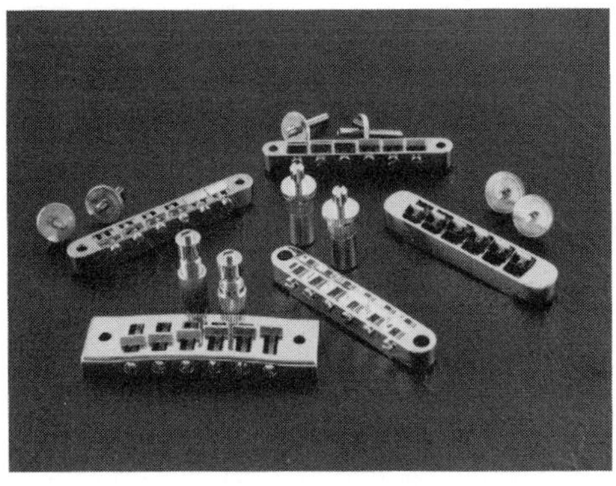

All Gibson bridge parts can be cleaned with lighter fluid and treated lightly with sewing machine oil or Teflon lube.

Matic bridges, however, need certain adjustments that the simple, flat-plate, Fender-style bridges don't. Tune-O-Matics are die-cast, with individual channels for adjustable string inserts. Periodically these bridges need to be dismantled, have their parts cleaned and refit, or be replaced altogether. Here are some set-up and maintenance tips for owners of these Tune-O-Matic–style bridges.

Gibson has offered five different adjustable Tune-O-Matic bridges since the original ABR-1 was first used in 1957: the Three Point, the Top Adjust, the Wide Schaller, the Nashville, and the original ABR-1. Parts or complete bridge assemblies for the Schaller, Nashville, and ABR-1 are currently available; the Three Point and Top Adjust have been dropped, and their parts are no longer available. We'll deal with the bridges and parts that are still offered by Gibson.

■ A wider bridge provides more travel for the saddles. All three of the current bridges are similar in that they raise up or down and their inserts adjust back and forth for intonation. Since the wider bridge offers more travel for the saddles, there is more latitude for setting accurate intonation when it comes to action height and string gauge. The Schaller is the widest, the Nashville in between, and the ABR-1 is the narrowest. With the original ABR-1, if the bridge isn't mounted in just the right spot, getting the correct intonation is difficult. The other two bridges offer more string-length adjustment, so one way of correcting poor intonation is to mount a wider bridge in the same mounting holes used by the ABR-1. Another method is to first plug the ABR-1 stud holes, and then relocate and redrill the stud holes without switching bridge styles.

■ One of the most solid of all the bridge mounts, the Schaller was introduced in '72 as a stock item on SGs, and then Marauders, L5- and L6-S models, and other Gibsons. Its height-adjusting studs screw into heavy steel anchor bushings that are pressed tightly into the top. Older Schaller bridges often suffer from flaked plating and metal deterioration caused by sweat, and it's often necessary to replace the pitted bridge saddles and sometimes the entire assembly. The saddles may appear to be permanently locked in by a machine screw with a slot-head on each end, but they're not! One end of the machine screw threads into the other and is super-glued in place. Since you won't know which end is glued (it's usually the backside, away from the headstock), heat *both* bolt ends with a hot soldering iron (40 to 45 watts) to break the glue joint, and then unscrew the bolts from each other. Replacement saddles for the Schaller come in a set (#10176) and are numbered from 1 through 6. Be sure to install them in the right order!

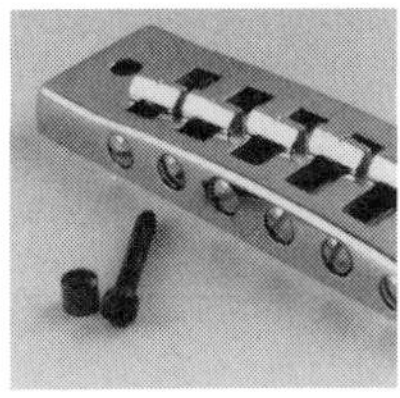

■ The Nashville bridge is the "new, improved" version of the ABR-1. It looks very similar, but it has more travel since it's wider by $\frac{7}{64}$", and it doesn't need a retainer spring to hold the saddles into the bridge body. (Neither the Nashville or the Schaller have the thin wire retainer spring that the ABR-1 uses to keep the saddles from popping out; this is a plus to some players.) It mounts on threaded flanged inserts that are pressed into the body, although the inserts aren't the same as the heavier Schaller anchor bushings. If your guitar is equipped with the Nashville bridge, you may find that the body anchors pull out too easily; in some cases, they want to fall out. I prefer a tighter fit than this for good tone transmission. You can carefully line the hole in the body with epoxy, white glue, or super glue, let it dry, and then refit the bushing. This tiny increase in the walls of the hole usually makes for a tight fit. If it becomes too tight, you need to scrape the walls slightly to remove excess glue. Working with glue—especially super glue—around a finish can have disastrous results, so be careful. A safer way to firm the bushing is to omit the glue, and instead wrap the bushing with Teflon plumbing tape before pressing it in.

Here's a neat trick for Nashville bridge anchors, taught to me by my friend Bob Pettingill of Carrollton, Georgia. Besides being a top-notch guitarist, Bob is a machinist by trade. He put his machining mind to the task of making the loose anchors on his Gibson Les Paul more solid, and here's what he came up with. He took a short (2" to 3") length of 10-32 threaded rod and turned a small section (about ½") of it down in size to .136" in diameter. He then threaded the turned-down part with a 6-32 tap. Next, by carefully measuring to the bottom of the anchor bushing hole in the Les Paul body and carefully trimming the original 10-32 section of his part, he got the new bridge stud to bottom out on the wood at the hole's bottom (above), while leaving the new 6-32 threads above the body surface. Now he can raise or lower his bridge with standard ABR-1 thumbwheels used on the turned-down 6-32 thread section. Going through the anchor bushings and down to the wood, the custom studs are very rigid, appreciably improving the tone and sustain!

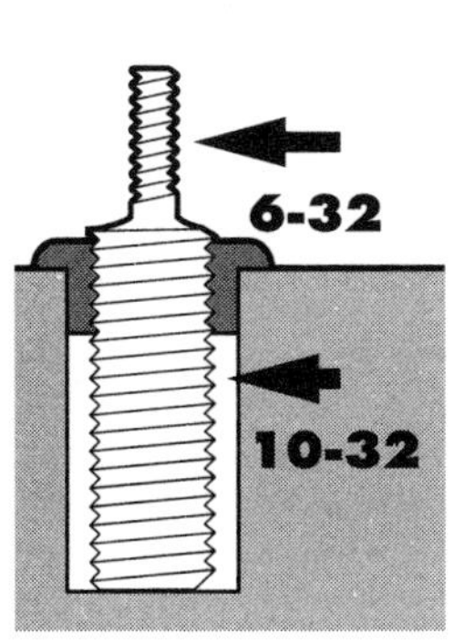

10-32 threaded rod turned on lathe and given a 6-32 thread

■ Unlike most imported copies, all three Gibson bridges are available with saddles that aren't pre-notched. Be sure to specify that you want them this way. The replacement saddles have no notches, either. This allows the player or repairman to individually notch the strings into the saddles for custom string placement. The imported ones—even Gotoh, which I like—come pre-notched, and this is less desirable.

■ To say that the Nashville bridge is new and improved implies that something is wrong with the ABR-1, which isn't really the case. In fact, when properly located for intonation, I prefer the ABR-1, because it's the bridge I grew up with, it looks "right," and it has a certain tone. While the only drawback of this original Tune-O-Matic is its narrower string travel, it does have a few quirks of its own. The ABR-1 retainer spring, which holds the saddle inserts into the bridge body, has a tendency to spring upward and buzz against the strings. You can correct this by pressing or "kinking" the spring downward in between the slotted screw heads with a small screwdriver tip.

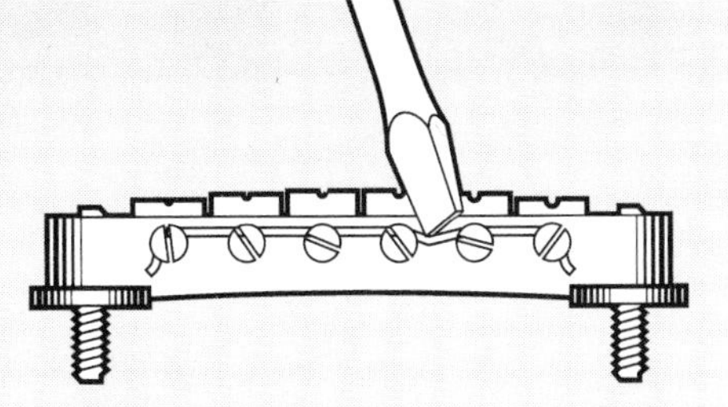

Not all retainer springs cause problems, though, especially on vintage instruments. With the Nashville and Gotoh bridges, you will find some variation of a snap ring or spring clip holding the insert into the bridge body; these must be carefully pried loose before you can remove the bridge screw and saddle insert (the Schaller has a double-ended bolt, as mentioned above).

■ Some owners of vintage Gibsons equipped with the ABR-1 may notice a buzzing problem or strange-feeling action caused by a warped bridge. This isn't common, but I've seen it often over the years. Perhaps the problem is caused not only by metal fatigue, but also by a player resting his hand heavily on the bridge while picking. Sometimes you can flatten out the warp, and sometimes you can't. Don't try it yourself. Take it to a qualified repairman or to a machine shop where the craftsmen are familiar with all the metals and stresses involved. With the bridge supported on each end, an arbor press or C-clamp can be used to gently push in the middle until the warp straightens out. You actually have to press the casting past the original point of flatness to get it to spring back true—a tricky task. Too much pressure or too fast a change can cause the casting to crack, so go easy.

On some current Gibson bridges, parts are metric. For example, new Nashville bridge studs are 5mm x .8mm, not 10-32. Check thread sizes before you start drilling or tapping!

■ On older instruments, especially those that were played hard, the studs that support the ABR-1 bridge have a tendency to loosen, bend, and/or lean forward. The most obvious solution to this is to redrill (enlarge) the stud holes and replace them with modern steel inserts and a modern bridge—either Schaller or Nashville. But this could harm a guitar's resale value, and we try not to alter guitar history, right? Here are *some* of the alternate ways to fix worn stud holes, made possible because the ABR-1 mounting hole spacing is so close to that of the Schaller, Nashville, and Gotoh replacement bridges. As a general rule, they're interchangeable. The hole-to-hole stud centers for the various bridge bodies are: ABR-1, 2.891"; Nashville, 2.926"; Wide Schaller, 2.891"; Gotoh ABR-1 copy, 2.891"; and Gotoh Nashville copy, 2.904". There are exceptions to every rule, so always double-check all measurements before making any changes. You might have a *little* trouble getting the Nashville (2.926") and the ABR-1 (2.891") to interchange; it depends on the individual situation. Also, if you're doing any drilling, tapping, or parts-switching, practice the operations on a scrap block of wood to be sure everything fits!

HERE ARE VARIOUS WAYS ABR-1 BRIDGE STUDS ARE REPLACED:

1 If the wear is minor and the bridge is just a little wobbly, remove the studs and coat the walls of the holes with super glue. This not only increases the hole size, but hardens the thread cut into the wood by the stud. Next "chase" (that is, follow a thread lightly with a cutting tool) the threads in the wood with a 6-32 metal tap to re-cut accurate threads, and again coat the new threads with super glue to harden them. Chase the threads one last time with the tap, and you should have tight-fitting studs.

2 Drill the worn hole to enlarge it, fill it with a hardwood dowel, then drill a fresh hole and install a new stud. Use the 6-32 tap to cut threads into the wood before screwing in the stud. Warning: This drill and plug method is quite noticeable unless you can do a very artful touch-up.

3 Stay with a metal stud-into-wood design like the original, but switch to the Nashville mounting studs without the anchor bushing inserts. These have a larger thread (10-32) than the ABR-1 (6-32), allowing you to quickly and simply oversize the sloppy original hole with a #21 drill bit and then rethread it oversize with a 10-32 tap; this method eliminates having to use a dowel plug. A Nashville bridge stud fits the new hole, but you'll need to find someone with a metal-working lathe to turn the top part of the Nashville stud small enough to fit the ABR-1 stud clearance holes. The thumbwheel attached to the Nashville stud may need turning down a little, too.

4 Using the same oversize tap method, switch not only to the Nashville bridge *studs*, but use the Nashville *bridge*, as well. Again, don't use the Nashville anchor bushings. Mount the new studs directly into the top wood using the appropriate drill and tap listed above.

To get into these drilling, tapping, pressing, and fitting modifications, you're going to need a full drill index with fractional, number, and letter bits, as well as a good assortment of standard and metric taps and dies. You can buy bits and taps one at a time, as you need them. You need a pair of dial calipers, too, and the inexpensive ($25) plastic kind will do fine. Ask your local hardware store for an index that lists the decimal sizes for drills and taps, or check with any good machine shop. If you choose to install the Nashville flanged anchor yourself, note that a "J"-bit fits tight, while a $\frac{9}{32}$" gives a nice press fit. For the wide Schaller anchor bushing, the $\frac{7}{16}$" is a finger-press fit, while $\frac{27}{64}$" is a pretty tight machine-press fit.

Replacing worn bridge saddles is fairly simple, at least mechanically. But once the new saddle has been replaced, cutting a new string notch requires skill and special tools. Many of the techniques in the Nut Work chapter apply to shaping bridge inserts, so look ahead if you wish. Here's a brief rundown on the basics:

Whereas Strat-style bridge saddles don't necessarily require a notch to keep the string in line, the Gibson style does. This is mostly due to the different string angle to the bridge saddle caused by having the separate tailpiece located behind the bridge. I use my nut-slotting files on a bridge although metal saddles are tougher on the tools than the bone, Micarta, or plastic used for nut making. Notch the saddles just deep enough to keep the string from moving to either side as you pick. This should never be more than one-half a string's diameter. Traditionally, the ABR-1 comes with the top three or four bridge saddles facing front and the bottom (*E,A,D*) saddles facing rearward for the best intonation.

However, it's more difficult to shape the saddle peak that faces the rear because of its sharp edge, and I've found that I can often turn the bass side saddles around and notch them like the others and still get good intonation, provided the bridge has been well-placed. If you turn around a saddle that's already notched, you may have to replace it entirely if the notch is out of line. File the string notches with a slight taper toward the front edge, and de-burr any wire edges left on the saddle. Once you set the intonation, the result should be a clean-sounding, accurately intonated string.

Cleaning and de-rusting bridge saddles

At one time or another, most of us run into rusting, dirty, and corroded "adjustable" bridge inserts that no longer move. As a result of wear, sweat, or corrosion, some bridge parts may be beyond repair. But many bridges, inserts, screws, and springs end up being junked unnecessarily when, with a little care, they could most likely be made to work. Here's advice on breaking rust joints, removing caked dirt, and on cleaning, degreasing, and lubricating metal bridge parts in general. I'll use the Fender bridge as my example, since it is both height- and length-adjustable, and therefore requires the most cleaning. Fender and Gibson guitars, however, are not the only prey of the dreaded crud monster. These techniques for cleaning, rust-breaking, and lubrication work on all metal electric guitar bridges, without harming vintage parts.

There are two likely rust problem areas for electric bridge inserts: at the height-adjusting screws that raise and lower the insert and control the string height, and at the length-travel screws that are used for

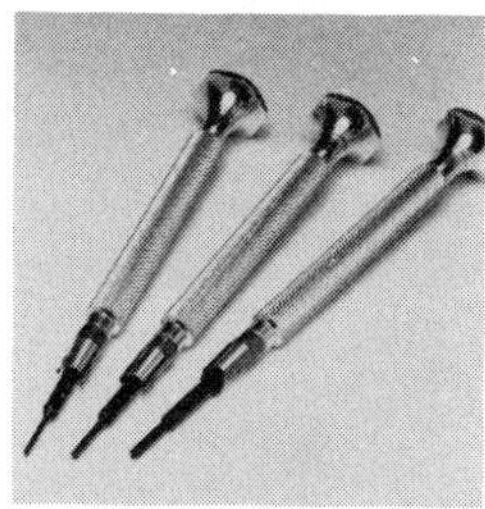

I just can't say enough about the screw extractors. For years, I didn't even know they existed—gotta keep my eyes open!

setting the intonation. Of course, the basic bridge body, which is usually a stamped or die-cast housing that the inserts sit on or in, needs to be cleaned, too. This is much easier to do if you can remove the parts first.

Remove the bridge from the guitar (with a Tele, gently remove the pickup first). Then, before trying to disassemble any parts, pre-clean them with lighter fluid. Pour some into a jar and apply a wet coat to the inserts, screws, and springs with a small, stiff brush or toothbrush. *Remember to wear safety glasses, and work in a well-ventilated area!* You may submerge the whole bridge in naphtha if you wish. After the parts have soaked awhile, remove as much crud as possible with a dry toothbrush. An air compressor can be a great help in blowing out dirt, if one is handy. Next, apply more naphtha with a little light oil added to it—the two mix together, with the naphtha thinning the oil and helping it run down into rusted threads.

Now, before turning any screws, clean the Phillips or flat-bladed screw heads. Remove as much dirt and rust as possible. I use the sharp end of a straightened-out dental probe to scrape the walls; a pin, needle, or sharp X-acto blade also work. Slot heads are easy to clean, but the Phillips type require more work. Often the Phillips' criss-cross slots are partially stripped from removal attempts made when the head was packed with dirt. In this case, even cleaning the head won't allow the screwdriver to get a grip. Screw extractors work best in this situation, or you can try blunting the tip of the screwdriver on a grinder (as in the drawing at left). By shortening the sharpest part of the tip, the screwdriver can then get a grip on what's left of the original slots. Don't fight the hard-caked dirt. Scrape a little out, and then soften the remainder with naphtha. If you're dealing with rust, dab a little Liquid Wrench or WD-40 onto the rusty area. Eventually you'll get the length-adjusting screw to turn, and you can back it out of the insert.

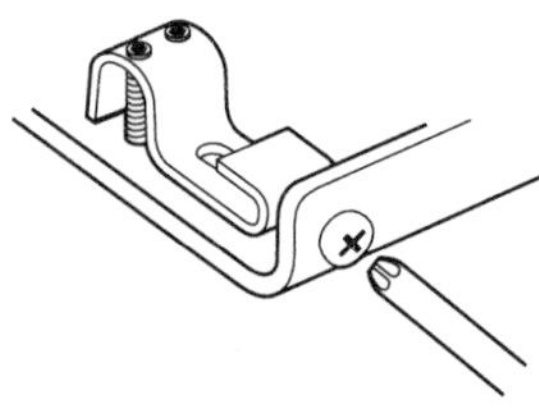

The height-adjusting screws on Fender-type electrics —in particular the Allen-head type—may be frozen with rust and dirt. It takes a very small, sharp tool to scrape the dirt from the screw's six corner walls. Careful soaking and scraping will, nine times out of ten, finally allow your Allen wrench to slide in properly. Don't try to turn the screw until you're sure the wrench is in far enough that it won't cause stripping!

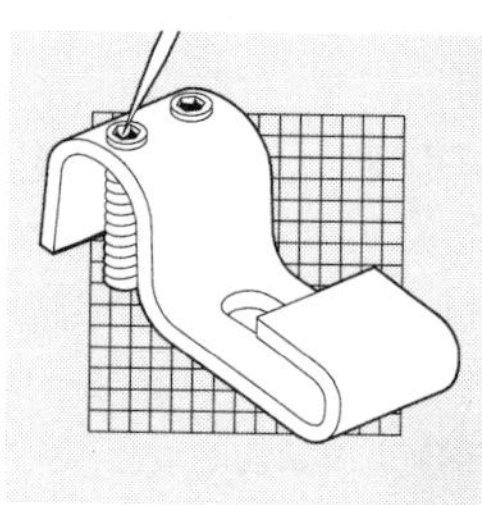

In some cases, even with the wrench well fit into the Allen slot, the screw still won't back out. Try going forward all the way through. If this doesn't work, don't get rough with the part. If the part's free of the guitar, apply a little heat with a propane torch, which causes the parts to expand and contract and often breaks the rusted bond. Do this gently, since overheating could cause premature cracking of the plating, although this has never been a problem for me. *Caution: Be sure that all solvents and explosives are removed from the area, that the part is completely dry, and that there is plenty of fresh air.* If the screw still won't budge, relax and try the following.

With a small pair of Vise-Grip pliers, grip the very end of the screw from the underside of the insert. With the insert clamped or held firmly, remove the part slowly down and through the insert. If a small bit of thread becomes crushed from the grip, either rethread it with a 4-40 thread-cutting die, or leave it alone, re-installing it from the bottom up after it's cleaned. This way the crushed thread won't get hung up in the insert's tapped hole or cause damage to the insert threads.

If your height screw's head is so stripped or rusted that you can't get it to work (and you either can't find a replacement, would rather use the vintage part, or have to play in an hour), try this: With the smallest razor-saw blade (.012") or a .010"-.016" nut-slotting file, file a screwdriver slot on the bottom of the adjusting screw. Use the new slot to help remove the screw for cleaning. Then when you replace the screw, re-install it upside down (slot toward the top). This modification switches the Allen head to slot head, with the part now being adjustable with a screwdriver, like with Tele-style bridge inserts. This works great!

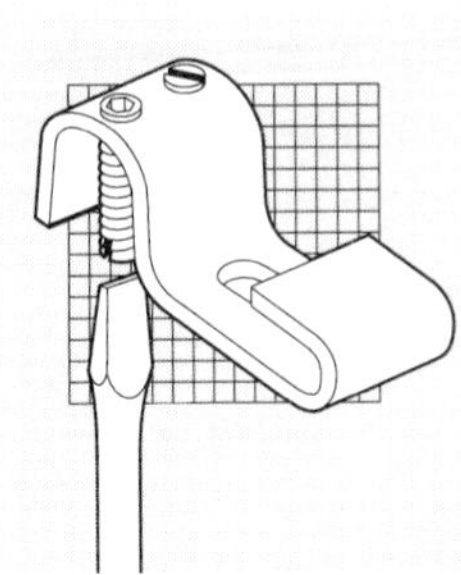

Once all the parts are disassembled, submerge them in naphtha. I like to keep all the parts from each insert together, so they don't get mixed up. Trying using a plastic ice cube tray for this, marking the separate compartments *E A D G B E* with an indelible marker. After a good soaking, dry the parts and brush them well with a toothbrush before reassembly. You probably won't even need to oil the parts to get smooth movement after cleaning, but if they're still a little stiff, lubricate the threads with sewing machine oil, Teflon lube, graphite, etc.

Sometimes the effect of a good cleaning causes a height screw to become so clean that it vibrates loose and allows the insert and string to drop in height, lowering the action. Sometimes this happens regardless of whether or not you've cleaned the parts. If this is your trouble, adjust the insert to the proper height and fingerboard radius, and then back each screw out slightly. Use a toothpick to put a drop of glue on the threads right where they enter the insert itself. Then readjust the screw to the desired position and let it dry. While not actually a bond for metal to metal, the glue will set the threads and stop them from coming loose. A good product for this is the Titebond or Elmer's Carpenter variety of white glue. I've also seen inserts that have a dab of clear silicon bathtub caulk spritzed on the underside around the loose screw. This method is sure-fire, but it might dampen the tone.

When cleaning parts, don't expect every bit of color or rust to disappear. Metal and plating that have been extensively corroded will never appear new. Just try to get the parts functioning again. Once you've reassembled all the inserts and re-installed the bridge, put a very light coating on the threads, using any of the lubricants mentioned earlier. Also, brush the parts off periodically—say, every few months (depending on how much you sweat) or during a change of strings.

Bolt-on necks

What's the most indestructible electric guitar ever built? Many would bet on the Fender solidbody with its bolt-on neck.

When's the last time you saw a Strat or a Tele with a broken headstock or a cracked body? Aside from the basic set-up, fretwork, and occasional electrical maintenance that all electrics require, these guitars can outlast their owners. However, the neck-body joint can be a troublesome spot for bolt-on owners, since its alignment controls the instrument's action and playability. Although attaching a neck to a body by means of four screws sounds simple, by understanding several key adjustment techniques you can get your guitar to play its best. Besides offering advice for vintage Fender owners, these pages on bolt-on necks should be required reading for kit guitar builders about to design and assemble their first instruments, since the biggest problem these new luthiers face is getting the neck set into the body so that the action feels right.

The techniques of filing and chisel-trimming the neck pocket to size can be used for fitting new parts, too. When I get a kit neck and body that fit too tight, I'm happy—I want a snug fit!

The most common adjustment made on bolt-on guitars is the realignment—or shifting—of the neck. This becomes necessary when the strings are falling off either edge of the fingerboard, even when you're playing the simplest of chords. When you're looking at the guitar from the front, the two outer *E* strings should line up equally to an imaginary center line, with neither being closer to the fingerboard's edge than the other. Because Fenders are designed with fairly wide bridge spacing and a fairly narrow fingerboard, the outer two strings are quite close to the fingerboard's edge to begin with. If the neck is even slightly out of alignment, the high- or low-*E* string will lean too close to either edge.

To correct this problem, slightly loosen the four mounting screws. Then hold the guitar in the playing position, edge down, on a table by gripping the body between your chest and one arm. With your free hand, give the neck a slight sideways pull in the direction that you wish to move the strings. Because the screws are only slightly loosened, enough grip should remain to hold the neck in its new position while you retighten the screws. If the neck still remains out of place after you shift it and retighten, you may have to use force to hold it in position while you tighten the screws (this can be tricky if you have only two hands). Some necks can be shifted without even loosening the screws—simply give the neck a quick jerk in the right direction.

A neat trick for keeping a neck in alignment is to slip a piece of metal screen-door mesh between the neck and body. The mesh embeds itself into each surface's lacquer, creating a friction that makes it hard for the parts to shift. This slightly raises the neck's height in the body cavity, so you'll have to readjust the bridge and pickup height.

If the fit between the neck and body is so tight that there's no gap on the side you're shifting toward, you won't be able to move the neck without removing a small amount of wood from the body cavity. If doing this makes you nervous, have a pro do it. But if you'd like to try it, go slowly and carefully. Avoid chipping the finish, removing too much wood, or removing wood in the wrong place. Lay a strip of masking tape on the body close along the neck, with just the right amount of body/finish showing that you feel should be removed. (The arrow in the drawing below shows where wood may need to be removed to provide more room for the neck to move from side to side.)

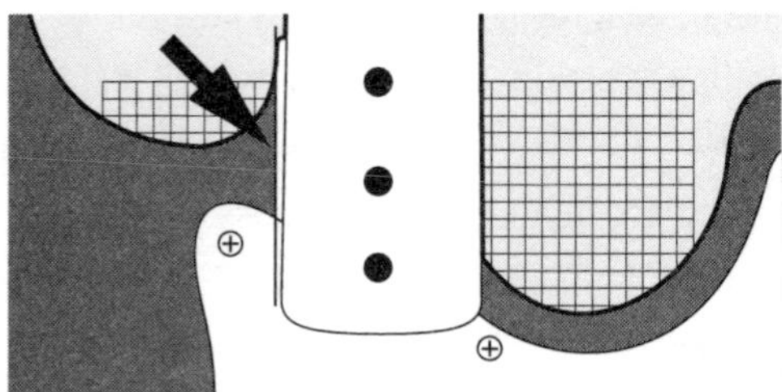

After removing the neck and pickguard, use a smooth file held at an angle to file the paint back to the tape line (see below).

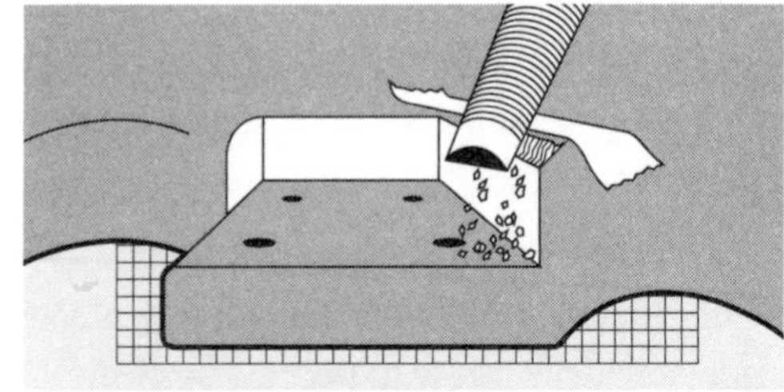

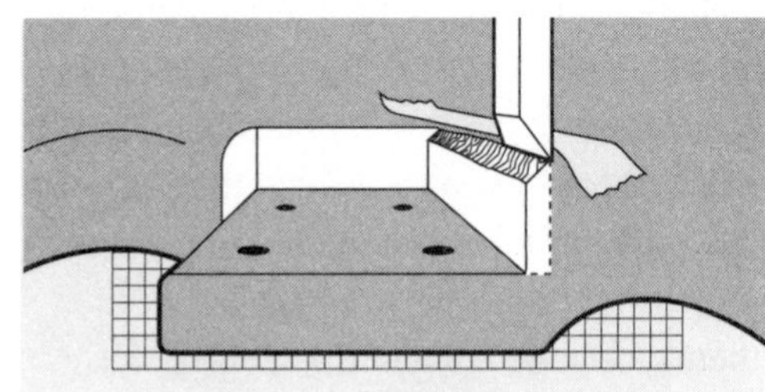

When you've filed to the tape, stop. Switching to a sharp wood chisel held at right angles to the body, pare away small bits of wood until you've removed the proper amount. Use the tape as your guideline as you chisel away the obstructing wood. Avoid touching the paint with the chisel, since paint chips easily. If you have a tight-fitting pickguard, you may have to file a small amount off that, too, before replacing it.

A bolt-on guitar's string height and action is controlled by adjusting the height of the bridge inserts. It's not uncommon to find a guitar with strings that are too high, even though the inserts are as low as they'll go. You may also find one that has strings that are too low, despite the bridge pieces being in their highest positions. In either case, the neck needs shimming. Begin by setting your bridge pieces at the center of their height travel (up or down) and at a radius that conforms comfortably to the fingerboard radius. This way, you'll still have room for fine-tuning the inserts' height after shimming the neck angle.

Shimming involves slipping a piece of thin cardboard, wood, or plastic between the neck and cavity. Very little thickness makes a drastic effect in the action. Time-proven shims have been fashioned from playing cards, matchbook covers, and flatpicks. I once even found the tooth of a comb used as a shim. If your strings are too high, making playing uncomfortable, put the shim at the

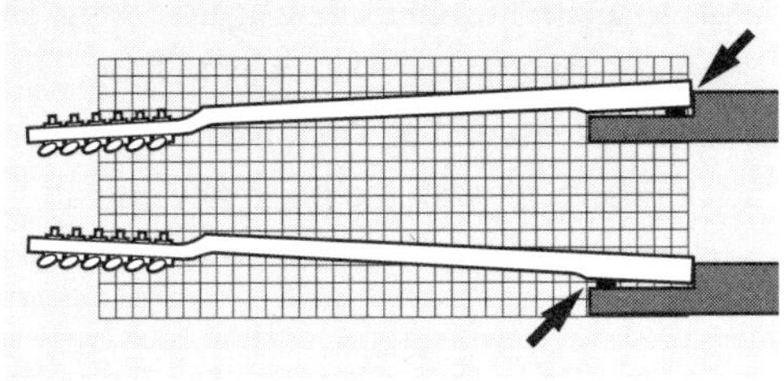

end of the neck that's closest to the inside end of the body cavity. If the strings are too low, place the shim towards the front of the cavity just ahead of the two forward mounting screws. Proceed by trial and error—put in the shim, refasten the neck (holding the guitar as level as possible to prevent the shim from sliding out of place), and retune to pitch. It's best to start off using a matchbook cover; one thickness usually works, and two thicknesses are usually too much. Experiment, and remember that screen-door mesh not only keeps the neck in place, but makes a good shim, as well. You should have a comfortable action when done.

Now we'll look at stripped neck holes, mounting a new neck by drilling your own mounting holes, and making a tapered, full-size wood shim.

FULL SHIMS, KIT NECKS, AND STRIPPED SCREW HOLES

Let's take a look at how to install a full-size, gap-filling shim between the neck and body, at ideas for mounting a new kit neck on a body you already have, and at tips for repairing stripped mounting-screw holes in a vintage neck.

First, here's a reference for the drill sizes used in this section: For the four holes in the neck that the screws thread into, use a #30 bit. For the clearance hole where the screw passes through, use a 3/16". A #13 bit is used to enlarge worn-out neck holes in preparation for plugging. Use whatever snugly matches the body clearance holes (usually a 3/16" bit) as a centering marker for layout of the four holes in the new neck.

The small neck shim described earlier leaves an air space between the joint. However, many players feel that they suffer a loss of tone unless firm contact is maintained between the neck and body, so they prefer a full-size shim that fills the entire gap. I make these full shims out of mahogany, which is soft enough to shape easily and hard enough to transmit tone. Before making the *full* shim, first shim the neck with a small sliver of wood as described earlier. This gives you the proper thickness of the new shim at its thickest part. Measure this test shim with a pair of calipers that read in thousandths of an inch, or use a feeler gauge. Next, trim and fit a piece of cardboard to fit the cavity perfectly (see drawing, next page). Hold it in place and mark out the four holes from the rear, using a 3/16" drill bit. Use this cardboard template to mark out the mahogany shim.

Here's an important bolt-on tip: When the neck's removed, seal its four neck-mounting screw holes with a drop of lacquer. This keeps moisture from absorbing into the tongue, which can cause a swelling or hump in the wood and frets. Try using a plastic pipette to add a drop of lacquer to the hole, and use an empty pipette to suction out the excess lacquer so the hole can dry. While you're at it, remove the truss-rod nut and seal up the hole bored into the end of the neck, too.

Start with a piece of wood that's $\frac{1}{8}$" thick and slightly larger than the cardboard template. The grain should run lengthwise with the body. Trace around the template onto the wood, drill out the holes, and file, whittle, or sand to shape. Use a few strips of

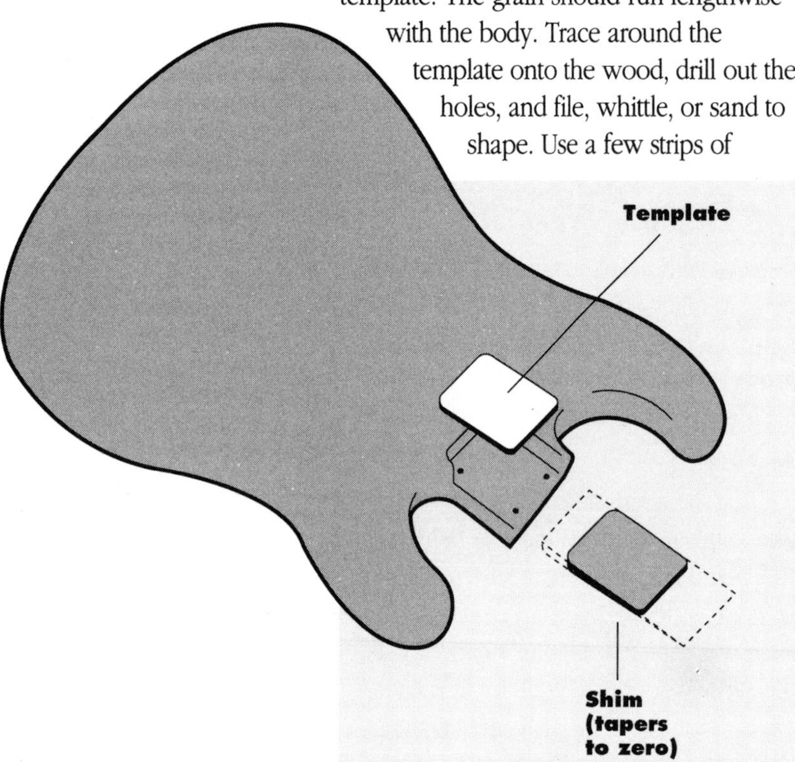

double-stick carpet tape to fasten the shim to a piece of hard, flat wood that's as wide as your shim and about 6" longer. This will be your backing support while sanding, with the extra length serving as a handle. Before sanding, lay out the taper of the shim with a sharp pencil, matching the thickest measurement that you made earlier at one end, and tapering the other to nothing. This line is your sanding guide. Hold the support block with the attached shim in one hand while using your free hand to press it against a belt sander equipped with a medium- or fine-grit belt. Although it may take several tries, you'll end up with a sliver of mahogany matching your thickest measurement at one end and feathered out to zero at the other end—very fragile!

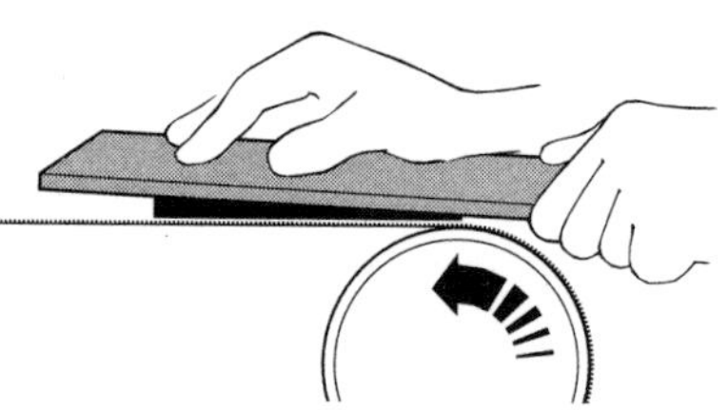

Replacement or kit necks often arrive without the four mounting screw holes already drilled. I prefer ordering them this way, since it allows me to really line things up properly. Set the neck into the cavity and clamp it while you install the two outside *E* strings for alignment. When the strings are in line with the fingerboard's edges, run the proper drill bit ($\frac{3}{16}$") through the hole. You'll feel when it touches the neck. Rotate the bit with your fingers to start the holes; then remove the neck and change drill bits to a #30. Finish drilling the holes, using the starter marks as a guide.

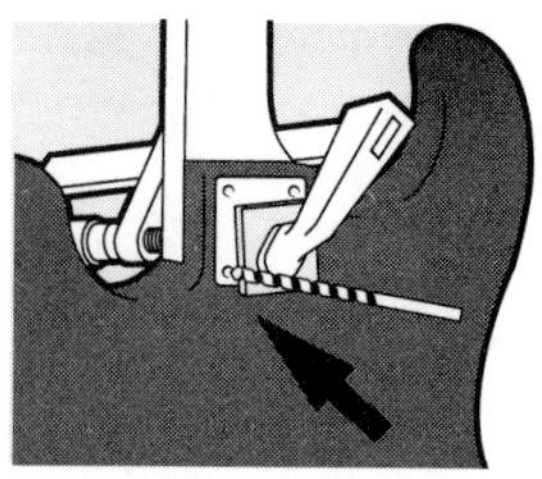

Most neck-mounting screws are standard-size, and the hole they thread into is smaller than the outside of the thread, which leaves enough wood for the screw to bite into. Use an electric hand drill or a drill press and be sure you drill perpendicular holes. If you measure the amount of screw showing through the cavity with the neck plate in place, you'll know how deep to drill without going through the fingerboard. Wrap a piece of masking tape around the drill-bit shank as a depth guide. After drilling the holes, prethread each hole with a mounting screw used as a tap. Rub the screw against some beeswax, paraffin, or paste wax to lubricate it before pre-threading each hole. Now mount the neck with the backplate and all four screws. It should line up with the strings.

If the four mounting holes in a used neck are stripped, try coating them with Hot Stuff Super T glue (the yellow bottle). This provides grip for the screw thread. Use a toothpick in each hole to spread the glue around, and let it dry for an hour or use Hot-Shot accelerator to speed up the cure. Repeat this operation several times, and then you can try rethreading the holes with well-waxed mounting screws. This usually solves the problem.

If the holes are too stripped, you need to drill each hole oversize, plug it with a

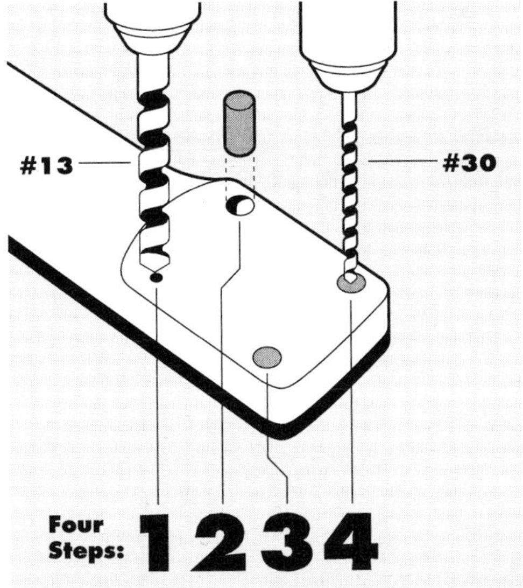

hardwood dowel, and redrill from scratch. Most worn holes may be plugged with a 3⁄16" wood dowel (above). To ensure a snug fit, you need to drill the oversized hole in the neck slightly smaller than the wood dowel; this is why you use the #13 bit, which is a few thousandths smaller than the dowel size. Regardless of whether you use a drill press or hand drill, remember that the neck is usually *hard* maple and may cause the drill bit to run off line, causing the hole to be drilled oversize or out of round. Always clamp an object that you are about to drill—especially maple.

After drilling the holes, cut four pieces of 3⁄16" maple or hardwood dowel (use a larger wood dowel and corresponding drill bit if the hole is really bad) approximately 5⁄8" deep, or whatever depth you have drilled into the back of the neck's heel. Coat the holes with Super T or carpenter's glue, and slowly drive the dowels into the holes, one at a time, with a small hammer. When the glue has dried, trim the dowel ends if they aren't flush, and then clamp the neck back into the cavity and proceed as you would when installing a new neck with no holes. If you've been careful with your work, the neck will tighten home snugly and serve for many years of playing.

BOLT-ON QUIRKS, SOLUTIONS, AND THE COMPOUND RADIUS

I'm definitely a Strat lover, and I basically agree with vintage experts who advise players not to alter old instruments. But many Strat lovers are caught between the vintage purists and the modern high-tech mechanical marvels. We appreciate the locking nuts and tremolo systems, and we can dig the high-tech sounds offered by electronic advancement, yet we don't want to see that stuff on our Strats. But we also find a need for certain repairs, and in some cases alterations, on guitars that we play and never plan to get rid of. Thousands of players own good but not exactly "vintage" Strats that would be more playable if they allowed their guitars a fret job, for example.

Forgetting twists, serious warps, broken truss rods, stripped truss rod threads (it's usually the easily replaceable nut that's stripped) and other subtle but hard-to-fix problems, we are left with two common Strat neck complaints: buzzing in the upper frets caused by a kinked neck or "rising tongue," and a fingerboard that's too radiused for bending strings without noting out. I, for one, don't think it's a sin to do fret work on a workingman's guitar, and I'll tell you why.

First off, I assume that you'll take your axe to the best repairperson you can find—someone who's capable of adjusting necks, removing frets, planing out humps, and refretting with barely a trace of the work showing when done. Second, I know that some guitars just can't be played unless some "surgery" is performed. If your guitar is correctly adjusted and really tuned up, yet you're still not satisfied, then the only thing standing between you and great playability (forgetting the electronics, of course) has to be the neck, and the fingerboard in particular. Here's how you go about solving these problems.

Buzzes up the neck are often caused by a swelling or hump that begins anywhere

If you have trouble seating a wood dowel into a tight hole (because of the hydraulic pressure created), try this furniture repair trick: With a thin razor saw cut several lengthwise slots in the dowel to let the air and excess glue escape—it will go in much easier!

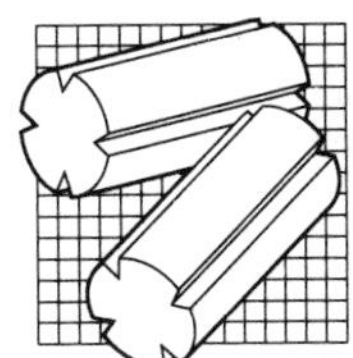

Compound or tapered radius fretboards aren't new. I recently worked on a lovely old C. Bruno guitar from the early 1900s that had a spruce top, Brazilian rosewood back and sides, pearl-inlaid soundhole, and an ebony bridge and fretboard —a compound radius fretboard which began at 5½" by the nut and tapered gradually to 12" at the end of the fretboard!

The best way to do a compound radius by hand is with the fretboard Radius Blocks designed by my friend Mike Koontz. This is one of the great new tools of the 1990s!

past the body joint. Many bolt-ons have a kink where the neck joins the body, due to the length and slimness of the neck, which is fastened abruptly to the body and placed under constant up-pressure from string pull. Sometimes these forces are more than the truss rod can correct. Also, the neck absorbs moisture through the four mounting-screw holes, as well as through the end-grain of the maple at the body edge. While lacquer is still my favorite finish for the neck and body, it doesn't impede the absorption of moisture as well as some other finishes. This moisture absorption can cause a slight swelling, noticed more often with rosewood fingerboards because of the extra swelling of the glue joint between the maple and rosewood. I've encountered fewer humps, swelling, or rising tongues on the old, pre-'59 maple necks.

Shims that are placed under the neck to change the tilt can cause kinks, too. The thin strips of fill material that are commonly used as neck shims create an air space that allows the pressure of the four mounting screws to act as a clamp, forcing a rising tongue! Combined, these forces can cause the last 10 frets to be higher than they should be, since the wood has risen. This isn't bad, and it's no one's fault: expect it with a guitar made of wood. These problems can be corrected with either a fret dressing, which will remove the buzz from the frets, or by a partial refret, in which the last eight frets or so are removed, the rise is scraped and sanded from the fingerboard, and the original (or replacement) frets are reinstalled. If you're a novice and any fret work is involved, take the job to a professional. You may be advised to do a complete fret job as long as you're at it.

A hump, kink, or rising tongue can be detected by placing a 12" straightedge on the fingerboard alongside any given string. The guitar should be strung to pitch, with the straightedge running from around the 10th fret to the fingerboard's high end. When viewed from the side, the fingerboard should appear flat, with the frets level with each other. If you see any gap or relief on this portion of the fingerboard, the tongue is probably high. The drawing below shows two necks: the top neck shows the upper part of a flat fingerboard; the lower one shows the same part of a neck with a rise. Put a small straightedge on the two diagrams and see for yourself—then have your neck checked by a pro.

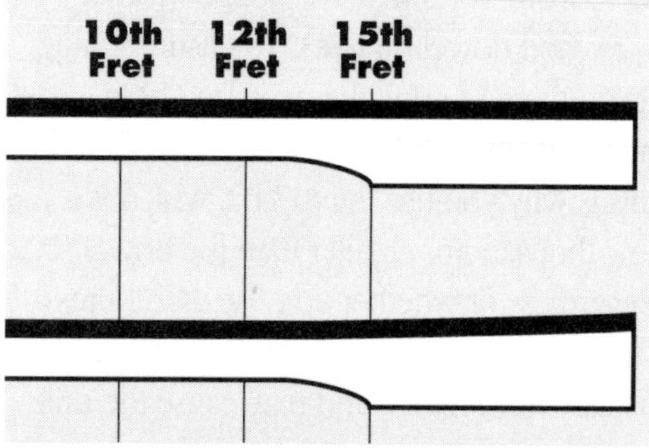

Bluesy bends that fret out or buzz on a guitar with medium-to-low action are caused by the very curved 7¼" radius of the standard Strat fingerboard. Many players like the feel and comfort of the curve when playing barre chords, and country and jazz guitarists find less need for far-stretching blues bends. Most blues and rock players, however, run into bending problems—especially on the high-*E* and *B* strings, and usually in the upper register's 10th to 21st frets. Sometimes the easiest solution is to have metal dressed off the frets in the tongue area under the

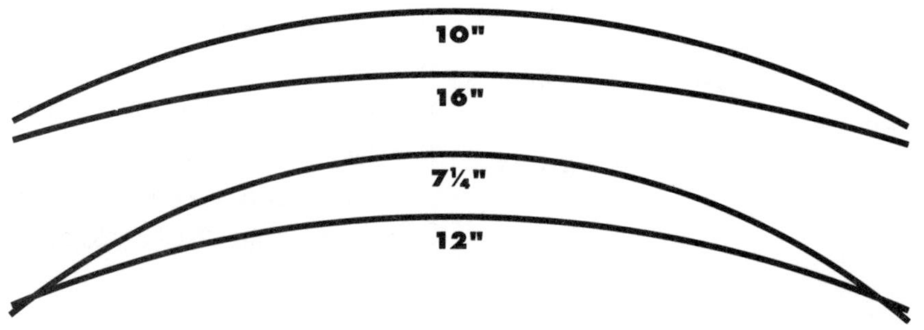

second and third strings—where the high-*E* and *B* strings end up when bent to their peak. But often this dressing solution is barely acceptable at best. The real answer lies in having a complete refret by an extremely good repairman experienced in tapering the fingerboard radius, gradually and subtly flattening it out as it goes up the neck and ending up with a 12" or 16" radius at the fingerboard's end.

Take a good look at a bend on, say, the first string at the 12th or 14th fret, going up to *G* or *A*. It ends up moving at an uphill angle towards or over the middle of the fingerboard radius. If you really need proof, remove the top strings and set a 6" straightedge on that same plane; if it rocks like crazy, that indicates a high spot or buzz. Since the strings taper on a long angle up and away from the fingerboard as they head toward the bridge, the fingerboard's radius need not be totally flat to be buzz-free. But a flatter radius is a help, especially in the upper register where the problem is most acute.

Repairmen were pleasantly surprised when the Warmoth brothers came out with Warmoth Radius compound fingerboards on their replacement necks. While these new necks can't help a vintage guitar's neck problems per se, they can save a lot of worry for players who question, "Should I do that to my Strat?" You can now buy a direct-fit replacement neck, usually for less than a high-class fret job, and try out its blues-bending capabilities while keeping the original neck stock. This can either be done as a test run before having a much-loved neck taper-radiused by a top fretman, or as a satisfying replacement that allows the original neck to be stored, unaltered and mint, until it's needed. I highly recommend the compound tapered radius for blues playing.

Ken and Paul Warmoth, along with their father, originated the non-factory replacement neck many years ago, and from the outset they perceived that players had some problems with a 7¼" radius. After discussing the situation with many repairmen, they decided to go with a fingerboard radius of 10", which is between Fender's and the Gibson 12". This 10" radius has since been the standard for almost all kit necks—so much so, in fact, that most locking nuts are made to match that radius. Therefore, if you plan to convert any guitar for a locking nut, check the fingerboard radius. You may find that you'll need to plane and refret the neck for optimum results. The arcs drawn on the opposite page offer a comparison of different fingerboard radii. The Warmoth Radius neck starts at 10" at the nut and tapers to 16" at the fingerboard's end.

If you end up having fretwork done, I recommend using Dunlop #6230, Stewart-MacDonald #148, or Luthier's Mercantile #FW7H fretwire. While these are similar yet subtly different, they all come close enough to the original Fender wire.

Blues-bend buzzing ceases to be a problem with a radius of 9½" and up. This radius, introduced by Fender in recent years, is a good compromise between the curved board of vintage Strats and the modern 10" and 12" fingerboards.

Fine-tuning a Stratocaster

With its slab-style body, bolt-on neck, and "automotive"-style construction, the Stratocaster is easy to work on from the repairman's point of view. However, setting up a Strat (adjusting the action, tremolo, intonation, etc.) is a different story, since it's the trickiest electric guitar to do perfectly. Understanding Strat quirks and knowing a few tricks of the trade can be a great help in adjusting your guitar for maximum playability. Here we'll cover some of the more common complaints players and repairmen have, as well as their solutions. I polled several of the nation's top repair and set-up specialists, asking them, "What are some of the simple problems that you constantly run into with Strats, and do you have any tips for adjustments that players can perform themselves?" Most of us were in agreement with the points discussed here.

This basic guideline for Strat set-up conveniently eliminates the most commonly found problems. Follow the outline in order, and your guitar will be playing its best when you're done. These are tips every player should learn. Have fun.

NECKS

The most common problem, the shifting of the neck in its pocket, was covered a few pages back in the section on bolt-on necks. Basically, you need only to loosen the mounting screws a tad, pull the neck into position, and retighten the screws when done. Before doing any set-up, be sure the neck is securely tightened.

Many Strats made during the '70s have a three-bolt neck mount with an adjustable tilt mechanism. These are a little more difficult to get snug, and I advise you to see your repairman for help. One solution—and I'm not necessarily recommending it—is to install a fourth bolt under the three-bolt plate. This bolt can be countersunk into the wood and completely hidden. Ask your repairman about this and other methods.

Some Fender Stratocasters, and most of their bolt-on clones, require that a thin shim be placed between the neck and body as an aid in adjusting string height. Once again, this was just covered, but I'm reminding you of it as we go through set-ups in order.

TREMOLOS

The most common and popular tremolo is the two-piece unit made from '54 until late '71. Fender has introduced several Strat tremolo designs since then, and when used with a properly set-up nut, they all work well. The nut is where most tremolo problems occur, as we'll see.

Whether you do it yourself or have it done by a specialist, adjustment of the standard two-piece tremolo involves much trial and error. In the end you must please yourself, and there is no one way to do it. Some players prefer that the bridge come to rest on the body as a positive stop or return point after being "dumped" (pressed downward to lower the strings' pitch). These hard-hitting, string-breaking players often like a positive body stop, so that the remaining strings don't all go instantly out of tune from the difference in string pressure caused by a broken string. The normal set-up, however, is with the tremolo plate raised slightly off the body at its rear, enabling players to cause the pitch to go slightly sharp by pulling up on the arm.

Before setting the tremolo, adjust the six mounting screws that fasten the bridge plate—if they're screwed down too tightly, the tremolo won't have the proper freedom of movement. Sometimes friction between the plate and screws causes jolting, catching, and sticking. One way to track down that problem (and often it's just one or two screws) is to remove the four center screws. Test the tremolo function with only the outer two screws holding the bridge down, and then by replacing the screws one at a time you'll find the problem. You can remedy this by carefully filing and fitting the holes to the screws as outlined in the Tuners and Tremolos chapter that follows. Actually, the two outside screws alone are able to hold the bridge sufficiently for playing. Stevie Ray Vaughan sometimes uses only two—proof of their strength, considering his high action, heavy strings, and hard-hitting blues attack. It's a good idea to loosen the screws slightly, regardless of the number, and then retighten them slowly until they just touch the plate.

A different approach used by some set-up men is to hold the tremolo forward in the tilted position, and then tighten the screws against the plate, preventing undue pressure on the screws when the tremolo is in use.

Use whatever method suits you. I've known some players who prefer using two mounting screws, yet would rather keep the middle four screws for looks. This can be accomplished by drilling clearance holes in the plate so that the screws aren't actually touching or holding anything. The instrument is altered, however, which could affect its value.

No absolute rule exists regarding the number of springs used and onto what claw hook and into which tremolo block hole they should be placed. Some guitarists who favor light-gauge strings beginning with an .008 use only two springs with the claw backed most of the way out; .009 players often use three springs with the claw still backed out quite a bit. Most players, however, end up using either three or four springs and adjusting the spring claw to get the desired tremolo feel and return point. Some use five springs with medium or heavier strings (Stevie Ray, for instance, uses strings gauged .012, .015, .019, .028, .038, .058). I feel that five springs are too much, and I don't like the way a tremolo plays this way. String gauge is extremely important when adjusting tremolos, and you should decide on a favorite gauge before making any adjustments.

When experimenting with the number and placement of the tremolo springs, try two at first, placed on the second and fourth hooks of the claw and extending to the two outside holes of the block (as shown at left). If you want to add another spring—and most players do—place it in the center of the claw and block but relocate the other two springs to the outside hooks and holes. With four springs, simply omit the center one—the idea is to balance the springs for good equilibrium.

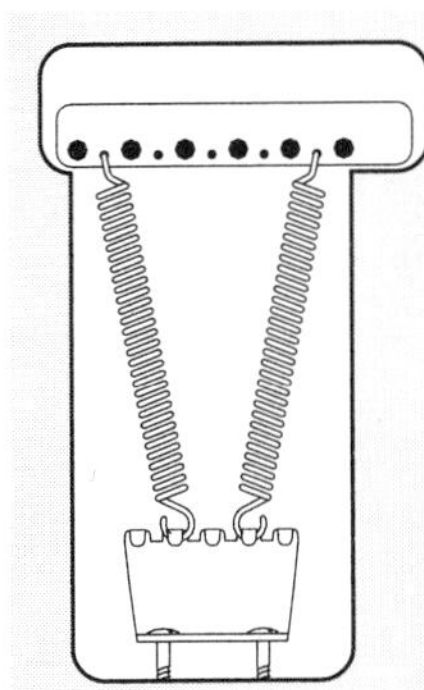

Here's a common tremolo set-up trick that pleases most players: With the strings tuned to pitch, adjust the spring claw tension so that the bridge leans slightly forward, with the plate slightly off the face of the guitar ($^1/_8$" maximum). Fret an *A* at the 5th fret on the high-*E* string, and pull up on the tremolo arm until the plate hits the body and stops. Adjust the spring tension until the note played at the 5th fret is *Bb* when the plate hits the body. After this "half-step sharp" test is completed, you'll be able to pull up on the arm slightly. Of course, if you change string gauges or alter the number of springs, you have to start all over again.

PICKUPS

One famous quirk of Strat pickups is that if they are adjusted too closely to the strings, the magnets' strong fields can hold a string's vibration in a vertical pattern, not letting it vibrate freely in a more natural oval or elliptical pattern. This causes the low-*E* string (and sometimes the *A* and *D*) to go crazy. It produces unwanted harmonic overtones that may be perceived as "double notes" or dead notes, and makes the proper setting of the intonation practically impossible. Besides the harmonic overtones, you may notice a general out-of-tuneness on the bass strings, especially as you play up the neck. A pickup that's too close may also cause buzzing on the upper frets, because the magnets actually drag the strings down and against the frets, especially with light-gauge sets beginning with .008s or .009s. This buzzing shouldn't be confused with a kinked neck, rising tongue, or worn frets. Before setting the intonation or string/action height, you should lower the pickups a few turns to eliminate their pull, especially on the bass side. Later, when all the action and intonation adjustments have been completed, you can slowly raise the pickups to find that most of your bad-note problems have been eliminated.

Many of the vintage 7¼" Fenders have no buzz problem because they're broken in from years of playing.

SETTING THE ACTION

Now, with the neck tight (and shimmed if needed), the tremolo adjusted, and the pickups' string pull eliminated, you're ready to set the action and intonation. Be sure that the neck is adjusted properly at this time. If you're after quite a low action, adjust the truss rod so that the neck is pretty much straight (little relief), and then play with a light attack. If you wish to play with .010s or heavier strings and use a medium action with a strong attack, loosen the truss rod slightly for some relief in the fingerboard to prevent buzzing. Go back and reread the section on neck adjustment if you're in doubt. If you're still unsure of yourself, go to a good set-up man to have your guitar neck adjusted. Offer to sweep the floor or take out the trash if you can be allowed to watch, so that in the future you can do the adjustment yourself. This approach might get you somewhere—it would in my shop!

In setting a Strat's action, you must understand that vintage Fenders have a very curved fingerboard radius of 7¼", as compared to Gibson's 12". Some Elite Strats built in the '80s changed to a 12" radius, and the American Standard and Strat Plus have a great 9½" radius, but we're dealing here with the standard vintage fingerboard.

Because of the curved board, many players perceive the action as being higher than it actually is; perhaps this is caused by a slight optical illusion. In general, I think Strat players should learn to accept a medium to medium-high action, because that is the way a Strat plays best. And unless they're willing to turn the fine-tuning (as well as any fret dressing or neck adjusting) over to a pro, players should try to get used to a Strat the way it is.

Once you're satisfied with the neck adjustment, lower the strings as close to the fingerboard as you like until you get too much fret buzz—when that happens, stop and back up a little. The strings at the bridge should follow the fingerboard's radius, rising slightly upward as they go toward the bass side. Raise the

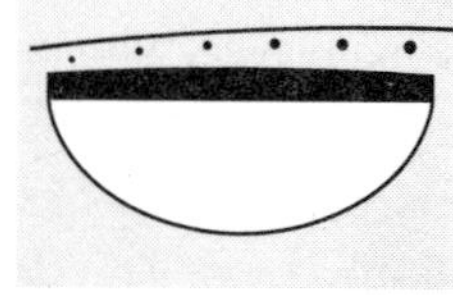

strings up or down, of course, by turning the two sockethead set-screws with a 4-40 Allen wrench. If you have older screws that are rusty and hard to turn, a little WD-40 or Liquid Wrench will help loosen and lubricate them. If the socket/Allen holes are filled with dirt, carefully clean them out with a sharp tool such as a dental probe; if you don't, the Allen wrench won't stick down deep enough for a good grip and may cause stripping or cracking.

NUTS AND TUNERS

At the same time you're setting the height at the bridge end, you must also check the string height at the nut. If either or both get too low, they cause buzzes between the string and 1st fret. If the nut is simply worn out, with the strings in really deep grooves that cause buzzing on the fret, see the section on making a nut, or have the nut examined by a professional. He'll tell you if the nut needs replacing or simply refitting. Be sure to seek good advice here, since the nut is the most important part in getting a tremolo to work well. Consider the following tips when setting up a nut, and if you decide to hire someone to do it, be sure that he's familiar with them.

Most experts prefer bone to Formica or plastic (Eric Johnson, however, prefers the plastic). The string angle, which comes from

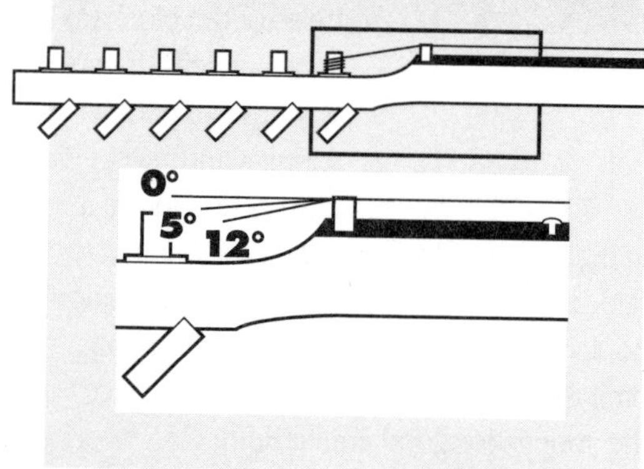

the tuner or string tree and breaks over the nut, should not be too steep when viewed from the side. A proper angle is somewhere between 5 and 12 degrees off the fingerboard plane—no more, no less (as shown at the bottom of the opposite page).

All Strats have a string tree for the *B* and high-*E* strings; on models made after '59, this tree is supported by a plastic or metal spacer. Often players remove the spacer and screw the tree down to the headstock face—don't do that! The angle becomes too steep, and the spacer is an improvement. Be sure that the string tree is de-burred and polished, and use it. Strats made since '71 also have a tree for the *G* and *D* strings. The trees and spacers put enough angle on the nut to keep the string from popping out, but not so much that they cause the string to bind from friction and not return in tune. Combat friction at the trees with Teflon gun oil or Magik Guitar Lube—just a drop on the underside is a great help.

With the four highest strings, two or three windings around the tuner maintains a proper angle between the tuner and string tree. If you remove the tree that holds the *G* and *D* strings or own a pre-'59 one-tree Strat, experiment with the number of downward windings (toward the bottom of the tuner post) needed to achieve the correct string-to-nut angle. On the low-*E* and *A* strings, any more than two downward windings causes too great an angle, and the strings will bind when the tremolo's in use. A neat trick is to wind the string up toward the top of the post, to let you control or alter the angle.

The nut's grooves or string slots should be no more than half the diameter of the string in depth and have a round bottom, and the slot sides should bear slightly away from the string. Nuts intended for tremolo use need to be slightly flatter on the bottom than others, so that the slot's round shape doesn't grip the string as it moves. The nut should also be slightly dressed away from the string on the back side to allow free movement (shown at right).

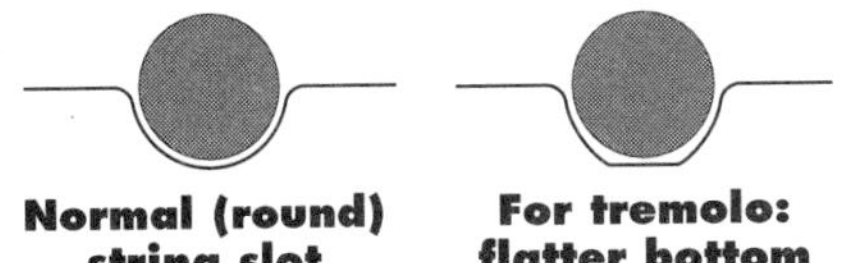

Normal (round) string slot **For tremolo: flatter bottom**

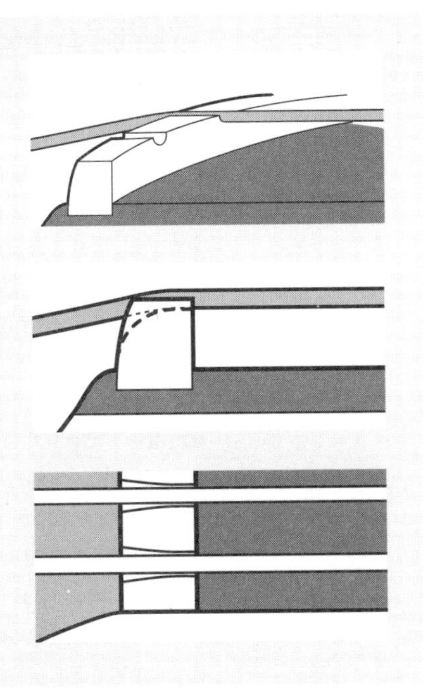

As a final step when you finish any nut—especially one designed for tremolo use—give a glossy polishing to the string-slot bottoms with 1000-grit wet-or-dry sandpaper; this relieves friction and improves tone. A drop of Teflon oil is also in order here, but be careful not to leave any on the headstock or fingerboard.

Don't blame all tuning problems on the nut or string trees. Be sure to check the guitar's tuners, too! At the very least, if the guitar has a good set of die-cast tuners, tighten the screws on the tuning buttons. This makes the tuner stiffer and harder to turn, but helps eliminate string-post wobble and slack storage (see the section entitled "Adjusting a Strat tremolo"). I've known repairmen who remove the small, crimped spring washer on the tuning button shaft in order to stiffen the string post and keep it from moving.

Occasionally a repairman or manufacturer will hastily file nuts with too sharp a back angle. This puts all the load and friction at one very small point at the front of the nut. While the string should "take off" at the nut's front (where it meets the fingerboard and the actual string length begins), it should have some "meat" or backing behind it and gradually slope up to the front edge. String slots that are cut too deep pinch the string and don't allow it to return in tune. They also cause a muting effect. Slots that are too shallow don't hold a string when it's bent from side to side, plus they can cause a string to pop out when least expected.

SETTING INTONATION AND PICKUP HEIGHT

When the nut and the bridge saddle height are perfectly set up, set the intonation before raising the pickups. Intonation is discussed at length in the next chapter, but in a nutshell: If a string is sharp, you need to move the saddle back away from the nut, increasing the string length and lowering the pitch by turning the saddle screw clockwise. If a string notes flat, shorten the string length to raise the pitch by turning the screw counterclockwise. Test the sharpness or flatness of a string by striking a harmonic at the 12th (octave) fret, and then fretting the actual note at that fret. Adjust the saddle forward or backward until the two notes are the same.

Finish your set-up by readjusting the pickup's height as suggested earlier. Properly set-up Strat pickups are closer to the strings on the treble side than the bass; they actually slant downward across the body. Likewise, the neck pickup is further from the strings than the bridge pickup. You'll find the right height by experimenting. The overtones described earlier are found mostly on the bass strings, especially the *E*, and usually further up the neck. Simply keep raising the pickups until the overtone phenomenon begins to happen, and at that point back off a hair. By not getting too close, you'll find a cleaner sound with no bad notes, and eliminate potential buzzing in the fingerboard's upper register.

If you've followed these basic set-up tips, you've also encountered most of the Strat's problems, eliminating them as you went along. Problems other than these and certain custom modifications—even fret work—can involve altering a vintage instrument. In cases like this, the choice is yours. There is certainly no disputing the fact that collectors of vintage Strats want them as mint and untouched as possible, and some are broken-hearted if you've even blown the dust off the pickups or from under the bridge saddles. So you could drastically affect the value of your guitar by performing anything other than stock maintenance. If in doubt, contact a pro, and basically don't remove from, or add anything to, a vintage piece without first getting permission. Any serious Strat lover should buy A.R. Duchossoir's *The Fender Stratocaster 1954-1984.*

Special thanks to Jim Werner, who was extremely helpful in steering me toward many of the repairmen and collectors contacted on this subject. If you're interested in Jim's list of Fender instrument serial number and neck dates, contact him at R.R. 1, Box 236, Letts, IA 52754. Jim works hard to preserve the past, and we can all thank him by sending him any information on Fender instrument serial numbers, neck dates, models, colors, and other pertinent features that help date an instrument to a specific era.

Also thanks to the following repairmen for their generous help in the preparation of this section: Ron Lira of Honest Ron's Guitars, Oklahoma City, Oklahoma; Larry Brooks in Denver; Bob Christopher of Screaming Strings, Decatur, Alabama; John O'Boyle of Thoroughbred Music, Tampa, Florida; Mark Erlewine of Erlewine Instruments, Austin, Texas; Danny Thorpe of Heart Of Texas Music, Austin; Doug Phillips of Sound Electronics, Norfolk, Virginia; Charlie Longstreth of Light's For Music, Springfield, Oregon; Lyndal Anthony in Cedar Rapids, Iowa; Paul Mundan in Davenport, Iowa; the old crew of Bryan Galloup in Big Rapids, Michigan; Pete Moreno in Oshtemo, Michigan; Eric DeBarr in Battle Creek, Michigan; Mike Koontz of Zoppi's Music in Detroit; Gary Brawer of San Francisco Repair Shop, San Francisco, California; Rene Martinez of Zack's Guitar, Dallas; Mike Lennon of The Apprentice Shop in Springhill, Tennessee; and most of all to Michael Stevens of the Fender Custom Shop in Corona, California.

Pro set-ups: Stevie Ray Vaughan and Jeff Beck

Great guitarists have the ability to make their instruments talk. Doing so takes a special gift, a lifetime of practice, and a great guitar. Haven't you always hoped that the guitar had *something* to do with it? Wouldn't you guess that a great player's guitar is set up to play really well? If you're like me, you'd like to know just how their guitars are set up (and I don't mean simply with what gauge of strings, or whether the action is high or low). You wonder how *their* guitars might feel in *your* hands. Would you play better?

In November 1989, I had a chance to try out the guitars of Jeff Beck and Stevie Ray Vaughan when these great guitarists played the Ohio Center in Columbus. I was anxious to see how their guitars would measure up to my expectations. Then I decided to do just that—measure them—so that you, too, would have a chance to adjust, set up, and compare the feel of your guitar to those of these top players.

PHOTO: BRIAN BLAUSER, ATHENS, OH

Rene Martinez using a Dremel Moto-Tool on Stevie Ray Vaughan's Number One.

Before the show, I spent the day with Jeff's and Stevie's guitar techs—Geoff Banks from Witley, England, and Rene Martinez of Denton, Texas, respectively. Geoff has worked with Trevor Rabin of Yes, Robert Plant, and most recently Jeff Beck, Phil Collins, and Genesis. Rene honed his skills for years as a repairman for both Charley's Guitars and Zack's Guitars in Dallas. I was interested in the simple but subtle set-up and action adjustments—the everyday stuff of being a tech for a guitar mogul. Of course, I was all ears for any other tips, tricks, and secrets Geoff or Rene might divulge. Here's what I found out:

Jeff and Stevie Ray were traveling with nine guitars, all of them Strats. Jeff's four included a yellow Vintage reissue model made by Fender's George Blanda in '86, as well as three custom-ordered Strat Plus models recently handcrafted and set up by ace guitar man Jay Black of the Fender Custom Shop. The Strat Plus models are equipped with Wilkinson nuts, Lace Sensor pickups, and the American Standard Tremolo, and are actually prototypes of a Jeff Beck Signature Model. One significant change is the size and shape of the neck. Jay Black notes: "Jeff wanted the biggest necks he could get—like baseball bats—so I patterned them after a 1935 Gibson L-5. Each neck is big, but different in size, shape, and feel. The seafoam green one, which Jeff favors, is close to an inch thick all the way down."

Stevie's guitars are all pre-'63 models, except for "Charley" (outfitted with the Danelectro "lipstick tube" pickups, it was made from kit parts at Charley's Guitar Shop in 1984). They all have names, too: Number One, Red, Butter Scotch, Charley, and Lennie. The only significant change from stock on these Strats has been the addition of 5-way switches and a good coat of shielding paint in the control cavities. Number One, the beat-up sunburst that we all know, is Stevie's main squeeze.

If you can set-up a Stratocaster, you can set-up any electric guitar—and you don't need a guitar tech to do it for you. Just keep reading!

As this book was being completed, we got word of Stevie Ray's death. We've all lost him just as he had come into his own as a major force in the Blues. We miss him.

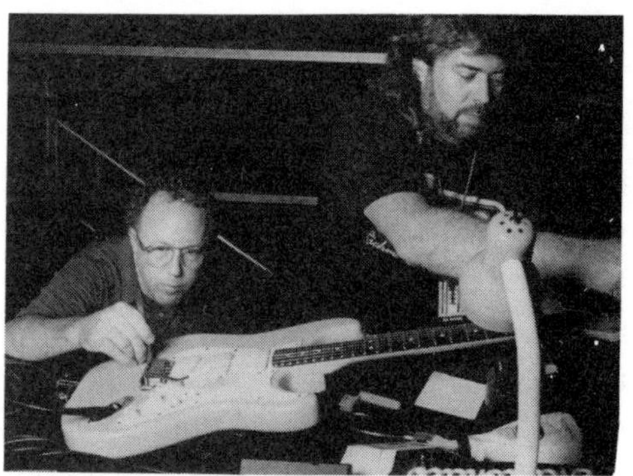

PHOTO: BRIAN BLAUSER, ATHENS, OH

Geoff Banks strings up Jeff Beck's Strat while Dan takes measurements at the bridge.

NECK ADJUSTMENT

With all the guitars, neck straightness is the first thing I checked, sighting down the fingerboard. A fingerboard should either be dead-flat or have a slight up-bow, known as relief, in the direction of the strings' pull. Stevie's guitar had approximately .012" of relief around the 7th and 9th frets, and then leveled out for the remainder of the board. Jeff's fingerboards are flat—adjusted straight as an arrow. Jay Black said, "I gave them a *little* relief, but .007" at the 7th fret would have been generous."

STRING GAUGE

Stevie tunes his guitar to *Eb* and uses GHS Nickel Rockers measuring .013, .015, .019 (plain), .028, .038, and .058. On this particular day, Rene had substituted an .011 for the high-*E* to keep down the sore fingers that blues bends can cause. Jeff performs his acrobatics exclusively on an Ernie Ball set gauged .009, .011, .016 (plain), .026, .036, .046. Both Geoff and Rene change strings every show for each guitar that gets played.

No other guitar—not even the Les Paul—has been so popular for so long. I've been fixing the darn things for almost 30 years!

FRETWIRE

If you're trying to evaluate action, it's nice to know what size and shape of fretwire is used. Number One's frets measure .110" wide by .047" tall. These frets would have started out at .055" tall when they were new, and were probably either Dunlop 6100 or Stewart-MacDonald 150 wire. Jeff Beck's frets aren't quite as big. According to Geoff Banks: "Jeff went with the Custom Shop's recommendation of a .098" wide by .050" tall fret. This is what Fender is now making as a 'vintage' wire, although it's taller than the fretwire used in the 1950s and early '60s."

STRING HEIGHT

I measured the distance from the underside of the strings to the top of the fret at the 12th fret on both *E* strings. Rene Martinez describes, "I set up all of Stevie's the same: 5/64" on the treble *E* string and 7/64" at the bass *E*." Geoff Banks: "Actually, I don't measure them. I do it by feel, and what I know Jeff likes." (I measured slightly over 3/64" on the treble side, and 5/64" on the bass. Later, Jay Black told me: "I set them up at 3/64" [treble] and 4/64" [bass], but I did this with the string fretted at the 1st fret; I like to eliminate the nut when making this measurement."

FINGERBOARD RADIUS

Knowing the fingerboard's radius can help in setting up a comfortable bridge saddle height and curve. Stevie's Number One was somewhat flatter than the vintage 7 1/4" radius. Rene has refretted the neck at least twice, and in the process the fingerboard has *evolved* into a 9" or 10" radius in the upper register. This isn't the result of a purposeful attempt to create a compound radius, which allows string-bending with less noting-out; it just happened. Jeff's custom Strats have a compound radius, too, starting out with Fender's currently popular 9½" radius, but flattening out further on up the board. Jay Black hand-shaped them, and from about the 12th fret up they flatten out to an 11" radius.

BRIDGE SADDLES

The bridge saddles on Jeff's green custom Strat Plus were set at the Fender Custom Shop to the same 9½" radius as the fingerboard. The new-style Fender saddles

PHOTOS: BRIAN BLAUSER, ATHENS, OH

Plastic tubing protects Vaughan's strings from breaking.

Stevie's polepieces are highest on the bridge side.

Stevie's standard vintage tremolo uses all five springs.

are formed with a smooth groove to follow the string angle, and support it gradually up to the point where the string takes off at the saddle's peak. While these saddles aren't overly prone to string-breaking, Jeff did manage to break a *D* and high-*E* string or two later that night. This was more a result of his exuberant attack, though, than evidence of any bridge saddle troubles.

Stevie's Number One, however, wants to break high-*E* and *B* strings at the saddle every chance she gets. Rene showed me why the strings break, and how he takes care of the problem: As a string comes out of the vintage Strat tremolo block/bridge top plate, it "breaks over"—or contacts—the metal directly; this causes a slight kink that weakens the string. With the bridge saddles removed, Rene uses a Dremel Moto-Tool to grind the hole's edge until the lip is smooth and gradual, and any binding is eliminated.

Number One uses vintage replacement saddles (the originals wore out long ago), and they're not all alike—some have a shorter string slot than others. The high-*E* and *B* strings may contact the front edge of this string clearance slot as they rise toward the takeoff point at the saddle's peak. The kink formed by the contact stretches onto the saddle peak during tuning, and breaks right at the crown. Rene elongates the slot, again by grinding, and then smooths any rough metal edges. Finally, he slides a $\frac{5}{8}$"-long piece of plastic tubing (insulation from electrical wire) over each string to protect it from the metal break points. He uses the heaviest piece of tubing that still fits down into the tremolo-block hole. Even with this, the high strings still cut through the plastic quickly, and strings break—sometimes in only one set. Rene plans to try a Teflon wire insulation if he can find the right size.

NUTS

Jeff's Vintage reissue has a standard Fender-style nut. The three custom Strats are set-up with Fender/Wilkinson roller nuts, like those used on the Strat Plus. Stevie's Number One, Lennie, and Charley have standard Fender-style nuts, but Rene makes them from bone. Stevie prefers the sound of bone, although for studio work he had Rene make brass nuts for Scotch and Red.

TREMOLO SET-UP

Measured at the rear of the tremolo plate, Jeff's American Standard Tremolo shows a healthy 3/16" between the bottom of the plate and the guitar top. He uses three tremolo springs mounted in the two outer and one center hole in the tremolo block. The springs connect to the middle three fingers of the claw, and are tensioned so that when he plays, say, the 3rd fret of the *D* string, it provides one whole-step if the bar is pulled up until it stops. His standard Vintage tremolo is mounted with all six screws and uses all five springs. It's tensioned so that the plate returns flat onto the top; I measured 7⁄16" between the spring claw and the cavity wall where the claw is attached.

Rene prefers the durability of the stainless-steel Fender tremolo bars. He puts a small wad of cotton at the bottom of the tremolo-block hole to keep the bar from over-tightening and becoming hard to remove if it breaks. He emphasizes the importance of lubricating all the moving parts of the tremolo system, preferring a powdered graphite-and-grease mixture (the grease holds the graphite in place where it's needed). He lubricates everything that moves: mounting screws/plate, all string breaks and contact points (including the saddle peaks) where the springs attach to the block and claw, the nut slots, and the string trees. Many other lubricants work: Vaseline, Magik Guitar Lube, Tef-Lube, etc.

PICKUP HEIGHT

As a reference point, I laid a precision steel straightedge along the frets for making this measurement. Jeff's Lace Sensors have little magnetic string pull, and therefore can be set quite close to the strings; in fact, they work best that way. On the treble side, the pickups were all within 3⁄64" of the straight-edge; on the bass side, they touched it.

Stevie's pickups were raised fairly high. I measured from the straightedge to the pole-piece tops: On the treble side, the bridge pickup touched the straightedge, the middle *almost* touched the straightedge, and the neck pickup was 1⁄16" away. The bass side measured 1⁄32" at the bridge pickup, 1⁄16" at the middle, and 1⁄32" at the neck.

TUNING MACHINES

We've covered about everything except tuners, and there's nothing secret here. Except for the yellow Vintage reissue, Jeff's Strats are equipped with either Sperzel or Schaller rear-locking tuners. Stevie Ray's tuners are the originals, and each has three full string winds for the best angle at the nut.

Well, that's the end of this story. You'll need an accurate 6" ruler to do the set-ups, and you can pick one up at any hardware store (General makes a good one). Don't be surprised if you go through a few sets of strings while you experiment. Good luck, and I thank Geoff and Rene for all of us! I had a lot of fun gathering this information, to say the least, and I hope you like it.

Electric bass set-up

The electric bass has come a long way since Leo Fender introduced the Precision Bass in late 1951. You might say the electric bass has come of age, with companies such as Pedulla, Tobias, Steinberger, Modulus Graphite, Ken Smith, Alembic, and others *specializing* in electric 4-strings and offering extremely high-quality 5-strings, 6-strings, headless, fretless, and other models, as well.

Bass players have evolved along with the instrument, with a whole new range of percussive and/or melodic styles of playing. Now more than ever, proper set-up is the key to getting the best bass for the buck. When your bass is set up properly, it means that the nut, bridge, and neck have been adjusted to obtain the best action possible for your playing style and choice of string gauge. With a little practice, you should be able to make most of these adjustments yourself. Here's an outline for getting your bass to play its best, followed by a description of the important steps:

1 Install the strings you prefer. If the bass is new, play it awhile to get the feel of its action.

2 Sight the neck, looking for straightness or relief.

3 Make basic neck adjustments before adjusting the nut or bridge.

4 Adjust the bridge and nut together.

5 Re-check the neck adjustment.

6 Adjust the pickup height.

With Fender slab-style necks that have no headstock angle, install the strings with enough downward wraps to create good pressure on the nut. Basses with angled headstocks require fewer wraps to achieve good down pressure. Expect to go through several sets of strings until you find what's right for you. Begin with the manufacturer's string recommendation, and go from there. These basics may help you choose a set:

■ String tension is important. Equal tension from string to string gives a balance that feels right to both the fingering and plucking hands. For hard-to-adjust necks or those that tend to have up-bow, choose a light-gauge, low-tension string. Within a given gauge (regular, medium, light, etc.), flat-wound strings have the highest tension, half-rounds the second highest, and round-wounds the least tension.

■ Round-wound strings are bright in tone and easy to intonate, but cause finger squeaks. They have the most fret buzz.

■ Flat-wounds eliminate finger squeaks, but trade off tone and brightness. They're harder to intonate, but have the good ol' upright sound.

■ Half-rounds combine flat and round shapes into a string with low finger noise, decent brightness, and good intonation.

■ Core-contact (or "taper-core") strings have an exposed *core* that contacts the saddle rather than the outer string wraps. Some bassists feel that these are easier to intonate.

■ If you're a 5-stringer looking for the optimum low-*B* string, D'Addario's Jim Rickard, noted expert on all matters related to guitar design and construction, recommends a .145" gauge.

All bass necks are either straight, back-bowed (convex fingerboard), up-bowed (concave fingerboard), or somewhere in between. The straighter the neck, the closer the strings can be to the fingerboard for easy action—but you must play with a light touch close to the bridge to avoid buzz or fret rattle. Conversely, if you play close to the neck and dig in, you'll need some relief to avoid buzzes.

A "perfect neck" is one that, under string tension, adjusts straight for low action and easy fret dressing, has a slight back-bow when desired to counteract heavy strings, and loosens from straightness into controlled relief. A properly relieved neck (below) shows a gradual up-bow going from around the 9th fret toward the nut, but remains straight from the 9th to the last fret. The overall curve in the fret tops between the 1st

Bass necks are the hardest of all to adjust, keep straight, and refret. They're so long, it's hard to expect a truss rod to keep all that straight.

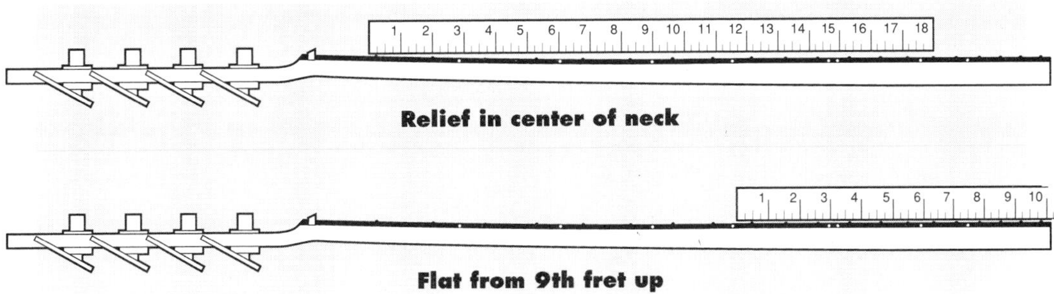

Relief in center of neck

Flat from 9th fret up

fret and the body joint mimics the string's long elliptical pattern as it vibrates when plucked. This eliminates a lot of fret buzz.

Sighting a neck is the simplest way of checking if it's straight, back-bowed, up-bowed, or in controlled relief. Hold your bass on its side in the playing position to get a true reading from the neck. Support the body, not the neck. Sight from the nut toward the body, and if you have trouble looking along the fret tops, sight along the glue joint between the fingerboard and the wood of the neck, using the line as a straightedge. You can also check by holding down a string at the 1st fret and at the body joint, since a tight string is a good straightedge. Or, to get a truly accurate reading, use a precision-ground 18" straightedge for comparison. This sighting of the neck determines if, and how, any adjustments should be made.

Loosen the truss rod by turning counter-clockwise.

To tighten, turn the nut clockwise.

Most bass necks are adjustable by tightening or loosening a truss rod nut. Tightening—turning clockwise—straightens an up-bow and removes relief. Loosening counter-clockwise allows some back-bowed necks that warp *away* from the strings to pull straight, or into relief. An old rule for tightening a nut that sounds silly but works is: "righty-tighty, lefty-loosey." Keep these few thoughts in mind when making any adjustments, and follow these steps in order:

■ The adjustment nut on many bolt-on, slab-style necks is at the body end. It's usually accessible only after loosening the strings and removing the neck.

■ Always *loosen* the truss rod nut first, since it may already be as tight as it goes. You'd hate to break it before even getting started. In fact, remove it completely and brush or blow any dirt from the threads of both the rod and the nut. Follow with a *tiny* dab of lubricant on the threads inside the truss rod nut (use Tri-Flow, Vaseline, Magik Guitar Lube, or oil), being careful not to get any on the bare wood. Lubricating the threads makes for a smoother adjustment, especially on older instruments.

■ Without putting tension on it, reinstall the nut until it's just snug. Then make a small pencil or pen mark on both the nut and the neck. When the marks line up, that's your snug starting point—a nice reference when making adjustments.

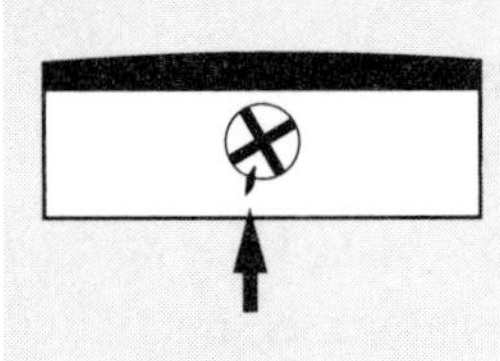

■ One half-turn on a truss rod nut is a lot. Once a nut reaches snugness, tighten it one-eighth to one-quarter turn and then check your progress. Expect to remove and install the neck several times during this process.

■ The effect of a rod adjustment can take days or weeks to be complete. You may adjust a neck perfectly, only to find a day later that the neck has kept moving from the rod's tension—becoming *too* straight or even back-bowed. Don't panic if this happens; simply re-adjust it.

■ If the truss rod barrel nut is extremely tight on the rod or recessed far into the hole, watch out! It was probably over-tightened by a previous owner or amateur "repairman." Some ill-informed people really crank those truss rods, which is a great way to break them, causing your bass neck to become permanently non-adjustable. Over-tightening can also cause the wood to compress, without straightening the up-bow. In this case, follow the removal, cleaning, and lubrication steps above, and then add one or two thin washers (see below) before

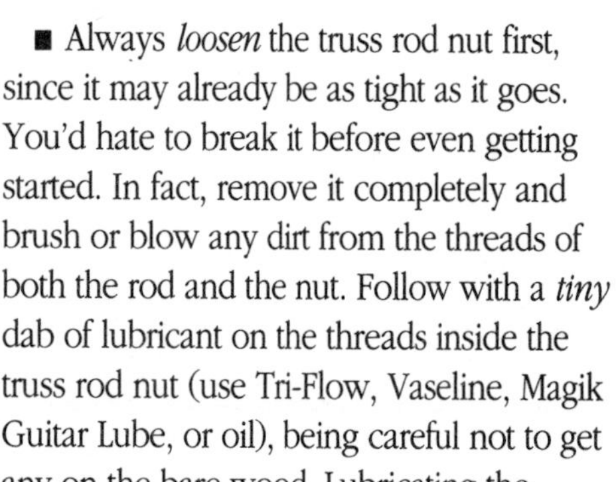

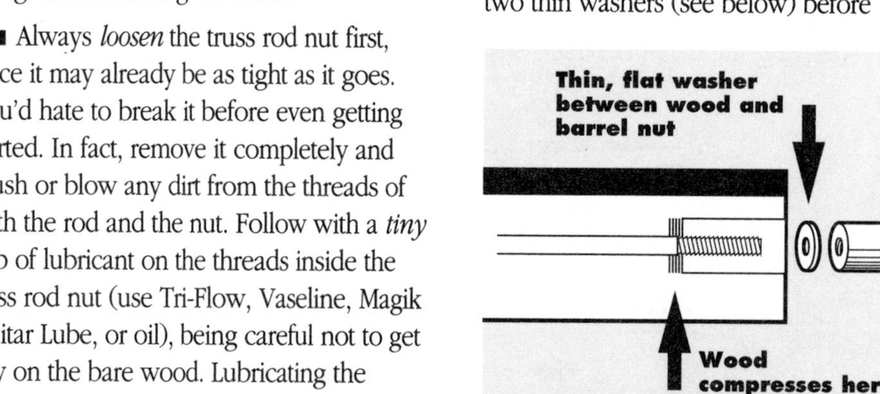

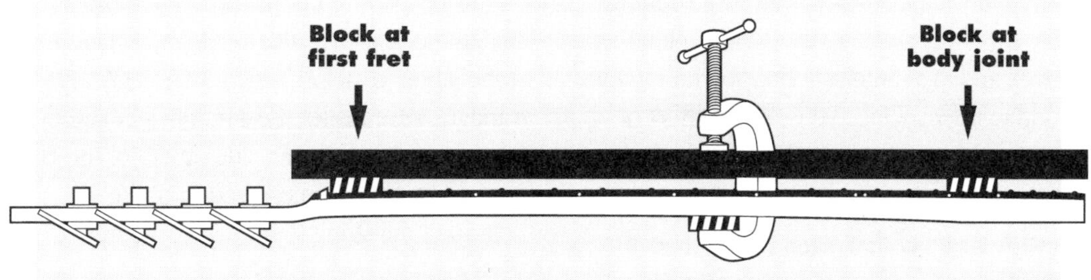

threading on the nut. Often this will give the nut a new grip on life and allow the rod to adjust further.

■ With a stubborn neck, sometimes it's best to loosen the rod completely, clamp the neck into straightness (or even a back-bow as seen above), and *then* tighten the truss rod nut. This method generally works when all else fails.

String height at the nut is critical. If the nut's string slots are too deep or the nut itself is too low, the heaviest strings are sure to buzz against the 1st fret. With a little luck, after any neck adjustments are made, you'll still have a nut that's slightly tall, allowing you the option of lowering the strings a bit. But if the strings are too *low* at the nut, have a new nut made or the original shimmed. Removing a nut without breaking it can be difficult, so leave this work to a professional.

Measure string height at the nut between the bottom of the strings and the top of the fret. A *low* action measurement taken this way would read: *E*–.035", *A*–.030", *D*–.025", *G*–.025". When I make a new nut, I stop lowering the strings at .050" on the *E* and at .030" for the *A, D,* and *G.* From that point I prefer to lower the strings gradually, with a customer's specific attack and playing style in mind.

Players with a strong attack, especially those using slap-style techniques that pull the string up and almost out of the nut slots, should use a fairly low-profile nut with string slots that aren't cut too deep. This way, the edges don't break off as the string is strained in its slot. From half to a third of a string's diameter is a good depth for the string slots. While bone is a preferred nut material for guitars and many basses, if your style is hard-hitting, stick to resilient plastic, graphite, or phenolic materials, which have less chance of breaking.

Bridge adjustments aren't hard to make, but are certainly no piece of cake, either. Expect to spend several hours getting things right, and if your first attempts aren't perfect, it's worth your while to keep on trying. A delicate balance exists between neck, nut, and bridge, and their combined effect determines your action. Bridge set-up controls the height of the strings, matches the curve of the saddles to the fingerboard radius, and sets the intonation. Here are the basics:

■ String height is raised or lowered at the saddle by adjusting small set-screws with an Allen wrench or screwdriver.

■ Lengthwise saddle travel controls intonation. If a string notes sharp at the 12th-fret octave, move the saddle back away from the neck. If a note is flat, move the saddle forward toward the neck.

■ Matching the arch of the saddles to that of the fingerboard makes the action comfortable to both hands. A radius gauge for measuring fingerboard and bridge comparisons is a handy set-up tool.

■ For low action and the least fret rattle, combine these approaches: 1) Get the neck as straight as possible with very low action,

A neck jig is a big help in fretting and setting up the electric bass.

and then eliminate any buzz by loosening the truss rod to add relief. 2) Straighten the neck and then eliminate buzz by raising the bridge inserts. Once you see the effect of both methods, *combine* them for the best action and least buzzing.

■ Remember that some buzz between metal strings and metal frets is normal.

String height measurements vary from manufacturer to manufacturer. I discussed bass set-up particulars with a panel of experts: Michael Tobias, Ken Smith, Roger Sadowski, M.V. Pedulla's Brett Carlson, and Bob Malone at Alembic. All of their string height measurements are between the bottom of the string and the top of the fret, and here's what they had to say:

Michael Tobias: "We never measure, because each bass is different. But our set-ups *start out* with 1/8" at the last fret all the way across, following the fingerboard radius (15" to 17"). This gives a height of 1/16" to 3/32" at the 12th fret. When you press a string at the 3rd fret, it should clear the 1st fret by .010" or .012". No bass will play without some relief. As a measure, hold down a string at the 1st and 15th frets—you're using the string as a straightedge—and adjust the neck until, at the 8th fret, you can just slide a Fender thin pick in between the string bottom and fret top; that's your relief. Our stock strings are private label in .040", .060", .080", and .100" gauges."

Ken Smith: "I use taper-core Ken Smith strings on all but the *G* string, in gauges of .044", .063", .084", and .106". You must have relief, between 1mm and 2mm at the 9th fret, even up to 1/16" at times. Really, all basses must be set up on an individual basis. I don't actually measure string height at the nut, but prefer an action where a player can depress a string without having to press hard, and with no buzzing on an open string. I consider a *low* height at the 12th fret to be 1/16" all the way across."

Roger Sadowski: "I shoot for a mostly straight neck with a *little* relief, and prefer a string gauge of .045", .065", .080", .105". My standard set-up is for the string height at the 12th fret to be on the fat side of 5/64" for the *G*, and 3/32" for the *E*—measured from the bottom of the string to the top of the fret."

Brett Carlson: "We use relief, except on fretless models—with those we get the neck perfectly straight. Our relief, measured by holding down a string at the 1st and last frets, is set it at .015". String height at the first fret is .025" under each string, and at the 12th fret I shoot for 3/32" under the *G* and 5/32" under the *E*. All our nuts are brass, so we don't have a problem with the string slots breaking. Our standard strings are D'Addario round-wounds in the .045", .065", .080", and .100" gauges." (Brett's .015", by the way, is a *slight* relief.)

Bob Malone: "In a set-up you can't go beyond what you have to work with. It all comes down to how straight you can get that neck. If you can get it straight to begin with, then your set-up can go from there. I like a very slight relief, but I don't measure it; it's all by feel. For nut height, when a string is pressed at the 3rd fret, it should just barely touch the 1st fret. Alembic basses are built with brass nuts."

Well, that's the bass set-up story. Finish up by adjusting the pickup height to suit your tastes (just don't raise them so high that the strings either slap against them, or get pulled into the upper frets by the magnets). Remember that none of us learned these tricks overnight, so be patient.

Troubleshooting bridge problems before set-up

Certain things must be understood about an acoustic guitar before you can even *think* of set-ups. And some adjustments—often those made to a bridge—fall into the "repair work" category. We'll look at the problems here, and then deal with their solutions in the Acoustic Repairs chapter.

The set-up of flat-top acoustic guitars often borders on repair work. It's not like electric guitars with their mechanical, easily-adjusted bridges.

No part of the acoustic guitar is more important than the bridge, which transmits sound from the vibrating strings to the guitar's soundboard. And if the bridge has problems, the guitar's tone and volume have problems. Therefore, players of acoustic guitars should become acquainted with the telltale signs of bridge trouble and learn what constitutes proper set-up. There are many problems common to the glued-on, flat-top guitar bridge, such as splits, warps, and saddle faults. Arch-top bridges, because they're removable and adjustable, usually have fewer problems, but we'll touch on arch-top basics, too, such as the proper fit between bridge base and guitar top and the clean cutting of string notches for a clear sound. This bridge overview should help you in evaluating your own instrument, whether you do the work yourself or have it done by a specialist.

Bridges separate from the top for many reasons, not all of which can be detected from the outside. Because of this, I always look inside a customer's guitar before quoting a bridge repair job of any sort. Buy an extension-shaft inspection mirror at a hardware or auto parts store. Then, with the guitar tuned to pitch, use a desk lamp for light and inspect the guitar's insides, paying special attention to the bridge plate (photo, next page) and the main braces. If any braces are loose, you will see a gap between

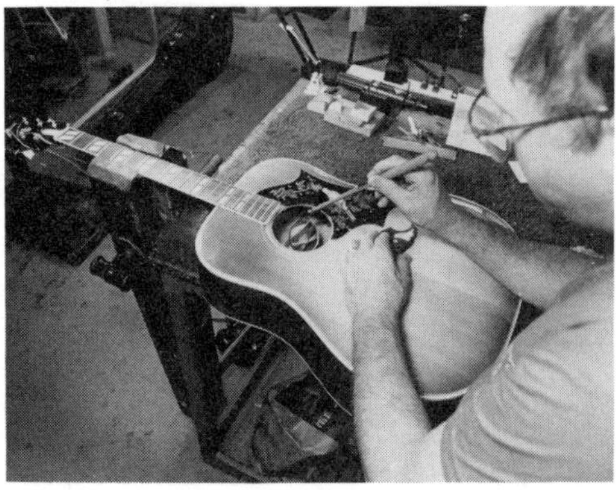

the brace and the top. Learn to use the lamp and mirror together, reflecting the light source against the top while you look.

On inexpensive guitars and many imports, the two main X braces often show a large gap just under the bridge area. This allows the guitar top to bow or hump, and of course the flat-bottom bridge does not want to stay glued to a curve. Sometimes these guitars' bridge plates have obvious gaps, or they're made of thin, warpy plywood instead of a proper hardwood. These are best replaced by a qualified repairman.

Gaps are common here

On a lesser guitar, a combination of gluing the braces and replacing the plate can flatten a humped top and help lower high action at the same time. This is accomplished with a reverse-warp board or a caul used during gluing. Rarely will the bridge plate on the better American-made guitars such as Martin, Guild, and Gibson need to be replaced, so you might get a second opinion if a repairman suggests this.

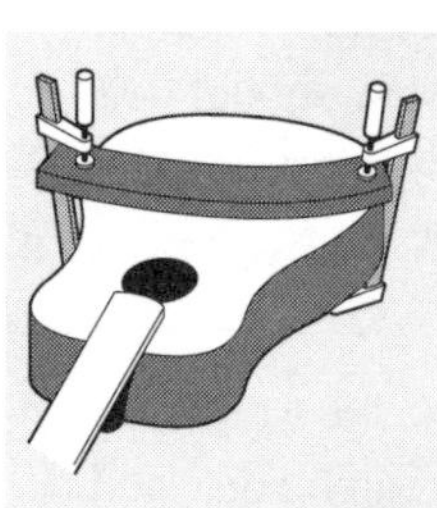

In checking for a partially loose bridge, use the flap of any string package as a feeler gauge. Try to slide the paper between the guitar's top and the back of the bridge while the instrument is tuned to pitch. If you can get a ½" length or more of paper under it, the bridge should be removed and reglued. If there is only a hairline gap, often glue can be worked into it while the string pressure helps keep the loose joint open. The strings are then quickly removed, proper clamps and cauls are applied, and the joint is left to dry overnight. This process is discussed later in this chapter.

When a bridge has come off entirely, you must choose between regluing the same bridge or using a replacement. I often replace a bridge if one or more of these problems are involved: serious splits in the bridge, a warp in the guitar top or bridge (making a proper refitting impossible), poor intonation, or a cheap original bridge with a saddle that raises or lowers by means of adjustable thumbscrews (I like to replace these with a standard bone saddle). Consider all the facts—and don't be hasty in slapping a bridge back on.

Minor splits running from the top of the bridge through the bridge-pin holes can be filled with a sawdust/glue mixture or a slip of wood, and usually the repair will last. I advise this method of repair if you own a vintage instrument and wish to keep the original bridge to preserve the guitar's value. However, some vintage guitar owners prefer a handmade duplicate of the original—except for an improved location of the saddle, which yields better intonation. As a player, I approve of this important adaptation and suggest that you consider it if your bridge is off. Splits through the saddle slot usually get worse, and often a repair here won't last long due to the tremendous string pressure.

Often a lovely vintage Martin will have a bowed top. *Don't let anyone try to flatten it.* Instead, fit the unglued bridge to the warp. Most often, we flatten tops only on cheaper guitars in order to get the bridge to hold and perhaps to bring down the action. However, the proper method of lowering action on a good old guitar is to remove and reset the neck or by clever fingerboard leveling and refretting. On guitars with a good, flat top, it's usually best to treat the bridge for what it is—a piece of warped wood. Throw it away and make a new bridge. If instead you grind a warped bottom to fit the top, you'll end up with a very thin bridge that will later split from its lack of mass and thickness.

Although you can correct poor intonation by slightly changing the position of the saddle (filling the original slot, then recutting one), if the bridge is removed, you may choose to replace it with a handmade bridge with the saddle positioned properly. I prefer this, because filling and recutting the slot hampers tone.

On many acoustic guitars with adjustable bridges (some Gibsons and many imported copies), I find a tremendous improvement in sound from filling the holes in the top and replacing the bridge with a solid-saddle, non-adjustable model. If you own that type of guitar, discuss your options with a repairman. Since these guitars' bridge plates can usually be replaced easily, a repairman can remove the bridge plate and any thumbscrew hardware, plug the holes in the spruce top, replace the bridge plate with a new piece of wood, and custom-make a bridge with a standard saddle and bridge pins drilled closer to the saddle. This gives you a better string angle and bearing on the saddle, thus improving power and volume.

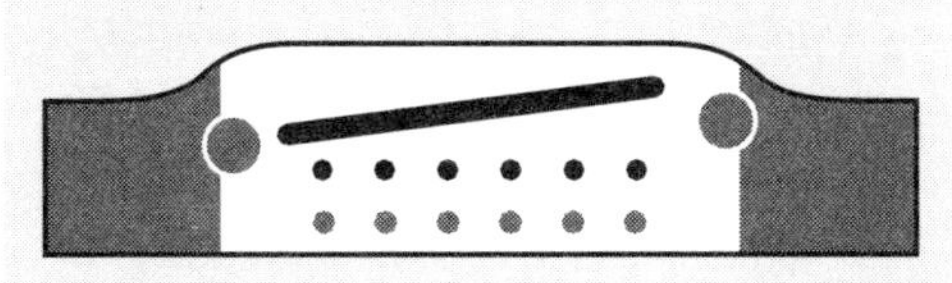

In the drawing above, the dark areas indicate where the new bridge-pin holes are located, while the lighter areas show the original holes to be plugged.

Arch-top and flat-top bridges

The last few pages discussed many of the common problems that can befall an acoustic guitar bridge, including top and bridge warpage, loose braces and bridge plates, splits, and other serious ills that may require total bridge replacement or serious repair. Of course, any such work must be completed before you can set-up an instrument. Now let's look closer at set up particulars such as shaping the bridge-pin holes and string notches, as well as the various aspects of saddles, including size, shape, and slots. If you're an arch-top player, we'll discuss the proper set-up of your instrument, too.

If your old Martin has a bowed top, don't let anyone try to flatten it!

The flat-top bridge has two functions: to hold the strings and to transmit their sound to the body. Any problem in either of these functions results in loss of both volume and sweetness of tone. Every detail counts. For example, on a well-made bridge, the bridge-pin holes should be reamed carefully so that the pin fits snugly but not too tightly. Also, I prefer to see a slight chamfer (countersink) on the bridge top so that the head of the pin has clearance around it. This chamfer not only looks attractive, but allows the pin to sit lower in the bridge.

Each string, being a different diameter, requires a properly sized notch in the bridge. This allows the ball-end wrapping to sit forward in the notch, with the string's end pulling up against the hardwood bridge plate. When the bridge pin is inserted into the hole, the string is locked into the notch. And if the fit is snug, good volume and tone follow. The string notch should be radiused toward the saddle where the string breaks as it comes out of the hole (shown at right). You can clean the bridge notch yourself by using, for example, a coping saw blade

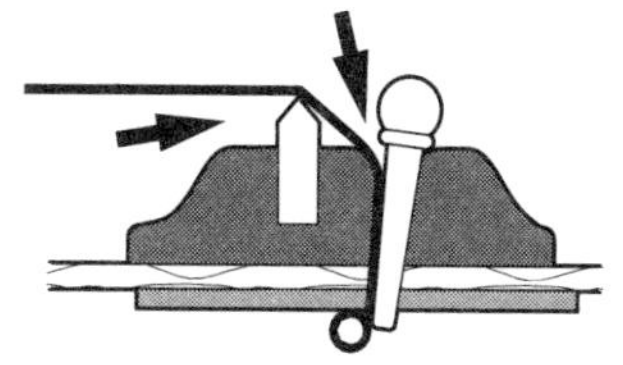

mounted in a wooden handle (above); carefully create a notch if you don't have one. Saw with the teeth pulling up so as not to fragment the wood on the inside. After sawing, use a small needle file to smooth and radius the slot's top.

Sight across the bridge from the side, looking lengthwise along the saddle. If it looks curved or warped or seems to tilt forward, have a qualified person clean up the slot and fit a new bone saddle. Or read on and do it yourself. This "squaring the slot" is important, since there is a huge difference in power and tone transmission when the saddle fits well. A saddle should be somewhat difficult to remove, due to its tight fit. In fact, you should be able to grasp a well-fit saddle with a pair of pliers and pick up the whole guitar with it (but don't try it!). However, a saddle that's too tight or forced into its slot could cause the bridge to split.

The correct shape for the saddle top is smoothly rounded and free of sharp edges. The saddle should be showing 1/8" to 3/16" exposure above the bridge. This ensures a string angle steep enough to produce good volume. Going over this height can cause the saddle to warp, and it exerts too much pressure on the slot. A height much less than 1/8" does not give the guitar's body enough chance to sound.

If you have a slight intonation problem (the string sounds sharp or flat), you can correct it by sloping the saddle's peak toward the front or back. If the string plays sharp, file the slope away from the headstock. If the note sounds flat, slope the saddle toward the headstock. (This method of correcting intonation troubles is called "compensating" the saddle, and it's covered later in this chapter.) The saddle should conform to the fingerboard's basic shape, unless you have a certain action preference. Experiment with different-shaped saddles to find what suits you best.

Arch-top bridges often suffer from a poor fit of the bridge base to the guitar's top. The best fit can be achieved by hand, using a sharp knife such as an X-acto or a violinmaker's knife. It takes a great deal of skill to do this; however, as a substitute you can tape a piece of 120-grit sandpaper to the top and then slide the bridge base back and forth to contour it. The shape that a knife gives produces the cleanest fit and best tone. Good violin makers are the most adept at this bridge-carving technique. If you can find a person good at violin set-ups, see if they'll carve a bridge to fit the top; it'd be worth the effort! Some arch-top guitars have a solid, unsplit bridge base, while others are split. In either case, check the bridge fit under normal string tension, since the top and base bend. A perfect fit without string tension might be imperfect when the strings are on.

I prefer arch-top bridges that do not have metal Tune-O-Matic type saddles; the solid wood top pieces produce a better tone. These solid wooden "saddles" are often staggered for intonation compensation, especially on more modern instruments. The string notches should not be over one-half the diameter of the string in depth—just enough of a groove to keep the string from popping out when plucked. The notch should fit the string's shape and be slightly rounded to a dull peak—not a sharp point—with all burrs removed. I polish the string grooves on rosewood or ebony arch-top saddles with 0000 steel wool to burnish the wood and make it hard.

Arch-top bridges should not be glued into place. They usually leave a mark in the finish, so you'll know where to reposition the bridge when you remove the strings while cleaning the fingerboard or polishing the instrument. If the bridge seems to pull to either the treble or bass side and the strings won't line up with the fingerboard, the tailpiece may have to be moved slightly to either side. Have this checked by a qualified

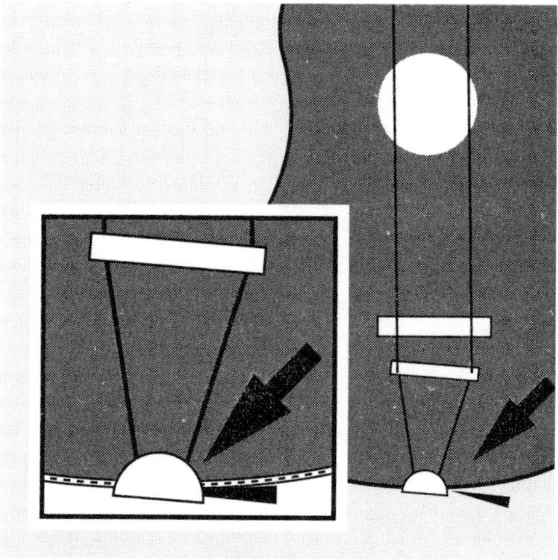

repairman, since the mounting holes *may* have to be plugged and re-drilled. But in many cases, this simple trick often solves the problem: Loosen the tailpiece and slide a small shim of wood, paper, cardboard, etc., under one edge of the tailpiece bracket on the same side that you want it to move toward (see drawing above). The shim forces the tailpiece into position—and it doesn't take much!

While there are some bridge problems that these pages haven't covered, you now know the basics and should be able to see how all the different factors relate. If you have bridge problems, think everything out and get professional help before doing any work that you may regret.

Fitting flat-top bridge pins

Flat-top acoustic guitars only sound their best when the strings are correctly installed and well seated in the bridge-pin holes. A string's ball end must fit snugly against the bridge plate on the top's underside. It should never be pulled up into the bridge plate, the top, or the bridge itself. Bridge pins that pop out or "creep" up, string-end windings that pull up onto the saddle, or a dull, muted tone are indicators that things aren't right down below. Often these problems are easily cured, and the advice given here applies to many situations.

Use a telescoping inspection mirror to look at the guitar's interior, especially the top, where much of the string pressure is transmitted. Check to see whether the string ball ends are pulled neatly against the hardwood bridge plate (at right) as they should be, or instead are working their way up into the plate, top, and eventually the bridge itself.

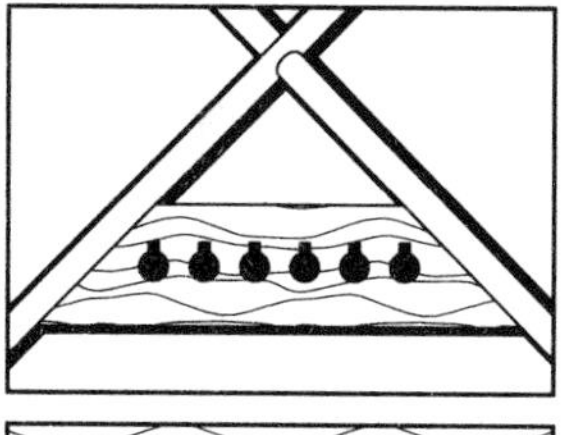

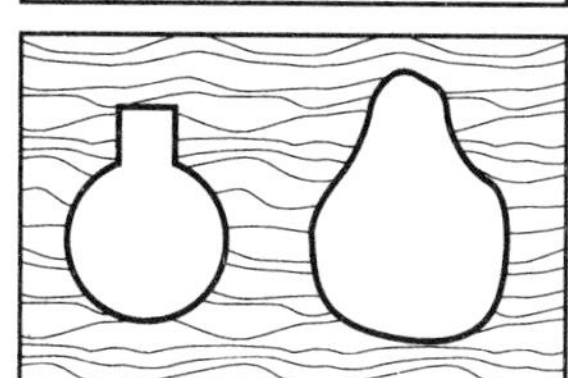

Ideally, bridge-pin holes should have a slight notch at the front edge for the string winding to pull into (see the "clean" hole at right). The pin's job is to keep the ball end shoved into this notch when the string is tuned to pitch. A properly fit string, notch, and bridge pin allow the complete removal of the pin with the instrument at pitch—leaving only the notch to hold the string!

Most modern bridge pins are installed with their flutes facing forward (a flute is the groove molded into the pin, which accommodates that portion of the string winding that isn't seated into the notch). Bridge pins do not have to be installed with the grooves facing forward: With older guitars and instruments with worn, overly-deep notches, turning a bridge pin 180°—until the groove faces the rear—helps hold a string in a notch, especially a wound string. This simple pin rotation often keeps a slightly loose bridge pin from falling out all the time, too.

Many bridges (generally on inexpensive guitars) have only very slight notches, or none at all. It's best to create or enlarge these notches until the string locks in. I use a miniature, wooden-handled jigsaw blade for slotting bridge-pin holes. I customized the saw by removing the blade, flipping it end-for-end, and then regluing it into the handle. Now the teeth of this "bridge-pin hole saw" point upward (toward the handle), and cut on the upstroke—avoiding the tendency to tear out bridge-plate wood, which can happen on a saw's down, or "exit," stroke.

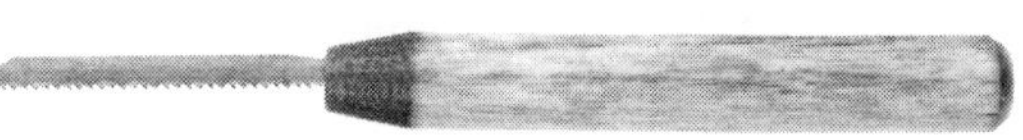

Although pin-hole slotting is a simple, inexpensive job, it requires finesse and experience, so consider having it done in a professional shop.

After a bridge is glued onto a guitar, the bridge-pin holes are drilled through the top. A hardwood block should be held on the inside to absorb the shock and keep the drill bit from breaking out wood as it plunges through. This step is often omitted, especially on cheap guitars or in work done by inexperienced craftsmen. Again, the mirror can tell you a lot in a hurry. If the bridge and plate holes *are* fractured, punched out, worn out, don't despair—the problem is fixable. Here's how:

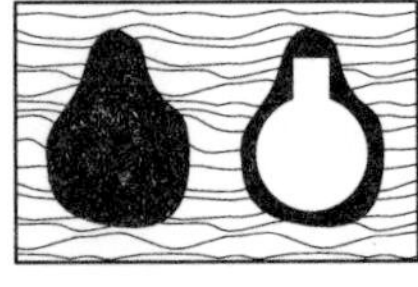

In many cases, it's possible to work a Bondo-type filler (represented by black, at left) into the worn or chipped holes. Use a rubber squeegee and wear a rubber glove. Once dry, remove the excess filler with small scrapers and sanding blocks, and seal the plate's repaired area with several layers of Special T super glue. Then carefully redrill the bridge-pin holes with a backer block inside, and create the string notches using the miniature jigsaw and an *upstroke* to keep from pulling the new filler out of the holes.

Another bridge-plate repair method that I've often seen, and done myself on occasion, is to glue a thin veneer of wood onto the original plate. This method is fine for some instruments, but the choice should be made by a professional. A too-thick piece of wood could harm the tone and value of a good guitar.

Here's a temporary solution for badly worn holes. It works well and may even add tone and sustain to lower-quality instruments: Slide a plastic, wood, or ceramic "spacer" (a bracelet or necklace bead) over a string's windings and up against the ball end. Now the bridge pin can properly hold the string and spacer against the bridge plate, as in the bottom drawing at right.

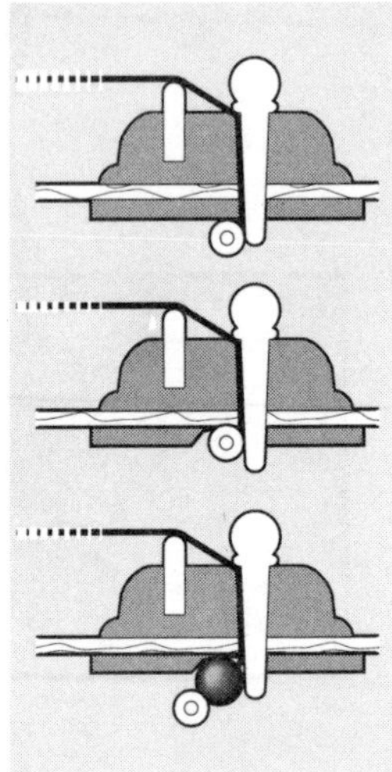

After enlarging the shaft hole with a drill, you can take apart a fishing lure—a Mepps Spinner—and use the cone-shaped brass weight as a spacer. It cost me six lures for my set, but they have a great tone, and I use them in my shop during this type of repair. Obviously, you'll have to string the guitar from the inside, since the beads won't fit through the hole!

Getting a string end to "lock in" at the bridge notch is simple, but requires skill, experience, and the proper tools. Also, this notching of the bridge may require some refitting of the bridge pins to their tapered holes. It's easy to end up with loose bridge pins that fall out after these adjustments. So if all else fails, don't hesitate to take your axe to a pro!

Refitting and replacing bridge saddles

Acoustic players who search for the utmost in tone and volume can't be particular enough about having a well-fit saddle. Made and installed properly, the saddle puts the finishing touch on expensive, high-quality instruments. The same attention to detail in fitting a saddle to a less-expensive model is probably even more important—it's amazing what a tone depressor a poorly installed plastic saddle can be. Here I'll describe symptoms of "saddle sores," and suggest methods for cleaning the bridge slot and fitting a new saddle into it.

Since the saddle is the final stopping point of a string's length, its placement is essential in determining proper intonation. More important, it's the transmitter of sound from the vibrating string to (and through) the bridge, causing the top to move. This creates the sound, tone, and volume that is unique to each individual guitar. In order of preference, my choices of saddle and nut material are: ivory or bone, Micarta, and plastic. Bone is the best all-around material for saddle-making, since it's readily available, inexpensive, and quite hard.

A saddle should be replaced when:

■ It fits loosely in the saddle slot and can be easily moved with the strings removed. This loose fit may not only cause vibrations and slight buzzes, but it also seriously inhibits the guitar's ability to produce volume—not to mention tone.

■ It has become pitted or grooved from years of use. To file or sand out these imperfections would lower the action—time for a new saddle.

■ It is made from plastic, and the player is looking for more volume and better tone. In my opinion, plastic just won't cut it.

■ The slot is too shallow, causing the saddle to lean forward and eventually develop a warp or crack. In this case the slot should be recut deeper before fitting another saddle (more on this later).

Note: If you feel like attempting your own saddle work, don't start on a guitar that's dear to you; search out a clunker for practice—they're easy to find. Regardless of whether you work on your best guitar or a yardsale special, record the saddle's height before removing it. Make a mark on the front and back of the saddle with a sharp pencil at the point where it enters the bridge. This will help you remember the saddle height after you have installed the new saddle blank and are ready to set the string height. Remove the saddle by gripping it with a pair of end-nippers or pliers, and gently rock it side to side slightly as you pull upward. Don't force anything, and remember that some saddles are glued in. If you have too much trouble, take the guitar to your local repairman. When the saddle is out, mark the bottom on the treble side with a small "X." This will help you remember which side was treble or bass when you're ready to trace it onto a new blank.

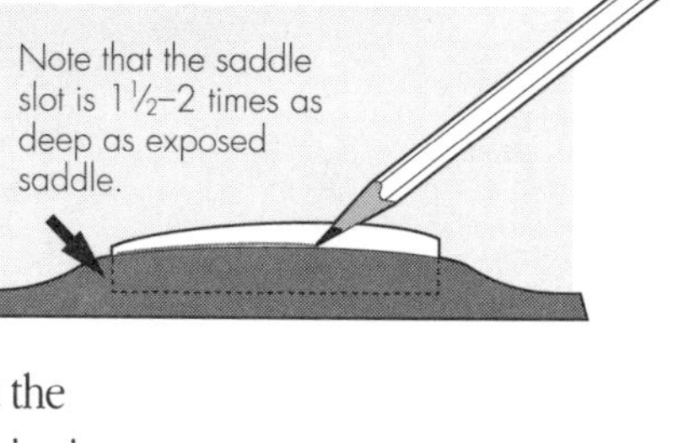

Note that the saddle slot is $1\frac{1}{2}$–2 times as deep as exposed saddle.

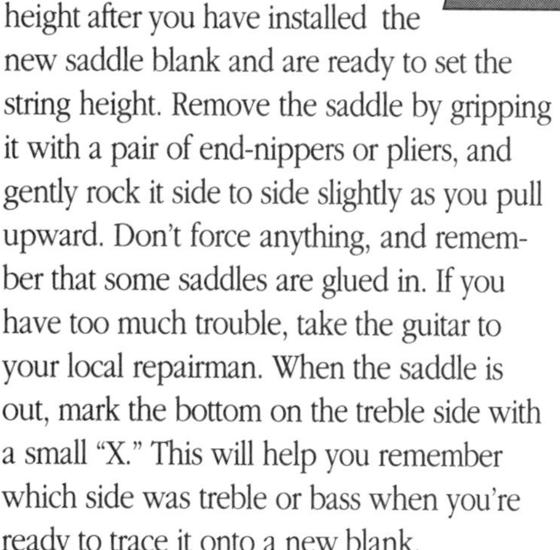

Before you can replace the saddle, you must be sure that its slot is well shaped and straight from end to end, with smooth, perpendicular sides that are square to the bottom. The slot should be deep enough to support the saddle well (approximately one-and-a-half to two times the saddle's exposed height above the bridge top). It's not uncommon to find sides that are shaped as those at right, with lines that are not perpendicular to the bottom or parallel to each other. Going slowly from end to end with a sharp, long-beveled chisel, you can pare the wood from the sides to square up the slot. A spark-plug file with the tip ground as shown can be

Practice saddle-making on scraps of wood or inexpensive Micarta and corian saddle blanks. Save the bone for when you're an expert!

used as a scraper on the push stroke, filing at the same time. It's also great for smoothing and straightening a slot from end to end, as well as for cleaning up any chisel marks. If the slot looks good to begin with, try inserting a standard blank into it and don't mess with trying to change its size—I haven't run into this situation enough times, however!

If the slot is too shallow, allowing the saddle to lean or fall over, it must be made deeper. The best method is to rout it with a Dremel Moto-Tool mounted in its router base. Actually a miniature router, this tool is well known by professional repairmen and serious hobbyists. The base can hold the router at right angles to the bridge, and with successive passes of 1/16" or so, you can quickly reach the desired depth. After routing, clean up any slight marks on the sidewalls with the chisel and file. Wear a dust mask while cutting or sanding bone or hardwoods.

Most saddle blanks range from 3/32" to 1/8" in thickness. While some replacement saddles drop right into the existing slot, most are thicker than the original by as much as 1/32", to account for the squaring-up and consequent over-sizing of the old slot.

I prefer the oversize blanks of bone, and usually size them on a stationary belt sander. Slower but no less accurate results can be achieved by hand. First smooth and flatten one side by rubbing the saddle against a mill file (the same file used for leveling frets; see the section on making your own files, or look into the fret levellers sold by Stewart-MacDonald, and designed by me!). After measuring the saddle-slot thickness, transfer the measurement to the new blank with a pencil or scribe, measuring and marking off the good, flat side. Remove material from the opposite side until you come to the measured line. This can be done by rubbing on the smooth file or against 180- or 220-grit sandpaper, or by using a scraper blade. When the blank begins to fit, trim it to exact length and round the ends to match the slot's dimensions.

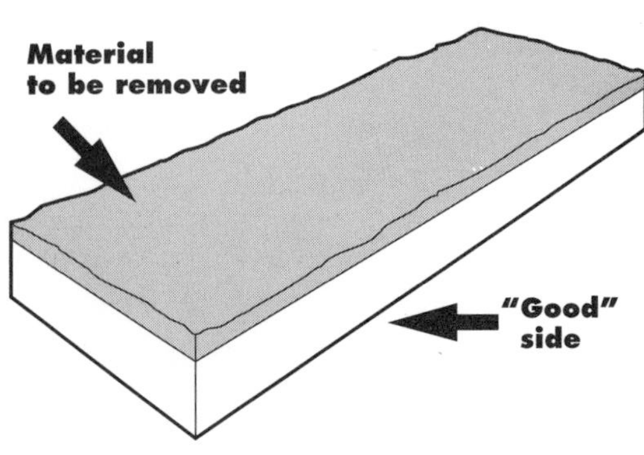

Rather than just drop in, a well-fit saddle "squeaks" when installed. Support the guitar under the bridge with your free hand while pushing the saddle in from above. A too-tight saddle might eventually cause the bridge to crack, or it may not go in at all. Once inserted, it will be hard to remove for shaping and action work, so practice on inexpensive instruments if you've a mind to do your own work. As I've said, if you were to grip a well-fit saddle from above with a pair of pliers or Vise-Grips, you should be able to pick up the entire guitar by gripping only the saddle!

When the new blank fits into the slot, recreate the former string height and saddle shape by referring to the original, which you've marked with a pencil. If you didn't like the feel of the original action, reshape the new saddle to suit your taste, raising or lowering the strings by degree. In general, the saddle should follow the fingerboard's curve somewhat, but rise slightly and flatten out a little as it goes toward the bass side. In other words, the bass strings should be higher than the treble strings to avoid buzzing. While roughing in the saddle, always be sure that its top, or crown, is rounded, so you won't be breaking strings each time you string it up to check the action. When you reach the desired action height, final-shape and round the saddle to a gentle curve and polish it with 400 or 600 paper. This final setting of the action is actually extremely tricky and requires much practice.

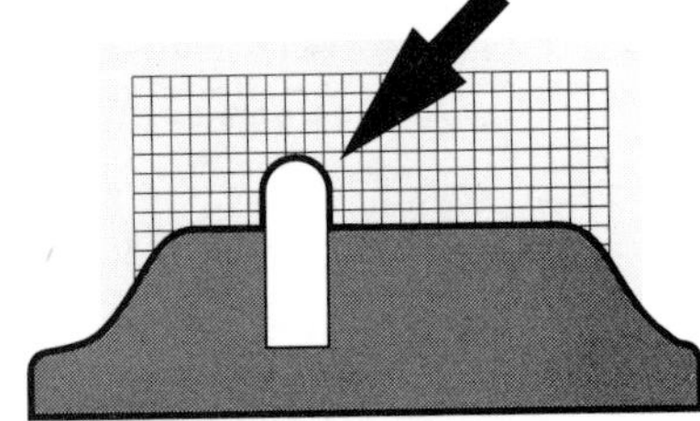

Setting up a classical guitar

Having the ability to adjust the action on a Fender bass, tweak the truss rod on a vintage Les Paul, or fit a perfect saddle into a Martin D-28 doesn't necessarily qualify a repairman to properly set up a nylon-string classical guitar. There are several major set-up differences between steel- and nylon-string acoustics. This section describes classical string installation, correct neck relief, action height at the nut and 12th fret, and the proper shaping of the nut and saddle. Most of the set-up techniques used here apply to adjusting a nylon-string "folk guitar," as well. (Braced for nylon strings, these guitars typically have a wider, flatter fingerboard than most steel-strings. Most American and European guitars made before the late 1920s fall into this category, and many of them have bridge pins. During the '50s folk boom, folk guitars were made by Goya, Favilla, Hagstrom, and other manufacturers from abroad. While these instruments are different from the modern steel-string, they aren't grand concert classical guitars, either. If you understand the set-up of both classicals and steel-strings, though, you'll be able to handle the folk guitar.)

I've set up my share of classical guitars, and once owned an excellent hand-made Yacopi. Like many of my peers, I learned Bach's *Bourrée*, studied the Carcassi method, struggled with Fernando Sor, and ended up playing the blues. So I'm no expert when it comes to the concert guitar, but I know experts. I contacted several of the best to get their opinions on set-up: William Cumpiano, a student of Michael Gurian and the founder of Stringfellows in Hadley, Massachusetts; Jeffrey R. Elliott, a master luthier and mentor to a thriving community of guitar builders in the Portland, Oregon area; and Richard Schneider, who collaborated with Dr. Michael Kasha on taking the design of the classical guitar to new heights. (After hearing a new Kasha/Schneider guitar, Segovia wrote: "To Schneider, in whose hands is the future of the guitar.")

Richard's guitars incorporate the principles of the Kasha design, and his avant-garde instruments are hailed for their beauty, playability, and superior concert tone. Although he sits at the pinnacle of the guitar-building craft, Richard is more likely to speak about design ideas or his students than about himself. He feels that his main achievement may be that he will one day leave behind him more students trained in his methods than any other builder in history. His students include such well-known builders as Abraham Wechter, Gila Eban, Jeffrey Elliott, Mark Wescott, Gregory Wylie, Peter Hutchison, Charles Merrill, John Mello, Italy's Enrico Bottelli, France's Michel Geslain, and Sweden's Fredrik Gustafsson. Schneider's Lost Mountain Center For The Guitar, a non-profit organization for the education of guitar builders and players, conducts an annual seminar starting the first Saturday of August; for information on attending, contact seminar manager Eric Hoeltzel at Box 44, Carlsborg, WA 98324.

PROPER STRING INSTALLATION

Nylon or "gut" strings (especially the wound bass strings) are more delicate than steel and must be handled more carefully to avoid kinks, nicks, breaks, and unwinds. To prolong the life of nylon strings, take special care while installing, de-tuning, or removing them. The nut slots and saddle crown must be perfectly shaped to avoid cutting the strings, and the ties used to install them at the bridge and tuners are important, too.

Most wound classical strings have a limp end and a stiff end, while the unwound treble strings often have a plain end and a colored one. The limp end of a wound string

If you work on classical guitars but don't play them yourself, you owe it to your customers to find out as much as you can about proper set-up. Visit dealers who handle good classicals, ask questions, and play on the better instruments.

is simply a result of the manufacturing process; it is not meant to be tied onto the bridge, although many guitarists mistakenly do this because it's easier to wrap. The limp, loose, wrapped ends break sooner, and will not only mar the tie-block inlay, but scar the saddle as well, causing buzzing and intonation problems. Often the treble string ends are color-coded to identify the string tension (red=high; yellow=super high). Don't tie the colored end to the bridge! As Jeff Elliott points out, "The color can transfer permanently to the finish of the top or the bridge, so I either clip it off or use the uncolored end. Whichever end you use for tying, heat it with a match or lighter to create a small ball end that helps it lock. To avoid burning it, remove the string from the flame the instant it begins to contract. If the nylon looks brown or burnt in any way, it will be too brittle, and break off. In this case, cut it off and try again." Ball-end nylon strings, such as La Bella's Folk Singers, are available through your dealer, but they aren't generally used on fine classical guitars. They're used to simplify string installation on folk guitars or lesser-grade classicals.

For the standard wrap at the bridge, work about a 3" length of string through the tie block and out the back side of the bridge. Then bring the string end up and over the tie block, run it under the string, and loop or twist it toward the back edge of the tie block (shown at left). Because the sixth, fifth, third, and second strings have a similar large diameter, two twists are usually enough; the fourth and first strings should have three twists since their diameters are smaller. Regardless of the number of twists, the final twist should be at the back edge of the tie block, where you'll often find a strip of inlay material. The loose end must be tucked in under the string as it exits the string hole in the bridge. This isn't the only tie used on classical bridges, but it's the most common.

The sharply trimmed string ends have a tendency to poke into the top after you've completed the wrap, so be sure to snip the string ends to avoid putting dings in the top.

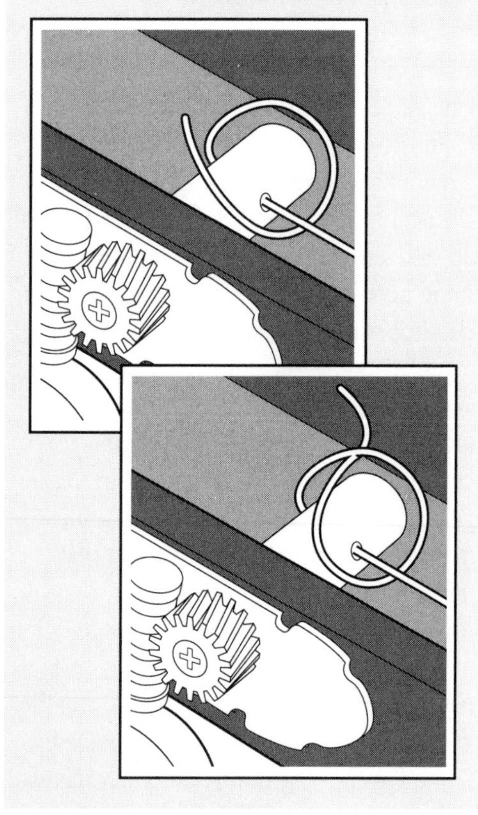

Tying the strings correctly at the tuning key shaft is important, too. For the simplest tie, poke the string through the tuner barrel (roller) twice so that it can't slip, and then wind. This is not the approved method in classical guitar circles, though. Here's the traditional method for obtaining a tie that's good-looking and self-locking: Run the string through the hole, and then back over the barrel and under itself. Then hold the loose end while tightening the string, locking it against itself (first drawing, above). Another similar self-locking tie runs back under itself and then threads up through the loop created by bringing the string back over the barrel (second drawing).

All makers don't necessarily wrap in the same direction or in the same way. William Cumpiano, for instance, believes: "You must have more than one wrap, and it's usually from three to five wraps by the time you get to pitch. Make the wraps around the barrel in the direction that creates the straightest string line to the individual string notches in the nut. Usually the *D* and *G* strings wind toward the center of the headstock, the outer two *E* strings wind toward the outer edges, and the *A* and *B* fall in between." Jeffrey Elliott, on the other hand, says, "Go through the barrel, keeping an inch or two of slack string, and come back up over the top and under the string as shown, but then wrap the string *around itself* twice. Then tighten the tuners, making the wraps around the barrel going *toward* the gears, unless the direction of the string won't get a clean shot from the barrel to the nut. Wrapping away from the gear causes the barrel to act as a lever, putting excess pressure and wear on the gear mechanism and shortening the gear's lifespan by years (especially if the gears are mounted poorly or have any loose components). But different guitars string up differently. The important thing is that a string doesn't touch another string, the channel, or the face veneer while on its way to the nut."

Richard Schneider advises: "Turn the tuning keys until the holes run almost up and down at right angles to the headstock face—maybe with the barrel holes leaning 5° or 10° toward the nut. Run the string down through the hole, up the side of the barrel away from the nut, and back over and under the string. Wrap around the string twice, and then tighten the key while holding the loose end. I don't worry about undue pressure on the barrel or gears, because the tuners I use have a bearing on the shaft end in the headstock center." All of these methods will work. You'll have to experiment to get the correct number of wraps in the right direction so that the strings look neat and miss each other as they go toward their respective slots in the nut.

RELIEF AND STRING HEIGHT

"Nylon strings have greater elasticity," points out William Cumpiano, "and therefore a greater vibrating arc than steel strings. To avoid string rattle, they require greater clearance all along the fingerboard. Fortunately, however, nylon strings are comfortable at a higher action setting, and they also intonate properly at a height where steel strings would play out of tune." Since proper classical set-up requires a higher action, the need for relief is less than you might think. In fact, the relief necessary to accommodate the vibrating strings of a classical guitar usually occurs naturally from the string tension (90 lbs of pull) exerted on a perfectly straight fingerboard. Relief is a very subtle measurement, and most makers expect to see from as little as .004" to as much as .040" when measuring the air space between the bottom of the strings and the top of the fret in the area in the 8th through 10th frets. According to Jeffrey Elliott, "Relief generally runs from a minimum of .004" to an average of .020" at around the 10th fret. More than .040" of relief is excessive, and too little relief can sometimes cause 'back-buzz,' where the string is laying on the frets between your fingering hand and the nut, causing a slight, but annoying buzz."

"I like to see a neck as straight as possible," claims Richard Schneider, "but some relief is inevitable and perhaps a help. Too much relief can cause *sympathetic* string vibration on the short string length between your fingering hand and the nut. This is a somewhat rare occurrence and is different than the back-buzz that Jeff's talking about, but it's annoying when it occurs. The average relief would probably measure from .020" to .040"." As a result of string tension, most classical necks take a permanent "set" or forward bow of as much as .020". This doesn't go away even when the strings are removed, so don't mistake this for a warped neck! Again, the higher action is not a problem for the player because of the softer

Feel like playing a little guitar? Take a look at this miniature classical guitar by Robert Steinegger of Portland, OR. It's only as long as your finger, but it's actually tunable!

touch used with nylon strings. Some makers may build a slight relief into their necks, while others remove extra wood on the bass side, starting at the nut and running "downhill" to the end of the fingerboard in the Ramirez and Hauser style. All these methods are correct, and all of the builders questioned approached relief differently.

THE NUT

Bone is the preferred material for making a good nut or saddle for any acoustic guitar. There's no need to go deeply into making a classical nut, since the same techniques described in the section on Nut Making are used to fit the classical nut. Because nylon strings are so delicate, the correct angle of the string slot to the tuner and a perfectly round shape in the nut slot bottom are even more important than with steel strings. It's especially easy for the wound strings to hang up in a poorly shaped slot, and when they do, they unravel and sound awful—just before they finally break! The classical nut has a flatter top to match the unradiused fingerboard, and like the steel-string, when viewed from the side the nut and string slots must taper at a gradual curve from the back side to the front edge at about a 10° angle.

Correct nut height can best be determined by eye, feel, and experience, but the novice can get close by measuring. Richard Schneider says: "The clearance, or air space, over the 1st fret with the string open and coming off the nut should be a little greater than the clearance over the 2nd fret with the string pressed on the 1st fret. A business card measures .005", so use three business cards to measure under the treble strings and maybe five or six business cards under the bass."

Of course, the overall action and height of the bridge saddle has a big effect on nut measurement. Use the same techniques shown in the nut making and saddle sections, balancing one end to the other and working the action down by degree. Another general rule for nut height that works for steel or nylon strings is to press a string at the 2nd fret, looking to see a slight clearance between the string and the 1st fret; as long as there is some clearance here, the open strings shouldn't buzz. The clearance should increase gradually from the high- to the low-*E*, because the lower wound strings must sit from .015" to .030" higher in the nut than the treble strings to avoid open-string buzz. Overall string height at the nut shouldn't get too low, since there's a strong tendency for nylon strings to buzz sympathetically between the fretted note and the nut behind where you're actually playing, just as they would from too much relief! Here's a final general rule for nut height: Measure the air space between the string and the top of the 1st fret, looking for a gap of ½ mm (.020") under the treble-*E* and around 7/10 mm (.030") under the low-*E*.

A traditional classical guitar fingerboard is flat from side to side, although some modern makers are introducing a very slight radius to make it easier to play barre chords: "This is a very gentle arch that's imparted with a plane," says Cumpiano. "It's not greater than a 1/32" offset at the fingerboard edge. It makes the instrument easier to play, and probably lets a player get away with a little bit less technique." The classical guitar's saddle should be flat, too, or match the shape of a slightly arched fingerboard. As with the nut, set the saddle action lower on the treble side, following the same 1⁄32" rise from treble toward the bass. Some makers taper and thin the fingerboard on the base side in order to keep a more regular saddle height across the bridge (this creates a more even angle on the string which exerts a more even tension on the top). Other makers who feel that the bass strings need to break at more of an angle than the treble strings disagree with this technique, since it eliminates that option.

ACTION/STRING HEIGHT

To set the action, use a small ruler at the 12th fret. Measure the air space from the bottom of the string to the top of the fret. Different builders prefer different readings under the two *E* strings: Elliott's preference is 3 to 3½ mm under the treble, and 4 to 4½ mm under the bass, while Cumpiano favors 1⁄8" under the treble and 5⁄32" under the bass. "A high action for a classical," he adds, "would be 5⁄32" treble and 3⁄16" bass." Schneider describes: "When fretting the string at the 1st fret, measure 3 mm under the treble and 4 mm under the bass. A good concert player can handle this action, although some prefer to have the action higher. After adjusting the action to these parameters, I make two more saddles: a low one measuring 2½ mm treble to 3½ mm bass, and another one that's 3½ mm treble to 5 mm bass. I also cut a second nut with the string spacing closer together by 1 mm. These are put in a little walnut and rosewood box that I deliver with each instrument."

Traditionally, the classical saddle isn't shaped quite as round as a steel-string's, because of the nylon string's tendency to unravel or break when it meets a sharp edge. Instead, the saddle is often tapered smoothly towards the front edge (above, right) so that the string "takes off" gradually, with full support from the saddle shape to avoid string breakage. This method of shaping is only valid if the exact compensation has been calculated into the placement of the bridge; otherwise the peak of the saddle may have to be slightly altered to get the most accurate intonation. Many classical builders prefer to use a gently rounded saddle top; either method is correct. The saddle should fit snugly into the bridge slot and have a well-sanded and polished top surface for optimum tone. There should be no sharp edges or notches cut into it, although John Williams, a great classical guitarist, has been known to prefer a notched saddle.

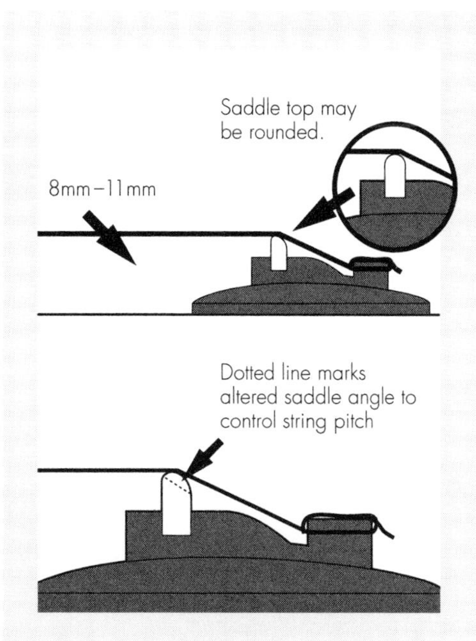

Jeffrey Elliott points out that the builder can control tone and string tension by altering the saddle's angle and thereby changing the pitch of the string to the tie block (above). This subtle refinement is probably beyond the scope of our needs, but it's the combination of such little subtleties that make one guitar sound better than another. Jeff also states that the height of the strings from the top is extremely important; from the bottom of the string where it meets the saddle to the guitar's top should measure somewhere between 8 mm to 11 mm for most instruments.

STRING RECOMMENDATIONS

What brands are good, and how often should they be changed? Cumpiano points out that a recitalist often changes strings every two or three days, and always before a performance. String deterioration has a dramatic effect on intonation, and sadly enough, classical strings are not only quite fragile, but expensive. Old strings lose pitch accuracy and tone. Cumpiano cites D'Addario Pro Arte Hi-Tension strings as a modern, well-built set, and he also uses Savarez Blues and Whites. Schneider prefers D'Addario Pro Arte, Savarez Crystal Solis, and GHS, which are all high-tension strings. "You might want medium- to low-tension strings for a recording situation," he adds, "because they're easier to finger, and some instruments do sound better with low tension." Kurt Rodarmer plays a Schneider/ Kasha guitar and only changes his treble strings every six to eight months, since they get rock-hard and stay that way, creating the best sound. He changes the bass strings every other week during normal practice, and always two days before a concert. (I encourage string manufacturers to market sets of bass strings only, because everyone always has scads of extra trebles!) Elliott favors both high- and normal-tension D'Addario Pro Arte and Savarez Alliance in Red or Yellow, which, he says, "are made of a new material that is smaller in diameter than most others, has less tension, provides a good tonal variety and response, and is extremely accurate and clear sounding." R.E. Brune, a famous luthier based in Evanston, Illinois, has recently begun importing the excellent Hannabach brand. Many players have been extremely impressed with these strings.

For more detailed information on classical set-up, read the books listed in the Recommended Reading section, especially *Guitar Making: Tradition and Technology* by William Cumpiano and Jon Natelson.

Twelve steps to replacing a nut

Many players are anxious to work on or make their own nut, since it's one of the guitar's most important parts, in terms of action, sound, and playability. While its perfect fit is best left to qualified repairmen where your favorite guitar is concerned, it is okay to develop your nut-making skills on inexpensive imports and old yardsale specials. This chapter describes the necessary nut-making tools (many of which you can make yourself), the best materials to use, and the basic steps involved. If you go about the process slowly, work on instruments of lesser value, and make a small investment in certain specialized tools, you should eventually be able to handle nut making like a pro. Remember, be patient and read the whole story before tearing apart any guitars—and don't wreck a good one while you learn!

Nuts need to be replaced for a variety of reasons: the string slots are too low and cause buzzing at the 1st fret, the string spacing is irregular or too wide or narrow to suit your taste, or the guitar isn't producing a strong, clean sound (this is most often caused by plastic nuts). Perhaps you've found a used guitar that would play, except for a chip right on a string groove at the nut. It doesn't take someone with a Ph.D. in guitar repair to know when the nut has to go—just follow your senses. In most cases, if your guitar plays well on the fretted strings and only annoys you on the open ones, the nut's just worn out. If you were happy with the nut's general shape, you can remake it, trying to copy the old nut's string width and spacing as closely as possible; simply leave the strings higher than before to eliminate buzz. On the next page is an outline for nut making, followed by advice on specialized tools that you'll want.

Bone is *white* because it's bleached. You'll also find a lot of yellow and off-white bone. I've been very happy with the blanks I get from Stewart-MacDonald and Luthier's Mercantile.

TWELVE STEPS TO REPLACING A NUT

1 Remove the old nut.

2 Clean nut slot of glue and residue, and square it up.

3 Choose new nut material and rough-in the blank to fit the cleaned slot.

4 Lay out string spacing.

5 Rough-in approximate string slots, without going too deep.

6 Trim off excess nut material from top as slots get deeper.

7 Lower and shape string slots, moving strings side to side, if needed.

8 Trim off excess nut material, rough edges, and overhang.

9 Final-sand and contour the nut's shape.

10 Polish with a soft rag and rubbing compounds (especially the bottoms of string slots).

11 Final-check the string height and shape, and string to pitch.

12 Glue in nut (with strings on, for clamp pressure).

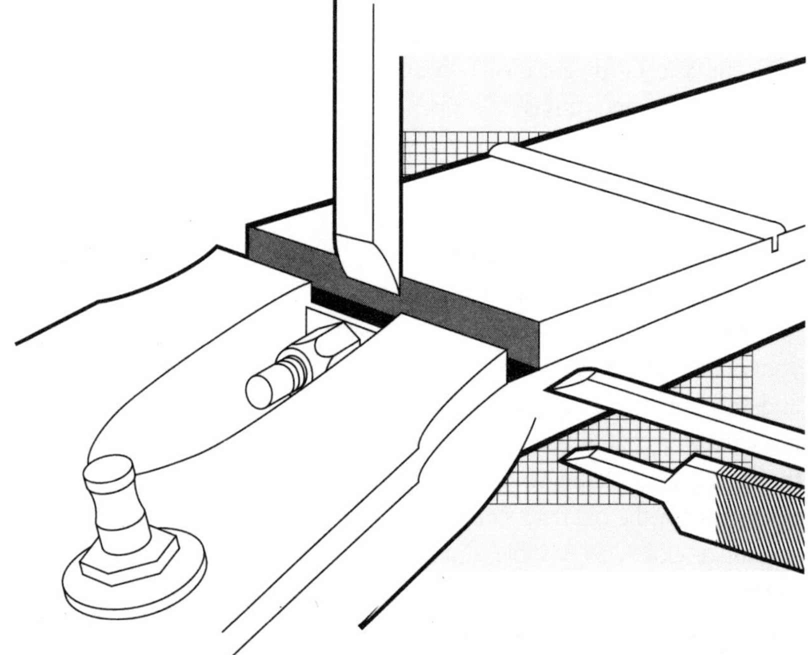

TOOLS

The right tools help make the job easier. You can make many of them yourself, and specialized items can be found at the luthier supply stores listed in the back of the book. Other items are available from hardware stores or wood-shop suppliers.

A sharp chisel is great for paring (shaving) and scraping glue off the fingerboard's end; I like a 3/8" or 1/2" bench chisel for this job. A 1/8" chisel that's ground slightly thinner in width is also good, especially for getting into a Fender-style nut slot (see drawing below). You'll find a smooth mill file handy for shaping the nut, cleaning away old glue, and helping with squaring-up. A small (6") mill file is also quite handy, since it's thin enough (.115") to file inside a Fender slot for squaring-up, and the file's tang becomes a great scraper, chisel, etc., when sharpened on a grindstone (note the tang-converted file in the drawing).

A set of feeler gauges is a help when measuring action height from the string's bottom to the top of the 1st fret. If possible, buy the kind that you can take apart by loosening a screw. In fact, feeler gauges are a must around any shop, for all sorts of uses. We'll use them throughout this book, so buy a full set.

X-acto makes a great razor-saw set with three interchangeable saw blades of .012", .013", .014" thicknesses. We'll use these to start nut slots, and in some cases to do the actual nut-slotting. An X-acto knife (or other brand) with #11 blades is also a must, since it's used to score the finish around the nut during removal. These saw/knife sets vary in size and price, and are available at many hardware stores and guitar supply sources.

Specialized nut-shaping files are available from Stewart-MacDonald, Luthier's Mercantile, and other companies. Custom-made for getting into nut slots, these round-bottomed files have smooth sides that allow you to cut the nut-slot bottom, but not the

slot's sidewalls. My favorite set—Precision Nut Files—has accurate, well-shaped, round cutting edges, and includes ten files ranging from .010" to .058". Full sets of files are expensive (in the $70 range), but worth the money if you are serious about getting into the business. The ten files that are my favorite can be purchased one at a time, and three of them would be a good starter set.

You'll need a 6" stainless-steel rule, preferably the hardware-store variety made by General. I've mentioned this tool often; everyone should have one. Notice that the fractions are converted to decimal equivalents on the back side; this is handy for string spacing. A dial caliper is always nice to have, but certainly not a must. Even the inexpensive plastic kind is plenty good enough for our needs.

Whenever you're making or adjusting a nut, remember that string height at the nut is directly affected by the height at the bridge. You may need to work back and forth a bit from the nut to bridge, by either raising or lowering an electric guitar's adjustable inserts or by filing, shimming, or replacing an acoustic guitar's saddle. You should be basically satisfied with the action and playability of the guitar as it is (with the exception of the buzzing from nut slots that are too low) before making a new nut, so that you don't discover at the job's end that the bridge was too high or low to begin with. Now on to making a nut.

Roughing in the blank

Before removal, score completely around the old nut with a sharp X-acto knife or razor blade. This way, if the finish starts to chip upon removal, the chip will stop at the scored line. Most often the nut comes unglued after being tapped with a block of wood and a hammer. Firmly but gently tap from the front (fingerboard side) of the nut, and then tap from the rear in the same fashion. Do this back and forth until the nut "rocks" out. Once loose, grip it with your fingers and pull it out carefully. I can't overemphasize the need to watch for finish chipping! It's a risk you'll have to take. Many imported guitars with thick polyester finishes are hard to score—but not impossible. Wear safety glasses while scoring the lacquer or polyester and while knocking the nut loose. With Fender-style guitars, you'll have to grip the nut with some end nippers or pliers after gently loosening it by tapping, and then pull it out like a tooth.

Once the nut's out, clean any glue or residue from the nut slot (the groove that held it in the neck). Even on cheap guitars, the nut slot is generally uniformly shaped at the factory, but it needs to be scraped clean of residue for a good-fitting blank. Common nut thicknesses range from ¼" to $\frac{3}{16}$" (for Martin, Gibson, Guild, and their acoustic clones) down to ⅛" (for Fender-style electrics). A variety of files and tools will fit in the slots for cleaning. I use a sharp chisel to remove any glue from the fingerboard's end grain and to trim any sticky stuff from the front edge of the headstock overlay. Held vertically and used with short strokes as a scraper, a chisel can be great for cleaning the bottom of the nut slot. The nut-seating files described earlier work the best. If you file the bottom of the slot, be sure to lightly file the lacquer's edge first, so that it won't chip

Many new nut blanks have tiny pits and crevices that you might not notice until the buffing stage. These holes may fill with compound or finger dirt, making the finished product look funky. For a smooth-looking job, try filling the holes with super glue before handling them.

It's hard to find perfect bone blanks, so don't throw out the pitted blanks; just save the really good ones for your primo jobs. And remember: Everyone else is faced with the same situation, so make do with what you have and don't complain to your suppliers—they're doing the best they can!

as you begin to file the wood. To avoid pushing a chip of lacquer off the neck, always file in from each side toward center.

I prefer bone as a nut material, and no longer use commercial ivory, which necessitates the slaughter of elephants and other mammals with tusks. Don't even mess with sellers of "legal" ivory—they're lying. Bone makes an excellent nut, and synthetic Micarta is also good (begin with Micarta as you're learning—it's cheaper).

Start with a blank that's bigger than the actual slot height, length, and thickness, and slowly bring it down to size. Use the saddle-making techniques described in the Acoustic Adjustments chapter as a guide for squaring up the stock and getting it to fit the slot. (Quick repeat: Flatten one side against a smooth file, mark out the desired thickness, and then sand, file, or belt-sand the opposing side to uniform thickness.) Be sure the bottom is shaped exactly like the slot; Martin nuts, for example, have an angled bottom. Leave a ⅛" overhang on both treble and bass ends to allow the nut to be shifted from side to side as you're laying out and filing the string slots. That way, if you happen to get a bit off on your string spacing, you can tap the whole nut towards treble or bass and relocate the string slots.

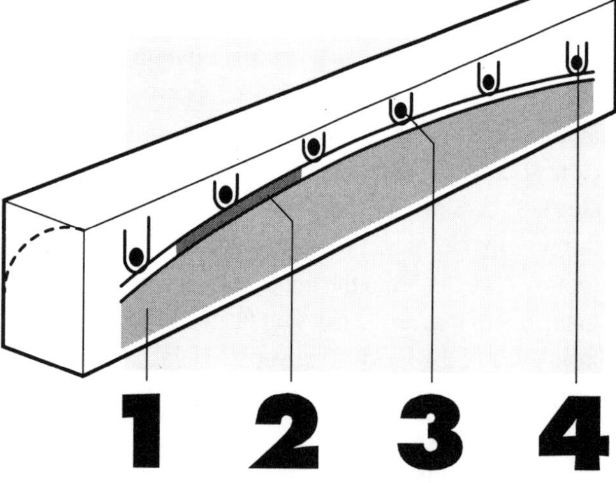

1 Start by tracing the fingerboard height/curve.
2 Add the fret height.
3 Here is the string height(the action).
4 Extra nut height above string thickness.

The nut should press into the slot and fit snugly. Viewed from the side or end, the blank should be gradually rounded toward the front edge (note the dotted line in the drawing below, left). If it pleased you, copy the shape of the old nut. When the blank fits, trace the fingerboard's shape (radius) onto it from the front side by running a pencil over the fingerboard surface. Remove the blank and finish laying out the nut in pencil by adding the thickness of the frets (say .035"), the height of the strings from the fret top, the thickness of the string itself, and a little extra for good measure. Most players prefer an action that's higher on the bass side than on the treble. (This treble-to-bass rise is illustrated in the previous two chapters.) Use care when taking the blank in and out, so that you don't chip the lacquer or wood as a result of the tight fit.

This is a good point at which to take a break, and review nut making up to this point. Spend time gathering your tools, and practice a nut rough-in on something that you know you can't ruin. Then we'll cut the string slots and finish the job.

Cutting string slots and finishing up

We just went through the steps for making a nut, described some necessary tools, and got through the roughing-in stage. Now we'll carry on with the job. Good luck!

Before proceeding any further, lay some masking tape over the headstock face and on the fingerboard between the nut and 1st fret to protect the wood and finish from an accidental slip of the file. Use as many layers as possible, until they get in the way of your work. On older guitars with brittle finishes, it's best to use the less-sticky draftsman's tape, which won't pull off the finish as badly.

Install the two outside *E* strings as far in from the fingerboard's edge as you like for spacing; do this by looking down from directly overhead. Mark the outsides of the strings on each side of the nut with a pencil and file starter notches to hold the strings. The best tool for this is a thin X-acto razor saw; it's also perfect for the actual filing/shaping of the slots for the high-*E*, *B*, and sometimes *G* strings. In general I use a specialized set of nut files that cut only on the thin edge and leave a round-bottomed slot. While the full set costs about $70 and is actually a great investment for anyone doing much set-up work, you can begin with three files (.016", .025", and .035"). These can cut most nut slots if you roll the file for extra width as you cut. This "roll-filing" action is the way to file slots. By using a file slightly smaller than the intended actual notch width and rolling on the forward stroke to widen the outside walls, you have more control and the file won't get stuck in its own notch.

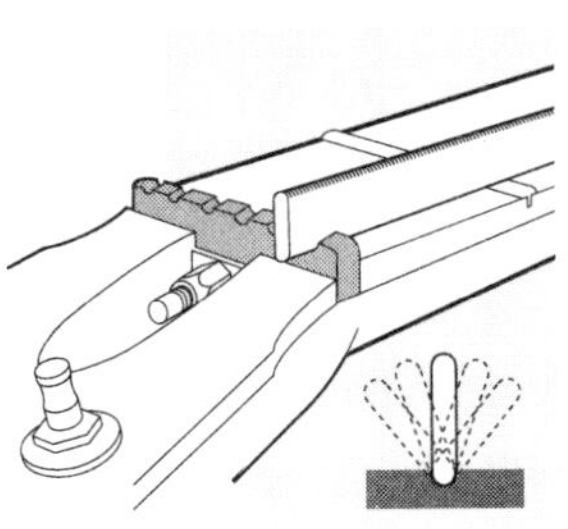

Once the outer strings are set in position, measure between their centers with the 6" rule or a dial caliper. Divide the distance by five for an approximation of the remaining string spacing. Use a calculator, because you'll be dealing in decimals—it's rare to find a nut width that's divisible by fractions. For example, if the outer *E* strings measure 1$\frac{3}{8}$" center to center, the decimal conversion is 1.375 divided by 5, which equals .275 from string to string. I refer to this measurement as approximate because the lower wound strings, being fatter, would actually be closer to each other than the unwound treble strings when spaced exactly evenly. Use the exact measurement only for the layout. File very light starter slots and then put on the remaining four strings. Adjust their spacing by eye as you file and lower them into the nut blank.

Once the slots have all been started just enough to hold the strings so that you can check them by eye when looking from directly overhead, switch to your nut files, X-acto sawblades, and/or ground-down, fine-tooth hacksaw blade. File at a back angle to the nut's front edge, so that the string will have decent downward pressure. To play properly in tune, the string's actual contact point should be at the very front of the nut. On guitars with angled-back headstocks, which are the most common, you basically follow the angle of the headstock itself. With slab-neck Fender-style guitars, you won't file as steep a back angle, so just file the appropriate angle needed for each string-post.

File the slots one at a time, starting with the high-*E*. Loosen the string and lift it out of the slot as you file. Then replace the string, tune it to pitch, and check your work. Expect to go back and forth from treble to bass several times before the slots get close to their final depth and shape. You'll need to keep filing the nut's top down as your strings get lower into the blank. In general, you want the strings to sit in round-bottomed slots, filed to the shape (diameter) of each string, and no deeper than one-half the string's diameter.

My friend Don MacRostie, who's an ace mandolin designer and repairman known throughout Ohio for his Red Diamond instruments, taught me the following method for knowing when the strings are dropped enough in depth. Here we use the feeler gauges described in the tool list given in the roughing-in section. You need to remove the protective masking tape from the fingerboard to do this:

Sometimes you'll work hard making a perfect nut, and right at the end of the job you'll go too low with your file, causing an open string to buzz at the first fret. You'll want to tear your hair out! It's called "blowing the nut," and we all do it. Either shim the nut, or start a new one. Sorry!

Although I've described how to measure and lay out the divisions of the strings before filing, I usually do it by eye. Learn to trust your own eye.

1 Measure the height of the first two frets, from the fret's top to the fingerboard, by laying a straightedge across the two frets and sliding different combinations of feeler gauge blades under it until they just touch the straightedge. Record this measurement (let's say .035" for an average, somewhat worn fret height).

2 Add to this from .005" to .010" or any figure you come up with after experimenting. New total: .040" (.035" frets, plus .005").

3 Stack up a number of feeler gauges that equal the total measurement (.040"), and hold them against the front edge of the nut while you file at a normal backward angle down to the metal. When your razor saw, nut file, or homemade hacksaw blade file contacts the hardened steel—you'll feel it instantly—it's time to stop.

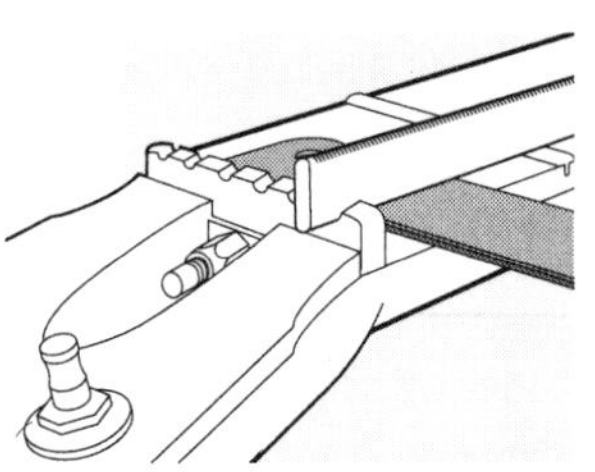

The nice thing about this method is that you can control the drop of the string and avoid accidentally going too low. Also, when you find a good measurement for high-*E* and *B* strings that is quite low and comes close to your final action, you can increase this amount by .002" or so as you go across the radius of the board toward the bass side, slightly raising these strings more than their treble-string counterparts. When you find good average measurements, record them as a guide to use some other time.

When the string slots are well spaced and deep enough, do the final shaping and finishing. Using a very sharp pencil, mark the excess nut-blank overhang and trim it off with your razor saw (file or sand if you prefer), leaving a slight bit of the pencil line showing so that you can file and smoothly sand it away without chips. For the final time, sand down the top to eliminate any too-deep slots, finish rounding and shaping the nut to look like your original or the picture in your mind's eye, and sand off any scratches using 320-, 400-, and 600-grit wet-or-dry sandpaper, in that order.

If you have any really deep scratches, you may find it easiest to remove them with your smooth mill file. Buff the nut on a soft rag smeared with a buffing compound and then a polishing compound, such as Meguiar's Mirror Glaze #4 and #7, in that order. I like to high-polish the slot bottoms with 1000-grit "Finesse" sandpaper wrapped around my nut files or razor saw. These buffing compounds and 1000-grit paper are available at most auto parts stores and from many guitar shop suppliers. Finally, dry-buff the nut surfaces on a clean dry rag. Care should be taken when sanding, smoothing, and polishing the nut. Stay on the exposed surfaces and lay off the bone that actually fits into the nut slot—too much buffing here can create a loose fit when it comes to the gluing-in.

To be sure that you have the action the way you like, string the guitar to pitch before gluing the nut. Recheck your string height and the relationship between nut and bridge. Don't be surprised if you have to take the nut in and out of the slot (stringing to pitch, as well) as many as a dozen times while you're learning. Expect a certain amount of string breakage, too, from the constant tuning down and up to pitch. Most professionals usually have a nut in and out of an instrument at least four times before completion, so don't feel bad.

If the final fitting meets your approval, glue the nut into place using a couple of light dabs of hide glue or white glue. I avoid using my beloved Hot Stuff super glue here, because its instant setting time won't allow you to move the nut from side to side when lining it up. Apply the glue lightly to the front wall and underside of the nut, set it in place, and quickly snug up the strings to help hold it in place. After the glue has set (one hour for a white/yellow glue such as Titebond, and three or four for a hide glue), you can tune to pitch and you're back in the business of making music.

Be sure to read between the lines here, knowing that I couldn't describe every approach to nut making, nor all the tools that can be used, without writing a book on just that one subject! I'm trying to offer enough information to help the do-it-yourselfer do a better job, and to educate those not interested in doing their own set-ups, so they'll be better prepared to shop for quality work.

Setting up the Wilkinson roller nut

Although I'm definitely a purist and prefer a bone nut on my '56 Strat, I still keep up with the times—and you should, too. So, to keep "Strat smart," let's look at the Wilkinson roller nut, Fender's non-locking alternative for tremolo players. Standard equipment on Jeff Beck's Strat Plus guitars, this nut substitutes steel rollers for the string grooves, or slots, that are normally hand-cut in a traditional nut. The rollers help ease the friction that occurs during tremolo use. Occasionally, this nut may need a minor set-up or adjustment you can do yourself.

The Fender/Wilkinson nut is a chrome-plated brass housing that holds six loose-fitting needle-bearing rollers at its front edge. At the rear edge, six additional rollers create down-pressure on the front needle bearings. The nut's six individual string slots measure, from treble to bass, .011", .014", .018", .028", .038", and .049". Deduct a half-thousandth (.0005) from each measurement for chrome plating, and you'll know what string gauges fit through the slots (a set of .010 to .046 works best, and an optional nut for .012 to .052 strings is also available).

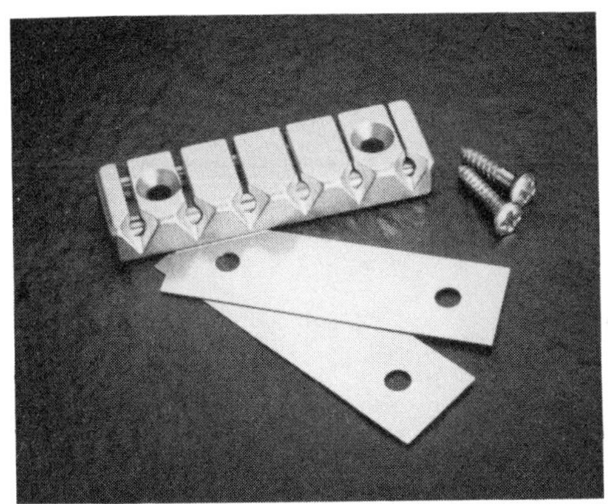

The Wilkinson Original Roller is an excellent tremolo nut that uses roller string trees, and it's offered in a variety of custom options. It's available through dealers and some guitar parts suppliers.

According to Dan Smith, Fender's Vice President of Marketing, "When we first looked at the Strat Plus, we knew we had a great unit in the American Standard Tremolo. We'd made 10 or 11 different tremolos over the past 15 years, and the American Standard was the best—it surprised even *us.* Taking advantage of this tremolo meant stabilizing what goes on at the headstock between the nut and the tuners. Trev Wilkinson happened along with his roller nut at just the right time. He redesigned it with exclusive, built-in hold-downs to do away with string trees on the headstock face.

"Our first model had rollers on the top three strings only. Soon, we installed them on all six strings to get better down-pressure on the wound *E*-, *A*-, and *D*-string rollers. This eliminated any chance of open-string buzz caused by either inadequate string angle or from headstock deflection. It's a little-known fact that a headstock can deflect—or bend up—toward the strings. This changes the down-pressure *slightly*, but enough to cause a possible buzz. Some headstocks deflect, and some don't, even when made from the same tree. A traditional nut *can* work well with a tremolo, if everything's perfect and if it's made by a skilled luthier. But those 'perfect' nuts have only a short lifespan before wearing low enough to warrant replacement—another reason we're using a roller nut on the Plus."

I've occasionally run into minor problems with the nut. A too-narrow string slot

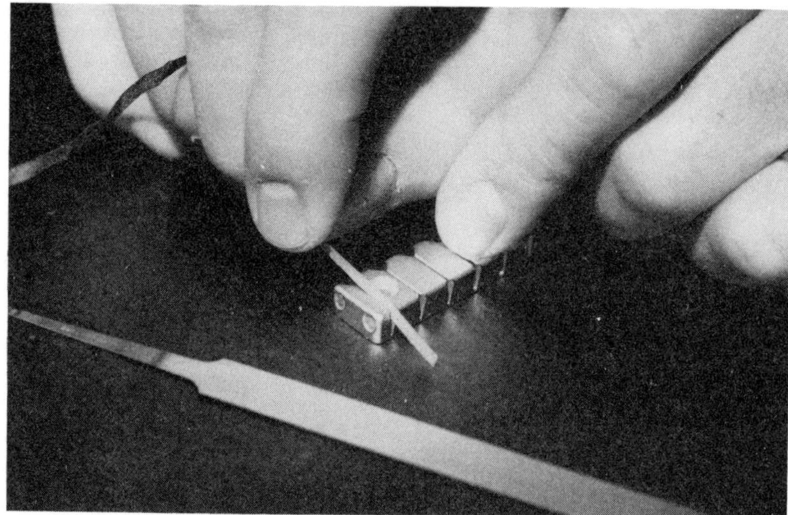

can cause a string to bind (usually the high-*E*), keeping it from returning to pitch or causing a buzz at the roller. Sometimes there's no binding trouble, but a slight buzz. Most likely, this sitar-like sound is on the high-*E*. Here are some solutions:

First, eliminate any binding in the slot. The binding may be caused by a warp you could never see or measure, or it may be due to a bit too much plating. I use a "lightning strip" to carefully de-burr the back edge of the string slot (pictured above). These thin metal strips are coated with diamond dust; your dentist uses them to clean between your teeth after a filling—ask for one. I also use my .010" Stewart-MacDonald Precision Nut File, again on the rear wall of the nut housing. Note: Don't scar the rollers. Before you do that, take it to a professional, please!

If a buzz isn't being caused by string-slot binding, most likely it's intermittent and will go away by itself (especially if you try to show it to your repairman). However, if you can't play it out, try any or all of these remedies:

- Simply put on a fresh set of strings.
- With the strings removed, tap lightly on the problem roller with a sharp-pointed tool such as an awl, ice pick, scribe, etc.
- Remove the strings and blow out the nut with compressed air.
- Loosen the nut's mounting screws, let the strings line the nut up naturally, and retighten. Often, just moving it like this solves the problem! Don't overtighten the two small mounting screws—just make them snug.
- Lubricate the offending roller after it's been blown out with air. To avoid attracting dust, use a non-oily Teflon type of lubricant. A little dab will do you.
- Rinse out a dirty nut with a spray-type tuner degreaser followed by a blast of air.
- To alter the nut height, your Fender dealer stocks stainless-steel nut shims in thicknesses of .002", .005", and .010".
- Finally, installing the nut involves routing a flat ledge and removing 1/16" from the end of the fingerboard. So, if Fender ever offers the nut as a replacement item, you'll have to make that woodworking decision.

Fretwire types and sizes

Before touching a file to your frets, read this complete chapter!

A customer with an old Les Paul "fretless wonder" asks, "Am I really missing anything by using a guitar with short frets?" Another wonders, "Will tall frets cause poor intonation?" The answers that I gave are the same as I'd give for any question about frets: The best frets for you—thick or thin, short or tall—depend on the feel that you like and the sound that you want. In the uncomplicated old days, most acoustic and electric guitars came with little variety in fret styles. Today, though, guitars are made with many different wire sizes and shapes. Let's see what's available in fretwire so that you can better choose your new guitar or your future refretting job. The following descriptions of tall, medium, or low wires may not necessarily coincide with some fret charts and descriptions that you may run across. This is my viewpoint on fretwire measurement, and the information is intended to simplify things for you.

Fretwire is available in three shapes—rounded, squared, and triangular. The most common fret shape, or profile, is the rounded head or "bead." You may have seen square and extremely low fretwire on a Gibson Les Paul or early SG. These guitars were nicknamed "fretless wonders," which they nearly were. This fret offered very low action with little drag on the fingers when moving up and down the board; sustain, tone, and easy bends were traded off for that action, however. A triangular-shaped wire has been pioneered by East Coast luthier Phil Petillo in recent years, and perhaps this will gain popularity with exposure. Round or "oval"-type wires (which have different heights, widths, and advantages) are far and away the most common, and therefore the most deserving of our attention here.

Tall fretwire ranges from .050" to .065" above the fingerboard (about the thickness of a dime). Not many tall wires are available. Here are some advantages: Tall frets are easier for string bends, since the fingertip has less contact with the fingerboard. They also offer more sustain, due to the greater mass and because the string isn't damped by as much finger/fingerboard contact, which draws away some tone, volume, and sustain. While tall frets don't offer the same advantages as the radical scalloped fingerboards described later in this chapter, they lean in that direction more than a short fret does, so you'll get better hammer-ons and pull-offs. They also outlast low frets and withstand more fret dressings between refrets. Some disadvantages: Poor intonation could result from pressing too hard, but this can be corrected with a gentler touch. Until the left hand relaxes, the frets may feel like railroad ties when you slide up or down the fingerboard, and the neck may "feel" slightly thicker, but this is minor. I enjoy playing on tall frets.

Regardless of width, medium fretwire is the standard that has commonly been used for the last 40 years. Some medium wires are called "jumbo," but this refers to the width, not the height. This wire ranges from .032" to .046" in height. Pros: With jumbo frets, the player can more easily achieve accurate intonation (again, this depends on touch), since the fingerboard wood stops the fingertip, not allowing the string to be pressed too deeply. Barre chords and slides are easier, and the guitar's tone is softer, since the finger has more contact with the fingerboard. Cons: To enjoy medium fretwire at its best, the fret work must be done accurately to ensure that you don't lose precious height during dressing. Medium wire wears out sooner because there is less height, and it allows fewer dressings between refrets. You'll still get years of playing out of medium wire if the fret work is good to begin with. Hammer-ons, pull-offs, bends, and sustain are not as easy as on tall wire, but most of us have been playing on medium wire for years and enjoying it; it's my favorite.

Except for the squared, low fretwire on the "fretless wonders," you probably won't run into low wire (.020" to 030") on a modern instrument. Expect to find low wire on used guitars that have seen much use and are simply worn out from years of playing and fret dressings. They're ready for a refret. While low wire is good for easy slides and fast action, it's not conducive to hammer-ons, pull-offs, string bending, and good tone and sustain. I do not enjoy playing on low wire.

A fret's width, regardless of height, affects playability and tone. Here you'll have to decide what you like. The increased mass of a wide fret offers a more "heavy metal" sustain than a narrow fret of comparable height, and wide frets wear longer than narrow ones. However, wide frets must be dressed more accurately than narrow ones to avoid poor intonation and buzzing caused by the string making contact off center (right), causing poor intonation, or flopping on a too-wide flat. Note: I dress a wide fret in two ways: rounded accurately to center, or semi-round like the top of a school bus (opposite). The "school busing," which is often preferred by my rock customers, wears longer.

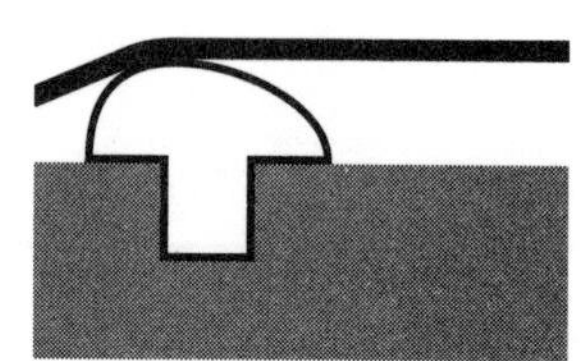

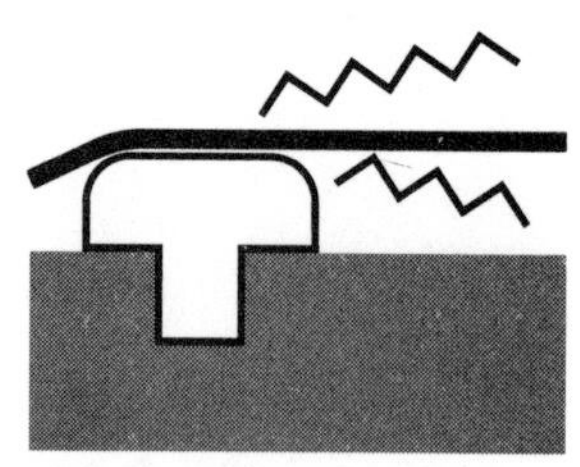

Narrow frets offer a unique sustain, due to a cleaner contact point between string and fret crown, as well as the most accurate intonation. They don't have any disadvantages that I can think of, except that thinner frets have a crisper sound—clean, like breaking a glass—due to the accurate contact made between string and fret. This clean sound is sometimes misinterpreted as buzzing, and may take getting used to. The choice of fret width can only be decided by you. I prefer narrow.

A fret's hardness is determined by the metallurgy of its alloy. Usually the choice is 18% nickel/silver (hard), or 12% (soft). Stick with the hardest wire you're offered—it wears longer. Some classical guitar players prefer soft wire, feeling that it is more gentle on nylon or gut strings. But in most cases, the harder wire is the preferred choice.

Phil Petillo's triangular wire may have advantages for the finicky player. This fret is hard and almost pointed (though there is a slight round to the top), which makes it very accurate when it comes to proper intonation. Petillo wire is installed using a patented, secret method that guarantees perfect intonation. As this wire gains acceptance, I'm sure many repairmen will stock it.

This basic information should help you understand the different types of frets. If you're shopping for a new guitar, ask the salesman to explain what size wire has been used. If you're looking for a refret, ask your repairman to show you samples; most keep enough different wires in stock to please anyone. But don't get too carried away worrying about fretwire—simply give it some thought while you enjoy playing what you have.

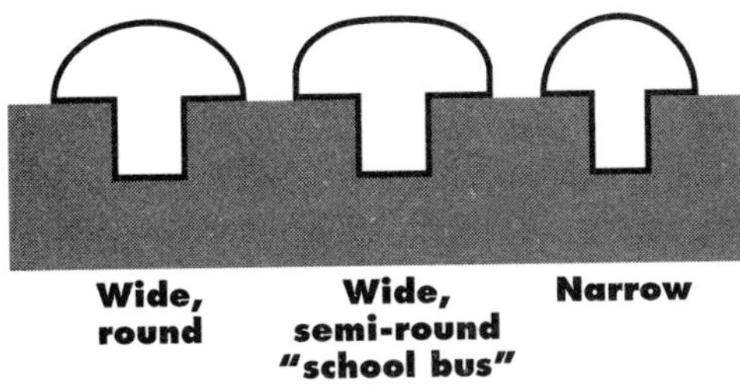

Wide, round **Wide, semi-round "school bus"** **Narrow**

Fretwire hardness and files

Don't run out and buy any tools until you've read this entire chapter—there are too many choices. Get what suits the job at hand.

While on the subject of fretwire and how tall or short, fat or slim it is, we should talk about fretwire hardness, too. Here I'll reprint a letter from a *Guitar Player* reader, William Dalziel in Strathclyde, Scotland, who asked two good questions. The answer to the first question addresses a topic that many builders, repairmen, and players have been curious about in recent years: Is fretwire softer than it used to be? The second question, regarding types of fret-crowning files, will introduce the rest of this chapter on fret work and give do-it-yourself fret workers help in choosing and using their first rounding file. Here's the letter:

"Touchstone Tonewoods lists two densities of fretwire—a medium Japanese wire and a hard Dutch 12% silver wire. Which is commonly used, and are there advantages in sustain when using the harder type? Also, the supplier advertises 'hand-made double-edged fret files' that are available in radii of 1.5, 2, 3, 4, or 5 mm. I am not sure which would most suit my needs. I plan on refretting a cheapish maple-fingerboard Tele copy with fretwire that measures 2.5 mm wide and 1 mm tall. I'll have to file the fret tops flat afterward to make them even, since this is my first attempt at fret work. Which file is best for the re-rounding, and what type of cut do these files impart?"

First, I'll answer William's fretwire questions. The most commonly used fretwire for steel-string acoustic or electric guitars is 18% nickel/silver. Classical builders often use softer wire. Harder wire produces more sustain, but a greater advantage over soft wire is its resistance to string wear. John Hamilton of Touchstone Tonewoods in Surrey, England, advised me that their 12%

Dutch wire is harder than the Japanese "medium" wire, so use it on your Tele. Relative fretwire hardness is a source of controversy in the guitar repair business. I've heard repairmen complain about customer remarks such as: "My guitar was refretted just a year ago, and the frets are grooved already." "My friend's '61 Strat has original frets that still play okay, with few worn spots. Are you guys selling us soft frets so you can get more work out of us?" Believe me, luthiers don't want their customers back in a year complaining of worn frets or expecting free remedies—*fret jobs just ain't that much fun!*

The FretBender

I checked with the fret manufacturers and found that they haven't changed their alloy specifications (as some of us have wondered). In the U.S., a 12% wire is considered soft wire, while the industry standard, 18% wire, is comparatively hard. The percentage—12% or 18%—refers to the amount of nickel in a given wire, not silver (fretwire *looks* silver, but it's made of copper, nickel, and zinc—with no silver at all). The alloy mix for an 18% wire is 65% copper, 18% nickel, and 17% zinc.

Fretwire is still made as it always was. It begins as a semi-hard round wire that is heated to anneal (soften) it, and it's then allowed to cool. It becomes "work-hardened" from being drawn through roller dies that compress the wire into a shaped fret. Once drawn, there's no practical way, at the manufacturing end, to increase fret hardness (in experiments, manufacturers found that rolling a too-hard wire, or wire with a nickel content over 18%, caused breakdowns in the machinery).

I sent old fret samples (saved over the years from vintage guitars), along with new ones, to a lab for the Vickers hardness test for precious metals. The results ranged from 184 to 205 points on the Vickers scale, with the modern wire being hardest in each case. The tests showed that large wire was harder than small wire. In the process, I began thinking about how hard copper gets when bent and unbent (those who have run copper water lines know what I mean) and ended up making what, for me, is a significant discovery. By running the fretwire through a FretBender, over-radiusing it, and then straightening it and rolling it again (repeating the process several times), the fret hardness gained from 14 to 20 points on the Vickers scale, which is appreciable. I was able to work-harden a smaller, Strat-size wire until the hardness matched that of the jumbo wires used in the lab test! Tell your repairman about this technique if he doesn't know it already.

I feel that the biggest reason for fretwire worry is the increased awareness of all facets of the guitar. Paying attention to every detail that improves technique causes one to notice worn frets sooner. Modern players are more aggressive than those in the '50s and '60s, utilizing considerable single-note playing, string bending, and a heavier attack, all of which causes more fret wear. Today's harder string windings also tend to wear frets faster. Also, many of the vintage guitars with original frets "still in good shape" were played with flat-wound strings—which aren't as hard on frets, perhaps accounting for some of the perception that frets aren't what they used to be. The real key to fret wear is playing time. It doesn't matter how old a guitar is; what's important is how much it gets played. Leave it in the case, and the frets will never wear out! Today's guitarists, though, play and practice more than ever.

As for fret-rounding files, Mr. Hamilton advises: "It's best if a rounding file is 1 mm or so larger than the fret size for proper clearance." So choose the 4 mm (.157") size, since being somewhat wider than the 2.5 (.098") mm fret, it will rest over the fret crown (facing page). A rounding file sits over the fret, but the radius of its teeth isn't deep enough to allow the file edges to touch or scratch the fingerboard wood; this could

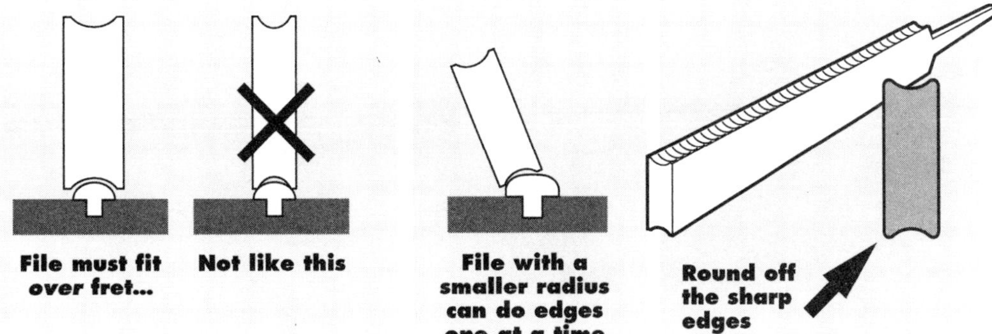

happen with an extremely worn or low-crown fret, however. Sometimes it's effective to use a rounding file with a radius that's smaller than the fret width for rounding just one edge of a flat-topped fret on either side of center (above). Another great fret-dressing tool is a 6" to 8" slim-taper, three-corner triangle file with its sharp edges ground smooth. This file is often used to smooth things after the rounding file (see the next sections for information on making your own fret files).

The *type* of cut imparted by a rounding file is round, of course. The file's function is to round off, or "re-crown," frets that are filed or sanded flat during the operation of fret dressing or leveling. The *quality* of cut depends on the make of file and how it's used. New files tend to chatter and leave hard-to-remove marks on frets. Here are a few tips for fret rounders: Avoid excess pressure with rounding files. Clogged metal in the teeth often causes scratching, so clean them often. Wipe a stick of paraffin over the teeth to act as a lubricant and help eliminate clogging. You can dull the harsh cut of a new file by rubbing a round chainsaw file back and forth over the teeth a few times. The edges of a file where the teeth run into the smooth side walls (as shown above) are often sharp; grind or sand them smooth along the entire file length to avoid gouging the fingerboard on each side of the fret as you're working. Practice on scrap to check the cut of a new file.

There, the topic of fret files—and the tools and techniques used for fret work in general—is now open! Learning about fret work is a long, uphill climb, but worth the effort. Coming along for the ride?

Fret-dressing basics

Few people seem to know what properly dressed frets are. But should only top professionals enjoy smooth action, easy bends, and a buzz-free sustain? Not in my opinion, and you'll agree when you see what a good fret dressing can accomplish. If you've been spending from $30 to $80 (the normal price range) getting your frets in shape, study the following tips on dressing frets, and consider putting a little money and extra effort into gathering the proper supplies and making the few simple tools needed to do the job yourself.

Much of this information was written over a period of several years. Because I change with the times, you'll see changes in my techniques, too. Learn all the techniques, old and new. They're all important!

Be sure you understand the fingerboard/neck evaluation and neck-rod adjustment explanation given in the Getting Started chapter before you attempt any fret work. And remember, before you touch a file to your frets, read this complete chapter, since it gives an overview of the fret-dressing process, as well as guidelines for determin-

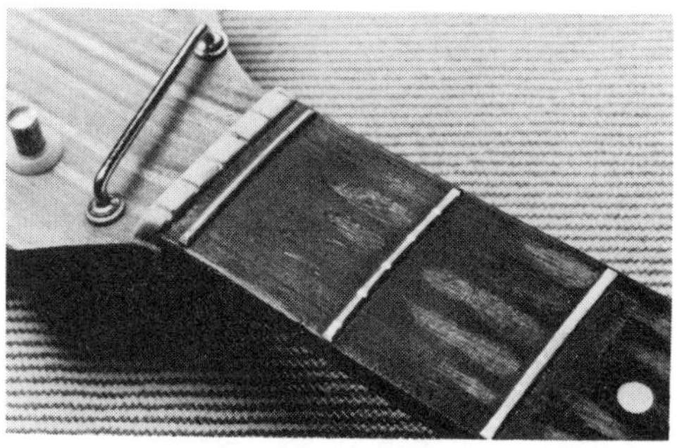

ing whether a partial or complete fret job is needed. Even if you're squeamish about dressing your own frets, you can use this information to relate better to your repairman or to help judge a guitar that you are considering for purchase.

Fret dressing refers to the leveling-out and re-rounding (or "crowning") of high, low, or worn spots on frets; these can cause buzzes and "noting out"—notes that won't play cleanly. Basically, here's what's involved in the process: Leveling is first done with a smooth, flat mill file, followed by 220-, 320-, and 400-grit sandpaper for smoothing. Next, the fret tops left flat by the leveling operation are re-rounded with a small triangular file or a fret-rounding file. Any jagged fret ends along the fingerboard's edge are rounded now, too. Finally, a good polishing with fine sandpaper and steel wool gives smooth, buzz-free frets that are a dream to bend on.

Many new guitars come from the factory with the frets leveled, but only a cursory job of crowning has been done. This is often why some factory-fresh guitars play less than perfectly. Since fret dressing is tedious and time-consuming manual labor, a deluxe job at the factory would raise the instrument's price. Crowning is necessary, though, since the flat tops of the frets will otherwise have more surface area for the strings to buzz against as they vibrate. Flat frets also cause problems in setting the intonation (since the strings can play sharp or flat to either side of dead center) and make the strings harder to bend due to the increased friction.

Guitars that have been played on for a while can develop grooves or pits in the frets, especially in the first five (above, left). If the grooves are too deep, you don't want to file all the good frets down to the level of those few bad ones for the sake of flatness and a level fingerboard. A general rule: When a pit or groove has been worn much lower than a third of the fret's full height (and definitely if the fret approaches the halfway mark in wear), have the guitar looked at by a repairman. You may be advised to have the worn frets replaced with matching fretwire (this is called a "partial refret") or to refret the instrument completely. Take the repairman's advice. If you do get a complete refret, you could explain that you would like to do the final crowning yourself. But be sure to ask the repairman to have the new frets leveled and ready for you. Of course, if you perform the crowning, you'll be offered no guarantees on the work.

Frets that are worn too flat are often found on inexpensive imports and sometimes even on fine American-made models. Rather than being pitted, the tops of these frets are extremely low and flat (above). This can be caused by years of playing or by a poor fret job that someone tried to correct by leveling without taking the extra time to crown. Although you may eventually need a refret, these low frets can be rounded with a lot of work. Find a bargain yardsale special with over-flat frets and practice on that.

Loose frets or a fret that is taller than those surrounding it will also cause a string to "note out"—in other words, you can't hear the intended note at all because the string is

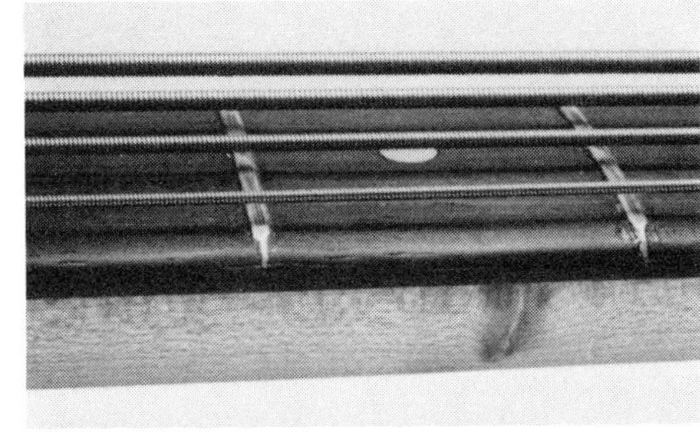

fretting at a higher fret. In most cases, this is caused by the fret working loose (above); it needs to be reseated. Although this is quite easy to do, I advise you to take your guitar to a repairman. It can probably be fixed on the spot. (Thanks to super glue and the repairman's knowledge in using it, instant repairs can often be performed while you wait.) After you've gained some experience, you can try reseating a fret yourself by following the information given later in this chapter in the section on loose fret ends.

The opposite of a too-tall fret is, of course, one that is too low, causing the string to note one fret higher. This is most often found on less expensive, off-the-wall guitars. It's usually caused by a fret that was somehow driven into the fingerboard too hard or by a mismatch of fretwire height. These frets should be pulled up to the proper height, or new frets should be installed. I'm not trying to drum up business for the Guild of American Luthiers, but once again, take it to your repairman until you've had some practice. This can be another instant repair, so take care of it before you attempt any leveling.

Jagged fret ends along the fingerboard edge are uncomfortable because they catch your hand as you slide up or down the neck. You may use the flat-leveling file to rebevel the fret ends if needed, and the triangular crowning file can be used to round and deburr any jagged fret ends. Due to wear or an imperfect fret job, some frets fall short of the fingerboard edge or have jagged ends (above, right). Don't try to bevel all of the ends to match these; either have the troublesome frets replaced or do your best to deburr the ends and make them feel comfortable until the guitar's refretted.

Dozens of different fretwires—thin or fat, short or tall, soft or hard—are used for guitars. Generally, a thin wire is used for most acoustics, while a wide, or "jumbo," wire is common for electrics. I like the taller wires better in either case because you can dress them more times between refrets. They also offer a better sustained note, are easier to bend on, and level and dress easier than low frets. For steel-string guitars, ask your repairman to fret with a hard wire; it lasts longer. A soft wire is fine for classical guitars, since the nylon strings won't wear grooves as easily, and the softer wire is much easier to level and crown. Here are my favorite fretwires: Dunlop #6130 and Stewart-MacDonald #149 for standard wide frets, and Dunlop #6100 and Stew-Mac #150 for extra-tall, jumbo frets. Stew-Mac #148 and Dunlop #6230 are unexcelled thin wires for electric or acoustic guitars. If you're serious about fret work, you should buy samples of any wire that arouses your curiosity, and check it out for yourself.

Now that you've got a basic idea of what the whole process involves, let's look into making some of the necessary tools—files, in particular.

Making fret-dressing files

If money's not tight, buy fret files from a guitar shop supplier and avoid screwing up good files on your own. Getting a good grind's not easy.

Fret dressing is one of the most common reasons a guitar ends up in the repair shop, and while you may never attempt your own fret dressing, these facts will help you better understand what's entailed in repairing an instrument that plays poorly because of fret problems. Fret dressing isn't always an easy task, and it's certainly not for all guitar owners. However, for those of you who are handy, let me introduce you to the simple and inexpensive fret-dressing tools that you'll need—tools you can make yourself.

These days I use the fine-cutting Japanese Finesse sand-paper instead of 3M. It cuts much faster and smoother.

Making the tools needed for fret dressing can be fun. At the hardware store, buy a 10" smooth-mill bastard file (choose one that's unwarped), a 6" or 7" smooth-cut triangle file, and a wire file-cleaning brush. Modify the files using my illustrations as a guideline. Caution: Unless you own a grinder with a good stone wheel, and are familiar with the necessary operational safety precautions, have your files ground at a machine, welding, or grinding shop. This is simple for them and inexpensive and safe for you. If there's a high school or trade school nearby, ask the metal-shop teacher if a student needs a small project. Your files can probably be ground while you wait. Note: Few people realize that grinders are danger-ous—even those little ones everyone has in the garage. The danger lies in stone wheels that are cracked or otherwise in bad shape. If these come apart while under speed, the exploding fragments could kill you or maul your face. This happened to a friend of mine; he's okay, but only because his father, a surgeon, happened to be home at the time. Don't get me wrong, I use grinders—but only with approved full-face protection, and I'm very cautious. Please do the same.

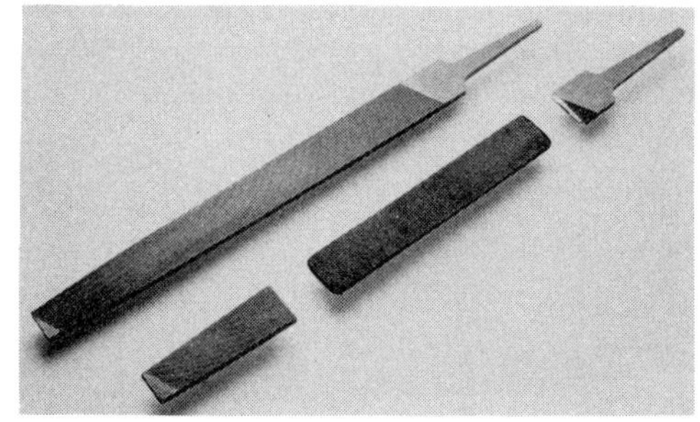

The 10" file should be cut into two lengths (above), approximately 3" and 6" long. These are the leveling files that will be used to rectify high or low frets and hump or rise, as well as to create fall-away at the high end of the fingerboard. To cut the file into the two lengths, you must grind a V-shaped groove on opposite sides until the cuts begin to meet in the middle.

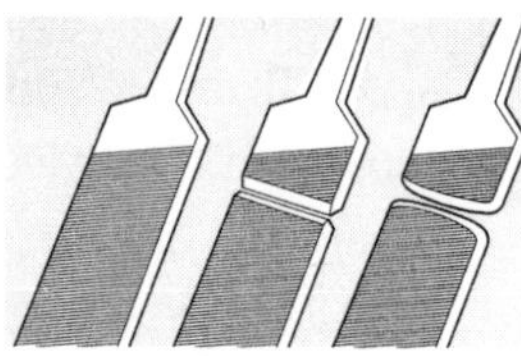

Then, with the file clamped to a tabletop or in a vise, break it along the scored line. Grind the broken ends into a smooth, rounded shape. *Always wear safety glasses when grinding and breaking!* You now have two leveling files. The smaller one is for leveling one or two problem frets (especially those on the section of the fingerboard that overlaps the guitar's body), while the longer one is the basic leveling file used for general smoothing of the whole fingerboard.

Although there are many rounding files specially made to crown frets, I think that the custom-made triangle file is the best. I learned to use one during my visits to the Gibson plant in Kalamazoo in the good old days. At the time, I had a beautiful flame-top Les Paul, and because I never trusted myself to work on it, the frets were dressed more than once at the factory. (In those days, you could make an appointment to have service done while you waited. I learned a lot by wandering around and watching.)

Your triangle file is used to round or crown the fret tops left flat after the leveling operation. It is also used to round over the

frets' ends and remove any jagged burrs along the fingerboard's edge. You must remove any trace of a cutting edge on all three corners of the file with a grinder or belt sander (here's a look at the file before and after). Also, blunt and round the tip, or nose, of the file. A poorly ground triangle file can scar the fingerboard wood on either side of the fret you're working on, even though you have taped off the fingerboard.

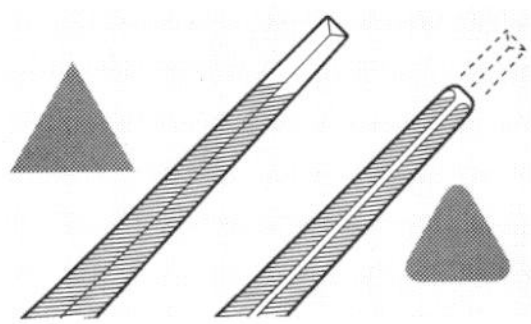

When you shop for your files, pick up one sheet each of wet-or-dry sandpaper in 320-, 400-, and 600-grits, as well as some 0000 steel wool and a file-cleaning brush (also known as a file card). My favorite file card has small metal bristles on one side and fiber bristles on the other; buy one if you can find it. Also, a brass-bristle mini-file cleaner is great for cleaning small, fine-cut triangle files.

A great tool for sanding and steel-wooling frets after leveling and rounding is a rubber squeegee from the 3M Company. This should be available at any automotive store selling finish supplies. Buy the smallest rubber squeegee available, and grind or file a groove along one edge of it. Eventually, you'll wrap the steel wool or sandpaper around this edge to do your polishing (look at the section on fingerboard cleaning for an illustration of how to shape the squeegee). Finally, pick up a roll of masking tape for taping off the frets while you file and sand them.

It will take you a little time to find and modify the proper files and to buy the sandpaper, steel wool, and squeegee. Again, finish this whole chapter before you start work!

Dressing the frets

We've defined fret dressing in detail and made the modified files needed for leveling and dressing the frets. Now, let's put this knowledge to use. Until you gain experience at fret dressing, practice on yardsale specials.

Until you gain experience, practice fret dressing on yardsale specials.

Using the neck evaluation and truss rod adjustment section of the Getting Started chapter as a guide, adjust your truss rod to remove any relief. Get the neck straight from the 1st fret to the 12th, using a metal straightedge for comparison. Then duplicate this straight, or "leveling," position with the strings removed. Lay a towel or pad on the table top, covering it and the entire work surface with newspaper to catch any metal filings. Rest the guitar's body on the padded part of the work surface, and cradle the back of the neck on a stack of books or anything else that can serve as a support (the neck rest shown in the photo is great for repairmen). Pad this cradle with a small rag and cover it with paper as well, because any filings could scratch the lacquer on the back of the neck. To avoid scratching, you will often have to vacuum or remove the filings. Check with your straightedge again to be sure that the neck support hasn't altered your straightness. If it has, move the support to a different part of the neck and/or make a slight truss rod adjustment.

Note: Even with the strings removed and the truss rod loose, some necks may tend to back-bow slightly (but this isn't common). These necks gain relief from string tension alone. In this case, support the headstock, not the back of the neck, and later you may either put slight pressure on the body or pull down on the neck's heel to straighten the neck as you file.

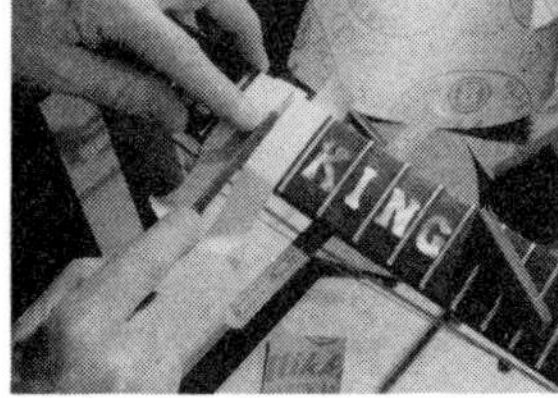

With masking tape, protect any part of the guitar that can be scratched by your files or sandpaper, especially around the fingerboard tongue and the pickups (which, if not protected, will magnetically attract and retain metal filings and steel wool dust). Although removing the nut is not always essential, it allows you to level the frets more effectively. First, carefully score around the nut with a sharp X-acto knife to break the lacquer. With a block of wood and a hammer, gently tap the nut to knock it loose, as described in the Nut Work section.

Several new fret-dressing tools have become available since 1985 when I started writing for *Guitar Player*. At Stewart-MacDonald I designed a long and short fret-leveling file with wooden handles and very smooth, long-angled teeth; and also a miniature, super-fine, three-cornered (triangle) file. Another tool, the Sand-Stick, is a small, plastic, spring-loaded belt sander used for sanding the fret tops after they've been crowned with the triangle file.

Most filing is done with the longer file held in the palm of your hand as flat as possible against the frets. The photo shows the Stew-Mac wood-handled fret leveling file. Remember that your goal is to create an accurate, smooth plane across the tops of the frets, so that no fret is higher or lower than any other. You want to expose new metal, or a fresh "flat," on each fret. Since most necks straighten easily and have no hump or rise on the tongue, you really won't have to do much filing—you'll only be "kissing" the tops. However, if you have a hump, rise, or high frets on the tongue, level those frets so that they don't cause the straightedge to rise up while you're checking for flatness on the main portion of the board.

To remove a hump or rise, use the short leveling file to work down any small, isolated problem frets. Check your progress constantly—a small amount of filing can make a lot of difference. Note: Many necks are not set at an exact 90° angle to the body, and a straightedge resting on the main fingerboard from the 1st fret to the neck/body joint may be on a different plane from the tongue, with the tongue naturally falling away because of this angle. This is normal, and should not be confused with a "hump," which is actually due to a swollen glue joint or high, loose frets. Usually, the most annoying problem on the tongue is a rise, where the last few frets are higher than the ones preceding them. Sometimes this takes a fair amount of filing to rectify, and in extreme cases it could leave those last few frets quite low and hard to round (but a careful rounding usually produces good results). Always file in a lengthwise direction parallel to the fingerboard's length, working the file from the treble side to the bass side and following the fingerboard's arc. Because a file cuts on the forward push stroke, you needn't work the file back and forth.

When you feel that you have eliminated any high or low spots on the tongue, restring the guitar to pitch, readjust the truss rod accordingly, and check the relief, leveling, and fall away as described in the neck evaluation section. Once the tongue problems have been eliminated, the straightedge will give you a much more accurate reading on the main fingerboard (1st through 12th frets). If all seems well, go on to those first twelve frets.

With the longer file, begin where the tongue filing ends and file in long, even strokes from the body towards the headstock, applying medium pressure. You will use many successive passes in order to cover a curved fingerboard's width, while on fingerboards with little or no arc, the file will cut its full width and you may finish sooner. I usually stop filing when my tool has just started to pass over the 1st fret. Then I back up and make another pass, continuing in this fashion until I've covered the width of the fingerboard from end to end. Once again, the straightedge must be able to rest flat on all the fret tops (except for a slight fall away) when the neck is in the straight filing position.

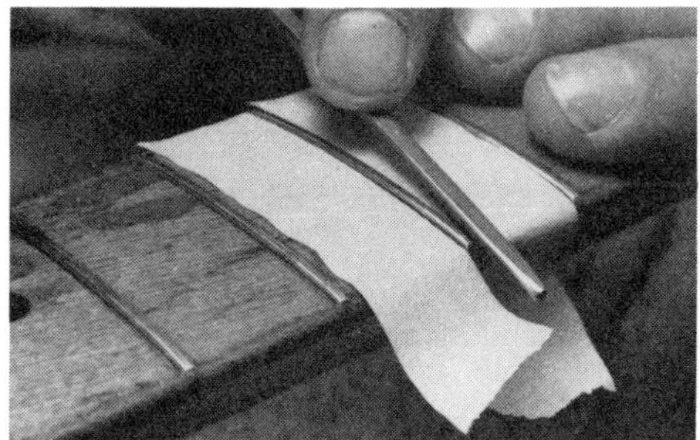

Use different pressures if you need to blend one section (for example, the 1st through 10th) into another (the 10th through 15th). If you know there is a high fret or a cluster of them, use your 3" file to work down that area. Follow with the long file to feather it in. A beginner should string to pitch often and readjust the rod to see how the feathering-in affects relief, leveling out, and fall away. You can always get the neck back into the filing position if—when you begin—you put a mark on the truss rod nut as an index and return to it every time.

When the tops of all the frets have been touched by the file and there are no high or low spots, smooth them with the 320-grit sandpaper that has been wrapped around a flat, palm-size wood block. Sand in a lengthwise direction, just as you did with the file (here, however, you may sand back and forth). Gently sand away all file marks from the fret tops.

Now, feel the fret ends. Sometimes they'll stick out beyond the fingerboard edge because the wood has shrunk while the metal fret hasn't. You can smooth the ends until they're flush with the wood by using the long leveling file held flat against the edge of the fingerboard. Avoid filing the finish any more than you must. If you do have to touch the finish, lightly sand any dull spots with the Japanese wet-or-dry Finesse sandpaper, using water as a lubricant, and return the original gloss by polishing with Mirror Glaze # 7 to finish the job.

Crowning the flat fret tops is easy using the triangle file. Always tape off the fingerboard on each side of the fret. Starting at the 1st fret, hold the file between the thumb and second and third fingers with the index finger on top, using the other hand's index finger to guide the file on the fret. With a forward stroke, apply light pressure, rolling the file to center (left) as you push it across the fret's length. Switch from one side of the fret to the other, using this rolling motion towards center. You are removing the square edge and re-rounding the flat top that you made while leveling.

You will see the flat top getting smaller as you work. "Round and roll" until the tiniest flat—or no flat at all—is left on the center of the fret. When you have finished crowning a fret, do a final clean-up on the fret ends with the triangle file, using a downward stroke that follows the fret's beveled end. One light downstroke should polish the bevel, followed by a series of downward strokes rolling to the center to round the end and remove any burrs. You will have to turn the guitar end-for-end or walk around your bench to get both sides of the fingerboard.

With the frets still taped off, wrap the 400-grit wet-or-dry paper around your homemade 3M squeegee fret polisher with the groove side down. With a series of back-and-forth strokes, polish the fret top and sides to remove any marks. Switch to the 600 paper and repeat the polishing process.

Now, wrap a thin layer of 0000 steel wool around your fret polisher and bring the fret to a high polish. Repeat this for each fret. When you're through with the polishing, remove the masking tape, always peeling it carefully from the outside edges of the fingerboard towards center; this avoids pulling off finish on the fingerboard's edge.

When all the frets have been rounded and polished, blow or vacuum off any metal dust and steel wool particles, and remove

Using the neck evaluation and truss rod adjustment section of the Getting Started chapter as a guide, adjust your truss rod to remove any relief. Get the neck straight from the 1st fret to the 12th, using a metal straightedge for comparison. Then duplicate this straight, or "leveling," position with the strings removed. Lay a towel or pad on the table top, covering it and the entire work surface with newspaper to catch any metal filings. Rest the guitar's body on the padded part of the work surface, and cradle the back of the neck on a stack of books or anything else that can serve as a support (the neck rest shown here is great for repairmen).

the tape from the body and pickups. Caution: On any guitar with an old, brittle finish, be very gentle in removing the tape to avoid pulling away the finish. As you peel the tape, rub gently with a fingernail on the tape's back just ahead of the bonding point to break the surface tension. String the guitar up to pitch, readjusting the neck rod to give some relief once again. If you use a straightedge now, be very careful not to scar the frets. If you've followed the instructions, you will have the best-playing guitar you've ever touched. Enjoy yourself—you've earned it.

Loose frets

Always wear safety glasses when using super glue. Remember that it can bond your fingers together, and keep a bottle of solvent handy in case of accident.

We're all looking for an easy way of eliminating buzzes caused by loose fret ends, which are hard not only on the ear but also on the fingers. While a complete fret job is sometimes needed to correct buzzes caused by warps, twists, and worn-out frets, just as often the problem can be solved by gluing down the end of the one fret that has raised up. In the old days, the resetting of a raised fret end was both laborious and time-consuming. But that was before super glue. Now the average guitar player can easily and safely solve this problem.

Fret ends raise up for a variety of reasons. It may be due to an oversized fret slot or an undersized fret tang (the part that is driven into the fingerboard slot to hold the fret in). It may be caused by insufficient glue: Some frets are held in with glue as an aid, while others are hammered in dry, letting the small beads on the side of the tang do all the holding. Dirt, grease, and oils may have loosened the glue or softened and weakened the wood that holds the fret. In extreme cases where much sweat and oil has been worked under the fret, the following method may not work, but it's worth a try; if it doesn't work, a partial refret or complete refret may be needed.

Begin by finding a wooden dowel at least ¼" in diameter and 6" long. Carve or file a slight notch in one end. This dowel is used for pushing the fret end down flush on the fingerboard while you wax the fret and its surrounding fingerboard area to aid in the clean-up of the glue. The stick also holds the fret in place while the glue sets.

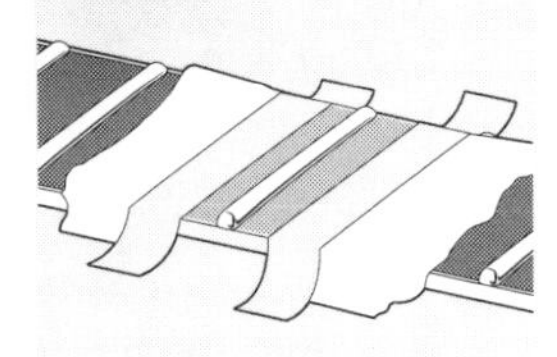

Next, lay a sheet of paper on each side of the bad fret and tape it down to within ½" of the fret. Wax the exposed fingerboard and fret edges, going over the side of the fingerboard or binding, as well, in case any glue might run over onto the neck. Use a Q-Tip to apply any sort of paste wax. Don't load the Q-Tip with wax; twirl it in the wax and wipe off any lumps. When you've finished waxing, release the fret. It should pop right back up, with no wax having gotten under the fret where you want the glue to do its work.

If you have more than one loose fret end (and often you will), don't try regluing more than one at a time. Use Hot Stuff Original Formula, which is water-thin and able to penetrate deep within the fret slot and tang area. You'll also need a bottle of accelerator to speed up the drying time and cause an "instant" cure. The reason we covered the rest of the fingerboard is so that all the frets don't become activated by the accelerator's effect, which lasts about 15 minutes.

The guitar should be fairly immobile while you're working, so block the neck with some books or something firm for it to press against. Apply a drop of glue to each side of the loose fret along the fingerboard edge as far back as your eye tells you it's loose, and watch it disappear as it runs deep into the problem area. Use a soft rag or tissue paper to remove any wet glue that doesn't run under.

Immediately follow with a squirt of accelerator on each side of the fret, and then quickly but smoothly peel off the tape and paper. While the glue is accelerating, it's wise to have your wooden press-stick in the other hand, ready to press the fret down. While pressing the fret flush to the fingerboard, you can use a straightedge or flat object to help judge when the fret is level with its nearest tight fret. The glue should set within 30 seconds. Don't press the fret lower than the frets on either side, since this will result in a fret that's too low and subject to buzz. The actual gluing and accelerating must be done swiftly and efficiently, so first practice the operation in a dry run. Follow this time schedule: Apply glue and clean up excess—5 to 10 seconds; squirt accelerator—2 or 3 seconds; remove tape—2 seconds; press fret down and level with straightedge or block—5 seconds.

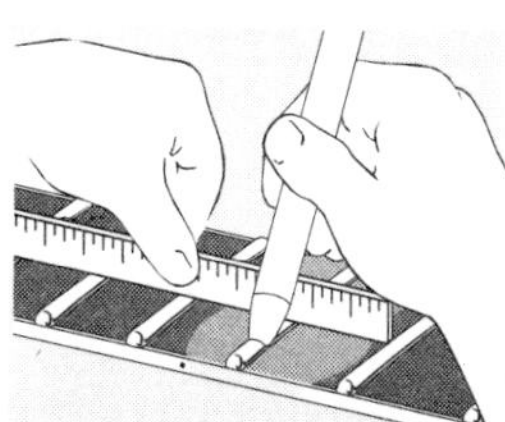

In less than a minute the fret should hold, sometimes leaving a small bead of squeezed-out super glue showing along the fret/fingerboard edge. Remove this glue with a sharp-pointed tool (pin, X-acto blade, chisel, etc.). Any glue that might remain on the waxed area of the fingerboard should be removed by scraping lightly (lengthwise with the fingerboard rather than across-grain) with a razor blade, and then polish with 0000 steel wool. If you still have a slight buzz, you may need to slightly level the fret with a smooth mill file or block of wood wrapped with #400 sandpaper, or use the Koontz radius blocks described in the next section.

If you have any trouble getting the fret level or if you feel that you didn't glue it properly, use a soldering pencil to loosen the glue bond and try again. Heat breaks a super glue bond in the same way that it loosens most any glue, including epoxies. *Caution: Heat causes some glues to vaporize. Do not breathe the fumes or allow them to get into your eyes!* Try to avoid getting into this situation. The second time around on a given fret may be more difficult because the hardened super glue is still under there. Don't use too much glue, and be especially careful not to let the glue run onto the neck. If it does, wipe it off immediately with some lighter fluid, which you should keep handy.

Wear safety glasses when using super glue, and remember that it can bond your fingers together. A short while back, a fret sprung up on me when my push-stick slipped, spitting super glue onto my prescription plastic-lens safety glasses. The glue hardened instantly and permanently. I had to buy a new pair of glasses, but my eyes were spared. Of course, avoid splashing a guitar's finish. Buy a bottle of solvent for cleaning glue from your fingertips and to help separate them in case of accident. Never use this solvent to remove glue from a lacquer finish, since it dissolves lacquer. Practice with the super glue and accelerator on objects that you don't care about before attempting a repair. This will give you a feel for the setting time and show you how quickly it runs.

Hot Stuff's yellow-label Super T can be used for loose frets, too. Practice on junkers, by all means. If you use Hot Stuff's red-label Original Formula, you don't have to use accelerator. Try it both ways.

Refretting

If you keep a guitar long enough and play it often, someday you'll be faced with getting it refretted. Most players get very nervous about letting just anyone pull and replace the frets on their favorite axe, and with good reason: Except for accidental damage, a poor fret job is the surest way to ruin a good instrument.

While lots of my advice in this book is aimed at do-it-yourselfers, I don't recommend that you refret your prewar Martin or '50s Strat without professional training. I'd like to help you understand why fret jobs are needed and what problems they can solve. I'll also describe how I like to see a fret job done, offer pointers on such things as fret-end finishing on bound and unbound fingerboards, and finally compare different fret job prices from around the country. I'm hoping to educate you before you pay big bucks for a fret job, so that you won't end up fretting about it afterwards.

A refret is an opportunity to correct most of your guitar's action and playability troubles. Abnormal buzzes caused by worn, high, low, or loose frets can be eliminated. High action resulting from too much relief, up-bow, or just plain old neck warp can also be repaired by actually scraping the wood of the fingerboard itself once the frets have been removed, rather than filing the fret tops. Perhaps a guitar's frets have been over-beveled, causing not only cramped string spacing at the nut but also a tendency for the strings to slide off the fingerboard during play. New frets that are less beveled make better use of the fingerboard's width.

Hard string-bending, overall stiffness, and sore fingers resulting from frets that are too low indicate the need for fret work. Many players will have a guitar refretted not because it plays poorly, but because they're after a different type of fret shape or size to accommodate a certain playing style. As mentioned earlier, tall frets are easier to bend on, jumbo frets have more sustain, etc. Traditionally, frets have been installed by carefully tapping them into the slots with a smooth-faced chasing hammer. In recent years, it has become more and more common for repairmen to remove the frets, slightly widen the fret slots with a small hobbyist's router such as a Dremel tool, and then gently press and glue the frets into place. I prefer the glue-in method and seldom do hammer-in jobs anymore, but either method is fine, depending upon how carefully it's done. There are many different ways of going about refret work, and no one method is right. I never fault fret work if it's done neatly and the guitar plays well. I do, however, have flaming fits when I see fret jobs done by so called "repairmen" who do nothing but yank 'em out and pound 'em in, paying no attention to the fingerboard's pre-fret preparation. The prep work separates the pros from the amateurs. Here's a synopsis of how I feel a fret job should be done:

FRET JOBS: THE GLUE-IN METHOD

1 Start by determining the customer's complaint with the frets as they are, listening to what he says and how he plays before forming an opinion. Special attention must be paid to playing style and string gauge. Choose a fretwire for the job.

2 Inspect the neck and fingerboard, looking for any problems such as warp, humps, and dips in the surface. Before estimating a fret job's cost, you must adjust the truss rod to its maximum looseness and tightness in order to get familiar with the neck. By checking the action of the truss rod, you determine if a neck has the ability to adjust perfectly straight, yet still offer relief when the rod is loosened. In my opinion, a "perfect" neck is one that can be adjusted perfectly straight under string tension, and

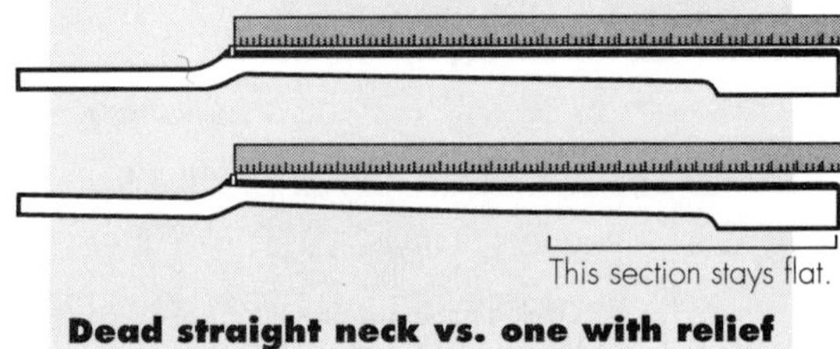

Dead straight neck vs. one with relief

yet pull gradually into relief when needed.

Note: The full effects of truss rod adjustment often take several hours or days to appear. Be sure to allow enough time for the neck to settle in after truss rod adjustment before any frets are removed and replaced. Also allow time for settling after the refret is done, and before the final set-up prior to going out the door. There are times when job must be done overnight for a pro on the road, and occasionally these may need a little redressing after the guitar has settled.

3 Before pulling them out with specialized end nippers, the frets are heated with a soldering pencil. This important step helps to avoid chips in the fingerboard. The inevitable small chips along the fret edge are easily glued back or filled in. Large chunks, however, are often the result of hasty work, and should not be tolerated. Keep your soldering iron's tip tinned (just as if you were doing electrical work), and the heat will transfer instantly. For a quick heat transfer, it doesn't hurt to put a little solder right on the fret, but be careful on maple fingerboards! Another neat tip is to remove a section of the "loop" on a Weller-style soldering gun, and then press the two cut ends against the fret to complete the circuit, sending the heated charge through the wire! If you're having fret work done, be sure your repairman is familiar with heating frets.

4 Fingerboard imperfections should be planed, scraped, or sanded out. This leveling is usually performed with files, scrapers, and sanding blocks. My favorite sanding blocks are the radius blocks developed by Mike Koontz of Ferndale, Michigan—and sold by several luthier suppliers. These eight blocks (pictured below, left) are perfectly radiused from 7¼" up to 20". Use 3M Stick-It paper to hug the block's contour. The work's progress is checked often by comparing the board to very accurate straightedges. Inlays, especially custom pearl-block types in badly affected areas, must often be removed to avoid being sanded too thin. They're replaced later just before the final leveling.

5 Once the board is properly leveled, the old glue is cleaned from the fret slots using a Dremel tool equipped with small router bits. The slot should be just wide enough for the fret to finger-press in snugly. This slot cleaning creates burrs on the fingerboard's surface, which are then removed by polish-sanding with up to 600-grit wet-or-dry sandpaper.

6 Each fret is bent exactly to the curve of the fingerboard radius with specially shaped pliers or with the FretBender shown earlier in this chapter—a tool that should be in every professional shop.

7 To ease in the later removal of any glue squeeze-out, the fingerboard is wiped with paste wax close to the fret slots.

8 The frets are glued, clamped into place, and left to dry. I prefer to glue in frets two at a time with a fast-set glue. The gluing process takes several hours. Since the frets are pre-radiused, they fit the board snugly all the way across and are held in place to dry by Plexiglas clamps known as cauls (right). The ½" top plate transfers clamp pressure to the plastic dowel rods, which in turn forces the flexible bottom sheet to hold the frets at the exact fingerboard radius. Later, the glue squeeze-out is carefully peeled away. Notice that the frets hang out over the fingerboard edge. This is to ensure that the fret ends are well seated. The ends are trimmed flush to the edge of the board after the glue has dried,

The full effects of truss rod adjustment often take several hours—even days—to appear. Be sure to allow enough time for the neck to settle before any frets are removed.

and smooth-beveled later. Fingerboards with binding are fretted in much the same fashion, except for some special fitting that will be explained in the next part of this chapter.

9 When all the frets have been installed, the rough edges along the fingerboard are carefully filed smooth and the fret-end bevel is created.

10 The fret tops are lightly leveled into one another with a very smooth file or a block wrapped with fine sandpaper (I use my radius blocks to hit all the fret tops at once). The small-size fret plane designed by Ken Donnell is also handy during the leveling; it's available from Stewart-MacDonald and Luthier's Mercantile.

11 Finally the frets are crowned and polished to a perfect finish. Follow the section on dressing the frets.

THE HAMMER-IN METHOD

With the traditional hammer-in method, you don't rout the fret slots, wax the fingerboard, or clamp in the frets (steps number 5, 7, and 8 above). Otherwise, the fingerboard preparation, fret leveling, and final dressing are the same.

When you clean the slots of dirt and old glue, use only probes and picking tools rather than a Dremel Moto-Tool, since you don't want to widen the slots. I prefer to do this with the thin back edge of a #11 X-acto blade held vertically, or with a small-size X-acto razor saw blade. You want the slot clean and deep enough to accept the new fret, but the slot's sidewalls must be left untouched so they'll hold the replacement frets. I usually clean and degrease the fingerboard with naphtha at this point, so that it dries while I'm preparing the fret wire. As long as the naphtha's out, use it to clean any oil from the fret wire, just as with a glue-in job. Then go ahead and pre-shape the frets to match the crown of the board (some repairmen hammer in straight lengths of wire, trusting the slot to hold the fret, but that's not my method). Pre-bent wire goes in easier and requires less force from a hammer.

Fretwire is available with many different tang and bead sizes, so choose a wire that will hold in the slot. The fit of the tang into the slot should be slightly loose to allow the beads that are driven into the wood to do the actual holding (above).

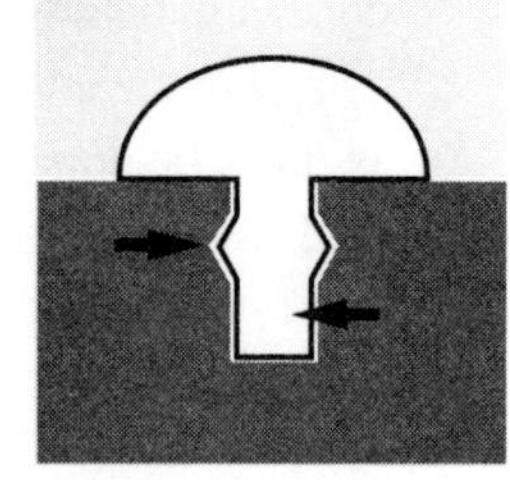

Most fret slots are about .022" wide when new. Fretwire generally has a tang width of between .018" and .020" (slightly undersize to the slot), and a bead width of around .030" to .033". With a difference of .010" to .015" between the slot and the bead measurement, pounding in a fret could back-bow the neck away from the strings. Because of this, oversize wire is often used to straighten an up-bowed neck. This technique was developed by Martin's repair shop for dealing with warped necks, and the company offers a good selection of fret wire with different tang sizes designed just for this purpose. To help choose the proper tang, measure the slot width with a feeler gauge. Knowing what size bead width to buy is tougher, since it depends on how many times a neck has been fretted and the condition of the wood, which could be soft and rotted. Experience is important, so practice on some yardsale guitars or replacement bolt-on necks, and study every book on the subject. It often takes several fret jobs to get the feel for it.

I use three fretting hammers (pictured). The homemade one is fairly heavy, with a 1" x 3½" head made from a piece of round brass bar stock. The second hammer is more delicate, smaller in diameter, and much lighter; it has a rounded brass face on one side and a nylon face on the other. I call the third one my "speed" hammer. It has a

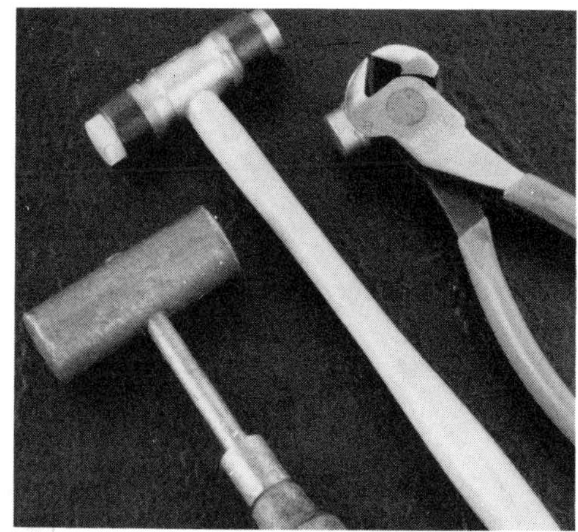

hammer head attached to a pair of flush-cutting end nippers, allowing me to hammer and clip with no wasted motion spent switching tools. I've seen these combination nipper/hammers used at Martin and Gibson. All three hammers come in handy, but you can also use a 16-ounce carpenter's hammer if you're careful.

The neck area where you're installing a fret should be supported to give resistance to the hammer blow. Use good supports that conform to the neck's shape, such as cloth bags filled with sand or buckshot. Sometimes I support the neck on curved blocks of wood or on the top edge of the neck vise on my workbench. Don't just support the headstock and then pound away at the unsupported fingerboard!

You can sometimes hammer in frets that are cut close to exact length, but only if the wood is quite solid (otherwise the frets have a tendency to pop up). I prefer to cut the frets with a 1/4" to 3/8" overhang on each side of the fingerboard, so that I can give them a little tap with the hammer to really get the ends down tight. Start hammering from one side (I work from treble to bass) and follow the board across. Don't drive the fret completely home, but tap it in from one edge of the board to the other—maybe three passes, by degree, until it's finally seated. You shouldn't have to *pound* the fret, just tap it until it comes to rest against the wood. On an acoustic guitar, the hardest area to fret is the tongue over the body, since there isn't a solid surface to hammer against. Here it's essential to hold a metal block or a sandbag inside the guitar under the fingerboard area. It can be very tough to get the frets well seated over an acoustic body, which is one reason many of us started gluing and clamping the frets in the first place!

The decision to use glue to hold in the frets is up to you; even large manufacturers do it differently. Certain repairmen consider gluing frets to be a bad joke to play on a future repairer. I don't feel that way, though, since frets should always be heated prior to removal to break any glue bond. You don't need glue on a perfectly good piece of wood that wants to hold a fret, although the glue's lubrication sometimes helps a fret go in easier. The most common glues for holding hammered-in frets are Tite Bond (aliphatic resin), hide glue, and shellac. (While not really a glue, fresh shellac does a great job of bonding metal to wood, especially frets. It was commonly used by guitar builders long before we were born.) The last time I visited the Gibson company in Kalamazoo, they were wiping hide glue into all the slots at once, quickly wiping off the excess with a damp rag, and then clipping in the frets with the combination nipper/hammer. At the Martin company, they wipe the fingerboard with water to lubricate the fret as it goes in and to swell the slot around the fret. I generally use either hide glue or Tite Bond, but I'd use shellac too. You can't use 'em all at once, so experiment!

Pounding too aggressively or too hard in one spot will cause dents or flat spots in the fret as you're going across the board. If this happens, you must remove the fret and either straighten or replace it. Likewise, not pounding hard enough leaves frets that aren't seated against the board. As a general rule, frets that pound in too easily and won't stay down may need to be glued or replaced with frets with over-size tangs. On the other hand, if you're pounding away and the fret isn't going in, don't keep at it. Either the slot isn't deep enough or the fret tang is too wide. Back up and review the situation.

If you use glue, let it dry overnight before clipping or filing the fret ends. Clip the ends until they are almost flush with the fingerboard edge (leave a little for final-filing to the wood, or you may get nipper marks on the bare wood or finish). Frets that are hammered in without glue have a tendency to pop up on the ends, so if that happens use a larger fret or check out the section on loose fret ends later in this chapter. With or without glue, use a downward pressure as you clip, being sure that you have sharp, flush-ground end nippers. To avoid fret-end pop-up, use a downward motion to clip the fret's crown first, and then the tang (left).

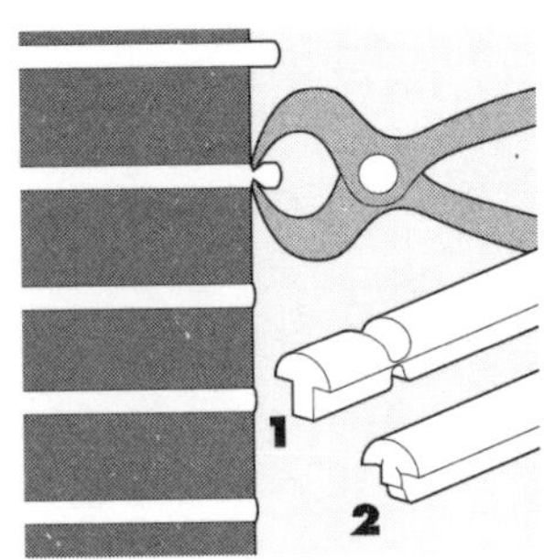

Once the frets are in, continue with the fret leveling and final crowning and polishing as described earlier. A hammer-in fret job can be just as perfect as the glue-in type. Learn all the methods and then use the appropriate one for the situation.

Bound fingerboards

Now you know some of the reasons why a guitar needs fret work, as well as what problems a refretting job can solve. I also showed how I go about the modern glue-in method. Let's continue by examining the treatment of fret ends during the refret and how to deal with fingerboards that have binding. I hope you'll find it enlightening to see the amount of set-up involved after the refret and to compare different fret work prices from around the country.

The shape of the fret ends is a matter of taste, and it's something you should discuss

with your repairman beforehand. Look at some samples around the shop. Remember the results of over-beveled fret ends: too narrow a string spacing at the nut and strings that fall off the fingerboard edge. An exaggerated bevel isn't necessary as long as the fret ends are filed smooth and don't catch the hand. A smooth, nicely rounded end is what you're after.

Bound fingerboards need special attention. There is seldom a reason to remove fingerboard binding when refretting, yet it's done often, perhaps in an attempt to save the "nibs" at the fret end, as pictured above. It's almost impossible to save the nibs during a fret job. It's best to pull the frets, level the board as if the nibs weren't there, and then fret it by either the hammer or glue-in methods. Also, removal of the binding involves much touch-up finishing, so don't be talked into doing it. (A rare vintage guitar can be fretted with its nibs left intact, but the job is so time-consuming and delicate that you'd best be sitting down when your repairman gives you an estimate.)

The frets can be installed so that the crown overlaps the plastic (facing page, top), as with most Martins and Guilds, or they may be trimmed flush to the binding and then beveled. Players getting a refret on a guitar with nibs (Gibson, Jackson, Gretsch, etc.) may prefer the fret/binding overlap, since it takes the place of the missing nibs and retains the feel. In the case of the overlap, the fret's tang is notched and filed smooth (bottom right) before installation. The tang is also beveled slightly inward to avoid pushing the binding out. The fret end is then finish-beveled to a player's taste.

If you've experienced action problems from a warp in the neck or humps in the board, the new fret job should enable you to set the action much lower without undue buzzing. But remember that a certain amount of clean, metal-to-metal string buzz is normal for any guitar, especially if one plays with a medium or heavy attack on light strings (.010s and under). Remember that repairmen are a sensitive breed. They're known to become offended when, after doing a painstaking fret job and then taking half a day to set up a guitar, the customer picks it up and whines, "It buzzes!" Any new fret job takes some time to break in, so be patient. It may take as long as a month for playing and fret wear to make things feel normal again.

When discussing price, few customers seem to appreciate the careful and tedious set-up involved after the fret work. Often the nut must be replaced or shimmed to accommodate the new, taller fret. Bridge set-ups must be readjusted, and there must be truss rod adjustment and general set-up. This work must be added onto the price of the fret job itself; there's no way around it. I spoke to several different repairmen from around the country, and they gave me some figures that may help you know what prices to expect when fret-job shopping. I'm listing the highest and lowest prices for normal fret jobs, along with prices for set-up and a new nut. As a rule, the highest prices were on the East and West Coasts, with New York being the highest. This list is current as July, 1990.

REFRET PRICES

With binding— $125 to $300
Unbound— $90 to $250
Maple w/lacquered fingerboard —$150 to $300
Fret dress—$25 to $80
New nut—$12 to $50
Action and set-up—$18 to $40

Consider action and set-up to involve truss rod adjustment, bridge intonation on electrics, string-height adjustment, and the final fit of the nut. For many acoustics, the saddle has to be refit or replaced by hand to accommodate the subtle action changes after a refret. These prices point out how much can go into an acoustic set-up alone:

ACOUSTIC ACTION SET-UP

Truss rod adjustment—same as electric
Final fit of nut—same as electric
Clean, straighten, square up saddle slot —$10 to $30
Install new bone saddle or shim old saddle —$10 to $30
Adjust action to fit the nut—$10 to $20

When shopping for a refret, consider the years of experience and training needed for one to do the job well. Consider the value that it adds to your guitar, and the enjoyment you'll get from playing when it's right. If you can't afford a first-rate refret, save your money. Price is important, but a botched fret job is much worse than no fret job at all.

For those of you who aren't intimidated by the complex nature of fret work and wish to learn more, these books are invaluable: Don Teeter's *The Acoustic Guitar, Vols. 1* and *2*, Hideo Kamimoto's *Complete Guitar Repair*, and Irving Sloane's *Guitar Repair*. I've made a videotape that offers an in-shop view of the subject, titled, of course, *Don't Fret*. It's available from Stewart-MacDonald.

Scalloped fingerboards

More than a few players seem to be looking for advice on scalloped fingerboards. Should they perform this modification? What does it have to offer? Is it reversible? Does scalloping a neck cause problems in the future? While many of you may be aware that John McLaughlin and Ritchie Blackmore used scalloped fingerboards years ago, I think that most of the current interest has been stirred up by Yngwie Malmsteen.

I thought scalloping was a dumb idea until I received a phone call from Pat Patton, a guitarist and instructor from Westlake, Michigan. Pat has been playing on a scalloped board for years and doing the scalloping himself. He came to me for instruction on doing the job neatly and to learn how to refret the neck when he was done. After only five minutes of listening to Pat play, I was totally knocked out! I hadn't been that excited about playing—and learning something new—for many years. You can teach an old dog new tricks after all. Here are the pros and cons of this modification:

Scalloping involves dishing out the wood between frets so that the fingertip has no contact with the fingerboard. It's difficult to do this well. If you're thinking of doing the job yourself, be sure to finish this chapter before you start—and you might decide to have it done by the very best repairman or builder that you can find. Expect the scalloping job to be expensive, and don't be surprised if you have to refret your guitar at the same time—this is not an absolute, but a good possibility. Factory-scalloped replacement necks are available from some of the suppliers, which gives you the option of leaving your original board stock—a great idea where vintage pieces are concerned!

When playing with a scalloped fingerboard, you have to develop a whole new touch in order to keep from accidentally pressing the strings too hard and going out of tune. I found that this light touch was easy to get used to. And, for the first time in my life, my fingering hand became so relaxed that I was able to play much faster and smoother, since my fingertips were no longer fighting the fingerboard wood in order to press the string onto the fret. This seems to be in direct opposition to Yngwie's view that "it's much harder to play fast with a scalloped fingerboard because the string action has to be much higher." I don't know why he says this.

The photo shows scalloping as Pat prefers it. These "radical" scallops are quite deep: $\frac{5}{32}$" to $\frac{3}{16}$" below the actual wood surface of the fingerboard that the fret seats against, and you can add to that the height of the fret itself. The scallops are complemented by either a good fret-dress (the tops are filed smooth and round, enabling the string to move smoothly when you press down into the scallop) or a complete refret

A salesman in a music store tried to tell me, "Scalloping ain't no big deal; tall frets will do the exact same thing." This is simply not true.

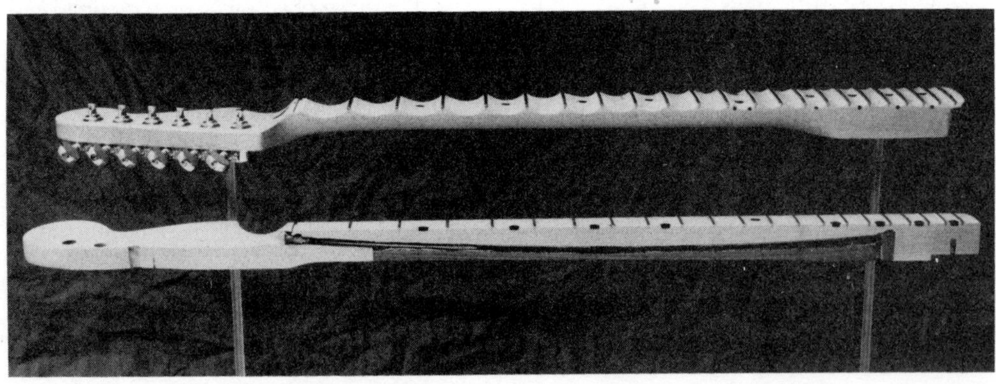

with a jumbo fretwire. I prefer the scallop to look a little asymmetrical—that is, not a perfect radius—with a little extra removed on the fret side that the finger plays against to accommodate the finger's ball end.

Since the guitar is a very personal instrument, the "benefits" of scalloping are subjective. Playing on one, I noticed the following changes in my playing: My fingering hand was relaxed, allowing me to play faster. Hammer-ons took less pressure in the attack, enabling faster trills and hammered chords. Pull-offs became easier, since the finger's flesh can reach deep down and really catch hold as you pull away, creating a distinctive percussive sound. A pitch bend (pushing straight down with the finger towards the fingerboard) could easily accommodate a semitone, and with a little practice, whole-tones and minor thirds can be done. Using this technique, you can imitate the sound of a pedal steel, for example, or even bend whole chords. I had never been able to do this before without a tremolo, and this produces a different sound.

OTHER BENEFITS

Due to the lack of pressure needed to hold down a chord, scalloping allows you to "rake"—or sweep—arpeggio passages, since your hand is free to move with the chord. This is an essential aspect of Yngwie's style. Bending blues notes has never been easier, since the finger can really get a good grab on the string with no slipping. This makes the wide, full-string vibrato of Yngwie or Ritchie Blackmore easier to achieve. Two-handed tapping techniques are also made easier, especially for the right-hand fingertip that is now able to pull off the string without first hitting the fingerboard. The violin-type finger vibrato also takes on a new sound since you can alter its pitch with a gentle pressing of the string. With scalloping, I find a more even, clear sound on all the strings in any position, probably because there is no longer any muting effect from the fingers touching the wood and drawing off some of the sound. Sounds good, huh? Now for the other side of the coin.

I wouldn't suggest that you scallop a vintage guitar if you have any interest in retaining its market value—you'll ruin it forever. Scalloping could considerably weaken any neck (aside from one you may have had custom-built with a scalloped board in mind), since the fingerboard is an integral part of the neck's straightness and stiffness. After scalloping, a neck might twist or warp, but frankly, I think any good repairman could compensate for this by adjusting the truss rod accordingly or making up for any problem with accurate fret work. Also, since the scallops must be quite deep, the position markers may need to be removed and re-inlaid. This is easy for dots, but if you have pearl-block or large, ornate inlays, you may have to settle for dot replacements or foot a very expensive re-inlay bill. The side dot markers may need to be moved or eliminated, as well.

OTHER CONS

The scallop is non-reversible. You cannot change your mind and simply have the neck refretted; the entire fingerboard has to be replaced. The tone of the guitar is going to change somewhat, too, and nobody could advise you as to what to expect there. I'd worry about this more with an acoustic guitar than a solidbody electric, yet even with electrics, I suggest scalloping a bolt-on neck at first. Buy yourself an extra kit neck and have it scalloped, leaving the original intact (or, try the scalloped Strat-style necks offered by several guitar shop suppliers). And if you're used to playing on strings that begin with a high *E* gauged .010 or heavier, be prepared to switch to .009s in order to gain the scallops' benefit. I found that my newly relaxed left hand compensated for the switch to lighter strings, and even though I don't enjoy playing on lighter strings, I really didn't notice a difference. (Pat suggests using

At first, try scalloping a fingerboard on an extra guitar, not your main axe! If you have any interest in retaining its market value, don't scallop a vintage guitar—you'll ruin it forever!

.009, .011, .013, .022, .032, .038 for acoustics or electrics.) Since standard truss rods curve up towards the fingerboard at each end of the neck (see photo, previous page), the scallop depth must be controlled accurately in these areas. Finally, scalloping is expensive and comes with no guarantees. Expect a fair price to be in the range of $150 to $200.

Recently a salesman in a music store tried to tell me, "Scalloping ain't no big deal; tall frets will do the exact same thing." This is simply not true. I may not have covered *all* the pros and cons of scalloping here, but you get the idea—give scallops a try if you've got the appetite.

The neck jig

The neck jig is the most important tool in my repair shop. Although only the most serious fret worker would actually build this tool, its basic concept should help all guitarists understand more about neck repairs and fret work. Many repairmen should profit from these pages, too.

Although I currently use the neck-stress jig for all fret work, it was originally designed to help correct problem fret jobs: necks with twists, warps, humps, and rises, or truss rods that don't work well. I wanted something that would duplicate the pressure of a fully-strung guitar, so that as I worked on a neck, it would be under the same stress—and in the same configuration—as when it was being played. Thus, the fingerboard shape had to remain constant. I also realized that because of gravity, the neck's straightness and relief when being held, or hung from a strap in the playing position, is different from when it's lying on the repair bench with its strings removed. By using the neck jig, it's possible to gain a greater degree of control over any normal neck, and more important, it's easier to salvage the problem necks that are often found on rare and valuable vintage instruments. When not in use (a rare occurrence), the jig doubles as a heavy-duty solid maple workbench. Here's how it works.

The body is first clamped firmly to the table with padded hold-down "dogs" that ride on cross-slots in the table (see photo at left). Under the body are padded spacer blocks to raise it off the table surface. At this point, the neck is suspended freely with ample space for stringing and unstringing.

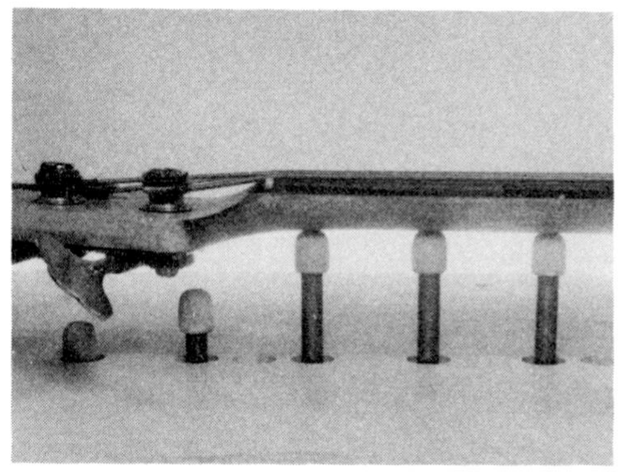

Now for the most important part: By loosening four lock pins, one on each corner of the table, I free the top to spin on centers. Next, the table top is tilted in the playing position at a 90-degree angle relative to the floor, and the guitar is tuned to pitch. Now the neck is read (analyzed) from the side, using a good straightedge while looking for the proper amount of straightness or relief, depending on string gauge and action height (above). I use a fluorescent Bright Stick as a backlight (see the drawing below). The light rides up and down on two rods, tilts to align with the fingerboard, and bolts to my rotating table top, following the work wherever it goes.

The tilting table eliminates the gravity factor, making it easier to adjust the truss rod, which controls the fingerboard's shape lengthwise. Note: With a properly working neck, there's always some pressure on the truss rod. With the strings in place, loosening a rod (turning counter-clockwise) gives a straight neck relief, while tightening it (turning clockwise) removes excess relief, or "up-bow." Of course, tightening the rod too much causes a back-bow away from the strings. Most players prefer a straight neck or one with a slight, controlled relief.

Once the neck is adjusted correctly, then I set the neck support rods (left). The steel rods have plastic protective caps and are set into accurately reamed holes in the jig bar, which is clamped to the table top underneath the back of the neck. First the rods are carefully slid up until they just touch the back of the neck, and then they are locked in place with set-screws. With the rods set, the strings are removed. Without the string pressure, the neck usually rises up slightly off the support rods because of the back-pressure from the truss rod. You must slightly loosen the truss rod until the neck sets back down onto the rods; when this happens, the neck is supported in the playing position. Thanks to the support rods, the table can now be rotated and locked into the level position for working, without gravity playing a major role in the neck's shape. The stress jig eliminates the guesswork in fretting and allows me to control the truss rod, especially in problem cases.

Many fine vintage guitars have problem fingerboards. A great guitar can still have humps, rises, warp, twist, up-bow, or back-bow. These are caused in part by the nature of the wood itself, but especially by years of playing with heavier strings and a tight truss rod. Remember that during the '50s and early '60s, light strings (beginning with a .010 high *E* and under) were not available, and most players used what today would be considered medium- or heavy-gauge strings, except for a rare few who used banjo strings to get those bluesy bends. Many of these necks have taken a definite "set" after years of truss rod/heavy string stress. This is not necessarily bad, but a fret dress or refret must be done

Support block slides on two rails.

Bright Stick light pivots on screw.

Clamp this block to your bench.

carefully in order to avoid needless planing, sanding, and scraping of the fingerboard. To me, the stress jig is a necessity in these cases.

Imagine the following situation: I received a '62 Fender Jazz Bass with severe problems. The neck was extremely back-bowed, which in itself is unusual, especially since the truss rod was completely loose. Worse still, the owner had tried to correct the problem (in exactly the wrong way) by tightening the truss rod, thereby breaking off the end of the truss rod along with the tightening nut. Suffice to say that I managed to replace the rod with one that worked, which got me back to the guitar's original problem: a back-bow with a loose rod. Here's where the jig helped greatly in solving the problem.

By stringing the bass up to pitch with the table tilted, I could see that the neck would become *almost* straight, but with none of the relief that most basses need. I supported the neck in this position, yet knew that with the strings removed, I couldn't loosen the truss rod to let the neck back onto the jig's rods. After removing the frets, I ran a guitar string through the empty fret slot at the 7th fret and used it to tighten the neck down with a turnbuckle that held it onto the rods. I was then able to scrape a little here, sand a little there, and by being careful where I worked, I managed to gain a little relief when stringing back to pitch. Next, I put some pressure on the truss rod by tightening it slightly. The neck was straight, and I rejigged it.

This time around, I could set the neck back onto the rods by releasing the truss rod. I then scraped and sanded again, mostly in the middle of the fingerboard, but also a bit on the tongue and some at the 1st and 3rd frets. The next time I strung to pitch, I had good relief with no rod tension, slight relief with some rod tension, and a straight neck with good truss rod tension. At that point, I was able to proceed with a standard fret job. To me, this minor miracle could only have been accomplished with the jig.

Tuner basics

There are many devices designed to help tune a guitar and keep it in tune. Electronic tuners and locking nuts have flooded the market, targeted especially at guitarists who use a tremolo. Many players never realize that one of the easiest ways to get in tune and stay there is to replace old, worn-out tuning machines that no longer hold their pitch. First we'll look at tuners in general, and then deal with their installation.

Tuners have three main parts: a plate or casting that holds the gear and shaft together, the drive shaft that's turned by the key or button, and the string-post shaft that's turned by the drive shaft. The drive shaft has a worm gear on one end, which drives the crown gear on the string post. The gears' housing is either the less-expensive, stamped-plate type made of steel, or a solid-metal enclosed unit known as a die-cast. The number of turns needed to cause the string post to go around one full turn indicates a tuner's gear ratio. Today most guitar tuners have a 14- or 15-to-1 ratio, while higher ratios of 20- or 24-to-1 are used on electric basses, which need the finer tuning capabilities due to their low-pitched, heavy strings (a higher ratio makes fine tuning easier).

Judge a tuner's quality by its "backlash"—the amount of free play felt when a peg is turned in an opposite direction without the string post moving. Also check to see if the post moves—thereby changing the pitch—without the tuning key being touched. Backlash is especially noticed by players who bend strings or use a tremolo, since when the constant pressure of the string at the post is altered, the string may not return to the original pitch. The locking nut is a good solution to backlash and post movement, but for vintage guitars, I feel that

Don't blame the poor tuners if you haven't mastered tuning yet!

the tuners should be replaced before a locking nut is even considered. By eliminating backlash, you might solve most of your guitar's tuning problems. Better tuners have low amounts of end play (up-and-down movement of the string post) and shaft wobble (back-and-forth string movement in the bushing, washer, or grommet on the headstock face).

For years all tuners were constructed with either open gears or a semi-enclosed, stamped sheet-metal housing. Kluson, Waverly, and Grover were the big manufacturers, with Kluson leading the field. Kluson's Deluxe (top photo, right) was not only the most widely used, but often the tuner most in need of replacement. They were notorious for backlash because their gears were made on a screw machine rather than a specialized, more accurate tool known as a gear hobber. Also, they made the worm gear from brass, when steel would have worn longer (all tuners today have a brass crown gear, but use steel for the worm). Kluson tuners had a backlash the day they were born, but no one knew enough to complain. There wasn't anything better, so players put up with them until Grover came along with the Rotomatic, the first high-quality tuner. Its die-cast housing enclosed well-machined gears that were lifetime lubricated and completely sealed. In addition, a threaded bushing with extra length replaced the press-in grommet to better support the shaft (right). This tuner became the replacement choice of repairmen around the country—much to the owner's delight—as well as a factory-installed standard on many higher-end guitars. Years later the Rotomatic was copied, then improved upon, by Schaller and Gotoh. Between Grover, Schaller, Gotoh, and the lesser-known but equally high-quality Sperzels, you'll find a size, shape, and style to fit any guitar or bass.

While die-cast tuners are no doubt the most precisely made and offer the least amount of backlash, they are also more expensive. And because of their larger size, you'll have to do some drilling in order to use them as replacements for the old-style

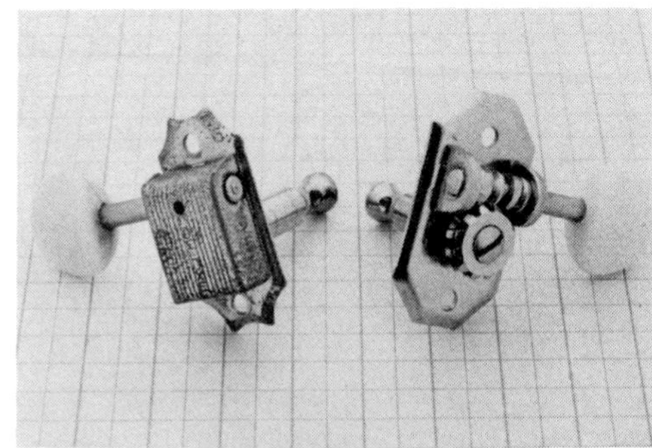

Two early Klusons: the "Deluxe" (left), and the "Ideal."

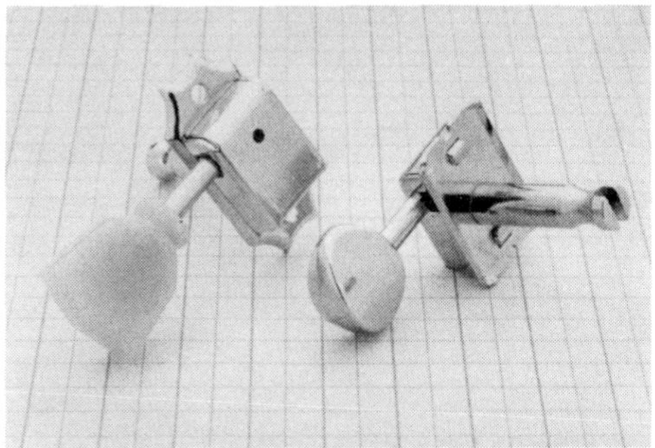

Two modern Kluson-style replacements: note the Fender style slotted "SafetiPost" and the trimmed plate.

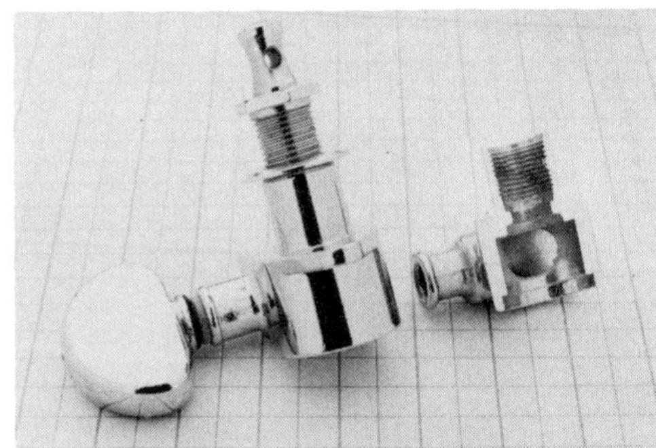

Modern Rotomatic die-cast tuner. Note the threaded bushing for extra shaft support.

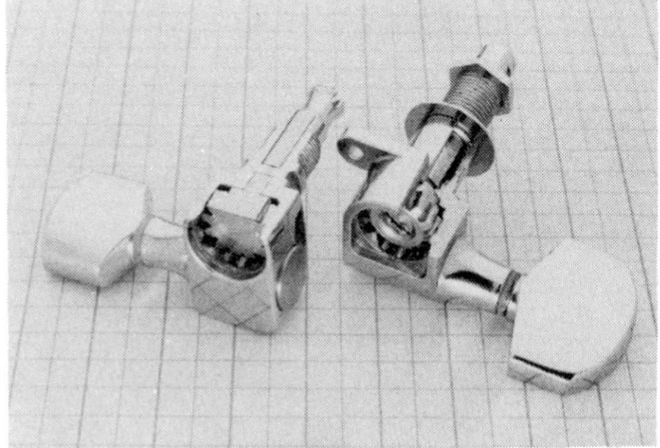

Sperzel tuner. Note the solid crown gear/post housing.

tuners with a smaller string-post diameter. Perhaps they're not a wise choice for a valuable vintage guitar or bass.

In the good old days, players had few choices when it came to solving tuning-key problems. You'd either install a set of die-cast Rotomatics or buy a new set of stamped factory replacements that were no better than the originals. Today's replacements for those old, low-priced Kluson Deluxe tuners are excellent. Modern Deluxe styles offer a 14- or 15-to-1 gear ratio, compared to the old 12-to-1, which means closer tuning capabilities. Also, the gears are accurately machined—regardless of which brand you buy—with nylon washers added to support end play on the worm gear, thereby eliminating much of the backlash. That means you're safe using them as an exact look-alike replacement, and you won't have to deface a vintage axe by drilling for the larger die-cast machines (you will have to enlarge the tuner bushing holes in the peghead face however, since Deluxe replacements use a larger shaft and bushing).

If you absolutely want the best machines and you don't mind redrilling, install die-cast pegs. Since many guitars manufactured since the late '60s already have die-cast tuners, replacing them is easy; the hole is already the right size, and no drilling is needed. But even die-cast tuners wear out or eventually suffer from backlash. So if you're shopping for a new set, there are several points to consider. The first is size: Mini die-casts are available for headstocks that won't accept the standard ones (Fender, for example). You can also choose color—from black, gold, and chrome to red and blue. Several other options are available, such as string locks—miniature locks that are actually built into the posts to help control string slippage. Sperzel offers staggered-height string posts for Stratocaster-style headstocks, which keep a good angle at the nut without using string trees; this is a real enhancement when using a tremolo without a locking nut. Perhaps you need Fender's slotted SafetiPost and trimmed plate to fit a Fender. Also keep in mind that some sets are heavier than others, and try to find pegs that match the original shape and mounting screw holes. If properly matched, they'll drop right in, probably even matching the original press-marks in the lacquer.

Many players have no idea of the variety of tuners available today, and since they seldom browse through the catalogs at their local music store, they assume that what they see in the showcase is all that's available. Ask questions and shop around, so you can really weigh the facts.

Locking tuners are a great invention. They really help avoid tuning hassles.

Tuner installation

Those are the *basics* of tuning machine construction—from costly die-cast tuners to the less-expensive, stamped variety. Almost any of today's well-made, inexpensive tuners are a good replacement value. Here are a few more tuner facts, along with some installation tips.

Not only are die-cast tuners the most accurate, but they also suffer the least from backlash. This doesn't mean that you can't tune well or won't be satisfied with stamped vintage replacements; you may well be. But die-cast tuners are the best, which is why you see them on most top-of-the-line instruments. (Would you put two-ply tires on a Cadillac?) Now, even die-cast tuners can develop backlash over the years: As the brass crown gear wears, the fit becomes looser. Another little-known fact is that if you tune a string too high—especially a wound string—and it suddenly breaks, the instant release of torque at the string post can loosen the screw that holds the crown gear to the post. This allows slop between the

Never assume that what you see in a music store showcase is all that's available. Ask for catalogs, and check the ads in music magazines.

Before drilling any tuning key mounting holes, be sure to read the over-oiled tuners section in Miscellaneous Repairs. People screw up this operation all the time. If you break off a screw—especially in maple—there's hell to pay getting the broken part out!

gears, and backlash can result. This explains why one tuner may occasionally develop tuning problems. You can't repair this, because you'd damage the tuner by trying to get inside it. Your music store, though, can often order a single replacement. Most of the various styles are available from Grover, Schaller, and Gotoh at competitive prices, and they are all equally fine tuners.

While researching this chapter, though, I learned that Sperzel tuners are unique. Their construction features totally eliminate backlash, end play, and shaft wobble. Not only are the machining tolerances extremely close, but the string post and crown gear are a one-piece, solid unit that is locked into the die-cast housing by a cleverly machined collar (see previous page). Also, the bushing threads are outside the housing rather than inside, allowing an even tighter fit between the post and housing and further eliminating any play. Since the string post and gear are solid, there is no screw that can loosen. Sperzel has been able to drill up through the shaft, thread it, and install a unique string lock that is adjustable with a thumbscrew from the rear; this Trim-Lock is an option. Another option is staggered post heights for Strat-style guitars, allowing the removal of the string trees while maintaining a good angle for the string passing over the nut. Sperzel tuners are a little more expensive, but they are definitely worth looking into.

Replacing stamped "deluxe" tuners is often simply a matter of removal and direct replacement. Installing die-casts, however, sometimes requires the enlargement of headstock holes. First remove the old tuners and mounting screws. Often the headstock grommets are quite snug, and you may have to rock them out, or at least loosen them by inserting a screwdriver shaft inside and gently rolling it in a circle until you feel it loosen. The grommet can then be pushed out from the rear with a blunt tool. Don't overdo the rolling motion, because

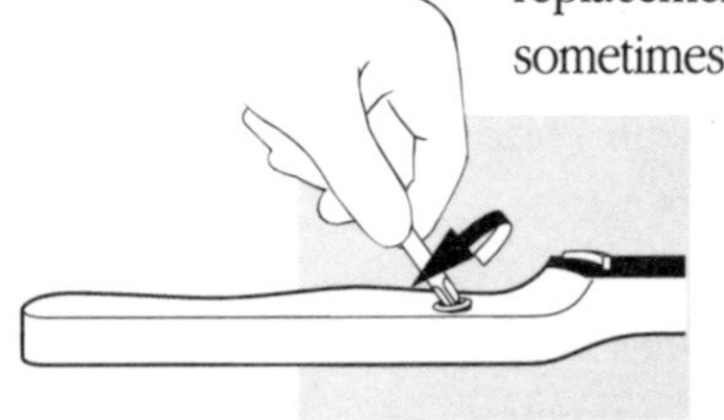

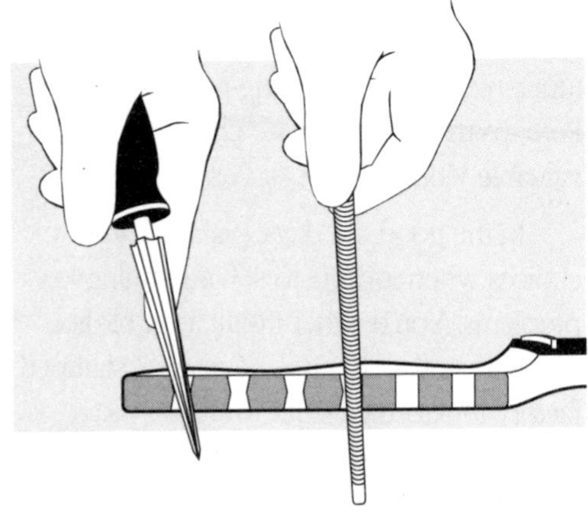

you could crack the finish. Now measure the housing's diameter: It will usually be around .380" or close to $\frac{3}{8}$", while the original hole will measure around $\frac{9}{32}$" or $\frac{5}{16}$".

This exact hole size would be important if we were going to use a drill, but we aren't; that's for pros or for people in a hurry. Enlarge the hole by using a tapered reamer (available from hardware stores and guitar shop suppliers). Ream halfway through from the front and from the rear, testing often with the new tuning peg until it fits. If the two reamed sides don't quite meet, leave a ridge in the center (above), removing this last bit with a rat-tail file. Be sure to hold the reamer at right angles, clean its blades often, and don't be in a hurry. Each hole may take you five or ten minutes. Wrap a piece of masking tape around the reamer's cutting flutes at the correct width of the new tuners to act as a depth stop.

Once all the holes have been cleared and the pegs slip in easily, install the tuners and tighten down the hex-nut bushing against the washer on the headstock's face. Now you can line up the tuners with the headstock shape in a fashion that both pleases your eye and allows the easiest turning of the keys. When the pegs look right, snug the hex nuts and drill the mounting-screw holes. Use masking tape on the drill bit as a depth guide to avoid drilling through the headstock's face! Be sure to use a bit that's smaller than the actual screw thread, so that the screw can bite into the wood. Thread each screw into the mounting hole to finish the job. The correct way to drill the mounting holes is illustrated and explained in the section on problems caused by over-oiled tuners.

You need to fill the old tuner holes to seal them from moisture absorption and to make the finished job look neat; remove the tuners to make the job easier. A local guitar shop or cabinet maker can provide small wood scraps (usually mahogany or maple) that match your neck. Carve or file small, round, tapered plugs that are slightly oversize to the hole for a snug fit. Glue them in with a white or yellow glue such as Franklin Tite Bond or Elmer's; use super glue only if you're experienced with it. If you "dry fit" the dowels to each hole, you can see where to trim them to length before gluing them in. This makes clean-up easier and lessens the risk of damaging the finish as you trim. A pre-trimmed dowel should push down into the hole until it's flush with or slightly below the surface. Don't expect the color or grain to be a perfect match, and seal the finished plug with a drop of lacquer or super glue as a drop-fill (the section on dents, dings, and scratches explains how). Of course, the plugged holes will be visible unless you totally refinish the headstock, but they should look good enough; and besides, that goes along with the installation of die-casts as a replacement for the old-style tuners.

When the finish dries, reinstall the new pegs, put on a new set of strings, and go find someone to play with—you've earned it!

Strat tremolo set-up

Tremolos have been the rage since the early '80s, when Floyd Rose hit the guitar world with the locking tremolo. Still, the most common tremolo question is: "How can I stay in tune with a Fender Stratocaster tremolo without installing a locking nut and modern bridge? I don't want to alter my vintage guitar." I spent some time with my friend Doug Phillips, a guitar repairman from Norfolk, Virginia, who is a Strat man all the way and a serious blues player. I was impressed by his four unaltered Strats that play beautifully and stay in tune. We spent many hours discussing the fine points of setting up the standard tremolo, and came up with the following modifications and adjustments that not only help the guitar stay in tune, but improve its sound, as well. And all this is possible without installing any of today's locking nut/bridge systems, all of which require alteration of vintage Strats. These tips will be a help to vintage Strat lovers who are trying to keep up with the modern music world.

There are many ways to adjust tremolos other than the one explained here. The best way is to sit down and fiddle with your axe for a while to see what *you* like.

The modern locking nut/bridge system is so popular because it basically eliminates the problem of slack storage—string tension that "hangs up" at the friction points outside the playing area in between the nut and bridge. When you tune a string or run it through the nut and string tree by depressing the tremolo, the friction points (nut, string trees, and less often the bridge) can make the string hang up, causing it to return sharp and throwing the guitar out of tune. The stored slack is held temporarily and usually releases the next time you make a bend or use your tremolo. If you retune this "sharp" string, it will be flat when it releases. Most slack storage occurs at the nut, at the string tree hold-downs behind the nut, and to a lesser degree at the bridge. If you eliminate these friction problems, your guitar will stay in tune.

NUT FRICTION

The first and easiest friction area to take care of is the nut. The string slots should be only deep enough to hold the string and keep it from popping out when played. The bottom of the nut slots should be rounded to the shape of the string, properly angled, and lightly lubricated with pencil lead, powdered graphite, Vaseline, or a Teflon lube such as Magik Guitar Lube. A well-fit nut allows the string to travel lengthwise without binding. You may be wise to have a troublesome nut replaced by a repairman who understands tremolo problems and will shape one carefully from a hard material, such as bone. Or, be adventuresome and try it yourself after reading the Nut Work chapter.

STRING TREE PROBLEMS

If you remove your string trees, expect to make an adjustment in your playing style. The upper two strings will probably seem harder to bend.

Eliminating the slack storage occurring at string trees can be done in a variety of ways, but the removal of them alone is not a solution, because then there will be insufficient down-pressure, or angle, at the nut, and the strings may pop out when struck. Also, without a decent angle at the nut, a great loss of tone occurs. Roller trees are available from a variety of sources (check your local music store—Wilkinson makes several). These are an easy retrofit for the originals, allowing the strings to move smoothly when the tremolo is depressed.

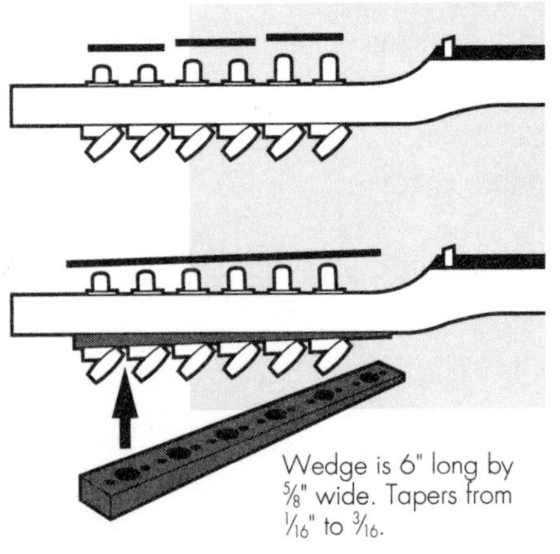

Wedge is 6" long by ⅝" wide. Tapers from 1/16" to 3/16.

You can eliminate the trees entirely by using replacement tuners with graduated shaft heights (left). Sperzel and Schecter offer graduated shaft pegs, so check with your dealer to find what's currently available. Installing these pegs, however, involves enlarging the tuner-shaft hole. Instead of enlarging the holes on his '62 Strat, Doug made a tapered hardwood wedge, drilled clearance holes for the tuners and screws, and slipped it between the tuners and the back of the headstock (below, left). This "wedge" solution works well, doesn't disfigure a vintage instrument, and is a simple way out if graduated shaft height solves your problem. Wilkinson also offers machined aluminum wedges just like Doug's, which work great. Note: If you remove your string trees, expect to make an adjustment in your playing style, because the upper two strings may seem a little harder to bend; you may have to push further to get the desired note. You'll be pleased, though, that the string has a little more resiliency at the top of the bend. Also, this extra resiliency results in a lot less string breakage, since the strings tend to give more.

STRING BREAKAGE

Breakage usually occurs where the string angles over the bridge plate. You can radius (taper) these holes with a small file and sandpaper or by grinding a radius on one end of a #4 counterbore and using it in an electric drill to bevel the hole evenly. This type of counterbore is generally used by machinists and is available at most industrial supply stores; any machine shop can quickly grind a radius on it. Besides eliminating string breakage, this bridge-plate modification also helps eliminate binding that occurs at the same point. An easier solution is to do what Stevie Ray Vaughan does: Slide a piece of plastic wire insulation over the string at the point of contact at the bridge saddle. This must inhibit some tone and sustain, although you can't prove that by listening to Stevie Ray!

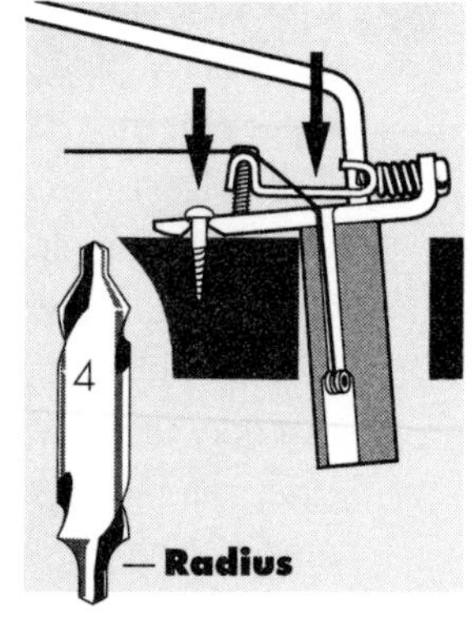

SMOOTH TREMOLO ACTION AND BETTER SUSTAIN

A tremolo often binds slightly as it rocks on the six screws that mount it to the body. With the bridge removed, inspect the six holes from the underside. You can increase the bevel by using the other end of the same #4 counterbore. This increased bevel gives more of a knife-edge pivot point to the bridge where it rocks against the mounting screws, and therefore noticeably increases the sustain. Many bridges are beveled properly and need no modification, but it won't hurt to have a look. The bevels should be the same. Concentrate on the rear edge of the hole—the edge that bears against the screw. Bevel (countersink) the underside of the holes until the remaining rim is approximately 3⁄64" to 1⁄16" thick on each hole. When replacing the bridge, tighten all six screws snugly, and then back off each screw a quarter turn; this keeps the bridge plate flat to the body while allowing enough room for the tremolo when in use.

SPRING ADJUSTMENT

The tension adjustment of the tremolo springs depends on string gauge and desired tremolo action—a personal choice. Many players want the plate to return to the instrument's face after use, but keep more tension on the springs than is necessary. Here's a good test for proper spring tension: Pluck the open low-*E* string and, at the 15th fret, immediately bend your top *E* string one-and-a-half to two steps. If the low-*E* holds true, the spring tension is probably correct. If it goes flat due to the additional pressure caused by bending the top string, tighten the spring claw until the low-*E* is close to remaining in tune. Experiment to find the springs that best suit your style. Not all springs are the same length, size, or material, so shop around. Players using sets beginning with an .008 to .009 high-*E* should experiment with two or three springs; .010s and up play best for me with four springs. Properly adjusted springs should ring clear when plucked, with no dull, plunking sound. A good spring tension and tone are important to a Strat's unique sound, since they create a natural reverb chamber.

If you follow these tips, you should find that your guitar stays in tune nicely and has marked improvement in tone. For many years, the Strat tremolo has been a great invention; it simply needs a little understanding and care.

Installing the Floyd Rose tremolo

Fitting a guitar with the Floyd Rose Tremolo and its partner, the locking nut, is work. This section begins by presenting the basics of installing a stud-mount, knife-edge tremolo. We'll cover installing the locking nut separately, and then explain setting up and fine-tuning the unit as a whole. If your tremolo is already installed, don't go away—there's something here for everyone!

While making a videotape on tremolo installation and set-up, I designed a set of related jigs and templates that require simple, clear instructions. Here are those instructions in abridged form, and I'll read between the lines for you, offering additional tips as we go along.

Routing templates and ball-bearing router bits make tremolo installation fairly simple. The body cavities are routed by using Plexiglas templates mounted to the guitar's face or rear; these templates are screwed to a guitar's existing holes—i.e., pickguard, pickup mounting ring holes, etc.—or held with double-stick carpet tape. Specialized ball-bearing router bits follow

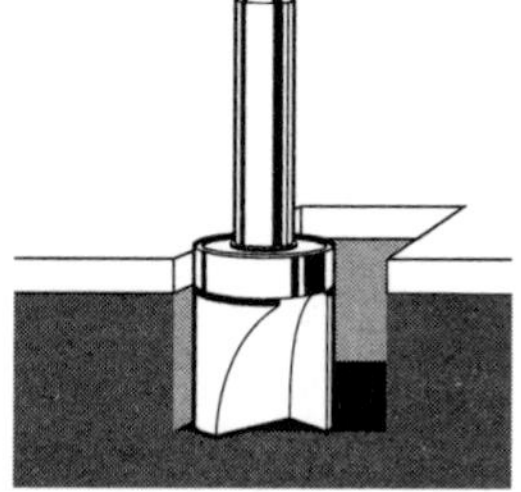

the templates' pattern (pictured at left). The bearing and router bit are the same size, so the cutter trims flush with whatever the bearing rolls against. Routing templates and ball-bearing bits are available from W.D. Pickguards and Stewart-MacDonald.

Typical installations involve either a modified rout for guitars with an existing standard Strat-style tremolo (the cavities need only to be enlarged in certain places) or a full rout for guitars that never had a tremolo, as well as for custom-built guitars and many kit bodies. The same rout depth, width, and clearance measurements used for the full rout apply to the modified rout, as well. We'll start by describing a full rout, using the templates mentioned above.

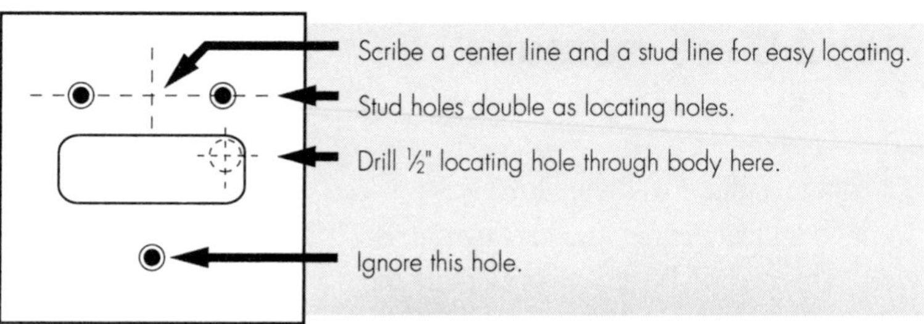

The clear Plexiglas top-rout template is most easily placed if you scribe locating lines on its underside. Scribe a line (laterally, when looking at the guitar) through the centers of the two mounting holes (above), and then scribe a second line at right angles to it; this is centered exactly between the holes. This second (longitudinal) line will correspond to a center line taken from the neck and laid out on the body. To find center, use a finely graduated rule and mark the center of the fingerboard at the nut and the last fret. With a long (30") straightedge resting on those marks, transfer the line onto a piece of masking tape fixed to the top in the area where the tremolo will be located. A taut piece of string (and a friend to stretch it) can also work if you don't have a long straightedge.

Now locate the template on the guitar top with line B on the guitar's center line, and with line A located the correct distance from the front of the nut. (Exact measurements for the bridge-stud centerline measurements are given at end of this section.) Mark exactly the two template mounting holes onto the guitar top; these should be 2$^{15}/_{16}$" apart, or 1.465" to each side of the center line. Drill the mounting holes with a $^{7}/_{64}$" bit, and use #6 x 1" drywall screws for fastening. The holes must be perpendicular to the top, since they'll later be enlarged and used for the tremolo pivot-studs.

Screw the top template onto the body and measure ¼" from each edge of its top right corner, marking this location with a center punch. Remove the template and, using a drill press and brad-point drill bit

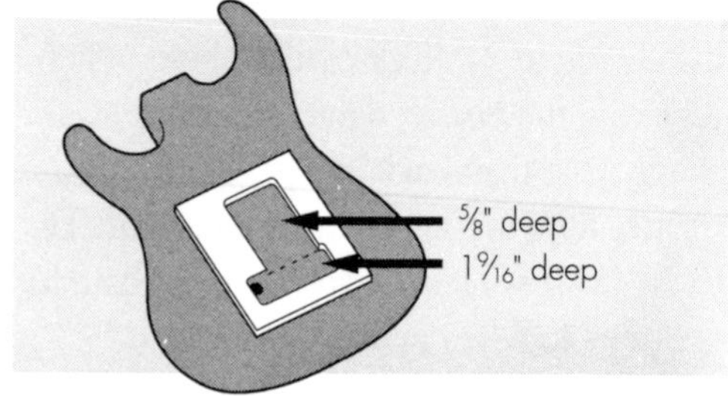

for accuracy, drill a ½"-diameter hole here, right through the body. This hole aligns the front and rear templates (the modified rout skips this step).

Remount the template. You're ready to rout, using a ⅜" ball-bearing bit. Eliminate plunging into the wood by starting each routing pass with the bit in the ½" locating hole drilled earlier. Rout the front 1$^{1}/_{16}$" deep, but go slowly—no more than ¼" per pass. The first rout is deeper than the others since, for the bearing to contact the template, the bit's full ½" cutting length must make the first pass (unless you shim the template up ¼" to get started, which is a good idea). Once you're ⅝" or more deep, remove the template (its thickness might keep the bit from going to 1$^{1}/_{16}$"). The bearing will follow the routed wall just created. Tape paper over the finish to avoid scratches from the router base plate. Stewart-MacDonald offers long-shaft bearing bits that permit chucking more shaft into the router collet—a safety feature I like. Never rout with less than $\frac{1}{4}$" of safely chucked shaft!

The rear template mounts by aligning one corner over the pre-drilled $\frac{1}{2}$" index hole (opposite). Square up the template lengthwise to the body. Drill mounting screw holes or use double-stick tape to attach the template to the guitar.

Rout the entire inside shape of the template to a depth of $\frac{5}{8}$". The rear rout will meet the front rout. Now the spring cavity is complete. Continue routing the block cavity (inside the template) to a depth of $1\frac{9}{16}$" for good tremolo clearance. The rear template can now be removed. Center the tremolo-spring claw on the front wall of the rear cavity, with its two holes $\frac{3}{8}$" from the back of the guitar. Mark the holes and drill them with a long $\frac{1}{8}$" aircraft bit.

Return to the guitar top, and redrill the two mounting holes $1\frac{1}{4}$" deep with a #10 bit; this is for the threaded portion of the mounting stud. Next, drill the holes again with a letter "I" bit, but only $\frac{3}{8}$" deep. This hole gives clearance for the stud shoulder; it's a close-tolerance fit, since it supports the shoulder during use. Install the studs. Note: Press-in anchor inserts with machine-thread pivot studs are now available as a substitute for the original wood-thread studs. These eliminate wood fatigue and the loose studs that can occur with prolonged tremolo use.

The studs, tremolo, claw, and springs could be installed now, but without the locking nut and strings, what's the use? Hold on until we get the nut on, and then we can play a few tunes.

Here's the mounting distance for five popular tremolos, measured from the nut's front edge to the center of the pivot-stud line. Figures for both long and short scales are given. A common installation error is to install the tremolo too far from the nut, causing the guitar to play flat, or the bridge saddles to hang over the unit's front edge. You'll be safe with these figures:

TREMOLO	**$25\frac{1}{2}$" LONG SCALE**	**$24\frac{3}{4}$" SHORT SCALE**
Floyd Rose:	25"	$24\frac{3}{16}$"
Schaller Floyd Rose-licensed:	$24\frac{15}{16}$"	$24\frac{1}{8}$"
Ibanez Edge:	$25\frac{1}{16}$"	$24\frac{1}{4}$"
Kahler Spyder:	25"	$24\frac{1}{4}$"
Gotoh Floyd Rose-licensed:	25"	$24\frac{1}{4}$"

Even with locking tremolos and nuts, you'll still have some kind of tuning problems. Nothing's perfect when you're dealing with guitars. Don't forget to enjoy playing!

Mounting the locking nut

Now that you've installed the Floyd Rose stud-mount tremolo, continue by getting the locking nut on. Once you're able to lock the strings at both ends, your tuning troubles are over.

When we shot a videotape on Floyd Rose installation at Stewart-MacDonald, I was worried about how I'd teach the nut installation so that it could be done with simple tools such as a router. (I'd been doing my installations on a vertical milling machine.) I actually dreamed up the following method right during the shoot, and it works better than I would have guessed at the time! Stew-Mac now sells this jig, and if you plan to do more than one of these operations, or perhaps to get into the business, it would be a wise investment. It's inexpensive and comes with extremely detailed instructions, and you'd need a machine shop to build one

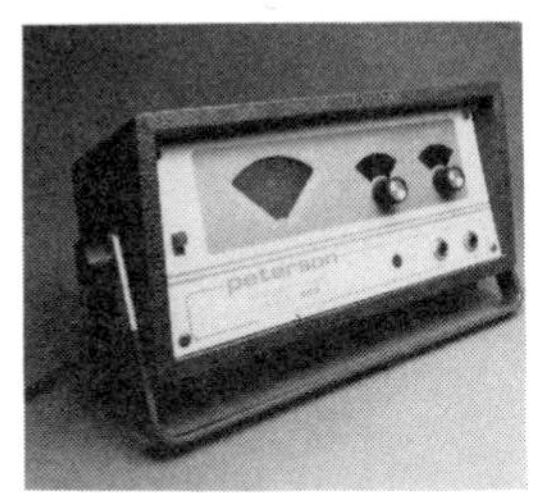

You'll find that an electronic tuner is a big help when you're setting the intonation.

as accurate. However, for one-time do-it-yourselfers, here are the jig instructions in abridged form, accompanied by illustrations to help you fashion your own router jig.

In a locking nutshell, the installation consists of cutting a ledge for the nut to sit on by removing a predetermined amount of wood where the original nut was installed. Then, holes for the nut's mounting bolts are drilled and countersunk. In an experienced woodworker's hands, a sharp chisel could cut the ledge quickly and easily, but it would be wiser for the novice to use a Dremel Moto-Tool to slowly machine the ledge. You players who are serious enough about guitar repair to install a locking nut yourselves should welcome an excuse to add a Dremel router to your toolbox.

Installation with chisel or router requires that you accurately measure the depth of the ledge, so that the nut ends up at the right level with respect to the frets. Having it too low causes buzzing, while having it too high creates a stiff action. A pair of dial calipers that measure in thousandths of an inch are a real help. Plastic-bodied dial calipers can be purchased for around $20—another invaluable addition to the tool chest.

When the outer two *E* strings are .010" above the height of the frets as they sit in the bottom of the nut slots, you're in the right ballpark. This is an average, slightly stiff playing height. You'd seldom want a higher action, and you can lower the nut if it feels too stiff. To rout the correct depth, you need one measurement: the distance from the locking nut's string-slot bottoms to the bottom of the unit itself ("A" at left). The nut described here is a Schaller R3 Floyd Rose-licensed model with an "A" measurement of .208". (Floyd Rose and Schaller designate neck/string spacing width with numbers ranging from R1 to R6; they're all slightly different at the "A" measurement.) Here's how to guarantee that the nut-slot bottoms end up .010" higher than the fret height.

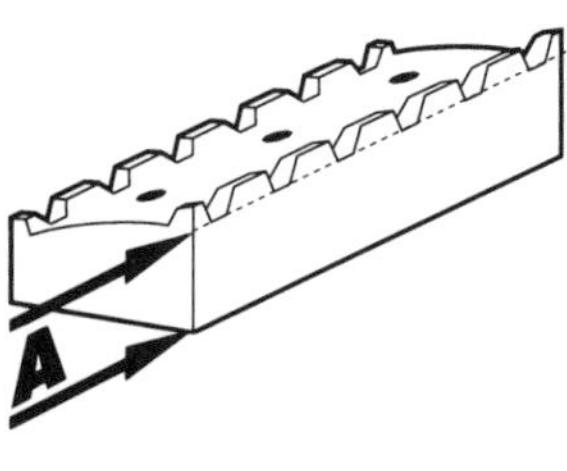

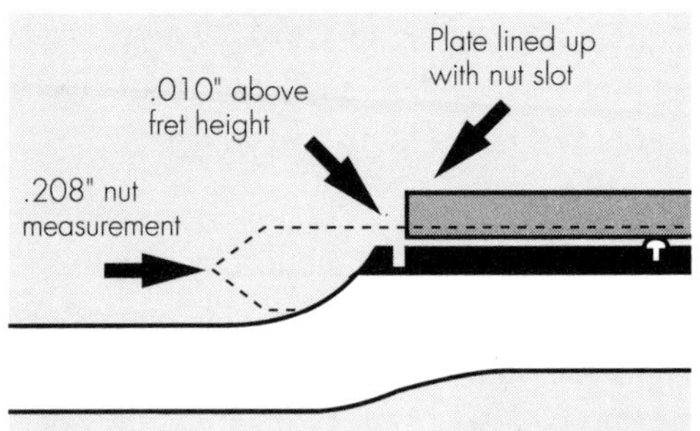

MAKING THE JIG

Clamp a flat, uniformly thick plate of wood, metal, Plexiglas, etc., to the first two frets, with its front wall flush to the original nut slot (above). Now, the bottom of the clamped plate is level with the fret tops, so if you use dial calipers to measure .010" short of the bottom, that's where you want the nut-slot bottoms to end up. Next, add the one nut measurement we took (mine is .208", yours could be different), and you'll have the distance from the top of the clamped plate to the nut bottom; this is the ledge to be routed.

The plate is more than a surface to measure from, however. With its front edge in line with the nut slot, it acts as a "fence" to guide the Dremel router base, keeping it from cutting into the end of the fingerboard. And routing the end of the fingerboard would change the overall string length—a disaster! The locking nut's front should be flush with the fingerboard end, with the nut bottom at a 90-degree angle to it.

Complete your installation jig by clamping a second platform of uniform thickness to the headstock face. This raises the Dremel Moto-Tool above the surface to be routed, allowing the cutter to be lowered into the wood by degree. You now have a usable facsimile of the jig I made, which is a single unit made of clear Plexiglas (the upper and lower plates are joined with threads and cap screws). The

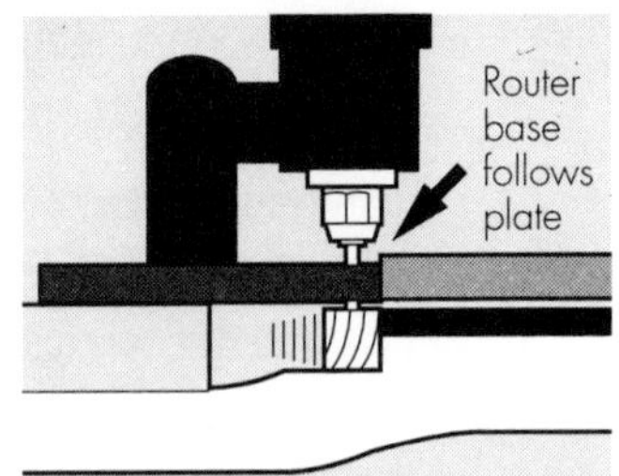

lower plate has a routing hole machined into it, and a built-in clamp holds it to the neck. There are two types of headstock: the straight, Fender style, and the angled, tilt-back Gibson type. With either, you remove the tuners in order to clamp on the platform (for the tilt-head, shim the table level with the fingerboard).

ROUTING

Use only a #115 Dremel router bit for the cutting. Rout no more than 1/16" per pass, and be sure that the bit cuts flush with the router's base edge. If the bit cuts more than flush, it could trim the fingerboard end. (If this happens, loosen the two mounting screws and wiggle the base into line, or put a couple strips of masking tape along the base edge to shim it away from the fingerboard.)

Measure often from the top plate as you rout, and when the ledge is cut, lightly glue the nut body (with string clamps removed) to the ledge. Spray Hot Stuff accelerator on the nut bottom and put two small drops of Hot Stuff Special T super glue on the newly routed ledge. Thirty seconds' drying time will set the nut firm. Then use it as a drill guide for a #30 drill bit. Drill down through the two mounting holes, right through the neck—the nut will hold the bit square. Now tap the nut loose using a block of wood and a hammer. Enlarge the #30 holes with an 11/64" bit, again drilling from the top side. Using a layer of wax paper in between, place a hunk of modeling clay under the rear of the neck/headstock area and press the neck into the clay to form it. The clay supports the wood as both the #30 and the 11/64" bits punch through with no splinters!

The countersunk holes are most safely drilled by using a step-bit. Stewart-MacDonald makes a step-bit with an 11/64" pilot to follow the 11/64" hole drilled earlier, and a 5/16" outer bore that drills a shallow flat-bottomed hole for the bolt heads. Extra care must be taken to avoid the bits' grabbing or tearing the wood by accident. From the rear, countersink the holes until three or four threads protrude through the ledge when the bolt is inserted. This is plenty to hold the nut tight—any more, and the bolt could come through the locking nut's top and touch the string clamps. Go ahead and mount the nut. If your nut ends up too low, it's common to shim it up to the right level. Good shim materials include 3M wet-or-dry sandpaper in the 400, 600, and 1200 grits, or mesh-like drywall sandpaper with a good grip (check your lumberyard).

Last of all, mount the retainer bar. Locate it 1" to 1 1/8" from the front of the nut, and centered from side to side as at right. Drill the two screw holes with a 9/64" bit marked with masking tape as a visual depth stop to prevent drilling through the headstock! Put your strings on, and check your work. You're done with the worst part. Now we'll troubleshoot any problems, cover set-up and fine tuning, and look at the recessed top-rout made popular by Steve Vai and the Ibanez Jem 777.

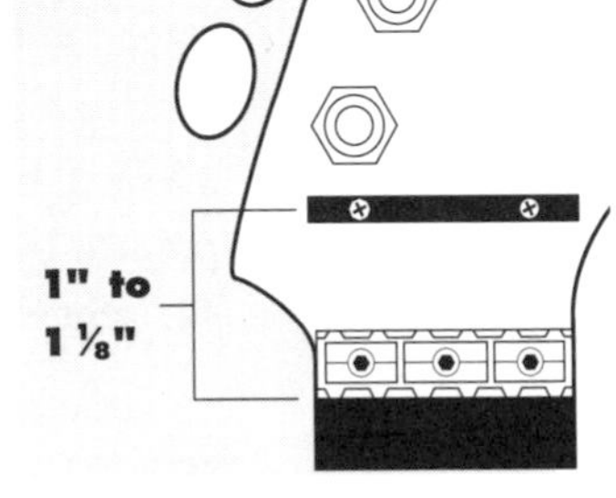

Setting up the Floyd Rose

Now you can relax, since the job of setting up your tremolo is easy if you learn these simple set-up basics: level the tremolo to the body by adjusting the springs and spring claw, set the string-to-fingerboard height by adjusting the two pivot studs, and adjust the intonation. *Guitar Player* magazine ran Mark Lacey's "Fine-Tune Your Floyd" in its Sept. '88 issue, and I suggest you read

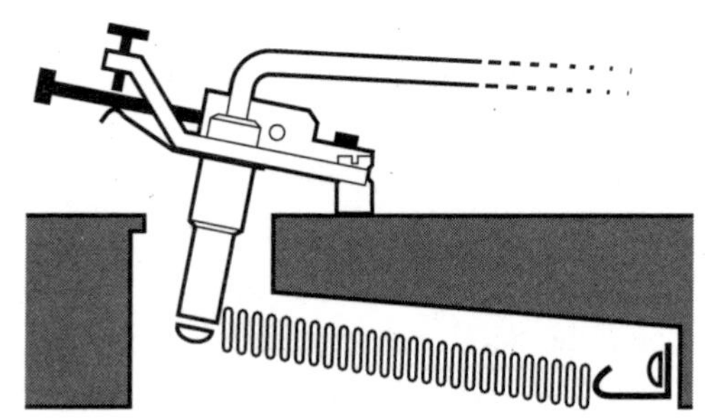

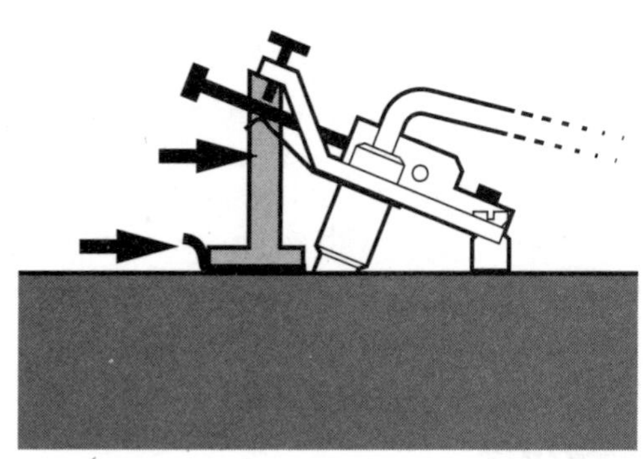

You may need extra clearance in the spring cavity (exaggerated here). Note the tapered back wall: The shallow end may be 5⁄8" to 3⁄4", while the deep end may be 11⁄16" to 13⁄16".

it; your library probably has a copy. Action and intonation are discussed in the earlier chapters of this book, so I won't bore you with repetition. I'll just skim through the simple stuff, making a few important points as we go. This will leave some space to take a look at the optional recess rout made popular by Steve Vai and the Ibanez Jem 777 series.

Leave the locking nut *unclamped* while you do the following work. First, level the tremolo parallel with the body by adding or removing springs in the rear spring cavity. Using a Phillips screwdriver, adjust the spring claw in or out until the unit is level. Most players use either two or three tremolo springs for string gauges beginning with .008 or .009, and usually three for .010 and up. Experiment until you get the right feel. Next, the string height from the fingerboard should be set before adjusting the intonation. Most players look for a low action that shows around 1⁄16" between the bottom of the strings and the top of the 12th fret. However, most players settle for a slightly stiffer action than this—say, 3⁄32". How low you can go depends on the adjustment of the neck and the condition of the frets.

Set the string height by simply raising or lowering the two pivot studs that the tremolo mounts on; this is much easier than with the individual saddle height adjustments common to Strats and many other guitars. Unless your tremolo uses machine-thread studs that adjust with an Allen wrench, use a flat-blade screwdriver with a sharp, well-ground tip that fits the stud slot snugly. This eliminates slippage that can not only mar the slot, but also cause the plating to lift away. As a general rule, most players adjust the tremolo so that the underside is from 1⁄8" to 1⁄4" off the face of the guitar; this provides plenty of forward dump and a fair amount of up-pull.

Keep in mind that a tremolo set close to a guitar's face has little clearance in the rear for up-pull on the bar. A tremolo that's set high off the top may require shimming the bolt-on neck to keep the strings close to the fingerboard (for advice on neck shimming, see the bolt-on neck section of Electric Adjustments). Also, a high-set tremolo may seem uncomfortable for players accustomed to resting their picking hand on or near the body (one solution, the recess rout, is explained later). And, depending on the cavity depth, a tremolo that's mounted high off the body may cause the springs to rub the bottom of the spring cavity. Ibanez and Kramer use a tapered cavity to solve this problem (above, left).

Floyd Rose saddles are made in three different thicknesses or heights. The tallest is used for the *D* and *G* strings, the medium for the *A* and *B*, and the shortest for the two outside *E* strings. This saddle-height combination creates a curve in the bridge saddles that matches the radius curve of most electric guitar fingerboards. Many players find that the "medium" saddle curve of the Floyd Rose plays comfortably with most necks. Custom-tailoring the saddle height is possible by

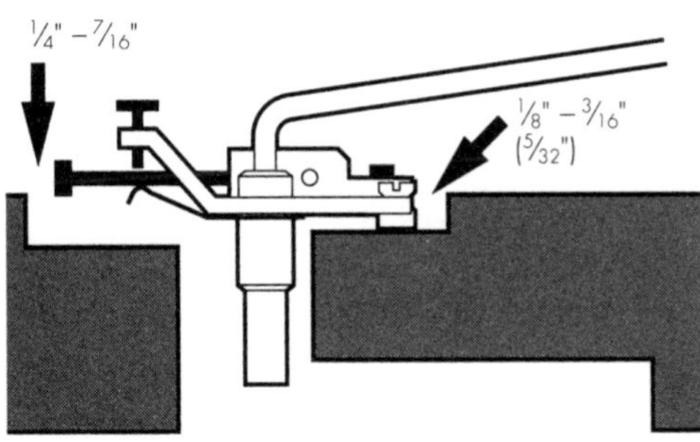

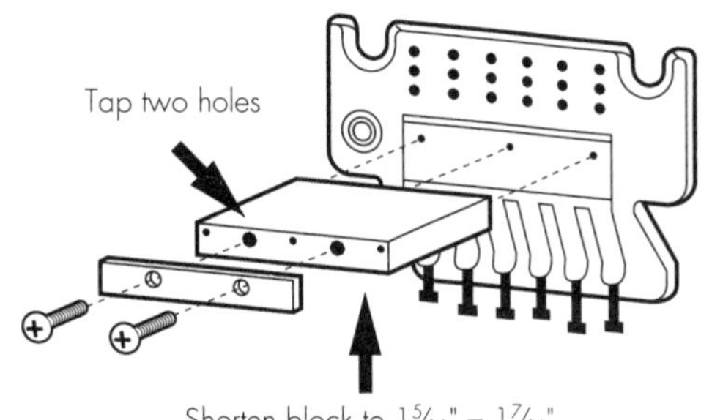

shimming the inserts with thin metal shim stock available from most automotive suppliers, or by carefully grinding the bottoms of the saddles to alter their height (this grinding is a tricky operation and should be left to a professional!). If you wish to experiment, replacement saddles are available directly from Kramer.

Setting the intonation of the Floyd Rose bridge saddles works on the same principle as any other adjustable bridge—if a string notes sharp, move the saddle back away from the nut; if the note is flat, move the saddle forward toward the nut. Since the string is clamped into the saddle itself rather than into a separate tailpiece, the saddles tend to slide forward from string pressure when you loosen the Allen bolt that holds them in place. This can be annoying if your intention is to move the saddle back, since you have to loosen (detune) the string in order to do so. Try "dumping" the bridge forward and inserting a bridge jack (facing page, right) to hold the tremolo up, keeping the strings slack while moving a saddle back or forth. I made my jack out of two scraps of hard maple and covered the bottom with felt as a protection for the finish. Of course, an electronic tuner is a help for setting the intonation. When your set up and intonation are correct, clamp the locking nut tight.

Here are a few tips on recess routs, which involve the removal of wood under the tremolo (below the surface of the guitar face). This allows the tremolo to sit fairly close to the top (1⁄16" is common) while still having clearance in the rear for up-pull. Also, many guitarists keep their palm, hand, or entire arm on or close to the top while picking, and the recess rout keeps the bridge closer to the body for this type of picking comfort. Recess-routing templates are available from some guitar shop suppliers. Most recesses are from ⅛" to 3⁄16" deep in the front portion of the rout, and deeper (¼" to 7⁄16") toward the rear for up-pulling (above, left). Since you can always rout deeper, start with the shallower measurements and follow the same ball-bearing routing techniques described earlier.

Recess routing may require shortening the tremolo block (above) to keep it from sticking out of the guitar's back. The amount you shorten it depends on how close to, or deep into, the top you want your tremolo. The Ibanez Edge block measures 1 5⁄16", while Kramer's shortened block for their guitars with factory-equipped recess routs measures 1 7⁄16". I shortened the block on my Floyd Rose-licensed Schaller to match the Ibanez Edge tremolo. Here's how to do it:

With a 1⁄16" drill bit, deepen the five spring holes by the amount you plan to remove (up to ⅜"). Using a hacksaw, remove up to ⅜" from the block's bottom, and then file it smooth to a length of 1 5⁄16" or 1 7⁄16", etc. Drill and tap the two spring holes on each side of the center-spring hole to accept a machine screw; I used a 10-32 truss-rod tap that I had handy. Finally, make a ⅛" x 2" x 5⁄16" flat spring retainer bar (⅛" screen-door aluminum stock purchased at the hardware store and hacksawed and filed to shape) with two clearance holes for mounting the bar to the tapped holes in the block. This will keep the springs from popping out when the tremolo's in use, especially on up-pulls where the springs go slack.

Well, that's about it for the Floyd Rose tremolo. For more information, read Mark Lacey's feature and check the Mar./Apr. '88 issue of *String Instrument Craftsman* for Chris Piles' article on Floyd Rose set-ups.

Kahler installation and set-up

I chose the Floyd Rose tremolo to teach measuring, layout, and routing basics, not only because it's popular, but because it's the hardest to install. If you can mount a Floyd, you're good with a router and can definitely handle any other installations. The most popular and readily available tremolos on the market are the Floyd Rose, the Schaller-licensed Rose, and the Kahler flat-mount. The last section covered installing the stud-mounted "floating" tremolos; now watch how you can apply those same skills to installing another excellent and popular tremolo, the Kahler Standard flat-mount.

Several features set the Kahler apart from stud-mount "floating" tremolos. It requires a much smaller body rout (removing less wood, and therefore less mass), and the rout doesn't need to go clear through the body, since it doesn't use a rear-rout for tremolo springs. Instead, the Kahler achieves its smooth operation by way of two small factory-installed springs, ball bearings, and a cam. Not having to rout clear through the body makes for an easy, good-looking installation on bodies that have never had a tremolo before such as Gibsons, hand-made guitars, Teles, etc. Here's how the Kahler's installed, but first a word of advice before you turn on that router.

My friend and one-time apprentice Charlie Longstreth helped me compile this Kahler information, and he emphasizes a good point: "The first question that should occur to anyone about to install the Kahler or any other tremolo is: Should the installation be done at all? It'd be tragic to modify a pre-CBS Strat, and many Kahlers are mounted on Strats. If you're lucky enough to own one of those rare birds, pick up a newer Strat and put a Kahler on *it*—and even then, remember that Strats that are new now will be old *someday.* Maybe you should build a guitar from kit parts." Okay, let's begin.

While Kahler makes a version of its famous flat-mount tremolo that can be installed on the tailpiece studs of a Gibson ES-335 or Les Paul, we'll use the Strat-style guitar for this installation. First, be sure that your neck is lined up to the body the way you want it, especially with reference to the bridge and pickups. Read the section on bolt-on necks carefully, and then remove any parts that could get in the way of your router, such as the pickguard, pickups, bridge, and the volume and tone controls. Next lay a strip of masking tape over the six factory bridge mount holes, and lay out the center line of the body using the same method described for the Floyd Rose. Another means of finding center is to use a straightedge long enough to lay along both sides of the fingerboard and extend out onto the body as far down as your masking tape (see drawing at right). Mark the straightedge line on the tape and find the center between the two marks.

With each tremolo, Kahler supplies a heavy cardboard template to use as a guide for laying out the area to be routed. To ensure correct lengthwise placement and good intonation, this template is located on a line measured out from the nut and marked at right angles to the body center line. Note: This cardboard is not a routing template; it's only for scribing the routing line on the inner edge of the template. I prefer using a Plexiglas template; this way, the cardboard piece can be omitted, since the Plexiglas template has the same inner shape and mounts on the same lengthwise line.

On a Strat, the two holes at the Plexiglas routing template's front edge mount to the outer two original bridge mount holes. To double check your work, scratch a center line on the routing template as we did with the Floyd Rose job (measure between the two holes), and compare it to the center line on your guitar. If they don't match, you have two choices: 1) plug the holes, line the template on the *body* center line, and redrill the holes; 2) go with the two factory holes and ignore the center line you laid out. The safest way to guarantee an accurate placement is to ignore any pre-drilled holes and measure yourself. Here's some help:

To correctly place the Kahler in regard to the string length, measure from the nut's front (where it meets the fingerboard) down to the masking tape on the body, drawing a line at right angles to the center line. This new line is for lining up the two mounting holes of the template; later these holes will be used to mount the actual tremolo, since they're the same holes. If the original Strat tremolo mounting holes don't line up with this line, plug the outer two and redrill them.

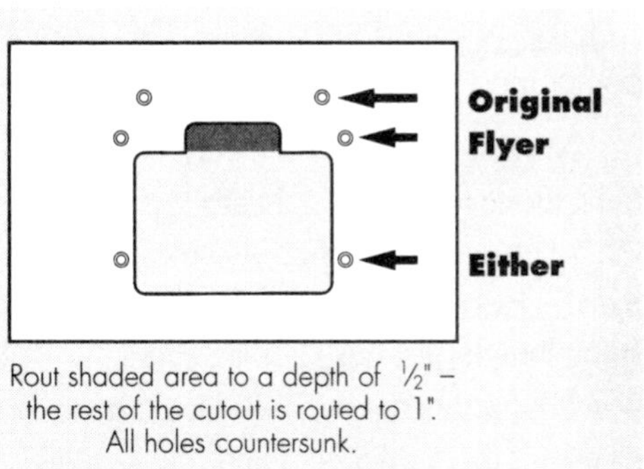

Rout shaded area to a depth of ½" – the rest of the cutout is routed to 1". All holes countersunk.

For a long Strat scale (25½"), measure 25¼" from the nut. For a short (24¾") Gibson scale, measure 24$\frac{7}{16}$". Once you've located this line, attach the routing template to the guitar body using double-stick tape, or screw the template to the guitar's face with wood screws. The Stew-Mac template that I use (below, left) has countersunk mounting holes and can be used for either the Kahler Flyer or the Standard flat-mount. The front two holes are for the Original, and the rear/front holes are for the Flyer; the back holes are the same for either tremolo. Mount the template with wood screws that are smaller than the final mounting screws, and make sure their heads are recessed and won't interfere with the router. After the template is mounted, scribe around the finish along the inside edge with a sharp scribe or X-acto knife. You'll be routing right up to this line, so scoring the finish first helps prevent chips when you remove the template.

Now I can take a break, and you can work. The routing's easy; just follow the directions given a few pages back for the Floyd Rose. The overall depth of the Kahler rout is 1", although many of us prefer to rout only ½" deep on the front part (the shaded area at left, which gives clearance for the two springs) to avoid taking away unnecessary wood, mass, and tone. When you've routed the cavity and vacuumed up the chips, lay a couple coats of clear lacquer on the bare wood to seal out moisture; you can even do this with a rag or a brush. If you want to get fancy, you can tape off the area and spray the new cavity with a matching paint. Sometimes I use black Magic Marker to darken the rout before the clear lacquer. That way, any part of the bare-wood cavity that you *could* see from the outside can no longer be seen. If your guitar requires a ground wire mounted to the bridge, run that wire now (on new work, you may have to drill a long hole from the tremolo rout to the control cavity, using a long ⅛" "aircraft" bit). You can get an adequate ground simply by screwing the tremolo base plate down onto a ground wire bent up the side of the cavity and wrapped over the edge. Keep this wire away from the workings of the tremolo! Go ahead and install the tremolo now, just to see how everything lines up, and then go on to the locking nut. But don't start playing with that wang bar yet!

Kahler offers three nut styles, not to mention one for their 7-string tremolo (not pictured). Two of them, the original Standard and the Deluxe no-wrench, flip-lever nut, are behind-the-nut locks that work together with a *real* nut. The third is called a Nut-Lock and is similar to the Floyd Rose, which requires that a ledge be routed for installation. Since we've already covered the Floyd style, let's briefly discuss installing the behind-the-nut style; it's easy.

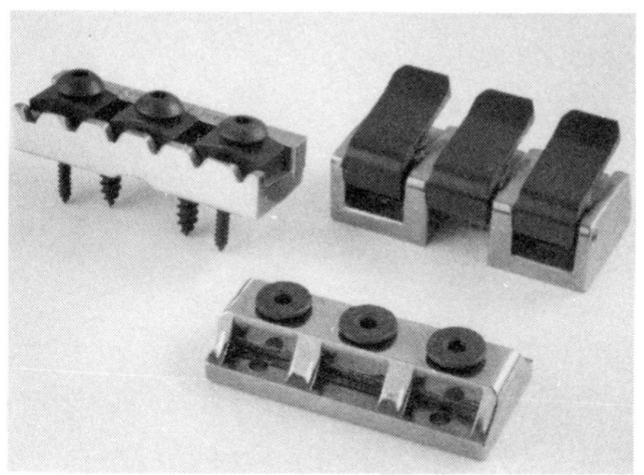

With a Strat, the only real work involved is in making a shim to support the nut at the proper height for getting good string angle through the nut slots. As with any nut, too steep an angle causes string binding or breaking in the slots, while too shallow an angle allows the strings to flop around, causing buzzes. Kahler recommends a string angle of eleven degrees (11°) between the string lock and the real nut; check this angle with a protractor.

Make the shim from a hardwood such as maple, rosewood, or ebony. Trace around the nut for the outside shape, mark the holes, and then drill them *before* shaping the shim; this eliminates splitting the delicate shim once it's shaped. Kahler offers pre-shaped and drilled Polystyrene shims that come in two shapes: a flat shim .068" thick (part # 8450), and a curved-bottom one (#8460) that measures .068" at the thickest part of its center, but tapers quite thin at the edges of the bottom curve. In certain situations you may wish to stack different combinations of these shims together. The string-lock should be as close to the real nut as possible, while still keeping the right amount of angle to hold the strings in their slots (about 1/4" to 3/8" from the rear of the nut). Too much distance between the lock and the real nut tends to store more slack than necessary. To keep from going clear through the headstock, use masking tape wrapped around your bit as a depth guide while drilling the four mounting holes (this is illustrated in the section in over-oiled tuners in Miscellaneous Repairs).

If you pick with a strong attack and are looking for big sustain, you might be interested in recessing your Kahler into the body. John Suhr of Rudy's Music in New York City inlays, or recesses, a Kahler flat-mount 5/32" deep into the body. This allows you to raise the roller bridge saddles to their highest point in order to get a strong string angle over the roller (saddle) without having overly high action. As a general rule, Kahler recommends setting the bridge saddle roller height so that a minimum of .475" and a maximum .625" shows from the bottom of the outer two *E* strings to the guitar body. With the *recess* method you get the maximum height (and more if you want), but still retain a normal string-to-body relationship, avoiding the necessity of shimming the neck in the body to keep up with the high rollers. Raising the saddle rollers really high creates better response and tonal quality, but the trade-off is more variance in tuning because you introduce more friction to the rollers with the increased string angle. This doesn't bother most players, though, so try it!

Note: If you recess the tremolo 5/32", you must move the bridge forward 3/32", since as the rollers are raised they also move *backward*—away from the nut—increasing the string length (just raise a roller saddle up and watch how much it moves). An alternate to recessing the Kahler is to raise the saddles high and then shim the neck to meet the strings; of course, the pickups have to be raised, too, and sometimes you just can't get them high enough. I should point out that Kahler doesn't recommend setting the saddles this high. There's nothing wrong with trying all these different setups and deciding for yourself; that's the whole idea of this book!

Kahler includes *Adjustment And Setup* with each tremolo; this pamphlet does a good job of teaching you how the tremolo works. They've also published a *Trouble Shooting Guide* and *Service Tips And Adjustments.* Even if you're not experiencing any trouble, ask your dealer to get you copies of these pamphlets, because they'll come in handy some day. For additional reading on Kahler tremolos, check John Carruthers' columns in the Feb. and Mar. '84 issues of *Guitar Player* and read Chris Piles' set-up tips in the May/June '88 issue of *String Instrument Craftsman.*

Tightening a loose Strat tremolo arm

Here's an interesting idea from Roger L. Scruggs of Lynchburg, Virginia: "In regard to Strat tremolo arms going limp, I have a remedy that works well on my '63 Strat. I removed the center spring from a small die punch cutter and ground a ¼"-long piece off from one end. This spring is about 5/32" in diameter and very stiff. I then dropped the spring into the tremolo arm hole and screwed down the arm until it hit the spring (above, right). By tightening the arm slowly until it met with resistance from the spring, there was enough up-pressure on the bottom of the arm to keep it from rotating. Being extremely stiff, this spring keeps the tremolo arm from being either too tight or too loose. I bought my punch/spring from Holiday Steel Rule And Die in Greensboro, North Carolina, but you should be able to find one at any die-maker's shop."

Roger's idea works great. Readers should note that this will only work on old-style Strat tremolos (made before 1970) that have a bottom to the hole; otherwise the spring would simply fall out. Readers can avoid having to buy a die-punch cutter by finding a hardware or industrial supply store with a good selection of springs; any stiff spring works. And remember, always wear safety glasses when using a grinder, and be sure that the wheel isn't cracked. Read the strict grinder safety precautions in the section on making your own fret files.

A Strat tremolo modification

Richard H. Ruth of Oklahoma City, Oklahoma, wrote to me: "I converted my tremolo from a face-mount to a semi-floating, knife-edge type. To do this, I bought some brass at a local hobby shop, bent it into shape, removed the tremolo, and mounted the new brass plate to the mounting holes on the body. Since the brass was bent to more than a 90-degree angle, it held the 'knife edge' of the tremolo when I replaced it. The only non-reversible alteration to my guitar came when I filed the underside of the bridge's leading edge to a sharper contact point. This modification changes the tremolo's pivot point from the

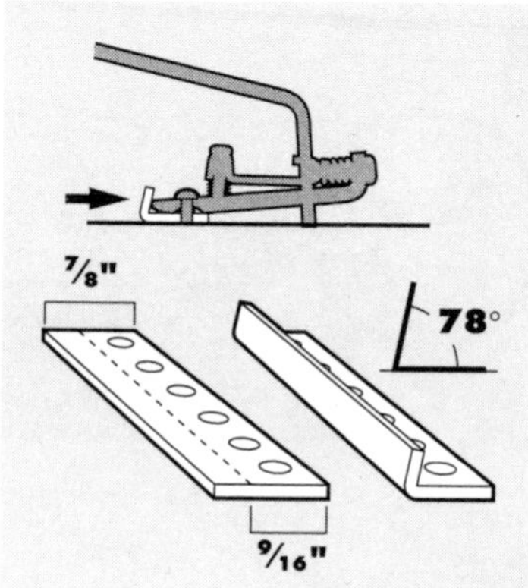

mounting screws to the front edge of the unit. The guitar returns to pitch almost as well as an expensive locking tremolo, and the tone is much improved. The only tools I used were a vise, a hammer, a 3/8" electric drill for drilling and countersinking the mounting holes, a hacksaw for cutting the brass to length, and a file. I replaced the original mounting screws with a countersunk variety having the same thread as the originals. The brass plate is 1/16" thick and around 7/8" to 1" wide, and I only needed to cut it to length. For a dollar I got enough brass to make two—and that was a good idea, since I messed up the first one (some experimentation was required to arrive at the proper bending angle so as to retain, but not restrain, tremolo movement)."

I asked Richard if I could borrow the guitar to try it out, and he sent it to me the next day. It works smoothly, and seems to return in tune well. Another nice thing about the conversion is that he enjoyed doing it. Many players love to customize their guitars and are looking for new jobs to do. Richard's idea is fairly easy to perform (above), and it doesn't really alter the guitar much. If you're squeamish about filing on your stock bridge, buy a replacement bridge/tremolo and use that instead—saving the original in its stock form—especially if you have a rare, vintage guitar. A "floating" tremolo is one that doesn't come in contact with the body of the guitar when it returns to pitch, since it's raised up from the surface. This enables the player to pull up as well as push down on the tremolo arm. In some cases, the neck may have to be shimmed in its pocket to accommodate the shimmed-up tremolo unit. Thanks for the tip!

The Trem-Setter

To conclude this chapter on tremolos, it's appropriate to say a few words about the Trem-Setter, a device that helps keep a tremolo guitar in tune in many ways. Designed by David Borisoff of the Hipshot Company, this tremolo stabilizer was first introduced in 1988. Since then thousands have been installed—not only by repair shops on a custom basis, but also at the Fender factory on their Strat Plus, Strat Plus Deluxe, and Ultra Strat guitars. Some players misunderstand the Trem-Setter's use and expect too much from it. So let's look first at what it will and won't do for a wang bar, and then I'll present some tips to make the installation even easier than it already is.

The Trem-Setter is an adjustable, spring-loaded device that replaces the center tremolo spring on locking or standard tremolos. It installs in the rear spring cavity, replacing the standard five-spring tremolo claw with two individual outer spring claws. This leaves the center spring area open for the Trem-Setter, which mounts on a hook (or "hinge-clip," as it's called) screwed to the cavity bottom. A brass pull-rod connects the Setter to the sustain block, so it moves with the block as the player works the tremolo and helps return the tremolo to the same spot after use. It also keeps even tension on the tremolo so that bending or tuning a string doesn't cause the other strings to drastically alter their pitch. The installation and adjustment instructions supplied by Hipshot and Fender are accurate, but a little too technical; they don't say enough about *what* the Trem-Setter does, or how it's done. So I talked with David Borisoff and Fender's George Blanda, both of whom had a lot to say.

"The main reason I designed the Trem-Setter," says Borisoff, "was to get away from the equilibrium, or balance, of the strings and springs controlling whether a guitar's in tune or not. The standard tremolo is like a bathroom scale—you can get on the scale twice and get two different readings. Or if you stand on the scale and shake, like shaking or bending a string, you'll make the dial flutter on both sides of your actual weight. This is what happens to a tremolo bridge when you bend notes, play certain notes with a strong attack, or even hit certain open strings: You upset the balance, and the tremolo flutters back and forth. The Trem-Setter's like a shock absorber in a car; it stabilizes the tremolo."

According to David, the unit accomplishes the following:

1 Improves the guitar's tone by controlling flutter. It stops the tremolo from absorbing or wasting the string's energy as it passes on to the body.

2 Helps the tremolo return to its "0" point in tune. This is not true, however, if the guitar has a poorly made nut, inadequate tuners, or improperly mounted strings. Locking tuners and the Wilkinson roller nut work well with the Trem-Setter, of course.

3 Keeps the remaining strings in tune when you bend a string. String-bending adds tension and causes the tremolo to "sag," or lean forward, which lowers the pitch of all the other strings. The Trem-Setter keeps sagging to a minimum.

4 Makes string-bending easier. Since the bridge isn't sagging toward the fingering hand, lowering the pitch, you don't have to bend nearly so far to get a note. Players who don't like tremolo guitars may find a change of heart if they try one with a Trem-Setter.

5 Keeps the strings in better tune if you rest your hand on the bridge or intentionally mute the strings. It's not a *big* factor, but the Trem-Setter can be set up with this in mind.

6 Helps make up for worn knife edges at the pivot point.

Let me point out the one thing it *won't* do: It won't keep a guitar in tune if you break a string. It was never intended to. The amount of tension needed to compensate for a broken string would detract from the Trem-Setter's sensitivity.

I asked Blanda if all tremolos have bridge flutter: "At Fender we call it 'warbling' when you get the bridge flutter that David's talking about. Any well-balanced tremolo guitar warbles a little, but that's the trade-off for having a sensitive tremolo that's free from friction and returns to pitch. The tremolo moves to accommodate the different tensions it receives from the oscillation of the strings. This movement is less pronounced with a vintage Strat tremolo, since the bridge plate has a solid rest on the body; it's not delicately balanced on two knife edges like the American Standard. If you *want* to make a two-point tremolo warble, just to know what we're talking about, pick the *G* string hard at the 14th fret, or pluck it with your bare fingers, and listen—you'll hear it if it's there. At Fender it's easy for us to take two brand-new identical Strats, one with and one without a Trem-Setter, and compare their sound. You can really hear the difference. The guitar with the Trem-Setter has a better, more solid tone, and any warble is stopped." I've heard that Leo Fender called the tremolo's sustain block an "inertia block" in the original patent drawing, showing that he knew that something was needed to smooth out the string-to-bridge vibration and put the energy to good use.

How much does the Trem-Setter change the feel of a tremolo as it's being dumped or pulled up? Blanda responds: "Not too much, and not at all when you pull up, because the pull rod moves *through* the spring on an up-pull, without affecting the tension at all. The tension of the Trem-Setter's spring is comparable to that of a normal tremolo spring. But rather than the spring *stretching* when you dump the tremolo, it *compresses.* A factory set-up for a Strat Plus uses three springs and

You can't talk about tremolos in the 1990s without talking about the Trem-Setter, because it works!

The knife edges on a new tremolo are sharp, and returning to "0" is not a problem. As wear causes the edges to round off, it may no longer provide the frictionless movement needed to return to absolute "0." The Trem-Setter overcomes that friction.

Playing a guitar outfitted with a Trem-Setter feels like playing a non-tremolo guitar.

usually .009"–.042" or .010"–.046" strings. A player who wants to use only two springs and .008" strings couldn't benefit from the Trem-Setter, since it's a three-spring system. Besides, we don't recommend using two springs on a tremolo in the first place. I should point out that all springs are not the same tension; springs used on locking tremolo systems are typically stiffer by as much as 15%. In a repair shop, extra springs end up laying all over the place, and if the wrong springs end up being used along with the Trem-Setter, the tension won't be right when you dive-bomb."

Sometimes I feel, or almost hear, a little drag when I press the wang bar on a Strat Plus. "This is not normal," Borisoff explains, "but it can happen. Over time we discovered that if too much grease was used on the brass pull rod, it actually vacuumed around the small stop-collar washer as it moved, creating a suction effect. Dismantle the Setter, clean off any grease, and when you re-assemble it, leave the washer dry or lightly lubricate it with WD-40. Be careful not to lose the washer when you take the device apart—the parts want to pop all over the place. We may switch to a *fiber* washer that not only won't vacuum onto the rod, but will also compress less, eliminating any possibility of slop. If you do take the unit apart, once the small slack spring that pushes against the stop collar is removed, you can see how the brass collar bears against the end of the threaded brass tube that the pull rod slides through." How much can the nylon thread nuts be tightened or loosened when the tremolo's tension is being adjusted? "You *can* tighten it a lot," says Blanda, "but you won't want it too tight. You'd never want to see more than 5⁄16" of exposed thread on the brass tube—experiment. As for loosening it, by temporarily removing the lock collar spring as we mentioned, you'll see that loosening the nylon thumb-nut counter-clockwise *too* much causes it to hit the brass stop collar—you don't want that! The whole trick in setting up the Trem-Setter is to get the brass stop collar to make perfect contact with the washer at the end of the threaded brass tube when the tremolo is sitting at its balance point. Then any lowering of the tremolo arm puts the Trem-Setter into operation instantly. You can loosen the thumb-nut tension as far as you like as long as it doesn't touch the collar. Hold one nylon thumb-nut while you tighten or loosen the other; otherwise they'll just rotate together, and nothing happens."

I asked Borisoff if he thinks there's a tone improvement when a Trem-Setter is installed: "I don't *think* there's an improvement, I know it. When the string's energy hits the bridge, you want it to transfer instantly to the body so that the sound comes from the bridge and body together. When a tremolo flutters at the balance point, the tremolo block and springs cancel out and absorb much of the string energy that you're working hard to get to your amp. The player puts a lot in, but not enough comes out. It's like running in sand, where half the energy just pushes sand behind you, with only half left to push you forward. Get on solid ground, and you can take off with a one-to-one transmission of energy with no waste." Blanda adds, "There's a better coupling between the tremolo block and the body, which produces a difference you can really hear."

One of the big questions, of course, is how well does the Trem-Setter work with a standard Strat tremolo? "Quite well if the guitar is set up right," insists Borisoff. "A vintage Strat has friction at the six mounting screws of the bridge plate, as well as at the nut slots, non-locking tuners, and string trees. Comparatively speaking, a Strat Plus looks pretty good with its roller nut, two-point pivot, and lack of string trees and locking tuners. So set-up is crucial on a vintage Strat. All friction points must be smoothed and lubricated so the strings can't hang up and store any slack."

INSTALLATION TIPS

Installation instructions come with the Trem-Setter, so rather than going through the whole operation, I'll just add my notes to what you already have. The installation only takes about a half-hour, and the tools needed are an electric hand drill, a small ruler, Phillips screwdrivers, and such. Adjust the stock tremolo to suit your tastes *before* you begin the installation, and take the time to set your guitar up right.

Since the original five-hook spring claw is removed and replaced with two individual outer spring claws, you'll be setting the tremolo equilibrium or balance point with *two* springs instead of three; the Trem-Setter has no effect, or spring tension, on the tremolo until you depress or lower the strings. This enables you to tighten the spring claws closer to the end of the cavity than you would with three springs.

The hinge-clip has two mounting holes; the front hole (closest to the tremolo block) is located $3\frac{3}{8}$" out from the sustain block. The hinge-clip mounts at right angles to the block and in line with the center spring hole. Use a center-punch to mark the hole and help the drill bit stay on center. Use a #50 drill bit for soft wood and up to a #80 bit for hardwood (the bits vary depending on the type of wood—practice drilling on scrap to be sure it works for you). *Drill only the front hole at this time.* Then temporarily mount the hinge-clip with *one* screw, and not too tightly. Now put the Trem-Setter onto the hinge-clip and snap the brass pull into the center spring hole of the tremolo block. Since the hinge-clip is slightly loose, it will line itself up naturally with the tremolo block. When it does, mark it, remove the Trem-Setter, and drill and mount the other hinge-clip screw.

The instructions call for drilling a $\frac{3}{16}$" clearance hole in the end wall of the tremolo cavity, but they *don't* tell you that you really should use a long aircraft drill bit. You can order such a bit through a hardware store, or have the hole drilled at your local repair shop. The long bit allows you to get the low angle necessary to allow proper clearance for the Trem-Setter's pull rod. The bit I use is 12"–14" long. I use a smaller $\frac{1}{8}$" bit as a pilot, and then enlarge that hole with the $\frac{3}{16}$", so there's less chance for the larger bit to run off course.

"I started out to make a completely 'stabilized' tremolo, but after finishing one prototype, I realized that I could get the same effect with the Trem-Setter and keep the cost down. Besides, most players would prefer not to replace their stock tremolo."
Dave Borisoff

I was thrown a couple of curves on two recent installations. The pull-rod hook and thumb-nut nearest to it scraped the back cover plate when the tremolo was dumped. The instructions advised rebending the pull-rod hook if this happens, so that its angle matches the angle of the hole in the tremolo block (it won't seat right if the angles don't match). I stuck a #50 (.070") drill bit into an empty hole so I could *see* the true angle of the tremolo block spring holes, and then bent the pull rod's brass hook to match. In one case this was the solution, but in another it wasn't—I found a different problem.

I was working with a replacement neck and body, an original Wilkinson roller nut (not the Strat Plus style), and a real American Standard tremolo that I got in a parts swap. By laying a straightedge across the back while working the tremolo, I could see just where it was rubbing, and that bending the hook wouldn't quite solve my problem. In this case the spring cavity was deeper than that of a real Strat ($\frac{11}{16}$" to $\frac{3}{4}$" as opposed to $\frac{5}{8}$"), causing the Trem-Setter's pull rod to rise at an angle where it hooked into the block. I used my Dremel tool with an abrasive mesh wheel to grind a groove across the bottom of the block (right), so the hook would sit deeper and at less of an angle. I *might* have been able to shim the hinge clip up $\frac{1}{16}$" to $\frac{1}{8}$" higher to get the same

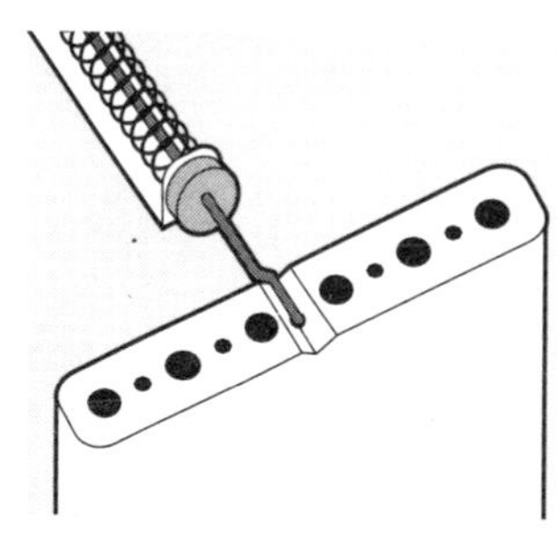

effect, but I took this route. You probably won't run into this problem, but if you do, you're ready.

One trick Dave Borisoff uses when the brass hook needs to be re-bent is to hammer on the hook with a center punch or nail set while it's in the trem-block; the block acts as an anvil, which shapes the hook to the right fit. I haven't tried this, but metal-working experience tells me it would work. The pull rod is made from a fairly soft brass, so don't hammer too hard—tap it!

In summary, I like the Trem-Setter. Here's what I think it can and can't do:

1 For me, its biggest feature is the way it eases bending strings and the fact that the other strings stay in tune when I get there.

2 It does a *good* job of helping a tremolo return to "0." It's perhaps 98% successful, so it isn't *perfect*: You should know that before you start. The slight 2% out-of-tune effect that may remain after dumping the tremolo can be straightened out by shaking the tremolo bar or hitting the bridge with the palm of your hand to settle it back into place.

3 As for the improvement in tone resulting from a better string/bridge/body coupling, if you can make an already great-sounding Strat Plus sound even better, I'm all for that.

4 String flutter or warble is something most players aren't bothered by, but for those who are we've now a way to eliminate it besides "blocking" the tremolo (many players shove a hardwood block between the sustain block and the body to improve tone, eliminate flutter, and stop the guitar from going out of tune).

5 The improved stability doesn't do *much* to keep the bridge from moving if you rest your hand on the bridge while you pick or mute the strings. It might do a little to help, but when you press down on the back of the bridge, you're pushing in the direction that the Trem-Setter's spring has no control over (this is the only claim of the manufacturer that I disagreed with). But David Borisoff explains that if you slightly loosen the two tremolo springs and then tighten the Trem-Setter's buck spring a little, your bridge should have more stability in the string-raise mode, letting you rest your hand on the bridge more.

PART 2 ACOUSTIC/ELECTRIC GUITAR REPAIR

The last 25 years of guitar repair

Twenty-five years ago, none of us imagined the changes and refinements that the guitar would go through, not to mention the scores of accessories and after-market modifications that are available today. With few exceptions, guitars are being built better than ever, and manufacturers are taking advantage of high technology without losing touch with craftsmanship. Many changes have occurred in the repair business, too, since 1965, with successful repairmen keeping up with the trends and improving their skills along the way. Now more good repairmen are available than ever before, thanks to repair schools, apprenticeships, and new books and video instruction. *Guitar Player*'s repair columns should take special credit for turning players into knowledgeable, finicky customers, and thereby causing all of us repairmen to keep on our toes and do our best work. Here are some observations on the repair business in general, along with a few good suggestions for those of you interested in this type of training.

Of course, great luthiers have been around for hundreds of years, but in 1965 they were much harder to find. Many of the repair shops grew out of the folk boom of the late '50s and early '60s. Some of the well-known ones included New York City's Folklore Center, the Herb David Guitar Studio in Ann Arbor, Michigan, and the shops of Randy Wood in Nashville, Don Teeter in Oklahoma City, and John Lundberg in Berkeley, California. I got my start at Herb David's in 1961. And unless you were within driving distance of such places, you were in trouble when the bridge popped off your Martin D-28. Nowadays most states have at least several skilled repairmen, many of whom are listed in the Yellow Pages. Most modern music stores offer in-house set-ups and minor repairs, and personnel can direct you to a qualified repairman for serious problems. It wasn't so easy 25 years ago.

I've known many good luthiers over the years who have called it quits and "gone back to school" in order to provide for a family; they would find a better living to be made in 1990. Guitar players and luthiers in general get a lot more respect these days. Because there are more players and more guitars being made than ever before, more instruments get broken or need professional set-up. The sheer number of customers out there makes guitar repair a viable way to make a living (not just a labor of love).

My friend and teacher, Herb David, surrounded by my brother-in-law John O'Boyle (repairman for Tampa's Thoroughbred Music), Shop boy David Surovell, and yours truly. Photo circa 1974. Over the years, many excellent repairmen have come from Herb's shop.

Guitar styles have advanced so much in the last few years that players must have far better set-up instruments than in the old days, when you used to hear excuses like, "My strings are too high," or "It won't play in tune" every time someone missed a lick. Today's styles call for a comfortable action, well-dressed frets that eliminate buzz, and proper intonation. This type of set-up work is usually performed by qualified repairmen after the sale. It depends on personal choice and can take several hours to do properly. I know repairmen in larger cities who do nothing but set up guitars and never get into serious woodworking on broken instruments. A good set-up man is usually a good player who gets lots of work by word of mouth. Never be surprised if it takes more than one trip to even the best of repairmen to get the feel you're after; in the old days, players would get rid of guitar after guitar simply for lack of a proper set-up specialist.

Thanks to new techniques in woodworking, new glues and tools, and the knowledge gained from experience, repairmen have improved each year. The newcomer to our trade finds many roads already paved and is therefore able to reach a higher degree of skill faster, especially after studying such great repair books as Don Teeter's two-part *The Acoustic Guitar*, Hideo Kamimoto's *Complete Guitar Repair*, Irving Sloan's *Guitar Repair*, and a host of building and construction books available at most luthier supply stores or local bookstores. If you are interested in repairing guitars, start acquiring a library on the subject. You can usually find all the *Guitar Player* back issues with repair columns by Rick Turner and John Carruthers on microfilm at a fair-sized library. Another good, simple book is Pieter Fillet's *Do-It-Yourself Guitar Repair*, which is inexpensive and geared for the average player. If you're a video-instruction nut, Harvey Citron and I have both made videos on the subject. Video courses are a good substitute for looking over a craftsman's shoulder, but in the old days I'd have given my eyeteeth for Don Teeter's books.

Personal instruction in building and repairing guitars and related instruments is available if you've the time and money to leave home for a month or two. Some repairmen augment their income or take a needed break from shop routine by taking on students for training. Although recently retired from the teaching business, I have taken on at least a dozen students in the last two years and know that in-shop training can be a great experience for teacher as well as for student. Several schools of lutherie of which I am aware are the Apprentice Shop (Box 267, Spring Hill, TN 37174), Roberto-Venn School of Luthiery (4011 S. 16th St., Phoenix, AZ 85040), Red Wing Area Vocational Technical Institute (Pioneer Rd. at Hwy. 58, Red Wing, MN 55066), the Renton Vocational Technical Institute (3000 N.E. 4th St., Renton, WA 98056), and last but not least

Bryan Galloup's Guitar Hospital (10495 Northland Dr., Big Rapids, MI 49307—Bryan took over my shop and school when I moved to Stewart-MacDonald). I have met graduates of all these programs and have been impressed by their work. Write for these schools' brochures.

A last major change is the incredible availability of specialized tools and supplies for the trade. In fact, many would be of interest to the average player who just dabbles in a little set-up here and there. If you're a woodworker interested in building and fixing guitars, send for all the supply catalogs listed at the end of this book. All in all, the guitar repair business is doing better than ever. And best of all, we're hearing fewer horror stories ("I took my guitar in for a fret job and got it back needing a new neck"), thanks to the larger number of skilled repairmen willing to respect their customers' interests. If you're not into the fix-it business, support your local repairman—he needs it.

Dents, dings, and scratches

Major guitar repairs such as broken necks, large cracks, splits, holes, punctures, and severe finish damage are best left to a trained repairman. Then there are the annoying little dents, dings, and scratches that are often easily fixed. About half of my customers care little about minor finish damage and are concerned only with their instruments' playability. The other half are upset by every little nick or scratch, especially if the guitar is new. Because many repairmen feel ill at ease when working in front of an audience, the customer never sees how simple many touch-up repairs are—repairs they could have done themselves. Here's a behind-the-scenes look at some simple touch-ups and finish repairs.

There are many types of finishes, past and present. In a nutshell, older guitars (up to 1930) were finished in varnish or shellac and are not so easy to clean or work on. Many of the finest handmade classical guitars have been "French polished" with a form of shellac, creating a beautiful finish that is hard to apply and needs special maintenance care. Since the advent of modern spraying techniques, lacquer has been used by many makers, the most notable being Martin, Gibson, Fender (until the late '60s), Gretsch, and Guild. Lacquer is the easiest to work on because it can be dissolved by solvents (thinners), dries quickly, and rubs out well. Most modern guitars, especially electrics, are finished in "poly"—polyurethanes, polyesters, epoxies, etc. These finishes don't "melt in" like lacquers and are hard to rub out, but you can do a lot with them.

Now to the problems. The most common and easiest-to-repair chip areas are on the edges of the instrument. Chips on the headstock, body binding, fingerboard edges, and the back of the neck are easy to touch up, because they don't show sanding and rubbing in the way that a larger, flat surface such as a guitar's face or back does. In general, avoid working on an instrument's main surface until you have much practice; sanding or rubbing in these areas usually shows, and the repair can be visibly different from the original finish. The professional usually manages to hide a repair by rubbing out the whole finish, often with expensive equipment such as hand-held power buffers or floor-mounted buffing jacks. Let's stick to the simple repairs.

First, you need some supplies. Any one of the following materials will effectively fill in a dent that has been made in a clear top coat (most colored guitars are usually top-coated with a clear finish of some sort, so you'll usually work with clear only; dealing with solid colors is explained later). If you wish to be well-armed for the job, try to get everything listed here, since each product has its own way of correcting a problem. First, go to a hobby store for some Hot Stuff super glue, which is available in three types: the water-thin Original Formula; Super T, a thicker gap-filler; and the very thick Special T. Also buy a spray bottle of accelerator for instant curing. Since most lacquers are bottled in quarts or gallons and you only need a small amount, ask your repairman or local furniture doctor to sell you small bottles of clear, unthinned lacquer and thinner.

Be *extremely* careful with cyanoacrylate glues! Always wear safety glasses and latex gloves while using them, and avoid breathing their fumes.

If you can't get super glue or lacquer, find a bottle each of clear nail polish and nail-polish remover (thinner); this works in a pinch. An auto-parts supplier is a good source for #600 wet-or-dry sandpaper (if they have it, also get a sheet of #1000 grit), as well as automotive finish rubbing and polishing compounds (I use Meguiar's #4 for rubbing and #7 for polishing). At the hardware store, pick up a spark-plug file. Finally, you'll need clean, soft rags for polishing and wiping. My favorites are baby diapers or flannelette (soft cotton flannel available at yard goods stores—buy plain, untreated flannel).

Since most dents, nicks, and scratches involve a low area in the finish or a spot where the finish is actually removed or chipped away, our job is to fill in the hole, let it dry, and then level and polish to a smooth finish. Practice on inexpensive yardsale guitars, the edge of worn-out furniture, clear objects such as chipped ashtrays, or even a marble—use your imagination. Be extremely careful with cyanoacrylate glues! Wear safety glasses and latex gloves (available at drug stores), since these glues stick flesh to flesh. Stewart-MacDonald sells a starter super glue kit that comes with a solvent that unglues fingers if you get in trouble; it can't be used for your eyes, however.

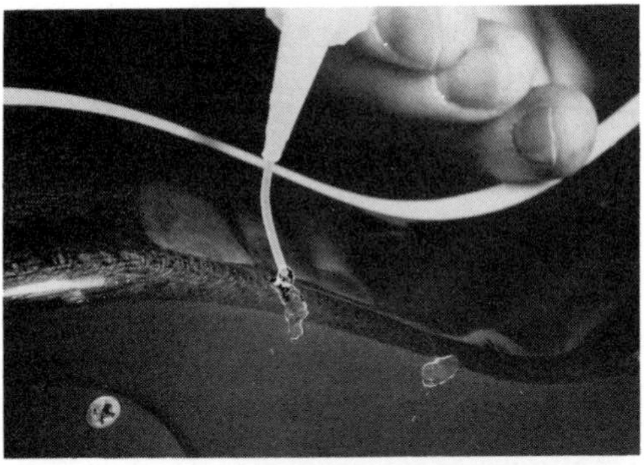

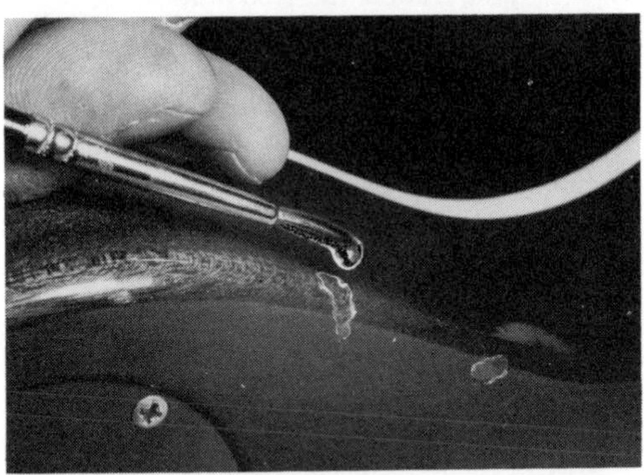

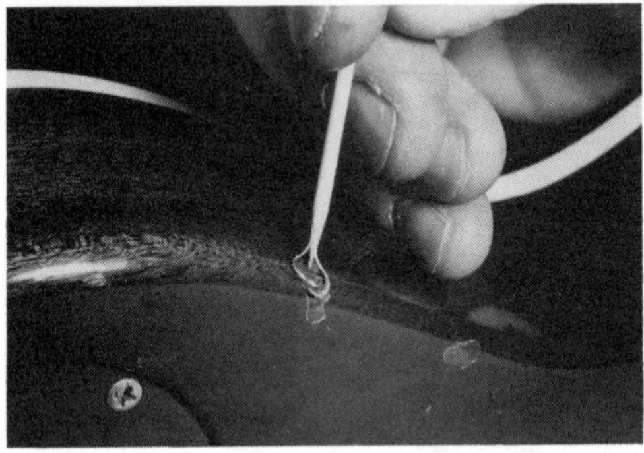

Practice filling in various holes with Hot Stuff. Try accelerator on some spots for instant hardness, and fill others with just glue, letting it air dry (you get a clearer fill this way). Use the flexible Teflon applicator hose to apply just a small drop (top photo). With the lacquer, use a brush to apply a small drop of thinner to a nick or scratch, both to clean the area and to help the lacquer melt in. Follow with a drop of unthinned lacquer as a fill (middle photo), letting it dry overnight or until hard (clear nail polish should also dry overnight). If a filler drop doesn't flow smoothly into a dent, use a toothpick to spread the liquid evenly (bottom photo).

Any of these drop fills will eventually build up higher than the surrounding finish and therefore must be leveled before polishing. The spark-plug file is good for quickly leveling a convex surface. Final-sand the area, using the #600 or #1000 sandpaper that has been dipped in water for lubrication and wrapped around a small, flat block. For final rubbing and polishing, use the Mirror Glaze #4 and #7. You'll soon begin to get the feel of the different materials—until you do, don't try anything on an instrument that you care about.

So far we've talked about dents, nicks, and scratches on an instrument's edge, where they are relatively easy to repair. Now let's learn more about finish types and consider which instruments you should or shouldn't work on yourself. This section further defines dents, nicks, and scratches, and shows how to go about making the repairs. Remember: If in doubt, take your prized instrument to an experienced professional.

First, let's examine the most common guitar finishes. If your instrument has a thick, glossy look—as if the finish had been applied by dipping it into a vat of liquid—most likely it's polyester or polyurethane. These surfaces are found on most imports and many American guitars made after the late 1960s. They are easy to drop fill, but hard to spray. These extremely hard finishes are also the safest to work on, because they won't dissolve from an accidental spill or overrun of thinner. For touch-ups, we use super glue.

Lacquer finishes are found on most instruments made since 1930. Always be careful with these repairs because the finish melts when touched by super glue, lacquer, nail polish, and thinners, all of which are used to touch up this kind of surface. Martin, Gibson, Guild, Harmony, Kay, Rickenbacker, Fender, and many other guitars have been finished with lacquer. In general, newer lacquered guitars have thicker finishes and are therefore easier to work on than the vintage ones with thin, brittle finishes that take very little sanding before bare wood is exposed. All lacquer finishes dent, chip, and scratch more easily than polyester. On lacquer, a thumbnail can dent the wood; on polyester, it won't.

Shellac, varnish, and French polish are often used on expensive handmade guitars—especially classical and flamenco—as well as American guitars made prior to about 1930. If you think your guitar has one of these finishes, take it to a good repairman and find out. I don't advise working on these finishes—they're hard enough to clean, harder to work on. No do-it-yourself repairs allowed here. (John Carruthers' Oct. and Nov. '78 columns in *Guitar Player* have good descriptions of various finishes and advice on their cleaning and maintenance.)

Now, a brief survey of accidents that can befall an instrument's finish. Dents are small pockets in a finish that result from the wood hitting a blunt object—the original finish remains, but is dented-in. A smooth dent with no cracks in the finish is an easy drop fill. With some dents, however, the finish is also cracked. Here you may prefer to chip away the broken finish before filling.

Nicks are usually the result of contact with a sharp object, and the wood shows bare. This repair is easiest on a clear, natural-wood finish. Stained wood is usually no problem: Simply apply clear finish over the nick. Some finishes, though, have color in them, and these are somewhat harder for the amateur to fix because the repair must match the original color.

Scratches occur when a small amount of finish is removed by some sharp object, neither denting the wood nor totally chipping away the finish to bare wood. Scratches come in all shapes and sizes, of course, and usually leave an opaque white mark. When they occur in inconspicuous areas, the

Finish touch-ups aren't easy. To do a job without a trace takes years of practice, and often you can't make a scratch or nick *invisible.* Whoever said you could mistreat your guitar and get away with it?

Wet-or-dry sandpaper should be immersed in water overnight before it's used. It works much better when it's soaked.

accidents are safe to repair. Beware of those that are away from the edges and out on the main body area—these can be tough to fix.

You can experiment on the guitar's finish beforehand. To test the finish on most electrics, remove the plate covering the control cavity and practice inside—it's the same finish. With an acoustic, remove a tuning machine from the rear of the headstock and practice on that newly exposed area. Before beginning a repair, clean and de-grease the area with a rag dipped in lighter fluid, allowing a few minutes drying time. *Caution: Use flammable chemicals only in well-ventilated areas, and never near an open flame.*

To repair a dent on an area such as the binding or the back of the neck, position the guitar so that gravity won't cause your repairing liquid to run while drying. The middle photo on the previous page shows a lacquer drop being applied by brush. Don't "paint" the lacquer on. Instead, use the brush to set a drop of finish into the hole; it may take several applications to get a build. Super glue is a good filler for lacquer or polyester. In the old days, we always used lacquer—that's all we had. But lacquer isn't so good on a polyester finish—it doesn't cling as well.

The Japanese Finesse sandpaper is the finest I've used. It's aggressive (an 800-grit cuts like 400), yet doesn't leave scratches. You must soak the paper overnight, and it lasts about five days.

The top photo at right shows a dent fill on the very edge of a headstock. Here you have two choices. In method one, pre-spray the dent with accelerator, wait five minutes, and follow with any of the super glues. Apply the glue sparingly; it sets fast due to the accelerator. You avoid runs this way, and should be able to achieve a full build-up in a matter of minutes by applying several coats. Use more accelerator between coats if the glue isn't drying. An alternate method is to use a piece of firmly attached masking tape to build a dam along the edge. This holds the glue and prevents it from running. You don't need accelerator with this method, although you'll have to wait longer for each coat to dry. This method does offer the clearest fill when the tape is pulled away.

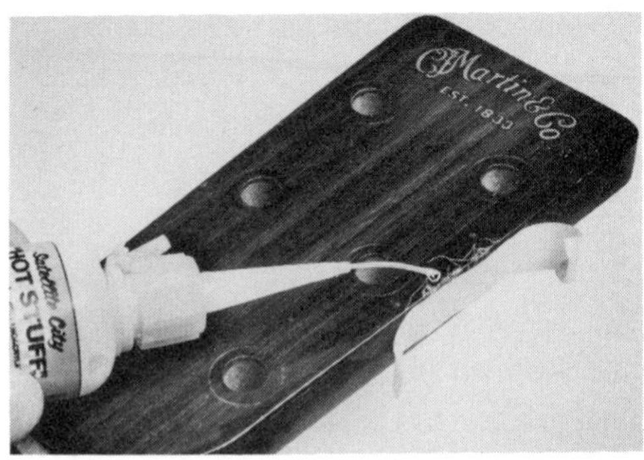

The next two photos show the proper method of leveling these fills using a spark-plug file. The hump from this filler should be made close to flush with the surrounding area before sanding. The final leveling should be done with #600 or #1000-grit wet-or-dry sandpaper or Finesse wet-sanding blocks. Wrap the paper around a small, flat block and dip it in water for lubrication. As the paper loads up with finish, dip it often and wipe off the particles with your thumb. Feather the spot away from the damaged area; if you just sand right over the fill, you'll get a dip.

Even better than the sanding block and wet-or-dry paper is the Finesse block, a small ($\frac{3}{4}$" x 1$\frac{1}{4}$" x 2$\frac{3}{8}$") block of pure abrasive grit.

Like Finesse papers, the blocks are left in water, and they last indefinitely. Finesse blocks are designed especially for leveling runs, sags, and imperfections in finishes. They're available in five grits from 400 to 3000.

Follow with two grades of Mirror Glaze rubbing compound—#4 and #7. If you've sanded to the very fine grits (1200 to 2000), you can start rubbing with #7, skipping the #4. Use a piece of clean, soft baby diaper or flannelette for rubbing. Don't use too much compound; a small amount will do. Whenever possible, always rub lengthwise with the grain. Don't rub too long or hard, but just enough to get the gloss back. When rubbing, take your stroke three or four inches away from the damaged area to blend in with the surrounding finish. Always use large amounts of elbow grease. After you've sanded with 2000-grit paper and used Mirror Glaze #7, follow with swirl-mark remover. Good brands include Black Magic, Pink-N-Glaze, and Mirror Glaze #9. Now we'll look at the trickiest fills.

More on dents, dings, and scratches

By now you should be getting more adept at using super glue and lacquer to touch up a well-worn guitar's many dents. Remember that you can use either super glue or lacquer for these drop fills, but that super glue works on instruments finished with lacquer or the modern polyesters, while lacquer is best used on *lacquer only*. In a pinch, you can use clear nail polish. So clean up your bench, and let's get back to work.

Dents that have a cracked or broken finish will look their best if the damaged

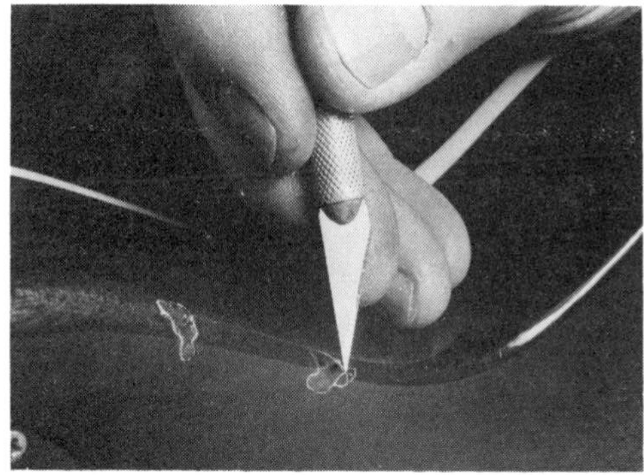

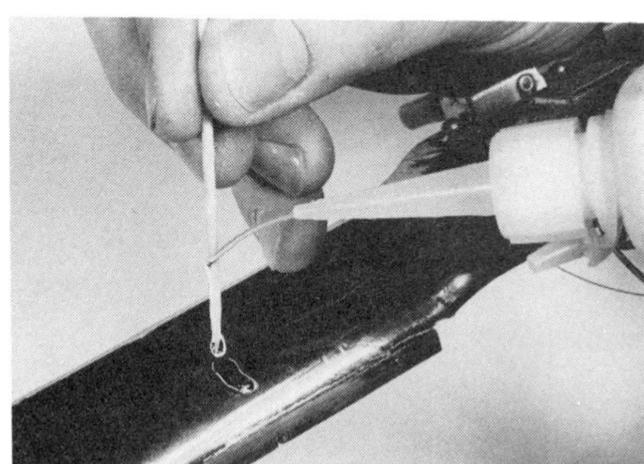

finish is carefully lifted out. Use a sharp X-acto knife to pry under the crushed finish and lever it out of the remaining solid finish (top photo). At this point you will have a jagged-edged hole with the bare wood showing—the same as a chip. Be careful not to pry into the wood itself. In the case of a lacquer finish, run a brush tip of thinner or acetone (not too wet) into the dent to dissolve the hole's edges. Follow immediately with a drop of unthinned lacquer. Use the brush to set a thick drop of lacquer into the hole, but don't try to brush it on with a stroke. The lacquer will probably take all night to harden, and it may shrink a bit, requiring a second coat. A proper fill should slightly rise above the surrounding finish.

If you're using super glue for this lacquer repair, you won't have to use any thinner to melt the edges. Super glue does its own melting as it cures with lacquer. Although the super glue Teflon applicator hose is handy for applying a small drop, you may find that sometimes you can't stop the glue from flowing, due to the siphon effect. Try holding a round toothpick in the dent and applying glue to it, letting the liquid run

Make your own drop fill by pouring some unthinned lacquer into a small baby-food jar and storing it with its lid off in a well-ventilated place for a few days. When it's thick and syrupy, it's ready to use.

Don't put too much drop fill into a hole at one time, or it may skin over and never dry clear down to the bottom.

down into the hole (bottom photo, previous page). This works for lacquer, too. Drop filling methods for chips and crushed dents are identical, and if the color has not been removed with the chip, you have a straightforward touch-up using clear fills. If, however, the color beneath the clear finish has been affected, you may wish to put a little color on the wood before using the clear.

Most electric and acoustic guitars that are not painted a solid color use shades of red, brown, black, and yellow. Good color matches can be obtained with Behlen's Solar-Lux Alcohol Stains, which come in these four colors and can be bought from woodworking and lutherie suppliers. These stains mix well with lacquer for light, translucent shades. They can be used straight or mixed for color match. They will not mix with super glue, but they can be covered over by it. I *have* found that super glue mixes well with certain lacquer "shaders" and with some dry powdered lacquer-soluble aniline stains. (Shaders are clear lacquer and thinner mixed with dissolved aniline powder; they add color but are otherwise transparent.)

An easy solution for color finishes is to use artists' felt-tip markers (top photos). When the colored ink is dry, follow with the clear drop fill. The colors may change under lacquer or super glue, so experiment. Usually permanent markers do a better job than the inexpensive discount kind that are meant for kids' coloring books. I have worked wonders in a pinch with Magic Markers in yellows, reds, browns, and especially black (great for black headstock-face touch-ups). With any colored pens or alcohol stains, always use less color than you think is necessary, since these stains darken in time and look different under the clear drop fill that follows. (For a color test, try practicing on pieces of glass, ashtrays, mom's furniture, or jewelry.)

Solid color finish repairs are quite tricky to pull off. Auto parts suppliers should have practically any color you'd need in acrylic

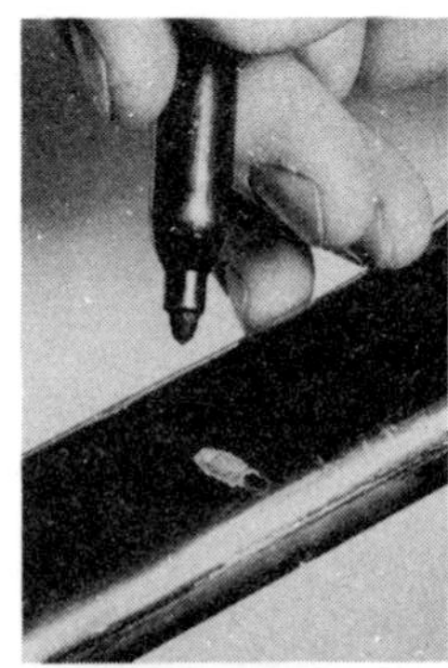

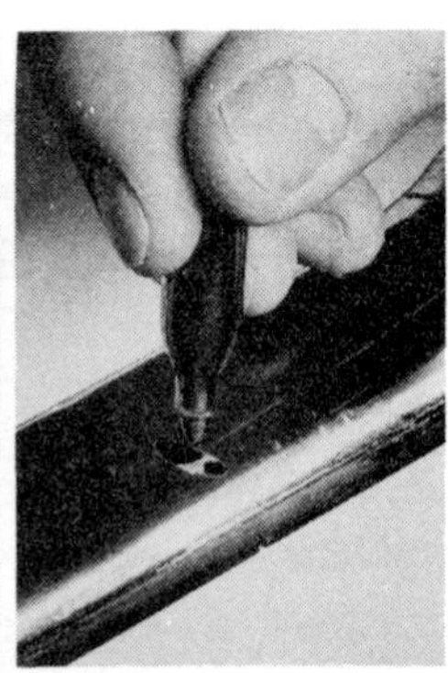

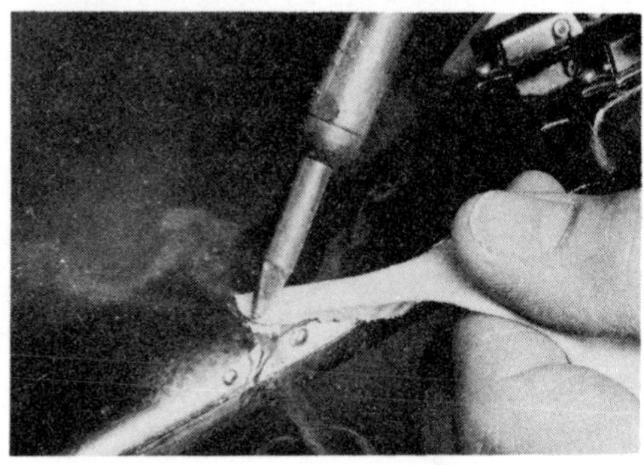

lacquer. Note: Used for furniture and guitars, woodworking lacquer is referred to as "nitrocellulose" lacquer and differs from acrylic. In general, the two don't mix well, but small amounts can be used for drop filling, as long as you give the paint plenty of time to dry. Follow an acrylic-lacquer color fill with a topcoat of super glue; don't use nitrocellulose lacquer. Good color matches take lots of experience, so practice on yardsale specials.

Deep dents that have crushed the wood fibers can sometimes be swollen back out. After chipping out the bruised finish, dampen the wood with a rag dipped in warm water. Squeeze out the excess water from the rag and hold a damp edge against the dent. Carefully steam the rag with a hot soldering pencil or gun (above), but don't overcook it. The steam can often raise the wood back close to its original shape—remember that the wood is still there, but only crushed. Allow several hours for the wood to dry, and continue with the drop fill of your choice. Dents that do not have a crushed finish can be filled as is. Look at these dents as smooth, clear-bottomed holes that need to be filled with finish—clear over clear. Super glue is my favorite for this; I allow ample time for drying and use no accelerator.

Scratches are the hardest touch-ups, since there isn't a clear-cut hole to deal with. Most scratches are irregular in shape and quite thin. On a lacquered guitar, brush a thin coat of lacquer thinner along the center of the scratch with a very thin, sharp-pointed artist's brush. This helps dissolve the line before the finish is applied. Apply the finish a dab at a time, once again using the brush tip to set lacquer into the scratch. Don't use a brush stroke; this can smear the work. Start at the farthest end and work your way towards yourself. If you have a good drop of lacquer on a brush tip, run a bead of it from your starting point for a good inch or so, until it runs dry, actually "pulling" the thick lacquer through the scratch. Never use a brush you care about with super glue, because you'll ruin it. If a scratch is well filled and doesn't need a second coat, let it dry many hours before leveling with well-soaked Finesse blocks or wet-or-dry sandpaper (1000-grit and up) that's been wrapped around a sanding block and dipped in water. Scratches in hard polyester finish should be filled with the super glue of your choice in much the same fashion, but use a toothpick dipped in glue instead of a brush.

All of the above touch-ups are to be leveled, wet-sanded, and rubbed out using the methods described earlier. Remember that all these touch-ups are on the instrument's edges, where it's easy to file, sand, and polish. Once again, I caution you not to attempt repairs on the face or back of your guitar unless you have a lot of experience. Sanding and rubbing-out in these areas will contrast poorly with the surrounding finish. Repairs on the sides of guitars (especially solidbodies) are easier, since the curved shape usually offers an easier access for the leveling file and wet-sanding block. The narrow width is also easier to rub out. When working on a side touch-up, rub well away from the repaired area, going along the nearest corner and blending in with the surrounding finish. Good luck!

A basic finishing schedule

Many players find that the only affordable way to own guitars with custom-tailored options is to assemble their own, usually from kit parts. My mail reflects this trend, with readers showing a special interest in products and techniques for finishing. They know that no matter how well a guitar is made, be it from scratch or a kit, it won't look great without a good finish.

Finishing is complex. Read all these pages, and that's just the beginning!

Modern guitar finishes are more complex, creative, and high-tech than ever before, and some would be hard for the best pros to duplicate. But anyone can do a respectable job of finishing, without expensive equipment, if they know what products to use and how to use them. The following pages dig deeply into low-cost lacquer finishing for the serious and patient do-it-yourselfer.

In 1989 I produced a video on finishing for Stewart-MacDonald; the tape covers the basics of lacquer spraying for the small shop or hobbyist. Here's the video's 10-step finishing schedule, which describes lacquer finishing using easy-to-get products and inexpensive tools. With the exception of the acrylic lacquer system described in Steps 5 and 6, we'll use nitrocellulose lacquer products.

First we'll describe each step and the various finishing products needed to complete it. Then we'll go through the actual steps for some common finishes. Not all finishes require every step, so skip those that don't apply in your case. Just don't change the basic order, and practice every finish operation on scrap wood. Put a complete finish on scrap before tackling the real thing!

Mineral spirits makes a great sanding lubricant, and it isn't bad with causing splits. Use mineral spirits in a well-ventilated area, wear gloves and a respirator, and keep it away from sparks or open flame.

WOOD PREPARATION

At this stage, major work such as rough sanding, shaping, binding, scraping, hole drilling, etc., should be complete. Minor problems in the wood surface are corrected, final sanding is done, areas not to be sprayed are masked off, and the instrument is well cleaned.

Pre-assemble all parts to make sure everything fits and lines up (neck/body, bridge, tuners, tailpiece or tremolo, etc.). This helps avoid drilling or last-minute "construction" after the finish is on (which often damages the finish by accident or causes lacquer to lift around newly drilled holes). Go ahead and string the guitar up. If the nut is to be finished, install it now. Continue by dressing the frets, especially their ends. You needn't wire the guitar.

FIXING DENTS AND CHIPS

Dents or dings in the raw wood can be drawn out with steam, since the wood is still there. Wet the dented area with warm water, let it sit a few minutes, and steam it out using a damp rag and soldering pencil. Use stainable, water-base wood dough to fill small chips. Its ability to accept stain is helpful if you're doing a natural finish, or it can be pre-colored with Behlen's powdered Fresco colors before the fill. Larger holes can be inlaid with wood or filled with auto-body filler (but body fillers can't be stained).

If slowly added to the chip in layers, super glues make a hard, clear fill; I use Hot Stuff. When dry, super glue does not take a stain, nor will a stain penetrate through it! So do any staining beforehand, and confine any fill material to the damaged area—keep it off the surrounding wood. Level a dried fill with a homemade, curved sanding stick surfaced with 80- or 120-grit paper. When close to level, switch to a sanding block for smoothing-in.

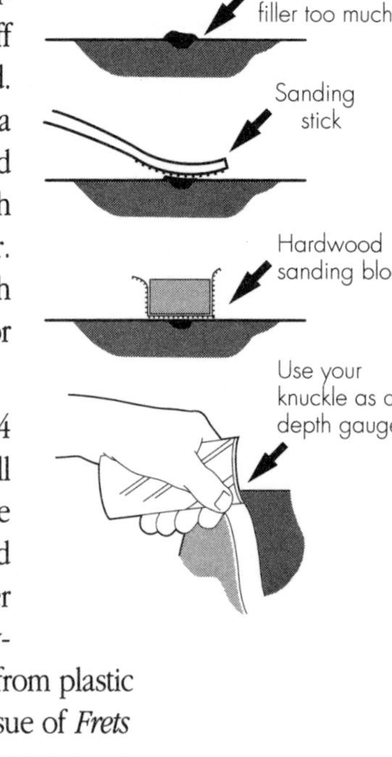

Scraping with a $4 steel cabinet scraper will remove scratches in side grains, in end grains, and in the cutaways. A scraper is also perfect for removing colored over-spray from plastic binding. The May '83 issue of *Frets* magazine has an article on scrapers—check your library.

SANDING

Some kit parts are so well sanded that they're ready to spray. Most, though, need final sanding to remove marks left by the factory. To save money, you can do your own sanding, following these rules: Raise the grain by lightly dampening the wood surface (don't soak it, though). Use a clean rag that's been soaked in water and well squeezed-out. When dry again, the wood fibers will be raised or firred-up, making it easier for the sandpaper to cut them off. Dampen the wood between every sanding to get a really smooth surface. Always wear a dust mask.

Don't use a sandpaper grit coarser than 120. Use either Fre-Cut silicon carbide or garnet paper. Start with 120-grit and progress through 150 or 180 to 220. A 220 final sanding will satisfy most of us. If not, continue sanding up to 320-grit. Sanding much finer can make a wood surface so smooth that lacquer has trouble adhering. Sand with the grain to avoid crosswise scratches. Block sand flat surfaces by wrapping the sandpaper around a flat-bottomed wood block. This spreads out the sanding pressure, so you won't create hollows in the wood from the roundness of your fingers. Keep moving, or you'll end up with an uneven surface. Don't use electric sanders until you have become proficient by hand, and blow off or vacuum the wood often to remove sawdust.

To remove the invisible sweat or oils left by handling, wipe the instrument with a naphtha-dampened rag before going on to Step 2. Wood preparation is the most important step of finishing, since the finish can only be as good as the wood underneath.

STAINS APPLIED TO BARE WOOD

There are many types of stain, many ways to apply them, and even more ways to screw them up. As your interest in finishing grows, experience will be your real teacher, and you'll come by knowledge naturally. To avoid confusion, I'll tell you what to use. By using the products and methods described here, you won't know all there is to know, but you'll get a healthy start.

Powdered aniline stains are most often used by luthiers. They're available in two forms: one soluble in water or alcohol, the other soluble in lacquer thinner or mineral spirits. We'll use a pre-mixed alcohol-type aniline stain known as Solar-Lux, since it's easier to use. You need red, yellow, brown, and black to produce most stained or sunburst finishes. An advantage of alcohol stains over water-soluble stains is that they are "non-grain-raising," or NGR for short. The stains can be applied by spraying or hand wiping.

Spraying gives the most uniform stain application. Inexpensive aerosol-powered "spray guns" with removable jars do an adequate job, and these units are self-loading (meaning that the user can add more or less thinner, stain, or lacquer at will). Some common self-loading aerosol brands are Pre-Val, Jet-Pak, and Miller. These aerosol power units will get cold and clog if you use them too long, so watch out! Otherwise, with care you can even use them for putting on the lacquer topcoats (after a good cleaning, of course).

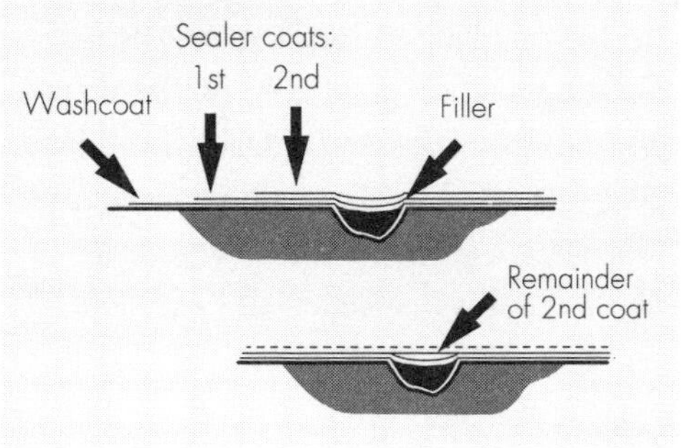

When dry, super glue doesn't take stain, so don't be sloppy while using it, especially for binding.

Hand wiping is a good, quick way to get a base coat on an entire instrument (like that on a red or brown Gibson SG). Yellow bases for sunbursts are often applied by hand. Retarder added to the stain slows down its drying and helps eliminate lap marks as stain is applied. In fact, the traditional sunbursts of the early days were hand-applied, very beautiful, and have a different look from the sprayed-on type.

NGR STAINS

Whether it's sprayed or wiped, Solar-Lux can be applied straight from the jar or thinned with reducer to weaken its color. Pre-dampen end grain with Solar-Lux reducer to keep too much stain from penetrating into those areas, making them darker than you might wish. A touch of fresh shellac or clear lacquer (say, a capful per cup) added to an NGR stain keeps it from soaking in too quickly and gives it body.

WASHCOAT BEFORE FILLER

Stained or natural, open-grain wood should be sprayed with a light washcoat of sealer or clear lacquer to keep the paste filler's color from over-staining the piece. Following the wood surface without filling the pores (below), a washcoat acts as a barrier between the wood and filler. The best washcoat is a vinyl sealer available from C. F. Martin's Woodworker's Dream, sprayed in one thin coat. It's compatible with the nitrocellulose lacquer.

During the wood-prep stage, carefully seal any holes or areas where wood grain might soak up water.

My most common criticism of beginners? Simple: They don't practice on scrap! And when you're doing the real finishing job, always keep a test piece of scrap handy.

FILLING THE GRAIN

Paste wood filler is used to fill open-pored woods such as mahogany, walnut, rosewood, and ash. It eliminates dust and air bubbles under the finish, and creates a flat surface for finishing by keeping the lacquer from shrinking into the pores as it dries. Filler isn't needed on close-grained woods like maple or alder, or on tonewoods such as spruce or cedar. Use natural wood filler (as opposed to pre-colored fillers) that can be used as is or colored with Fresco powders to produce darker shades. Stir the filler until it's mixed to about the consistency of thick cream. If necessary, thin it with naphtha in a well-ventilated area. Next "paint" the filler uniformly onto the wood and wait for a haze to form—your signal that the filler is dry enough to be rubbed.

When the haze forms, remove the excess from the surface with burlap or cheesecloth by rubbing across the grain. The trick is to keep from pulling filler from the pores when wiping, so don't fill too large an area. Do just the back, neck, or one side at a time, since filler that's dried too long is hard to remove (if this occurs, wipe the area with naphtha and start over). Filler shrinks about 10%, leaving very slight dips over the pores that will later be filled and leveled with sealer coats.

Protect areas not receiving the messy filler (spruce or maple tops, etc.) with paper and masking tape. Allow a week to dry before lightly sanding the filler residue from the washcoated surface with 320 Fre-Cut paper. After this light sanding, filler should remain only in the pores. For an in-depth treatise on filling and sealing, see Michael Dresdner's article in issue #3 of *The String Instrument Craftsman* (available from Pen-Lens Press, 142 N. Milpitas Blvd., Suite 280, Milpitas, CA 95035). I urge everyone to check out this newsletter—it's excellent, and back issues are available.

Remember: never mix acrylics with nitrocellulose wood lacquers!

PRIMER FOR SOLID COLORS

Nitrocellulose lacquer is commonly available in black and white, but it's hard to find in other colors, especially good-looking ones. You *can* mix your own nitro colors by using base-concentrate color (sold by Stew-Mac and many of the larger finishing supply houses) mixed with clear lacquer. Mixing good colors is hard, but fun to do. For pre-mixed modern solid colors, go "automotive" by using acrylic primer, color, clear top coats, and thinner. Primer (usually a neutral gray or white) hides the wood's natural color and builds a smooth surface. It builds quickly and sands easily. Martin Senour Lite Gray #3252 is a good brand sold at Napa auto parts stores. Dupont Lucite is also good. If you use acrylics, stick with the entire system—never mix acrylics with nitrocellulose wood lacquers!

SOLID COLOR COATS

When the primer has cured several days, acrylic color coats are applied. Four to six color coats can be applied as final topcoats and rubbed out. Or some finishers spray just enough color to cover the primer, then switch to clear lacquer or acrylic for the multiple-coat build-up. With clear over color, you must not sand until you're sure you've built enough lacquer to avoid sanding through; this takes two to three coats. To ensure compatibility, use acrylic primers, colors, and clears from the same company.

SEALER

Back to nitrocellulose. As gray primer was the "sealer" for acrylic color, consider sealer as a clear "primer" for nitrocellulose lacquer, sealing in the filler, stains, or sunburst. Thanks to a high solids content, sealers build quickly and act as a "bridge" between the wood and the finish, giving the lacquer something to cling to. For the novice, the best products are vinyl sealer, lacquer sanding sealer, or clear lacquer.

Sealer that's been sprayed and sanded correctly leaves a smooth matte finish, with few or no shiny specks indicating sinks or dips over the filled grain. Two coats of sealer (don't count the washcoat) sprayed by a pro using an air compressor and professional guns is plenty. Too much sealer (four or five coats) can cause cracking in the harder top coats and can add a slight milkiness to the clear finish. (But if you use the aerosol cans, they don't transfer as much lacquer per coat, so you may need four coats to get a true build). Sand sealer coats with Fre-Cut 320-grit until the small dips over the filled grain are gone. Any remaining shiny spots indicate an irregularity or depression in the finish surface. Try to get most of these now, or they'll come back to haunt you during rubbing out! This actually leaves a fairly thin finish, since most of the sealer is sanded off during leveling. Always be careful when sanding on sealer sprayed over colors; the risk of sanding through is great!

SHADERS, TONERS, AND TOUCH-UPS

At this stage correct any mistakes or sand-throughs. Sunbursts or colors can be highlighted with shading lacquer (clear lacquer colored with up to 10% Solar-Lux, or with lacquer-soluble aniline stain added). Sunbursts can be done at this time, over the sealer, and binding may be tinted for an antique look. An airbrush miniature spray (the Miller, Badger, and Paasche companies make good, affordable units) gun can come in handy for touch-ups. If you are using colored transparent finishes (such as the Pensa-Suhr and Paul Reed Smith types) and have skipped Steps 2, 5, and 6, you should spray them now, just before the clear topcoat is added.

CLEAR TOPCOATS

If possible, avoid sanding on any color touch-ups from Step 8. Unlike sealer, you can lay on the clear lacquer; four to six coats of lacquer is standard. Allow a three-hour minimum drying time between coats, and spray no more than three coats a day. To avoid breaking into the color coats, don't sand until after a two- or three-coat buildup. Even then, wet-sand *lightly*. Use water or mineral spirits as a lubricant (if mineral spirits are used, wear gloves and a mask, and have good ventilation), and sand with 400-grit wet-or-dry paper, drying off the finish with a clean, soft rag as you go. Whether you sand between every coat is up to you—some do, some don't—so experiment. Don't sand on sharp, exact edges; unsanded, they'll build up the extra lacquer needed to rub out nicely with the final finish.

Because of its thin viscosity, lacquer sprayed from pre-loaded aerosol cans builds more slowly than lacquer sprayed from spray guns or self-load aerosol units such as Pre-Val, Jet-Pak, or Miller (where the user has the opportunity to control how thick the lacquer is by adding thinner). In general, follow the manufacturer's thinning directions; usually a 50-50 mix (a ratio of 1:1) of thinner to lacquer is required for lacquer to spray smoothly. In humid climates, a dash of retarder should be added to the lacquer to help minimize blushing (the nasty white haze caused by trapped moisture).

WATER-SANDING AND RUBBING OUT

When the final coat of lacquer has dried at least a week (a month is better), wet-sand the finish to a dull, satiny patina prior to rubbing out. Once again, you want to remove dips. A felt-faced Plexiglas block makes a good backer for the sandpaper. Use 3M 600-, 1000-, or 1200-grit wet-or-dry paper, or Finesse paper in 1000, 1500, and 2000 grits. Water-sanding papers should be immersed in clean water overnight before using. Rinse the paper often in clean water to wash away any clogging particles.

Hand rub with a soft, clean rag and Meguiar's Mirror Glaze #4. Rub *with* the grain in a circular motion. Fold the loose corners

Never leave damp lacquer rags lying around the shop. Let them dry outside, and then throw them away.

of a rag into your palm to create a pad, then use liberal amounts of elbow grease. When you've developed a good, even shine, switch to Mirror Glaze #7 on a new rag, repeat the process, and you're done. Note: If you've used Finesse papers of 1200-grit or more, skip the #4 Mirror Glaze.

A good machine-rubbed look can be had by using a variable-speed electric drill equipped with a Meguiar's Finesse Pad. Using the same #4 and #7 polishes, these foam buffers have less chance of burn-through than conventional lamb's-wool bonnets, and give you a factory look. With either hand or machine buffing, squirt a thin line of compound onto the area to be rubbed, and pick it up with your rag or buffing bonnet as you work.

No matter how hard you try, some problems will befall you on your first jobs. The fun of solving these problems is what keeps me interested—and learning.

PHOTO: BRYAN GALLOUP'S GUITAR HOSPITAL

A large buffing wheel like this is a repairman's dream.

Spraying necks and bodies

We just looked at the different steps of lacquer finishing and the nitrocellulose-compatible products needed for doing them. Now here are basic spraying tips and safety measures, along with some specialized spray fixtures that you can make yourself. We'll start spraying with two simple finishes—a basic clear lacquer job for a bolt-on neck (both rosewood fretboards and "maple-necks"), and a solid opaque color on a kit body.

I like to compare finishing to cooking. The novice cook carefully follows recipes that guarantee success, while an experienced chef is more creative, instinctively adding a dash of this and a pinch of that while interpreting a recipe. Practice will allow you to experiment with your finishes, but for now let's stick to our "cookbook." To continue at this point, you must have digested the information given up until now. Before doing any of the finishes listed here, you should send for the various supply catalogs and acquire some supplies that suit your needs. Don't ruin a nice piece; practice all finishing on scrap wood until you gain a little savvy!

Whether you use a spray gun, aerosol can, or self-load aerosol, overlap the spray pattern of each successive pass from one-third to one-half the size of the pattern. The finish material thins out toward the edges of a spray pattern, so overlapping ensures an equal coat build and a uniform color. When you spray the next coat, spray at right angles to the direction of the first coat for more even coverage. Spray with the can or gun held between

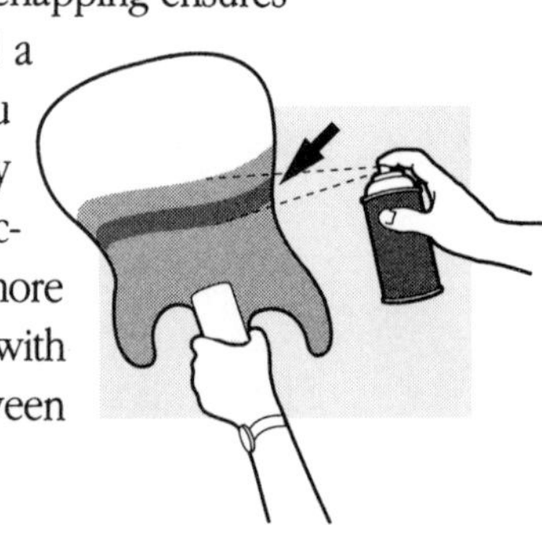

8" and 10" away from the instrument, and tilt what you're spraying away from the spray gun—don't hold it at a perfect 90 degrees. This tilting helps keep the spray from bouncing off the object, and allows the overspray to fall ahead of the spray pattern, to be covered by the next wet pass.

At times it's an advantage to spray *down* on an instrument that's lying flat. The lazy susan pictured below is easy to make and frees both hands to do operations such as sunbursting and touch-ups. You can spin it as you spray, which is great for spraying along the sides and in cutaways.

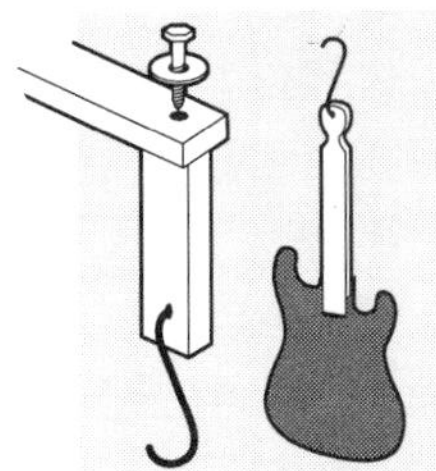

A length of two-by-four and a scrap of two-by-two make a portable spray hanger that can bolt, prop, or clamp anywhere. A clearance hole in the two-by-four allows the lag bolt to spin freely, along with the short two-by-two that it's tightly screwed into. A length of 1/4" steel rod that's bent into an "S" hook holds the hanging stick for a solidbody, or it can be slid through a tuning machine's hole on a headstock for hanging. An instrument can also be hung from a screw-eye placed in the butt end's strap button hole.

MAPLE NECK WITH ROSEWOOD FINGERBOARD

Spraying a clear finish on maple is the easiest to do, since there's no need for stain or filler. Here's the finish schedule for a maple neck with a rosewood fingerboard:

1 Wood prep if needed. Tape off the fingerboard.

2 Optional: For an aged look, stain neck with a weak wash of yellow-brown NGR stain. Pre-soaking end and side grain with reducer keeps these areas from absorbing too much stain. Experiment.

Skip Steps 3, 4, 5, and 6 (which were given in the finishing schedule a few pages back), since no filler is needed on maple and you won't be using solid colors.

7 Seal the neck. This calls for two light coats of shellac, vinyl sealer, or lacquer.

8 Skip unless you want to add color or highlights.

9 Spray four to six coats of clear lacquer that's thinned by a ratio of 1:1. Wet- or dry-sand as needed.

10 Dry one to two weeks. Wet-sand with 600-, 1000-, and 1500-grit sandpaper. Rub out by hand with Mirror Glaze #4 and #7. Carefully remove the masking tape from the fingerboard.

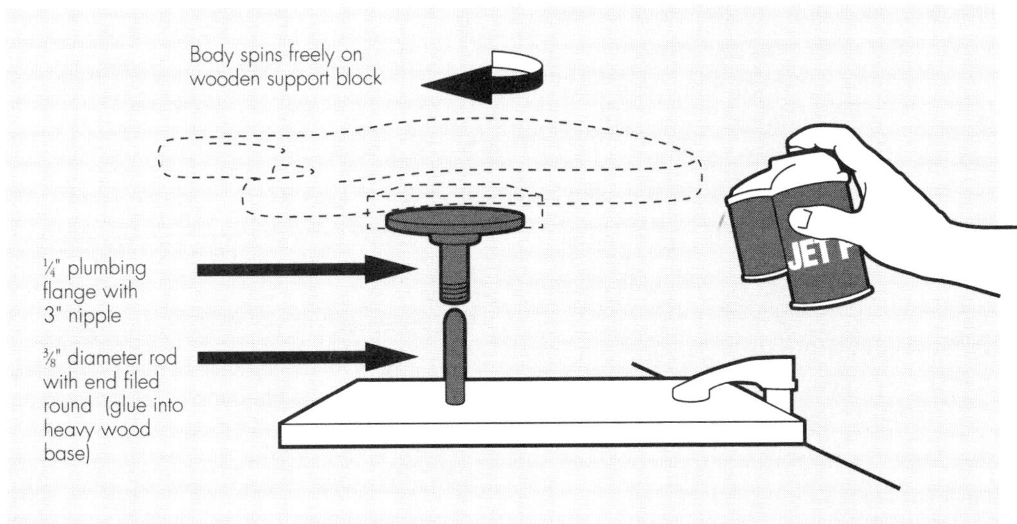

The secret to finishing a maple fingerboard is not to spray on too much lacquer. Use just enough to soak into the wood, and then build a slight gloss with three or four coats. Spray right over the frets, since the lacquer comes off when the frets are dressed.

You can't always expect the same results when using products such as Fullerplast, since temperature, humidity, and shelf life are involved. Don't blame me if it doesn't work for you; blame yourself for not practicing on scrap!

SPRAYING A MAPLE NECK

This letter from Al Valusek of Ann Arbor, Michigan, brings up the subject of spraying a maple fingerboard—a question often asked: "What kind of finish can I put on my late-'60s Strat's maple fingerboard after refretting? My repairman advised me that the fingerboard would have to be planed in order to remove some trouble spots, but he didn't want to take on the job because he's had poor luck finding the proper material with which to redo the wood (the original finish would be removed in the fingerboard-trueing process). Please help—I need a fret job!"

There are loads of clear lacquers, polyesters, enamels, etc., that will work when used correctly. I just use plain old lacquer, like Fender always did, and spray right over the frets—the lacquer will chip off during the fret dressing later. Suggest that to your repairman, but if he doesn't like lacquer, Fullerplast 353-00 Gloss, a poly-type finish, will do the job. He'll also have to buy the catalyst 353-50 and the Synal thinner 181-00. Two or three coats should be applied at two- to four-hour intervals all in the same day, so an early-morning start is advisable. He'll need spray equipment and a respirator (this is extremely toxic stuff that shouldn't be breathed). Sand lightly in between coats and follow the directions on the can. It can be sanded and rubbed out like standard lacquers. With polyesters and urethanes, I prefer to do the finish, rub it out, and then put in the frets. The finish will be hard enough the next day to complete the job. Note: You can leave the Fullerplast in the spray gun for the necessary spraying time, but dump it out immediately afterwards. Clean your gun extremely well to avoid ruining the equipment, since the catalyst acts as a hardener. Again, nitrocellulose lacquer does a great job—if you have cleaned the neck and fretboard well, of course!

LAKE PLACID BLUE METALLIC SOLIDBODY FINISH

I've found that the Lake Placid Blue lacquer used on a small number of custom-color Fender Strats in the early '60s is still available at my automotive store in acrylic lacquer (Dupont Lucite 2876-L). If you'd like to try this vintage metallic finish, you'll need one pint each of color, clear topcoat, and primer/surfacer, as well as a gallon of thinner (all acrylic-lacquer products). Spray the primer and color with self-load aerosols, and the clear with self-load or pre-filled aerosol cans (and of course the best job can be had with professional spray guns and an air compressor). I saw an original Lake Placid Blue Strat with the headstock face painted to match the body—it really looked great.

1 Prep wood as normal. Use acrylic spot putty for filling dents; this is available at an automotive supply store.

2 Skip—no stain needed.

3 Washcoat ash or open-grain wood. Alder needs no washcoat or filler.

4 Fill if needed; let dry a week or two.

5 Prime body with two to four coats of white or gray primer. Sand after the first two coats and after the last two. Allow three to four hours between coats, and let final coats dry three days. Sand the finish level.

6 Spray two to four coats of Lake Placid Blue, or enough to cover. Allow four hours between coats and dry overnight.

7 Skip sealer.

8 Lightly sand with 320-grit to remove dust. Touch up with blue if you sand through.

9 Spray four to six clear topcoats. Wait three hours between coats, and only do two coats a day. Sand as needed after first three coats are down.

10 Dry two weeks, wet-sand, and rub out as described above.

VERY IMPORTANT SAFETY INFORMATION

I realize that finishing products come with specific safety precautions printed on the label. However, I would like to caution you to:

- Wear rubber gloves when handling most of these products.
- Use a respirator (available at an auto supply store) approved for organic vapors, and spray in a well-ventilated area (like outdoors—just watch the bugs).
- Always wear eye protection.
- Don't smoke around spray products and don't spray around gas flames or pilots, hot light bulbs, or electrical appliances, including fans that aren't "explosion proof."
- Don't leave damp lacquer rags lying around the shop—the smallest spark can ignite them. Let them dry outside. When they're dry, throw them away.
- Never pour these chemicals down the drain. Pour all unused chemicals into an empty can with a good lid, and mark it "Used." When it's full, make sure that it goes to the proper chemical waste disposal station—check with city hall or a school's chemistry department to find out where.

Advanced finishes and sunbursts

You're never done when it comes to finishing—there's always lots more to learn. Perhaps you've experimented with some of the different finishing materials and have begun to develop a feel for them. Now you can really put yourself to the test by studying the schedules of two expert builder/repairmen: Mark Erlewine of Erlewine Guitars in Austin, Texas, and John Suhr of Rudy's Music in New York City.

Creator of the Automatic, Lazer, and Chiquita guitars, Mark Erlewine does a great "vintage cherry sunburst" that imitates the faded finish of a 1960 Gibson Les Paul. Mark was the first builder I know of to feature binding and carved tops on Strat-style guitars. John Suhr, besides handling the day-to-day repair needs of his customers, also finds time to create the Pensa-Suhr guitars for which Rudy's Music is famous. John sprayed the finish described here on a guitar made for Mark Knopfler in June 1988.

These two finishes deal with instruments with a mahogany body and flame-maple top. You can do the same type of finish on other wood combinations, such as ash or alder bodies with maple tops, by staining the lighter wood with walnut stain (alcohol aniline) to "imitate" mahogany during Step 2—otherwise Step 2 is omitted for mahogany. Both of these finishes require the careful taping and scraping of binding, as well as grain filling. They also involve careful, step-by-step planning. I chose them for this reason, figuring that if you can do these, you can do anything.

Finishing products change all the time as the government gets stricter about what goes into them. This is fine with me—I'd like to keep the earth around for my kids to play on.

MARK ERLEWINE'S VINTAGE CHERRY SUNBURST

1 Prepare the wood, mask binding, and protect the flame top with a paper cutout held in place by masking tape (tape the paper up to, and right over, the binding masking tape). Protect the headstock, fingerboard, and neck binding the same way.

2 This applies to alder or ash bodies only. Stain the back and sides of the body a brownish red, with brown being predominant. Use alcohol stains.

3 Washcoat the mahogany neck and body with lacquer mixed 1:3 (one part thinner and three parts lacquer).

An affordable (and excellent) little air-compressor/spray outfit is the Miller 2000. I can't say enough about this rig—especially to get you through your first few years.

4 Fill the grain with brown-red filler and let dry three days. Spray two coats of clear lacquer to lock in the color.

5 Color the filled mahogany with transparent lacquer shaders. (Wolf makes these premixed, or you can make your own shaders with lacquer-soluble anilines.) Spray two coats of red transparent lacquer mixed with a little brown and a touch of yellow on the mahogany. When these "shader" coats are dry, seal them with two coats of clear lacquer to help stabilize the color—this isn't the sealer step yet.

6 Expose the flame-maple top, and mask off the mahogany with paper. Run the paper right to the edge so that the tape sticks to the binding, rather than the cherry shader you just sprayed (the shader could pull loose, since it's uncured). Hand stain the maple top with alcohol aniline stain mixed eight parts yellow, two parts brown, and one part red. It looks dull when it dries, but don't worry. It will make the figure of the curly maple bolder, and it comes to life when it's hit with lacquer. Seal this color with two coats of clear lacquer just as you did the mahogany in Step 5. By sealing these colors from each other, you get less "bleeding" between the top and side colors. We're not done coloring yet. After the two clear coats have dried, spray two coats of Wolf Lemon Yellow transparent lacquer (thinned 1:1) over the top. Now watch the flame pop out! When this dries, seal and melt it with one coat of clear gloss lacquer.

Now for the "burst." Use Wolf Ruby Red as is, but thinned enough to spray. Sunburst the edges of the top with your spray aimed off the instrument. Use a small pattern, and hit only the edges while sunbursting—don't spray toward center! Spray this first pass no more than 3/4" in from the edge; this creates a fairly strong red. Then, mix the same red with equal amounts of brown transparent lacquer. Spray lighter, but go in 1½" to cover a larger area. Next, use just brown transparent lacquer to lightly mist the entire burst going in 2½" from the edge (this must be done lightly to duplicate the fading of this famous type of sunburst). When this dries, shoot one coat of clear over the burst to set the colors. Remove the tape and paper from the body. Scrape the binding to remove any color that may have bled under the masking tape.

If your headstock is already black (some headstock overlays are black fiber or plastic), remove the masking, and seal it with the rest of the instrument in Step 7. If you need to spray it black, do it now. Tape off the neck around the headstock face and spray enough black lacquer to cover the face. Let it dry, and scrape the paint from the pearl inlays.

7 Seal the entire instrument with two or three coats of clear lacquer (of course, the fingerboard itself should be masked).

8 If you want the aged look, color the binding with some top color that's been lightened with clear and has a dash of brown and red. An airbrush does this best. Don't overdo it, or it'll look fake. I use a homemade lazy susan to rest the instrument on while antiquing. It also comes in handy for spraying sides and sunbursts. There are many times when it's helpful to spray one side of a piece while it's lying flat, especially for avoiding runs. If you do get a run or "sag" in the finish, wet-sand it out with a Finesse block or 400 wet-or-dry sandpaper wrapped around a small Plexiglas sanding block with rounded corners. Rock the block on the bump to "feel" it and sand it level.

9 Spray from four to six clear coats of lacquer, sanding as you wish.

10 Rub out as usual.

JOHN SUHR'S PENSA-SUHR FINISH

Mark Knopfler's guitar has a mahogany body with a flame-maple top and ivoroid binding. The bolt-on neck is made of maple with a rosewood fingerboard that's also bound with ivoroid. The binding runs around the headstock, as well, which calls for quite a lot of scraping. And it's got a unique twist—the Watco Danish Oil. Watch how John's methods fit into the schedule.

1 Prep wood as normal.

Skip Step 2.

3 Skip washcoat, but wipe one coat of Watco Danish Oil onto the curly maple top. This keeps the filler from coloring it, and brings out the grain. Rub it on, and wipe off the excess.

4 Fill the mahogany with brown paste wood filler—no washcoat—and let dry three days. Clean the binding with a scraper afterwards.

Skip Steps 5 and 6.

7 Seal the whole body with one wipe-coat of Watco Danish Oil to mellow out the filler. Wipe one coat of Watco Oil onto the maple neck, too. Let both dry for one day, and then spray one thin coat of clear lacquer over the body and neck. This melds the Watco with the lacquer. Dry one day, and then finish sealing with clear lacquer mixed 1:1 with thinner. (As a rule, John's thinner is made up of two parts thinner to one part retarder; this is more than the manufacturer suggests, so experiment first.) Spray five or six coats of clear; after three coats, sand between coats with 400 Fre-Cut *Gold* sandpaper, which John says outlasts many others. Final sand until the finish is level. This ends the sealer stage.

8 Mask off the binding and top with newspaper and 3M Stripers tape (a pale green, latex-backed tape that is perfect for this type of work). Mask the fingerboard and neck binding, too. Spray the mahogany back and rims with Wolf transparent red and brown shading lacquer mixed three parts red to one part brown and thinned 1:1 with thinner (add some clear lacquer to this if you want a weaker color). Spray two or three coats. A good way to spray a body is to screw a holding stick in the cavity in place of the neck, and make a hanger as shown earlier. This allows you to rotate the body by hand while spraying or to spray with the body hanging. Let dry two hours, and then scrape and clean the binding. If you let lacquer sit too long (four hours or more), it becomes too chippy, and if it's not dry enough, it drags with the scraper. Two hours is right.

Now for the golden see-through top. Mix a transparent shading lacquer using mostly Wolf Golden Yellow as a base, adding a little Lemon Yellow and brown to suit. Mix in one-fourth clear lacquer, and thin the mixture 1:1. Mask off the sides of the binding, but don't bother trying to mask off the thin top of the binding, since it's easier to scrape that edge. Spray no more than two or three coats for the right color. Wait two hours, and then remove the tape and scrape the binding's top edge. Spray the same golden color onto the maple neck.

Now we lightly shade the binding. Pour off some of your top color, and add clear lacquer and a little Lemon Yellow. Spray the body and neck binding lightly. Since you don't have to worry about the slight overspray on the surrounding finish, an air brush is handy for this. This completes the coloring. Let dry overnight.

9 Shoot clear lacquer, thinned 1:1, over the body and neck. Sand after three coats, and then as needed every coat after that. John sprays 10 to 15 coats of lacquer. You probably won't need that much, since your brand of lacquer may not be as thin as John's to start with.

10 Let the finish dry one month before wet-sanding and rubbing out. If you use the 1000

I'm doing lots of experimenting with water-base lacquer, which will be the way of the future. It's not very toxic, nor a great polluter.

and higher grits of paper, try skipping Meguiar's #4 and go directly to #7 (see what suits you). John also uses a 3M liquid polish (Prep Team 05939), and his buffer is a Porter Cable 305 that runs at 2000 rpm.

Both of these finishes involve, among other products, the use of clear lacquer that is colored. You can mix these using lacquer-soluble anilines, or they may be purchased ready to spray. The Wolf lacquers mentioned here are pre-mixed; check your suppliers. Clear colored lacquer has always been part of traditional sunbursts, and has only lately become popular in creating see-through tinted finishes over highly figured woods.

For more information and different viewpoints, read John Carruthers' four-part treatise on finishing in the Feb., Apr., May, and July '83 issues of *Guitar Player* magazine. Other invaluable sources: H. Behlen's *Guide To Wood And Wood Finishing*, Sam Allen's *Wood Finisher's Handbook*, and the appropriate chapters in Melvyn Hiscock's *Make Your Own Electric Guitar*, Roger Siminoff's *Constructing A Solidbody Guitar* and *Constructing A Bluegrass Mandolin* (this has a very good color section on hand-applied sunbursts done with alcohol stains), William Cumpiano and Jon Natelson's *Guitar Making: Tradition And Technology*, and Don Teeter's *The Acoustic Guitar, Vol. 1.* My video with Don MacRostie, *Finishing Techniques For Stringed Instruments*, is offered by Stewart-MacDonald.

Well, that's it. I hope you'll profit from this advice. Remember to practice on scrap, and don't set your goals too high at first.

Dealing with humidity

Read this section on humidity every fall, just before heating season. Then follow its advice—I do!

Acoustic owners need to care for their delicate wooden instruments during the cold, dry months. Paying attention to humidity won't hurt electric owners either, so here's the skinny on chapped lips and cracked guitars.

In the humid summertime, guitars may suffer from becoming too wet, getting such symptoms as higher action (due to a more swollen top, which occasionally causes a bridge to loosen, as well) and a flat, "tubby" sound. Solve the high-action problem by having a lower "summer saddle" made for your guitar. The tubby sound goes away by itself in the fall, or whenever you have three or four nice, dry summer days in a row. Summer conditions aren't as dangerous as winter ones, however, since the wood seldom cracks due to over-humidification.

Low humidity occurs in the winter in most areas, and all year long in some desert and high mountain states. Heating your home, especially with forced air, adds to the dryness problem. When a solid-wood guitar dries out, the wood shrinks across the grain. The fingerboard shrinks, and the fret ends poke out from the sides. Tops flatten out or cave in, lowering the bridge and allowing the strings to buzz on the frets. The back may also flatten, and glue joints anywhere can come apart. If the wood dries too rapidly, the finish may check. In extreme cases, braces can come loose and the back, sides, and especially the top can crack. Most of these troubles can be avoided by adding moisture to the guitar's environment.

Use a hygrometer to measure your home's relative humidity; combination thermometer/hygrometers aren't expensive. If you're fortunate enough to have a furnace with a whole-house humidifier, use it; if you

Ontek's Lifeguard model 100L.

The Ontek Lifeguard in use.

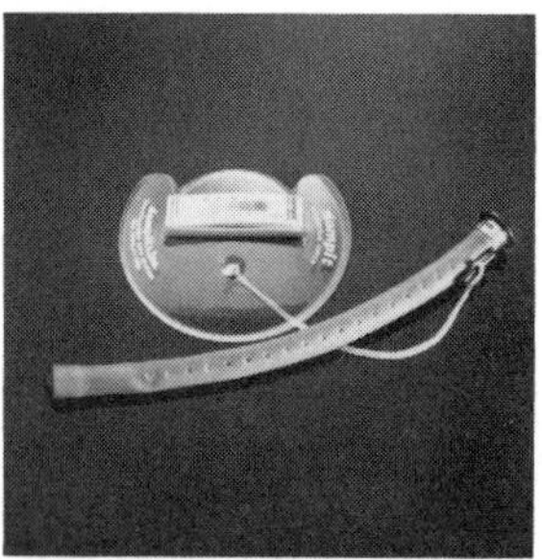
The Dampit system (with humidity gauge).

Like the Ontek, the Dampit covers the soundhole and slowly distributes moisture to the body.

don't, consider having one installed. Check out the portable room humidifiers available through Sears and other companies. A natural approach is to leave bowls of water to evaporate on wood stoves and heater grates. Any of these measures will help, but they may not be sufficient protection against the dreaded crack monster.

Lately, soundhole humidifiers have gained popularity with many players and manufacturers. Two companies, Dampit and Ontek, manufacture soundhole humidifiers that sell for about $12.00. Simply put, these devices are dipped in water and then mounted in the soundhole when the guitar's not in use, and they slowly distribute moisture inside the guitar body. These humidifiers have soundhole covers that must be used to work properly. With the proper use of these humidifiers in the dry season and possibly a lower saddle in the wet season, your guitar should play consistently all year round. I asked acoustic guitar experts Dick Boak from Martin, Bruce Ross at Santa Cruz Guitar Co., and Bob Taylor from Taylor Guitars for their thoughts on humidity and soundhole humidifiers:

Bruce: "Humidity control is most crucial to newer guitars. Once a guitar makes it through its first four seasons, it comes to terms with itself. Use the soundhole humidifier with care. I've seen them harm guitars, too, from over-wetting, which lets water drip inside."

Bob: "Lack of humidity control is the single source for over 90% of guitar problems. How you wax, clean, play, tote, strum, strap, oil, or loan a guitar is your business. These things don't matter a whole lot—the guitar will stand up to them. But when it comes to humidity, a little attention each time you play your guitar will make it last forever."

Dick: "Guitars sound terrible when they're full of moisture. But sometimes humidifiers are necessary—more so with newer guitars—and we sell both the Ontek and Dampit here at Martin. New guitars need special treatment for the first few years. Mostly watch the heat when it first comes on in the fall—don't 'force dry' your guitar. If all the drying happens in one day, you're in trouble. Keeping it in the case when you're not playing is a big help—with or without a humidifier."

Bob: "Try to keep a new guitar from any real shock (whether dry or wet) for three or four years. Lots of unnecessary and wasteful repair work is avoided by using a soundhole humidifier during the dry months. At Taylor, we include a Dampit with each guitar because it works. The Dampit is almost useless without the soundhole cover, but magic with the cover. We know of repair shops that use Dampits to fix guitars!"

Don't oversoak the humidifier; be sure to squeeze it out enough. Check the guitar's progress daily. Let your guitar tell you when it needs moisture. If the action's low and buzzy, and the top shows little or no arch, then you probably need to use your humidifier. If you're using a Dampit or Ontek for the first time on a guitar that's already dried out, expect to refill it after the first day—your guitar's thirsty. Keep your axe in the case during weather extremes, and learn to "read" your guitar—it's a great humidity gauge. When needed, use a humidifier from fall till spring. Soundhole humidifiers are inconvenient, but they're better than facing major repairs.

No system is perfect, especially when dealing with delicate wooden instruments that exist in a variety of climates. What's good for my guitar may not be good for yours, but many guitars will benefit from the use of a soundhole humidifier.

Top repair tools and techniques

My cousin David reglued the bridge on his Silvertone by stacking volumes A through F of Encyclopedia Britannica on it, and it stayed on for a month! Not a bad job, eh? Amateurs attempt more top, bridge, and brace reglues than all other serious guitar repairs. That's why these pages are devoted to common repairs for the good old flat-top. First, we'll look at the specialized clamps that have been developed for repairing acoustic tops, and then learn how to use them the way the pros do.

Shown at right are the five common types of bridge and top clamps: the wooden cam, as well as models made by Ibex, Herco, Pony, and Waverly. Here's a description of these clamps and the jobs at which they excel, which should help you choose the right clamps for your toolbox.

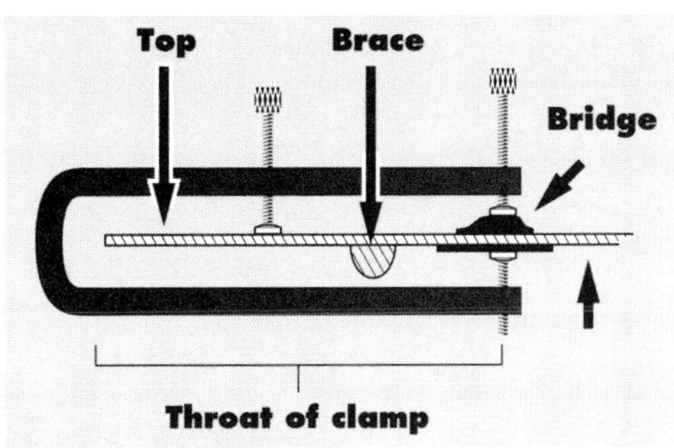

Clamps are chosen for their throat (reach), opening, weight, and strength, and are measured as illustrated above. Waverly and Herco clamps have an adjustable bottom jaw for getting around bracing—the size and shape of this bottom jaw is important—while the Ibex, Pony, and cam clamps have no bottom jaw at all.

Ibex clamps are cast aluminum, weigh 1 lb, and have a 6¼" throat and a 2¼" opening. Their lack of a bottom jaw gives them good grip and balance when clamped directly onto a brace or onto an interior caul (this caul is a hand-shaped scrap of wood used to protect against clamp marks, to spread gluing pressure, and to cut down on the number of clamps needed for the job). If I were allowed only three clamps for steel-string bridge reglues, I'd choose the Ibex variety. (Note: The most recent versions have substituted a plastic knob for the standard sliding T-bar handle. The plastic knob is not an improvement, and I encourage Ibex to go back to the old style.)

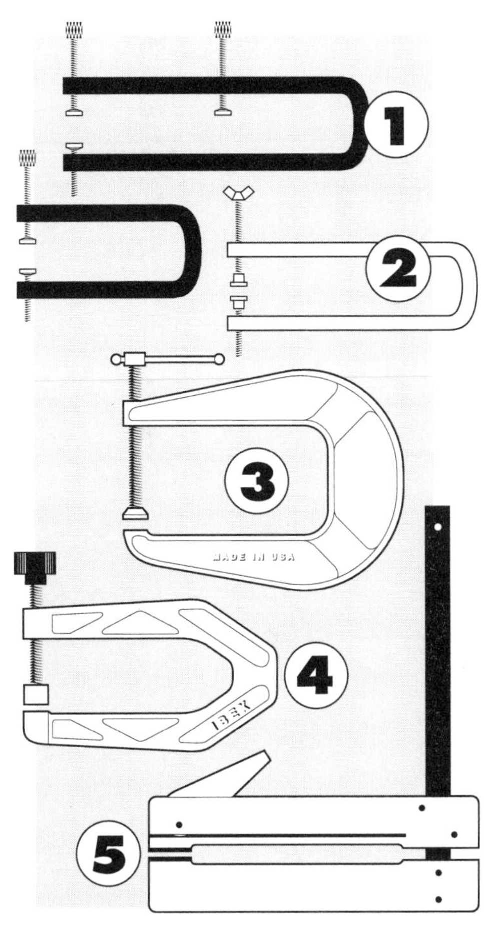

1 Waverly clamp
2 Herco clamp
3 Pony clamp
4 Ibex clamp
5 Cam clamp

The Klemmsia was the first commercially produced wooden cam clamp, but now several brands are available. Because of their large 8" opening, they perform all sorts of guitar repair and woodworking tasks. They're available in three throat depths: 3½", 5⅝", and 7¾", and weigh ½, ¾, and 1 lb, respectively. Like the Ibex, cam clamps have shallow, non-adjustable bottom jaws that balance and grip well (the cork-padded jaws' large surface area spreads gluing pressure well, and even without cauls, these clamps normally don't leave marks). With appropriate cauls to space around the braces, cams make adequate bridge clamps, and they are excellent for leveling cracks, gluing bracing, and many general shop tasks.

Herco bridge clamps are long C-clamps with a 2" opening, and are available in two throat sizes, standard (6⅝") and long (8½"). Each weighs just under 1 lb. Made of ½" x ¼" flat bar stock that's bent to form the "C" shape, these clamps tend to spring apart if too much pressure is applied, so don't over-tighten them. This style of clamp is important because you can fit lots of them in a soundhole, and the adjustable bottom foot allows you to get around the depth of the braces, as seen here. The long model is good for reaching way back to glue bracing, as well as for some bridge reglues on classical guitars. I often use the standard length to help out Ibex clamps during tricky bridge jobs, since they easily squeeze in between other clamps. Herco clamps are best for brace, crack, and bridge pad repair, or when used as helper clamps for bridge reglues. Herco has recently substituted a wing nut for the old knurled thumbscrew (like the Ibex plastic knob, not an improvement). I wish these clamp makers would leave well enough alone!

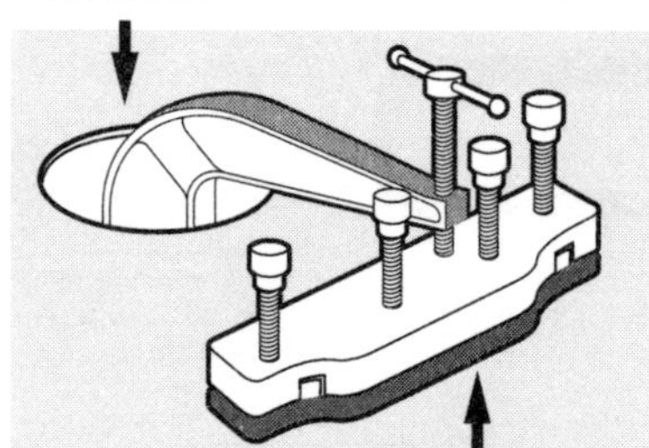

Ponys are the strongest. These heavy-duty cast clamps are used at Martin for bridge clamping—a long ($6\frac{1}{4}$" throat) model for classical bridges, and a short ($4\frac{3}{4}$") one for standard models. Martin uses only one clamp per bridge, relying on a special caul to do the rest of the job (above). Pony clamps have a $2\frac{11}{16}$" opening, and weigh as much as $2\frac{1}{2}$ lbs. Because these clamps are cumbersome and heavy, you would seldom use three, for example, to clamp a bridge. But for certain advanced repairs such as flattening a top, bridge pad replacement, or Martin-style bridge gluing, their incredible strength is just what's needed. Sometimes I'll use one Pony and two Ibex clamps for a bridge job.

Waverly is a newcomer to the long C-clamp market, and its products are available in three throat depths: $4\frac{5}{8}$" (short), $6\frac{7}{8}$" (standard), and $8\frac{3}{4}$" (long), with jaws opening to $2\frac{1}{2}$". Like the Hercos, they're made of bent steel, but they're thicker and don't spring easily. Built-in leveling jacks are an option on the standard and long models (see drawings, previous page). The levelers support the weight of the clamps by screwing against a caul laid across the top. Best of all, the jacks give extra pressure when needed to get perfect glue squeeze-out at the rear of a bridge. The short Waverly is able to clamp the entire shoulder area, and the area from the bridge in toward the soundhole. Being short, the clamp has more strength than its big brothers, so I'd use this for bridge reglues where I might not want the longer, "springier" types.

Regluing bridges, clamping cracks and loose braces

Inexperienced do-it-yourselfers should never attempt bridge removal and regluing on good instruments—it's hard enough to find a pro who will do it perfectly. Cracks are no different, and again you shouldn't learn on good guitars. A screwed-up crack repair, however, usually just makes a guitar look bad. It lowers its value, but at least you can still play the instrument. Screw up a bridge, and the guitar's finished until you can find a pro to make things right. This section focuses on teaching you how to begin bridge and crack work on low-quality instruments, and it should help you communicate with a professional when your guitar needs this type of work.

Bridges that are cracked, warped, poorly placed, loose, or lifted can have a detrimental effect on your guitar's intonation, tone, and playability. Bridge work is tricky and often fairly expensive, so consider the following points before attempting or authorizing any repairs. The most common mistakes made during bridge regluing are:

1 Gluing the bridge on crooked (out of square to the center line).

2 Mounting it too far toward the bass or treble side, so that the strings fall off the fingerboard.

3 Not recognizing when a bridge should be entirely replaced rather than simply being reglued.

4 Trusting that the factory mounted the bridge in the perfect spot (professionals always measure for themselves).

5 Failure to check inside the instrument for loose braces, etc., before you install the bridge.

6 Not letting the glue dry long enough. Allow a minimum of 24 hours for Titebond or hide glue, although two or three days is best.

7 Underestimating your own ability to do the job well!

Bridges that are only slightly loose at their back edge can often be reglued without being completely removed. This is done by forcing glue into the gap and clamping the bridge in place to dry. As a rule, if you can slide one empty guitar-string package into the opening, take it in for a checkup.

When a bridge is removed, the goal is to break or loosen the glue joint between the bridge bottom and the top wood (usually spruce, cedar, or mahogany). This isn't easy to do, so beginners should only remove bridges on instruments with cheap plywood tops! Here are several accepted bridge-removal methods:

1 Use a heat lamp to warm the glue joint, being sure to protect the top area around the bridge with heat deflectors. When the glue joint is softened, the bridge lifts off.

2 Strike the bridge/top glue line with a wide chisel to impact or shear it off.

3 Rout the bridge a little at a time with an appropriate router table and top protectors, and then warm up and peel off the last paper-thin layer. This method may sound extreme, but when done properly, there is little risk of damage to the top. Obviously, the router method is only appropriate when complete bridge replacement is necessary, and it should only be performed by a professional.

HERE ARE SOME IMPORTANT POINTS TO KEEP IN MIND:

- Generally speaking, bridges shouldn't be removed with hot knives, since this method often scars the finish. Telltale marks from a bridge reglue are an unwanted and unnecessary side effect.

- Some bridges warp up, curling away from the top. Once removed, a warped bridge can often be flattened by heating it, and then clamping it flat to dry into the proper shape. I have straightened a severely warped bridge by first soaking it in water, and then clamping it flat to dry.

- Cheap guitars may have finish under the bridge, allowing it to pull loose. Remove the finish to get wood-to-wood contact.

- A bridge may loosen because it's too flat to conform to the top's arch; it's not uncommon to carve the bridge bottom to match the top, or to make a new bridge with an arched bottom.

- The original glue surfaces must be free of dirt and old glue. A small scraper or the back of a chisel is best for cleaning the bridge area on the top (*sometimes* with a little help from a gel-type stripper).

- After the bridge is on, wait at least 15 minutes for any excess glue to squeeze out along the edges. With a damp rag, clean along the glue line until there's no squeeze-out left; you may have to clean the line four or five times.

- Too much glue is as bad as too little glue—another reason that experience is important for gluing a bridge on properly. Over-gluing or under-gluing can weaken any wood joint; visit a good cabinet shop to get a feel for glue techniques. Spruce absorbs glue into the grain, so practice on scrap.

My videotape *Bellyaches* really shows bridge and top repair up close (its available from Stewart-MacDonald).

With the exception of normal bridge reglues, many poor bridge repairs end up being done as a means of avoiding a neck reset. Avoid ruining a bridge simply because you don't yet know how to reset a neck—send the guitar to someone who does!

Whatever it is, it can be fixed—somehow, somewhere, by someone!

■ When installing a bridge, make cauls that match the bridge shape (right). Cauls spread clamping pressure and protect against clamp marks. It's wise to protect the guitar's interior—especially bracing—with cauls.

Speaking of cauls, a sheet of clear acrylic (Plexiglas) in a 1/8", 3/16", or 1/4" thickness makes a great exterior support for crack and brace work. Being flexible, acrylic can follow a top's arch while still keeping both sides of a crack level with each other (right; note the extra leveling screw). Its great strength, even in thin (1/8") sheets, gives the top protection from clamp marks and supports the pressure of clamped braces. The ability to see through a Plexiglas caul is a plus when lining up a clamp with a crack, especially when gluing the interior wooden crack supports known as cross patches (right). Also, acrylic won't stick to most common top-repair glues.

■ The two glues most often used for top repair are aliphatic resins such as Franklin's Titebond, or fresh hide glue such as Behlen's Ground Hide Glue (my favorite). Hot Stuff has its place on el cheapo top repairs or in special situations, but only when used by a pro. For the novice, Tite-Bond is the best all-around top-repair glue because it allows the most working time before it sets. Use it for everything *except* cracks (its high water content causes some cracks to swell). For cracks, stick with hide glue—it swells less and dries clear and brittle, like the finish surrounding it.

Many experts use hide glue for all vintage top repair, not only because it's historically correct, but also because the brittle qualities of hide glue enhance tone. Since it has a relatively brief shelf life, always check ready-mixed hide glue for dryness before using it. The best hide glue is mixed fresh daily from dried flakes. It sets quickly, so consider leaving it to the pros!

■ With loose braces, any loose flakes of old glue must be cleaned from the gap

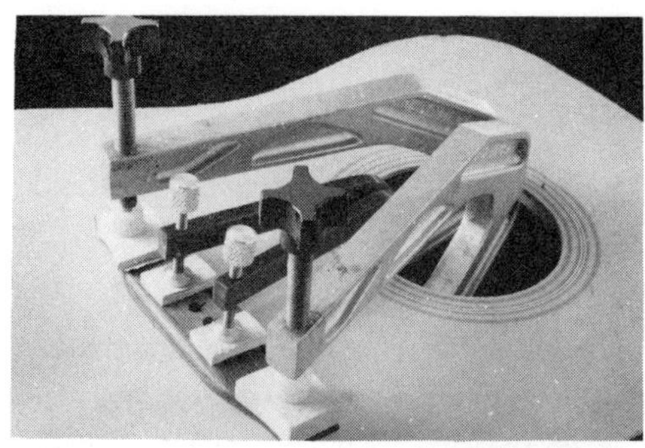

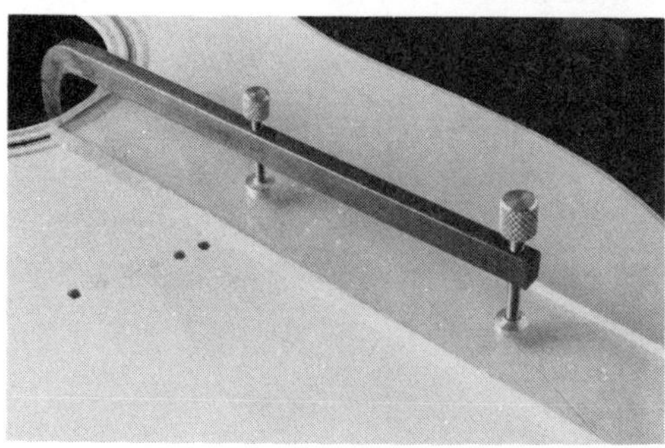

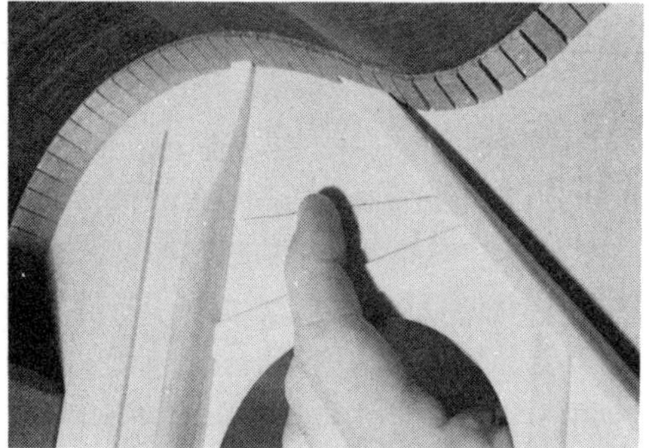

between the brace and the top before you'll get a good bond with new glue. You can get into these gaps with thin razor-saw blades, sandpaper, and feeler gauges to scrape, push, pull, and saw out the old glue. Most repairmen inject glue into the loose gap and then spread it around with thin metal feeler gauges to get good coverage. Again, be sure to use protective cauls on delicate spruce top bracing to avoid crushing the wood as well as to spread the gluing pressure over a larger area.

■ If you have any doubts about your ability to repair your acoustic's top, don't attempt it yourself. It can be fixed—somehow, somewhere, by someone. There are great repairmen (and -women) out there. Choose someone who will study the problem, and not just do the first thing that comes to mind. A person with the necessary skills, tools, and talent to do a given repair needs only the method—and that's often different every time. Since there's no one "right" way to do any of these repairs, figuring out the best approach is half the fun!

Winter cracks

Cracks are among the most common structural problems afflicting hollowbody guitars. Many a person has rushed his instrument to my shop, expecting me to read the last rites over his pride and joy just because of a simple split. While a split on the top, side, or back is certainly not to be ignored, if it's caught soon enough, it can be easily and inexpensively repaired—and quite invisibly, too. Guitars are, after all, made of wood, and wood splits. Of course, a mistreated guitar is bound to suffer damage. Too few people realize that lack of humidity can split even the best of instruments, causing as much of a crack as a sharp blow. In both cases, a simple hairline crack is easily repairable, often without the need of a professional repairman.

HAIRLINE CRACKS

These may be very hard to see; often you can only spot one when holding the guitar at a certain position in the right light. Hairline cracks can be mistaken for checks or crazes, which are finish cracks that should be left alone and are nothing to worry about (besides, they cannot be repaired without serious finish work that could hamper a guitar's tone and value). Many of us love a checked or crazed finish and feel that it adds to a guitar's charm and character.

Here's a simple test for determining whether a crack is actually in the wood: Using the ball of your thumb or fingertip, press very gently along the edge of the crack and watch for any movement of the wood. Avoid pressing your fingernail against the wood, since this could leave a mark. If the wood is actually cracked, you will see a slight movement of the wood—most likely on the side of the crack that you're pressing on, since the pressure won't transmit across the split line. For a round-hole acoustic, remove the strings and apply pressure from the inside. If you can reach it, get your fingertip right under the crack (see photo at bottom left), and press dead center. This should gently force the split open while you're looking from outside. Remember where you pressed, so that you can repeat the process later while gluing.

WIDE CRACKS

These won't close easily and cannot be repaired using the gluing method for hairline cracks about to be described. An open split that you can look into may need to be filled with a piece of matching wood. This process of splinting should be done by a professional. Often, but not always, a large crack will close up in the spring as humidity increases, and then it may be glued with little trouble and no splinting. In fact, if the crack was splinted when the humidity was low, the fill might be "spit out" by the wood as it attempts to close and return to normal. Therefore, let a professional determine whether a large crack should be filled during the dry season or left until spring and glued.

Hide glue is best for crack repair, although it's the hardest to use. Most profes-

If you use the granular hide glue, a Gerber's baby-bottle warmer makes a miniature "instant" glue pot. The one I use cost $9, and heats glue to 140° in 5 minutes! I use a kitchen meat thermometer to check the temperature.

sionals use dry hide glue granules mixed with water and heated in a glue pot, making a fresh batch each day. This hot glue sets quickly and takes practice in using. A high-quality hide glue is available from H. Behlen and many guitar shop suppliers. A good substitute is Franklin Hide Glue, which comes pre-mixed in small plastic bottles and has an additive that prolongs its working time. It can be found at most lumber yards and hardware stores; check the date, and don't buy glue over a year old. You can use Franklin Titebond, a well-known wood-working glue, but this can cause the crack to swell more than hide glue. It doesn't dry as clearly, and takes longer to dry thoroughly.

For the gluing and clamping operation, you'll need a bowl of warm water, some small pieces of clean cloth (3" x 3", some dipped in water and some dry), and good-quality masking tape that has lots of stretch. Squirt a dab of hide glue onto the fingertip of either hand, and then quickly use your free hand to move the crack in the same direction as you did earlier, only this time work the hide glue into the open crack. Work in enough so that when you release the pressure, a slight bead squeezes out. Wipe off excess glue with a damp rag, and then wipe the entire area dry in preparation for your tape "clamps."

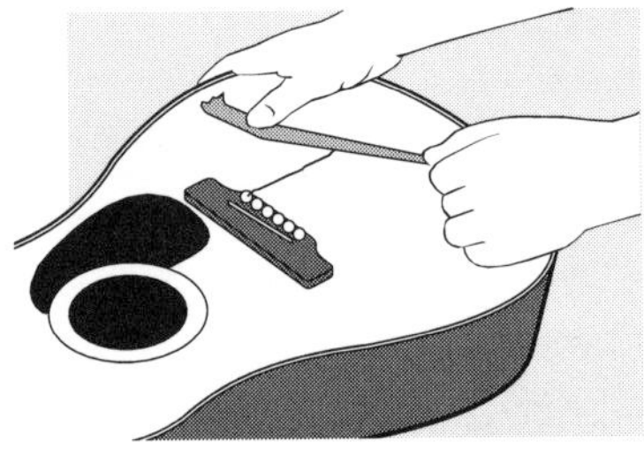

At a right angle to the crack's length, apply the masking tape by rubbing/pressing with your thumb two or three inches from one side of the crack. Stretch the tape up and over the crack—without actually touching the tape *to* the crack—and press it down again about two or three inches on the opposite side. If the tape is fresh and stretchy enough, the crack will close as the tape attempts to shrink back to size. Practice the taping operation with a dry run (no glue) until you get a feel for the tape's stretching qualities. Use as many pieces across the crack as necessary (sometimes I cover a crack completely for good pressure). If there's a glue squeeze-out each time you apply a piece of tape, wipe it off with a damp rag and re-dry the area so that the next piece of tape will stick. Let the glue dry at least 12 hours.

When the glue has dried, remove the tape by pulling at an angle (below). Peel it very carefully, since it's possible to remove small pieces of finish, especially on older instruments with thin, checked finishes. If you see finish coming off with the tape, rub the tape with your fingertip slightly ahead of the point where the tape is releasing from the body. This helps break the surface tension and allows easier removal of sticky tape. If you cleaned the glue bead well when it was still wet, you're done once the tape is removed. However, if there are still any dry glue beads that squeezed out, pick them off carefully with your fingernail or a sharp tool such as an X-acto knife. Buff the area with a soft, dry cloth and add any good guitar polish (Martin offers one).

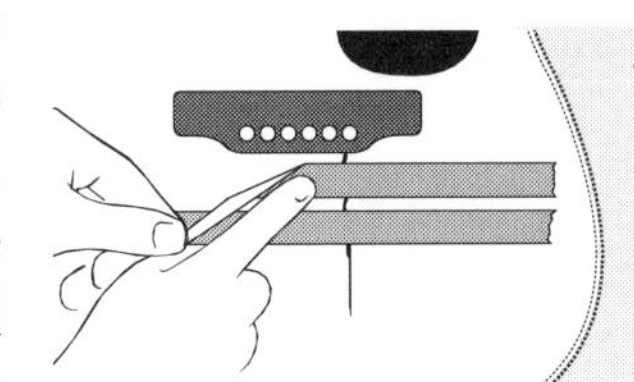

AVOIDING CRACKS

If you heat entirely with wood, keep a large kettle of water on or near the stove at all times to maintain some moisture in the air. Electric home humidifiers that are faithfully filled with water do a good job. There are also several in-case humidifiers available which were mentioned at the start of this chapter. You can make your own in-case humidifier by cutting a piece of kitchen sponge to fit a plastic soap box (the type used for storing soap when traveling) through which several small holes have been punched with an awl or icepick. Soak the sponge in water, squeeze out the excess until damp, and shut it in the plastic box. Kept in the accessory compartment of your case, this will help protect your guitar from cracks due to the excess dryness in winter.

Top cracks caused by curling pickguards

Being a Northerner from Michigan, I had adjustments to make when I moved south to Athens, Ohio—almost to the Mason-Dixon line. Things are different down here. Instead of "hello," we say "hey, bud," and the local term for "yes" is "yeah, boy!" The weather's different, too—an inch of snow closes the schools, and some years it's possible to play golf in February—on grass! But it's not always that way, and when there's cold weather and dry heat, it means trouble for guitars made of wood—especially acoustics.

Besides humidity, another dryness-related problem that affects acoustic guitars with solid wood tops is the shrinking and curling of the pickguard and the damage it can cause to the wood underneath. Martin guitars are especially prone to such troubles, as are most would-be Martin competitors. Here's a list of common pickguard problems, along with their symptoms and suggested repair methods.

Martin pickguards shrink because they're made from either nitrate (until '76) or acetate ('76 until present) plastic. Both are notorious shrinkers, with the older nitrate being the worst. But, along with their good looks, these plastics were chosen because they sound good, too—and Martin's tried them all. The shrinking plastic wouldn't be a problem if it didn't take the wood with it. That's why Martin switched to pickguards backed with double-stick adhesive in late 1987; this modern adhesive allows the wood to move.

Wood needs the freedom to shrink in the dry winter months and swell during the humid summer. Up until 1987, the backs of Martin pickguards were brushed with a solvent to melt the plastic, and "glued" directly to the bare wood before the finish was applied. These glue joints don't move well with the wood, and as a result problems could occur: shrink cracks at the pickguard's inner or outer edges; curling of the pickguard and the top wood, sometimes causing the top wood to pull away from the main X-brace; or the pickguard falling off totally.

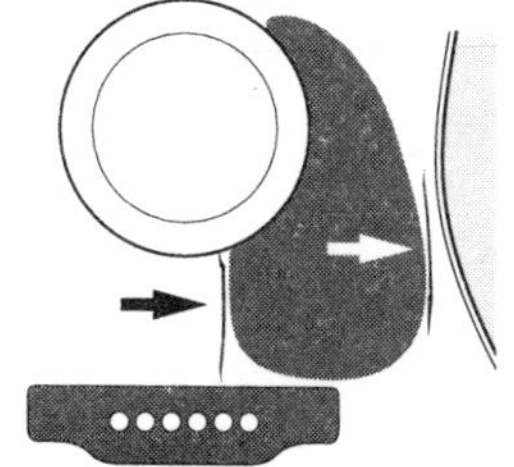

Shrink cracks along the pickguard's edge take years to get very big. Some aren't even visible, and lay just under the pickguard's edge, soaking in moisture, sweat, grime, and guitar polish, all of which make any problem worse. Caught early, a small shrink crack can be sealed with lacquer or glue; this keeps it small and prevents it from absorbing moisture until it stabilizes.

A crack that's wide and stable and no longer swells shut in summer can be splinted (filled with a sliver of wood—usually spruce —to match the top). Before gluing in a splint, I use a "crack knife" to clean dirt from the crack and make its walls parallel and slightly tapered to keep the spruce fill from falling through. This crack knife (pictured at right) was designed by the Martin repair department. You'll find a more detailed description of it on page 48 of Irving Sloane's excellent book *Guitar Repair*. Most of the photos in the book were taken in the Martin repair department, and a chapter is devoted to pickguard repair. A well-chosen splint of wood, matched in color and grain pattern and then carefully touched up with lacquer, is an almost invisible repair when done by a pro.

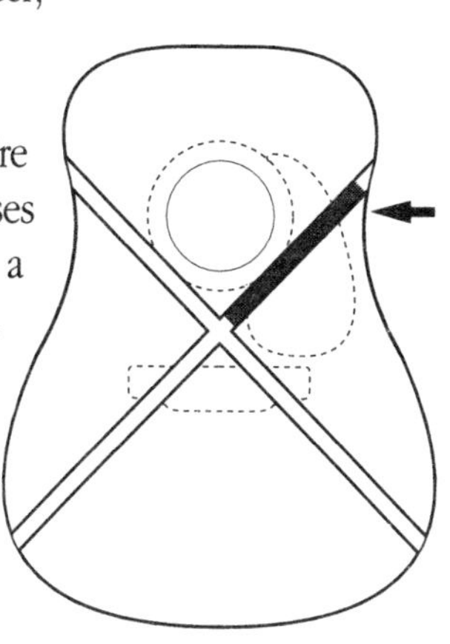

Curling pickguards, and the wood they're glued to, are upsetting—even mild cases look scary. Severe curling may create a concave dip in the top, pulling the wood loose from the main X-brace (indicated by the arrow on the drawing at right). By the way, loose braces should be fixed before using the crack-splinting techniques just mentioned. When appropriate,

I've seen very few good old guitars with nitrate pickguards that didn't have some sort of shrinkage problem—but it never kept me from wanting them.

the pickguard can be removed to let the wood relax and flatten before being reglued to the brace. Removing the pickguard without pulling up spruce is tricky, so only have it done by a professional shop with prior experience.

The mildest problems are pickguards that come either partially or completely loose of their own accord. The relief of stress often prevents any cracks, curls, or loose braces, so it's nice if nature does the job for you. A pickguard that's only loose around the edges can be reglued (at least temporarily) with white glue or hide glue and then clamped in place to dry. Don't use a permanent solvent-type glue such as Duco or super glue. In general, it's best to take a pickguard off and then reglue or replace it.

When a pickguard's off, any glue residue should be removed from the top, and the bare wood should be sealed before any remounting is done. I generally seal the bare wood with a coat or two of lacquer or shellac. Once dry and sanded smooth, the hard surface gives future adhesives something to cling to rather than the wood itself. As for the proper remounting glue, follow Martin's lead—use double-stick adhesive, or buy a real Martin pickguard. If you make your own pickguard, mount it with a spray adhesive such as 3M-77 or use double-stick adhesive carpet tape. And don't mount it on the bare wood!

Neck resets

If you own an acoustic guitar with a stiff, hard-to-play action, or if it isn't as loud as you might wish, don't be alarmed if your guitar surgeon suggests an operation called a neck reset. The life of your favorite guitar may depend upon your knowing the basics of this common yet difficult surgery. This is not a "how-to" for hobbyists, but a basic rundown of the neck resetting process as I know it.

The need for a neck reset is generally a natural result of the settling of an instrument's wood and joints. This movement of the top, sides, back, and neck block, coupled with the up-pull on the neck and top exerted by string pressure, can cause the strings to gradually rise further from the fingerboard. Other reasons for resetting a neck include improper fit to begin with (causing poor action that becomes more noticeable and unbearable with age), and glue joint failure (often due to dryness), where the neck is pulling away from the body. If the guitar has great action but isn't putting out the volume it should, it could be due to a low bridge saddle (backtrack to the section on saddle set-ups for details). Resets are often performed just to allow the luthier to raise the saddle height and drastically improve a guitar's sound.

A new guitar with any of these problems may be a candidate for factory warranty repair; your repairman will know. In general—especially with older guitars—don't blame the maker, but accept the settling as natural and often unavoidable for a delicately made acoustic instrument. Whether it's used or new, if you really care about your guitar, be willing to pay for the job out of your own pocket, and have it done by a skilled repairman with whom you can discuss the instrument. Use the following information as a basis for discussing the methods to be employed.

Before work is started, the luthier must determine the best method for separating the neck and body joint. Most often, this involves a "dovetail" joint (previous page). The preferred method is to first loosen the fingerboard tongue with heat, and then steam the joint apart by removing the fret just past the body joint. This is done by drilling a small hole and injecting steam into the dovetail joint. This method usually works for Gibson, Martin, Guild, Gretsch, Harmony, Kay, and most other traditional American guitars. Some of the joints and glue used on the less-expensive imports, however, have surprised more than one luthier, myself among them. Prior experience and quick decision-making are a necessity for good results.

Luthier Charlie Longstreth, who services both Light's For Music in Springfield, Oregon, and McKenzie River Music in nearby Eugene, came across a neck removal set-up that makes for a clean steam operation. It's an Erlenmeyer flask from a chemistry lab with two glass tubes in the rubber stopper top—one for the wet, boiling steam to enter (where it leaves much of the moisture behind) and the other for the "dry" steam to exit on its way to the neck joint (below). This is not a tool you'd try yourself, but a good one to tell your luthier about if he's using a steamer without a moisture trap. He'll know the safety precautions to take with steam. Dry steam causes less swelling and finish problems than the other methods.

After steaming, the neck is gently pulled up and out of the dovetail socket. Any excess glue is quickly removed while still wet, and the neck/fingerboard and top/neck block joints are gently clamped until dry (eliminating possible over-swelling of the joints).

Once the wood is thoroughly dry, a small portion of the neck heel is trimmed away with an extremely sharp chisel (right), changing the neck-to-body angle and bringing the strings closer to the fingerboard. Much experience and a keen eye are needed for knowing how much wood to remove during this heel shaping. If you get the opportunity, ask to see and play a completed neck set done by a shop you're looking into.

It's not uncommon for a neck reset to require some fret work afterward—either partial, total, or touch-up. The need for fret work can usually be judged beforehand, but remember that when wood is heated and steamed apart, a lot of changes such as loosened frets and swelling can occur. Remember, fret work is often the way of

There's a detailed article on neck resetting by William Cumpiano in issues 5, 6, 7, 8, and 10 of *The String Instrument Craftsman.* Find the back issues and check out those articles!

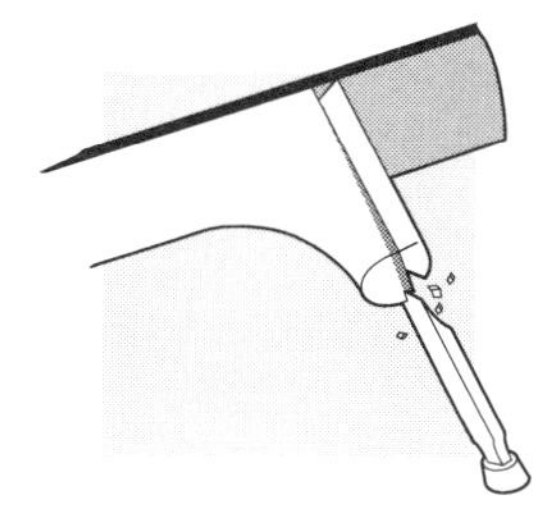

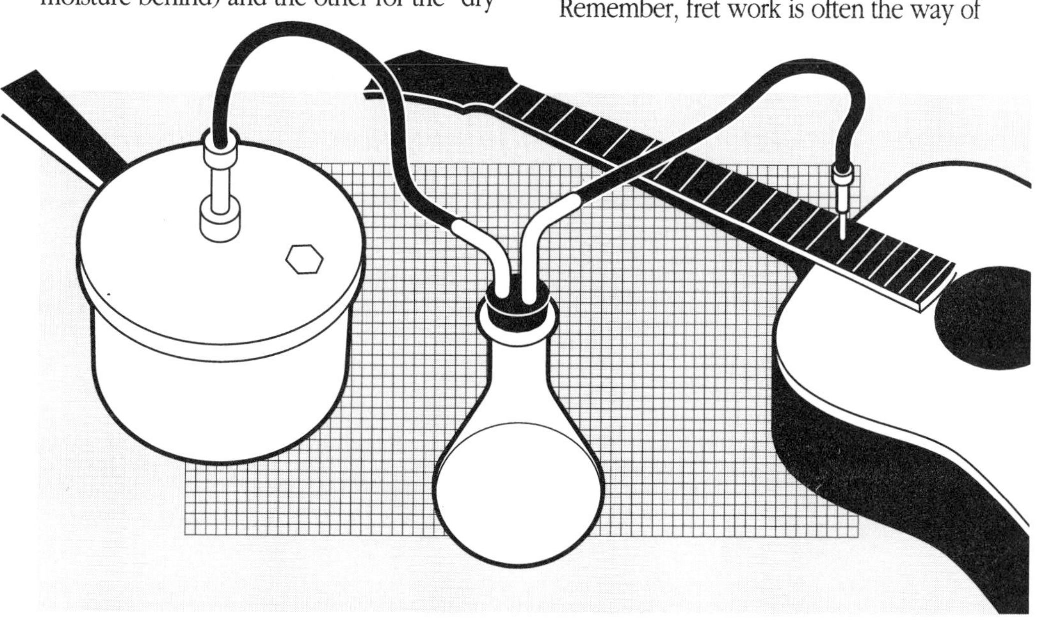

controlling the instrument's final playability. On a difficult neck removal, minor damage to the finish caused by escaping steam may also be encountered, requiring expert touch-up. This is something the luthier can predict in most cases.

The easy resets are the older guitars constructed with animal glue, which requires little heat and steam. The toughies are guitars built with modern glues and those with wide, thin heels (some Guild and Gibson models) that have more glue area. Wide heels tend to swell and crack from the steam, too. Guitars with fingerboard binding require special care to avoid burning or melting the plastic during the reset process. Neck resets aren't so simple, are they?

The principles governing flat-top acoustic guitar resets apply also to arch-top acoustics and electric guitars. As a rule, these guitars don't require resets often, thanks to their adjustable bridges. Exceptions are old Les Pauls with trapeze tailpieces, some mid-'70s SGs and Les Pauls with shallow neck angles, and occasional semi-hollowbody ES models, especially those with non-Bigsby tremolos. Most of these Gibson neck-set problems are solved by slightly grinding down the bottom of the bridge. When you find a Gibson solidbody requiring a reset, expect to lay out some dough, since they aren't easy, even for the factory pros. Early Gretsch guitars are often found to have loosened at the dovetail and fingerboard extension. But don't shy away from buying an old Gretsch because of neck problems—once fixed and set up right, they're hard to beat.

A variation for neck resetting involves removing the fingerboard tongue over the body to reach the joint, rather than removing the neck and fingerboard as one (when this method is used, the fingerboard should be cut a few frets up the neck—not at the body joint—to keep a strong wood joint). Another way is to loosen only the fingerboard and "slip" the neck by bending it back into perspective; or the back, side, and neck-block joints can be loosened to squeeze the heel in. Of these last three methods, the first is permissible in some situations, but the latter two "slip 'n' squeeze" methods should only be used on inexpensive quickies.

A neck reset is nothing to fear, but find the right person for the job. Get more than one luthier's opinion. Barring unforeseen problems, a neck reset will probably last 20 years or more, maybe even a lifetime, if the wood has truly finished settling. For getting a less-than-perfect flat-top to play and sound its best, neck resets are as important as good fret work and well-fit nuts and saddles.

The basic tools

With the exception of rare, vintage instruments, guitar electronics is one area of repair where a novice usually doesn't do much permanent damage. Sloppy solder joints can always be done over, and even if you burn something up, buying new parts is easy. Electronics never came easy for me, and I'm no Craig Anderton, Dan Armstrong, or Seymour Duncan—but I can teach you the basics, and let you take it from there. Here are some helpful books, listed in what I consider to be their order of importance as they pertain to electronics. They're all valuable, and are available through bookstores, music stores, and guitar shop suppliers: Donald Brosnac's *Guitar Electronics For Musicians*, Adrian Legg's *Customizing Your Electric Guitar*, Hideo Kamimoto's *Complete Guitar Repair*, Melvyn Hiscock's *Make Your Own Electric Guitar*, and Bill Foley's *Build Your Own Electric Guitar*. Let's start by outfitting a basic guitar electronics toolbox, and learn what each tool does. Then we'll put the knowledge to use.

Break open a few pots, mini switches, and other components, and you'll really learn how they work!

To excel in guitar electronics, you must be able to take guitars apart and put them back together with your eyes closed. Removing control cavity cover plates, pickups, pickguards, bridges, tailpieces, potentiometers, selector switches, and the like is common—even for the simplest repair. Use an ice-cube tray as a parts organizer, since losing parts is the nemesis of many an otherwise well-meaning repairman. And if you don't know guitar parts well, draw a map of which parts went where. Disassembly/assembly tools are the basis of an electronics tool box, and you may have many of them already. On the next page is a list of the basic tools, most of which are shown in the accompanying photo.

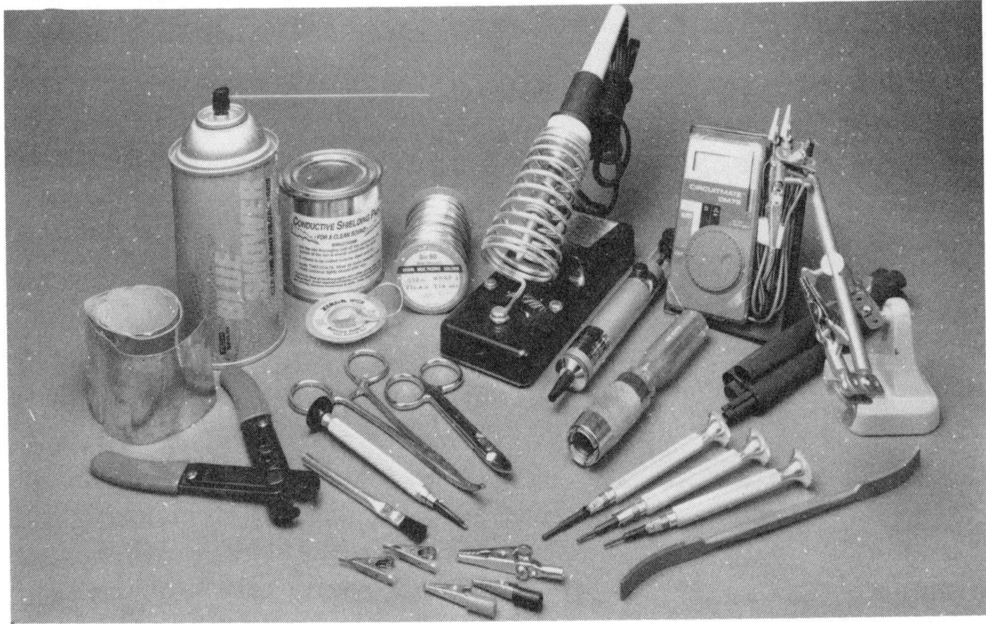

- Small screwdrivers from size 0 to 2 in Phillips and flat-blade.
- Sockets, open-end wrenches, and nut drivers in the $\frac{1}{4}$" to $\frac{1}{2}$" range (you'll find uses for these tools in metric sizes, too).
- Needle-nose pliers, wire cutters, small wire snips, and hemostats.
- An inspection mirror is handy for finding a problem without removing anything.

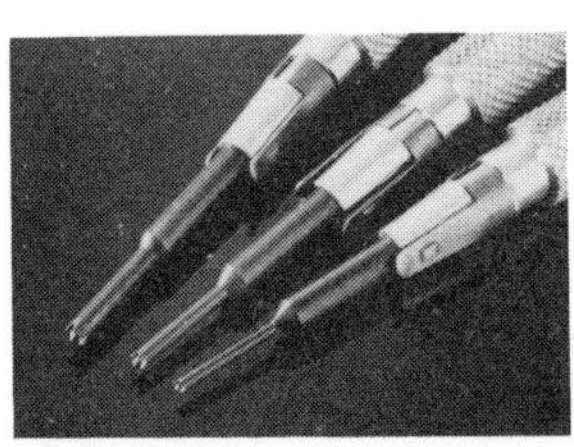

- Screw extractors to remove screws with stripped heads (left). You'll love this tool if you've ever tried to remove miniature screws with slots that are rusted, filled with dirt, stripped and mangled, or a combination of these problems (especially Gibson's Phillips-head pickup mounting ring screws!).

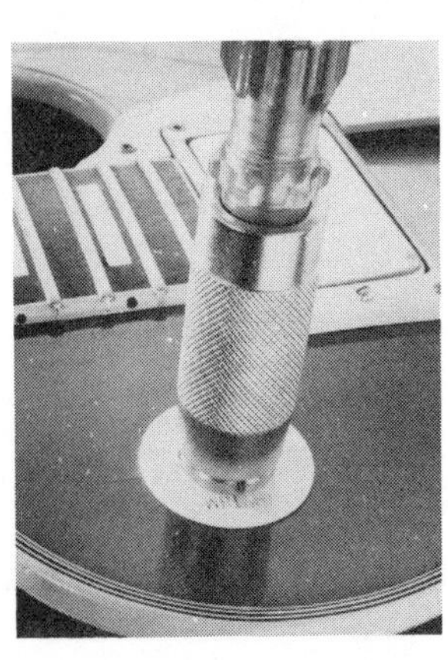

- Switch-nut wrench (left). This uncommon but valuable tool is used for removing the knurled nut on a toggle switch. Most repairmen have seen lots of vintage switch nuts mauled by slipping pliers or Vise-Grips.
- Soldering iron. I generally use an Ungar 45-watt pencil type with small and medium chisel tips, and an insulated stand to set it in while hot. With most guitar electronics, you want to get on and off the part fast, and the little 15- or 20-watt pencils don't cut the mustard (but they are handy for some delicate parts like transistors).
- A de-soldering tool, or "solder-sucker," is a mechanical device that cocks like a dart gun and creates a vacuum when you release the trigger. It's used for sucking molten solder away from parts. Another type uses a rubber squeeze-bulb; it looks like an ear syringe, but it's Teflon-lined so the solder doesn't burn through.
- Solder. Use a 60/40 resin core in a small diameter (.032"). Never use acid-core solder in guitar electronics!
- A soldering jig, also known as a "third hand," has a weighted base and adjustable arms with alligator-clip "hands" that keep delicate parts aligned for soldering. Several brands and styles are available.
- Wire strippers save a lot of time and hassle. Get one with an adjustable stop to control diameter. The simple type sold by General works fine.
- An X-acto or razor knife with the #11 blade helps in stripping insulation length-wise and for delicately cutting the insulation of small wire sizes before stripping.

■ Some sort of electronics probe or sharp, fine-pointed dental tool is needed to fish wire through holes, separate braided shielding, etc. The curved dental type can grab around potentiometer shafts and snake them through mounting holes.

■ Heat-sinks clip temporarily onto the leads of delicate parts being soldered or de-soldered. These clips absorb heat, keeping it from running up the wire and burning the part. The small (1" to 1½") brass, copper, or aluminum alligator clips sold at Radio Shack work well.

■ Jumper cables. Small lengths of wire with alligator clips at each end, these are used for temporarily checking a wiring plan before soldering it together.

■ A curved bottom file to remove plating or oxidation from the back of potentiometers that won't take solder; 220-grit sandpaper also works.

■ Tuner cleaner and lubricant is used to flush out and lubricate "scratchy-sounding" and stiff or sticky volume and tone controls. Blue Shower and Blue Stuff are two good brands.

■ The multi-meter, also known as an ohmmeter or VOM (volt-ohm meter), is the most important tool. It's used to diagnose most of a guitar's electrical ills. A good meter doesn't cost much—from $30.00 to $50.00 buys a nice one. Choose one that reads DC resistances of at least 500,000 ohms. Its main uses in our business are described in the deep guitar electronics section that follows.

These are the basic tools; use this as a shopping list as you add to your toolbox. Now, let's look at supplies such as wire, shielding materials, and switches, and then spend some time working at the bench.

Wire, shielding, and capacitors

One of the best all-around wire types for guitar electronics is tinned, stranded copper wire. Being stranded, it bends easily without breaking, and the tinning (which turns the copper to a silver color) means the wire's ready to solder with no additional tinning necessary. Choose a wire to suit your needs from the following list. Except for the last one, they're all tinned, stranded copper:

■ Single-conductor wire with a plastic insulating jacket. This is usually black, red, or white—your basic "hookup" wire; shielding isn't necessary.

■ Single-conductor, as above, but with Teflon insulation that resists soldering-iron heat. It won't melt in extra-hot situations.

■ Coaxial, or "co-ax," is a single-conductor wire with an insulating sleeve wrapped in a braided shield that protects the inner core from interference. This wire is used as a ground in many situations. Some co-ax types have a plastic outer jacket, while others have only the wire braid. Most Gibson pickup leads are this type of wire, having a stranded core, black cloth insulation, and an outer braid that's used as the ground.

■ Coaxial, as above, but with non-melting Teflon insulation.

■ Four-conductor with foil shield, a fifth—stranded—ground wire, and a plastic jacket. This "multi-lead" wire is used for four-wire humbucking pickup conversions. The foil shield is the best you can get—90% effective.

■ Last of all, it's convenient to have small-gauge (22 to 25) hookup wire. Usually solid copper, single-strand wire makes a good jumper for short runs such as criss-crossed terminals on mini switches, etc. It also makes a good, strong ground wire.

If you're doing electrical work, make it a *habit* to double-check your shop when you leave, making sure you haven't left on a soldering iron or anything else that might cause a fire. And if you wake up at 2:00 AM wondering if you left something on, get your butt out of bed and go check!

SHIELDING YOUR GUITAR'S CIRCUIT

This helps give you a hum-free signal. Using shielded wire wherever possible is a good bet, but you can further improve your sound by shielding the body cavities, wire channels, and pickguard with conductive shielding paint or copper foil. The paint is laced with nickel, which creates a conductive barrier that AC hum and radio signals can't penetrate. Shielding paint is easy to use, if you follow these directions:

■ Work in a well-ventilated area and use an OSHA-approved, vapor-barrier respirator.

■ Wear eye protection.

■ Use cheap, throwaway "acid brushes" to apply it.

■ Build up two coats, and test your work using your multi-meter set to its continuity scale. Touch two different areas to see if you get a beep or visual reading.

■ The shield is conductive, so it must not touch any part of the circuit other than the ground, or it could short the circuit.

■ When you're finished shielding, run a wire from the shield to ground. The more carefully you shield, the better your signal will be.

Copper foil is a great shield. Shielding a surface such as the back of a pickguard is easy with foil, and cleaner than paint. But doing a body cavity is a different story. Foil comes in rolls or sheets with a self-stick back; you peel away the protective layer, and it sticks to almost anything (mostly your hands). Shielding a cavity with foil is like making a slip cover for a couch or chair: You cut different pieces to shape (the bottom, sides, etc.) and then "paste" them in place with the self-stick. Let one piece overlap the other by ¼", and then solder each joint—this is the ultimate shield!

Heat-shrink tubing is God's gift to wiring. By sliding it onto one of two wires to be joined (or one wire to be insulated from another) *before soldering*, you can do away with sticky electrical tape or masking tape, which turns stiff, yellow, and crumbly. Heat-shrink, or "spaghetti tubing," as it's known, comes in a wide range of sizes for any wiring task, and it makes even sloppy work look professional. It insulates wires that shouldn't touch, and its stiffening effect strengthens connections.

Choose heat-shrink in a size that not only slides over a given wire, but fits back over the *solder joint* once a connection is made. Always use the smallest size you can get by with, and slide it as far away from a connection as possible while you solder. Wait until the solder cools before sliding the heat-shrink over the new joint; then heat it with a match and watch it shrink and compress tightly around the wires. Rotating the wire as you heat the tubing creates a uniform contraction (professionals use heat-shrink guns similar to small hair dryers). Multiple wires going to a common terminal point can be heat-shrunk together as a unit to make their combined diameter smaller; this makes it much easier to thread wires through drilled holes and wiring channels.

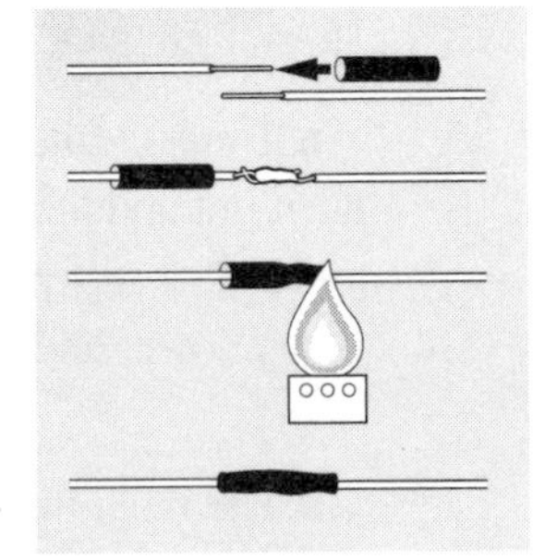

Capacitors play an important part in guitar electronics, since they control your instrument's tone. Older guitars have the "Tootsie Roll" type with multi-colored rings to denote their value, while more modern instruments use either thin ceramic disks or the square, plastic-dipped type. The job of the "cap" is to ground, remove, or bleed off the treble (highs) from the signal. Most single-coil pickups (such as those on Strats) use a .05μF (microfarad) capacitor, while humbuckers (Les Pauls) use a .02μF. As Gibson's Tim Shaw points out: "Gibsons have darker-sounding pickups and need smaller capacitors to cut off fewer highs. Our usual guitar capacitor value is .02µF. Fenders, on the other hand, have more top end and traditionally use larger caps to be able to roll off more highs. Fender's guitar caps are usually .05µF. Basses can be .05µF, or even .1µF. These values are for high-impedance circuits only. The lower the impedance, the higher the capacitor value. EMG pickups, for instance, use much higher capacitor values in their tone controls." Changing to a cap of a different value alters your guitar's tone without hurting anything, since you can always get back to your starting point. Learn more about capacitors in Donald Brosnac's *Guitar Electronics For Musicians* and Adrian Legg's *Customizing Your Electric Guitar.*

HERE ARE SOME SOLDERING TIPS TO KEEP IN MIND:

■ Use a soldering iron rated anywhere from 15 to 45 watts. In a novice's hand, the lighter-duty iron has less chance of burning up a part.

■ It's not uncommon to own and use soldering irons of several watt ratings. The 45-watter is *my* favorite all-around iron, although it's a little hot in some delicate situations.

■ Keep your iron's tip *tinned* (shiny with solder) from the moment you first turn it on, and clean it often during use by wiping it on a damp sponge.

■ A tip that doesn't get tinned the first time it's used may burn up and never do a good job of soldering.

■ Don't forget to use heat-sinks on delicate work (left).

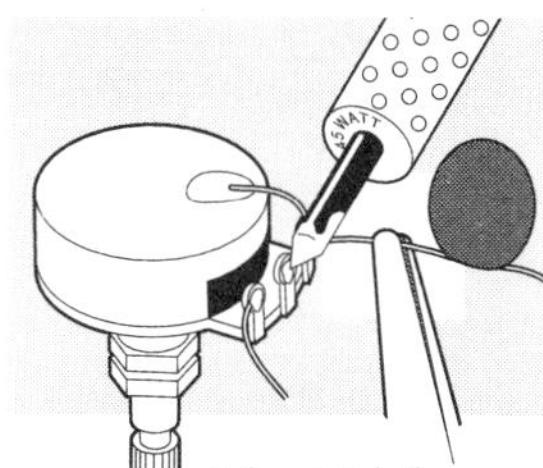

A heat-sink (here, a pair of hemostats) absorbs heat before it can pass down the wire to delicate parts.

Troubleshooting with a multi-meter

Guitar electronics runs deep. Only a fool (I saw that smirk) would suggest that the subject could be "taught" in a single chapter of a book. I'll be happy if you just learn these basics here: how to use a multi-meter to troubleshoot problems and test parts, how to replace a simple part like a potentiometer or an output jack, how to shield a guitar, the correct way to solder and de-solder, and how to replace a pickup. From there, you can dive on in and swim as deep as you like. Let's get started.

I use the "credit-card"-type multi-meter. The particular model is a Circuitmate DM78, although I'm sure there are other equally good brands. It's small, inexpensive (around $35.00), has a digital readout (a needle/scale combo can be hard to read, especially on an inexpensive meter), and auto-ranging, which means it finds the correct range automatically, and you don't need a degree from M.I.T. to use it! The meter's four settings are DC voltage, AC voltage, ohm scale (for reading resistance in ohms), and continuity. You won't be needing the AC voltage range for guitar electronics, but the other three settings are used all the time.

The DC voltage scale is handy for checking batteries. A guitar with a preamp, active pickups, or active circuitry needs its batteries checked often. Put the meter's black lead on negative and the red lead on positive for an instant battery check. Any 9-volt battery that reads less than 7 volts should be discarded. Using a meter sure beats laying your tongue across the terminals to see how big a charge you get!

Continuity testing's easy, and if your meter has a beeper, which mine does, you can see and *hear* continuity. In the meter's

When you find a bad part, *throw it out.* Repairmen tend to save broken parts such as pots and switches, thinking they'll have some use for them. Eventually the bad stuff mixes with the good, and you have to re-test everything. Chuck 'em!

continuity setting, touching both probes to any conductive surface or surfaces (ends of a wire, copper-foil or conductive-paint shielding, pickup-cover to ground, bridge to ground, etc.) lets you know if there's an uninterrupted connection or a dead short.

Working with the ohms scale always makes me feel like I know something. Use the ohms function to check pickups: Look at the output wire(s) coming from any standard single-coil or humbucking pickup, and you'll see a hot lead and a ground lead. These may be two separate wires, or a single-conductor (hot) coaxial wire with a braided shield used as ground. Touch one test probe (red or black, it makes no difference) to the hot wire and one to the ground wire. This gives you a reading of the pickup's DC resistance in ohms. A Strat pickup, for example, should read from 5.5–6.75k ohms, and a standard Gibson humbucker should read from 7.2k to 8k ohms (new ones are 7.6k ohms). Some hot humbuckers, such as Gibson Dirty Fingers and DiMarzio Super Distortion, read twice that—12k to 14k ohms. Since it has two coils, the humbucking pickup is generally more powerful than a single-coil, but not always. A modern 4-wire pickup has four leads coming out of it, and each coil can be read separately; they should read the same. Pickups or coils with weak ohm readings or none at all are defective and must be repaired, rewound, or replaced.

On the pickup at left, white is hot, black is ground. At right, the braided shield is ground and the inside is the hot lead.

TESTING, CLEANING, AND REPLACING POTS

Because of wear, dirt, spilled drinks, dust, etc., a "bad" pot either doesn't work at all (no volume or tone change), has a scratchy, dirty sound, or only works intermittently. In most cases, simply spray-cleaning a pot cures its symptoms. Two good brands of "tuner" cleaner are Blue Stuff and Blue Shower. Some brands don't do a good job and can actually cause a pot to freeze up—a nightmare on a vintage piece! Stick the cleaner's hose tip into the opening in the side of the pot's case, and spray liberally. Tilt the piece, so the cleaner can run back out as it flushes the pot while you turn the shaft on and off to clean the contacts. If your guitar has sealed pots with no hole to spray into, remove the knob and pull up lightly on the shaft. You'll see a little movement. Squirt here, and the very thin cleaner usually finds its way to the problem. Contact cleaners are available from radio/TV service shops. Don't forget to wear safety glasses, and be sure to protect the guitar's finish and your table top from the cleaner. If cleaning doesn't cure its ills, test the pot with your meter.

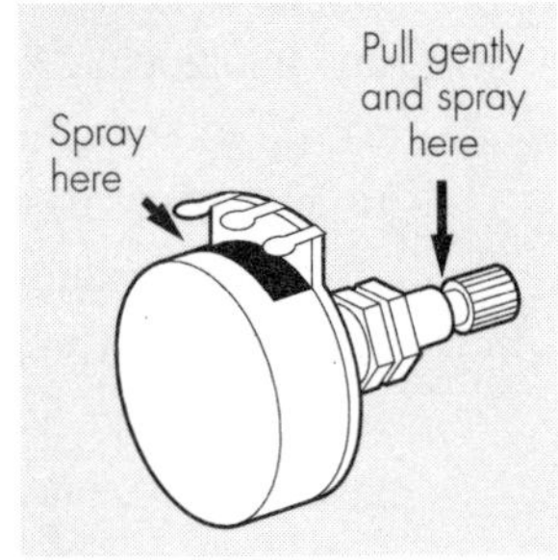

Again, set the meter to the ohm scale and practice on a pot that isn't wired into a circuit. Using both probes, touch one to each of the *outer* two lugs for an instant, true reading of the pot's resistance. Now, if you put the test probes on an outer lug and a *center* lug, the resistance will vary from 0 ohms to the true rating of the pot (250k, or whatever) as you turn the pot's shaft. You can test a pot that's wired into a circuit using the above method, but note: On a pot with a pickup wired to one lug and an outside lug bent to the case and soldered/grounded (as with most volume pots), you must de-solder one of these two connections—either the pickup or the grounded lug (above)—before you get the pot's reading. Without de-soldering, you simply get a reading of the pickup itself. If there is no pickup wired to a pot, the bent-back/soldered lug poses no problem, and you can test the pot normally. If a pot's good, re-solder the parts you disconnected, and you're back in business. A pot that isn't within 20% of its rating should be replaced.

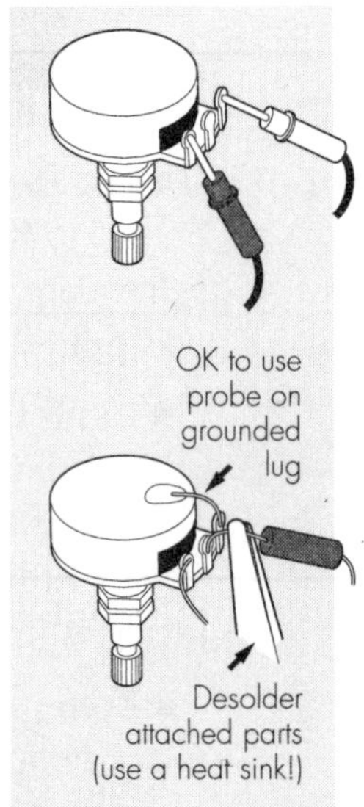

Soldering techniques

Replacing a pot is pretty easy, if you can get at it. Teles, Strats, and Les Pauls have easy access, but a 335 can be a toughie. You might be wise to make a drawing of which wires or parts went where. Most pots have delicate wires and many have a ceramic capacitor wired to them. Protect these parts by clipping heat-sinks to the leads before de-soldering. The operation is made easier if you use a solder-sucker, so it can't reflow and harden as soon as you remove the iron. When the pot's free, remove it and *throw it out*—you don't want to start saving them.

When you solder in a new pot of the same rating, *tin* the connections first; this means adding solder to the lugs and to the metal case before re-installing the wires (any wires or capacitors are still tinned from the original installation). When parts are tinned before soldering, the actual connection takes place much quicker. Touch the soldering iron to the part, let it heat up, and then flow the solder to the *part*—not the iron's tip. A good solder joint looks slippery, shiny, and silvery—not dull, grayish, and dry. Solder spits, so wear protective goggles, button up your shirt collar (and no shorts or short-sleeved shirts!), and protect any good finishes nearby (guitar, table top, etc.).

Mini switches

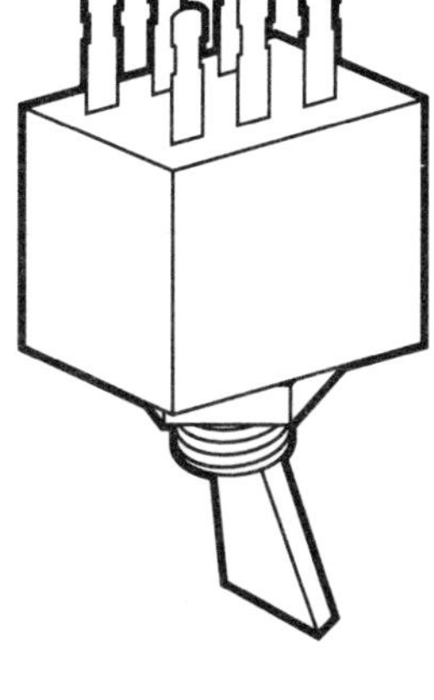

Still with us? Man, don't let these pages get you too "wired"! If it gets to be too much, take a break and do a fret job or something. Actually, this guitar electronics stuff should be a welcome change from super glue, wood scraps, lacquer, stains, loose bridges, clamps, and dirty hands—there's nothing here but good hot solder, the trusty multimeter, and nice, clean parts to wire.

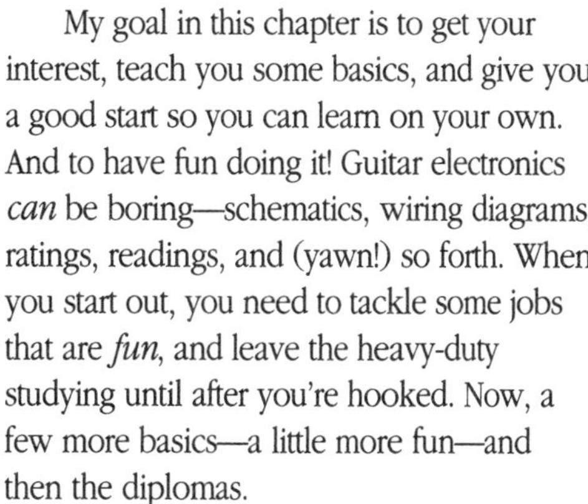

My goal in this chapter is to get your interest, teach you some basics, and give you a good start so you can learn on your own. And to have fun doing it! Guitar electronics *can* be boring—schematics, wiring diagrams, ratings, readings, and (yawn!) so forth. When you start out, you need to tackle some jobs that are *fun*, and leave the heavy-duty studying until after you're hooked. Now, a few more basics—a little more fun—and then the diplomas.

Mini switches are as important to guitar electronics as capacitors, potentiometers, shielding paint, and the like. These little toggle switches control most of the hot-rod and custom wiring options you're likely to try ("dual-sound," pickup phasing, coil cutting, series/parallel, etc.). Because of their small size, you can fit one or more of these switches into most control cavities without having to use a router to enlarge or re-shape the cavity walls; and for mounting, you only need to drill a 1/4" hole for the small shaft.

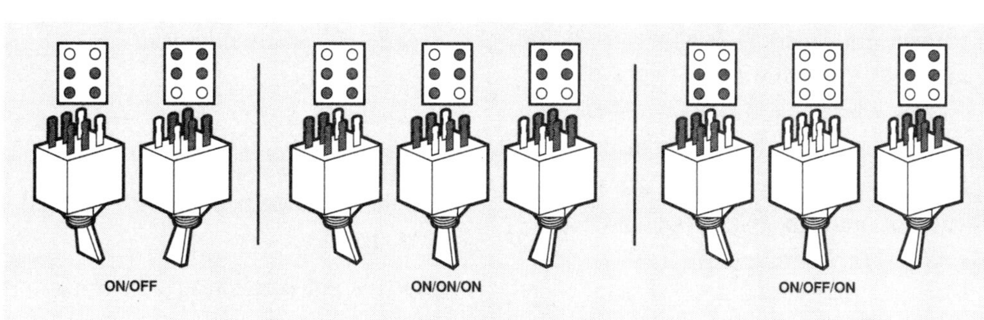

If space is tight or you don't wish to drill a ¼" hole in your guitar for a mini switch, check into push/pull pots. These are normal potentiometers with a piggyback mini switch that operates separately from the pot. Replace an existing tone or volume pot with a push/pull pot, and you'll *also* have the mini switch to do all sorts of fancy switching!

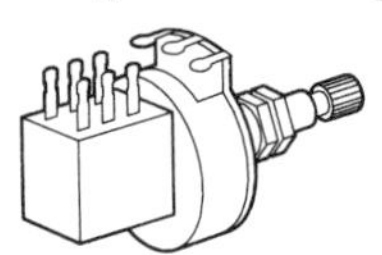

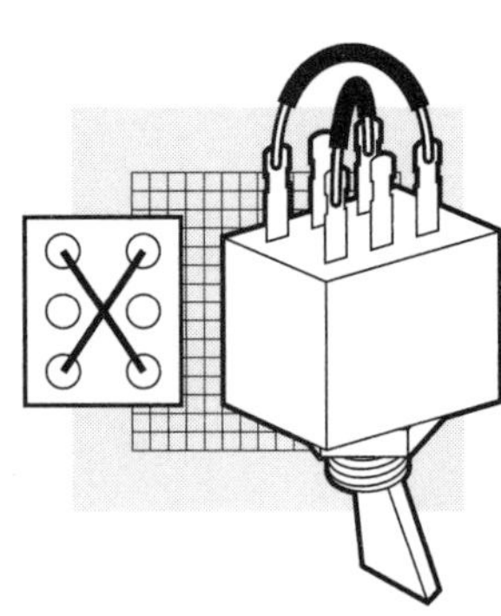

You can buy double-pole or single-pole mini switches. Double-pole switches have two sets of three terminals, or lugs (pictured on previous page), while single-pole have only one set. I stock double-pole, because even though they're a little bigger, they do anything a single-pole does, and more.

The three most common types of double-pole mini toggle switches are on/on, on/off/on, and on/on/on. On/on controls pickup phasing, coil-cut (or two pickups coil-cut at once), or series/parallel. The on/off/on variety puts a single-coil pickup in-phase, out-of-phase, or off, and may be used for pickup selection. On/on/on can work like a Gibson Les Paul toggle switch (lead pickup, both pickups, rhythm). It can give series, single-coil, and parallel selections for a humbucker, or act as a pickup selector switch for three pickups at once. And these are just some of the functions that mini switches perform. The drawings at the bottom of the previous page show which terminals are "hot" when the lever is thrown.

With double-pole switches, each side (or pole) has three wiring lugs. Each side is independent of the other side, although they can be used together. In fact, it's common to "jump" from one pole to another, like the cross-corner terminals used during phasing, for example (left). For short jumpers on mini switches, try this combination: Remove the plastic jacket from solid-copper wire and the Teflon jacket from a stranded wire, and then slide the Teflon over the solid core. This kills three birds with one stone, since the solid core easily pokes through a terminal's hole, it won't fall to pieces like a short strand, and its Teflon won't melt on the criss-crosses and cause a short. When wiring a mini switch, don't rest your iron too long on any one lug, because most switch bodies are made from plastic. In the next section we'll use a mini switch to control the wiring options of a four-wire humbucking pickup.

Installing a replacement pickup

So far you've learned wiring basics, how to read a meter, techniques for clean and safe soldering and de-soldering, and which parts are commonly used. Now you may carefully experiment with the electronics of your own guitar, and I'll bet I know what you'll do first—wire in a replacement pickup, right? Since replacing pickups is the most common job done by do-it-yourselfers, a few pickup-wiring tips are appropriate. Wiring a direct-fit replacement pickup is often simple: Using a wiring diagram, you just unhook one pickup and wire in the other. But there are plenty of pitfalls, too, and you can avoid them by considering the following points before buying a pickup or tearing apart your axe.

■ What sound are you after? If you're adding a pickup to existing pickups, will they be compatible? A well-stocked and knowledgeable music store can help you choose, and Bill Foley's book *Build Your Own Electric Guitar* includes an extensive chart that suggests which pickups sound best for different musical styles. Here's a sample:

HEAVY METAL RHYTHM/NECK POSITION:

Alembic: SAE, HB assembly
Bartolini: 1HC, VHC
DiMarzio: X2N, PAF, Super II, (2) HS2 or 3
Duncan: Jazz Neck, Invader Neck, Seymourizer II, JB
EMG: 85, 58, SA assembly with presence control
Lawrence: 58, XL500 neck, (2) L-25 XL
Schecter: Monstertone assembly

■ Is the alteration permanent? You often can't go back!

■ Do the polepieces match the string-to-string spacing?

■ Some older two-lead (hot and ground) humbucker pickups can be rewired as four-wire pickups. If vintage isn't an issue, perhaps you can rewire the pickup you have to get what you're after.

■ A direct-replacement pickup should drop right in with no additional routing, an important consideration with valuable vintage instruments. With careful disassembly and measuring, you can know if it fits before it's too late. Replacement pickups often have more depth than the original, so don't be surprised if you have to rout or drill the cavity to gain clearance.

■ Switching from single-coil to humbucking often requires routing the body cavity. This is easily done with templates, just like installing the Floyd Rose.

■ Universal routing is popular with many kit body manufacturers. These routs accept either single-coil or humbucking pickups, but you still have to enlarge the hole in the pickguard, especially when replacing a Strat-style single-coil with a humbucker. This, too, is done with a router and pickguard cutout templates.

■ Does the new pickup offer functions that the guitar's wiring system can't operate, such as phasing, dual sound, etc.? In other words, will you have to add mini switches, pots, and such. And if so, is there room?

■ If you're going active, you need someplace to put a battery.

■ Would routing a pickup cavity endanger the structural integrity of the instrument? For example, I've seen old Gibson SG single-coil guitars with a humbucker added in the neck position. There wasn't a lot of surface area in the neck/body joint of these guitars in the first place, so when you add some overzealous routing, the neck falls right off!

If you've read this checklist and still want to hot-rod your guitar, go ahead! Here are a few tips for installing a pickup:

What makes pickups work? In a nutshell, a pickup is made by coiling wire around a set of magnetic polepieces that are held in a frame, or "bobbin." The polepieces pick up string vibrations and "send" them—that is, induce a current—through the magnetic coil of wire that then changes the vibrations into an electric signal. The signal is received and made louder by the amplifier. Understanding how a humbucker works helped me better understand pickup wiring.

A humbucking pickup is a combination of two pickups (coils) in one cover. The two coils are wired together in-series/out-of-phase to eliminate hum. They're also charged magnetically opposite by turning the magnet around in one coil so that the two coils actually end up being electrically in-phase. This describes the traditional humbucker designed by Seth Lover for Gibson in the late 1950s. One set of magnets wrapped with wire makes a single-coil pickup, and single-coil pickups usually hum because they receive interference from AC current in the home, shop, onstage, or wherever. Seth applied for a patent (PAF) on his discovery that two single-coils can be connected together in a certain way with a common output and ground to make up a hum-canceling pickup.

In-series means that one coil connects, runs into, or is linked to the other coil end-to-end; this adds the resistances of both coils and gives us the famous humbucking power. The series link always combines matching ends of the coils (i.e., the finish wrap of one coil to the finish wrap of the other, or a start to a start). Most often the two finish ends of the coils are used for the "series link." Although each coil's wire is wound in the same direction on its bobbin, because the end of one goes into the end of the other, this is considered out-of-phase, hence the term in-series/out-of-phase.

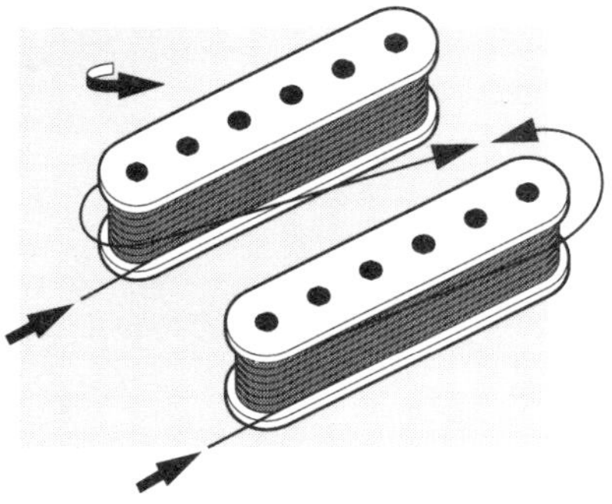

With any pickup wiring, it helps to have the factory wiring diagram, since wire color-coding is not the same from manufacturer to manufacturer; one company's green is another's red. If you don't have a wiring diagram, try your local dealer or the books mentioned at the beginning of this chapter.

At the same time, the coils of a humbucker are also magnetically out-of-phase to each other because the two rows of polepieces are on opposite sides of a common magnet. This gives one row of polepieces a "north" polarity, and the other a "south" polarity, which causes the wire of each coil to induce the current (signal) in opposite directions. This phenomenon not only allows the hum of one coil to cancel the hum of the other coil, but it returns the two out-of-phase coils to being electrically in-phase after all! It's the relationship of the north and south polarity and the particular way the two coils are wired together that gives the pickup its hum-canceling ability, its power, and its name. It must be pointed out, though, that the two coils don't have to be in the same cover. Any two single-coil pickups can be wired or switched together to make a humbucker. A Fender P-Bass pickup is humbucking, for example, even though it's split and sitting in different positions under the strings.

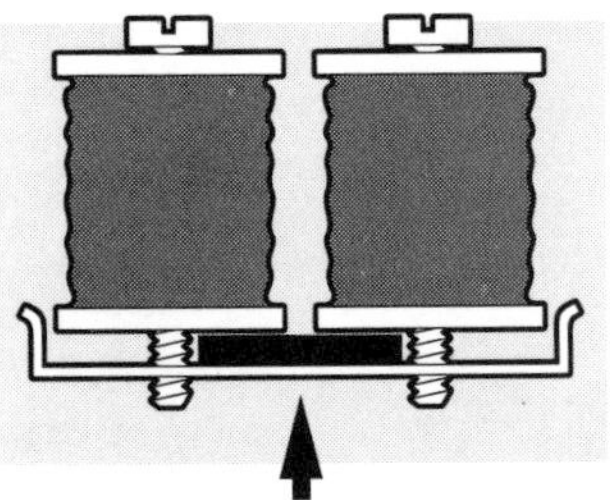

With a humbucker, usually the smooth-faced polepiece is north and the slotted adjustable polepiece is south. Of course, some pickups have two rows of adjustable polepieces.

COLOR-CODING AND START/FINISH WRAPS

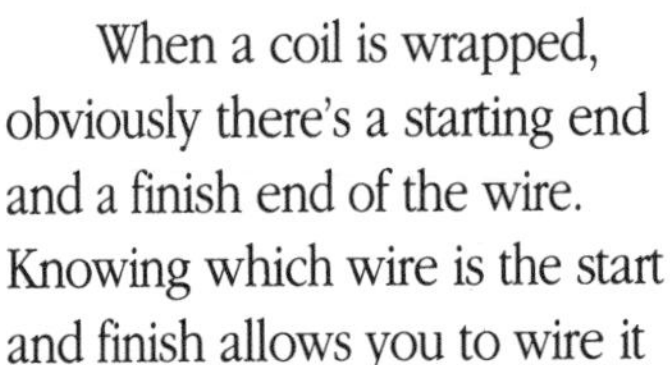

When a coil is wrapped, obviously there's a starting end and a finish end of the wire. Knowing which wire is the start and finish allows you to wire it without regard to factory color-coding and without a diagram. Some manufacturers use the same colors but not in the same order, so you can't use a DiMarzio diagram to wire a Duncan pickup! It's no big deal, but each time you discover the start and finish to a certain pickup, keep a record of it. Here's a list of the color-coding and the start/finish wraps for several manufacturers:

	FINISH	START
S. Duncan	*Red/White*	*Green/Black*
DiMarzio	*White/Black*	*Green/Red*
Schaller	*Green/Yellow*	*Wht/Brown*

Learn how to use your multi-meter to determine the functions of two unknown wires coming from a coil by reading page 51 of Donald Brosnac's latest edition of *Guitar Electronics For Musicians.*

SERIES/PARALLEL

Several times in this book you'll see the terms series or parallel used to describe the linking of electric components or the coils of pickups. Series linkage combines two components by wiring them end-to-end. Parallel linkage combines components side-by-side. If you're using these terms with regard to pickups or their coils, you're linking resistances. When two equal resistances are linked in series (i.e., the two coils of a humbucker), the result is the sum of the two; the series sound is powerful and bassy. When the same two resistances are linked in parallel, the result is one-quarter of their combined values. Parallel sound is weaker, but very bright and clean. The series or parallel wiring options are what gives today's versatile four-wire humbuckers their distinctive sounds.

FOUR-WIRE PICKUPS

If your guitar has a modern four-wire humbucking pickup, this means that instead of the coils being permanently wired together inside the pickup with only two leads coming out (a hot and ground), the start and finish ends of each coil are brought outside the pickup casing in a four-wire coaxial cable with a separate ground (either a separate strand or braid of wire). The two coils can be wired together in five combinations: 1) in-series/out-of-phase (a normal humbucker); 2) in-parallel/out-of-phase; 3) in-series/in-phase; 4) in-parallel/in-phase; 5) either coil by itself (a coil-cut). Of course, there are many more options when you begin to combine two pickups together. To learn more about multiple pickup options, read the recommended books and check out the videotape I made for Stew-Mac, *Guitar Electronics And Hot-Rod Techniques.*

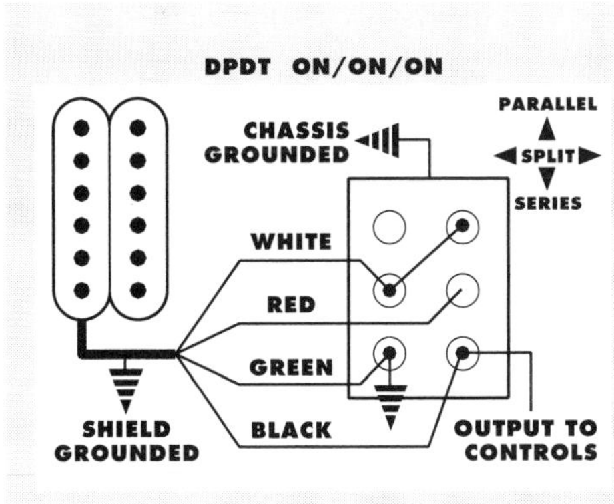

The five pickup functions are normally controlled with a mini switch (often supplied with the pickup) or a push/pull pot. Shown above is a sample Seymour Duncan diagram for wiring a humbucker in-series, parallel, or split-coil using a DPDT on/on/on mini switch. I don't need to give any more space to diagrams, since they're easy to read and the best way for you to understand the different wiring options is to hear them. Try this test, preferably on a "kit" guitar you're not too worried about screwing up:

Install the four-wire humbucker of your choice in the bridge position, re-install the strings, and bring the pickup wires out where you can twist (not solder) the leads together in the five different pickup combinations. Then solder two wires, a hot and ground, to an output jack and connect their free ends to two alligator clips. By connecting the alligator clips to the twisted ends of the colored wire combinations, you can plug a guitar cord into the jack and hear the sounds straight from the pickup to the amp. Once you've heard the pickup sounds, you'll be more confident when using a wiring diagram to install the mini switches that allow pickup options to be neatly switched with the flip of a lever!

The following list shows how to wire finishes, starts, and ground to get the five pickup combinations mentioned above. Remember, the pickup has five wires in all (two starts, two finishes, and a ground), and here's how they're designated:

F=finish, S=start, and G=ground.

SERIES OUT-OF-PHASE

The standard humbucker. F+F=series link, S+G=ground, S=hot (output). A powerful sound with lots of bass and not much hum.

SERIES IN-PHASE

The standard humbucker. F+F=series link, S+G=ground, S=hot (output). A powerful sound with lots of bass and little or no hum.

SERIES OUT-OF-PHASE

F+S=series link, F+G= ground, S= hot (output). This is no longer a humbucking pickup! Thin-sounding, it has less volume and bass than a humbucking.

PARALLEL OUT-OF-PHASE

F+S=hot (output), F+S+G=ground. This is a humbucker with a single-coil sound. Quite strong.

PARALLEL IN-PHASE

F+F=hot (output), S+S+G=ground. No longer humbucking, it has a thin sound, and it's not too strong.

COIL-CUT

S=hot (output), F+F+S+G=ground. One coil is grounded out (shorted) completely. No longer humbucking, but a good, strong single-coil sound.

INSTALLING A HUMBUCKER IN A STRAT

Now let's replace the rear (bridge) single-coil pickup of a Strat-style guitar with a humbucker. This is an easy job if you've learned how to use a router and routing templates. You can eliminate the hassle of re-routing the pickguard simply by buying a pickguard with the rear humbucker cut-out already made. These can be purchased from most guitar parts suppliers, and they allow you to save the original for posterity. If you'd rather rout your own, do it before removing the pickguard to rout the body. Lower the bridge pickup until it drops down, so that you can lay out the humbucking outline onto the pickguard. If you have a plastic pickup mounting ring, use that as a template. Otherwise, the usual humbucker rout is 1½" x 2¾" with a 3/16" radius in the corners (you could make a cardboard template for tracing). Better yet, use a plastic routing template to lay it out; you'll soon be using it to do the routing, anyway.

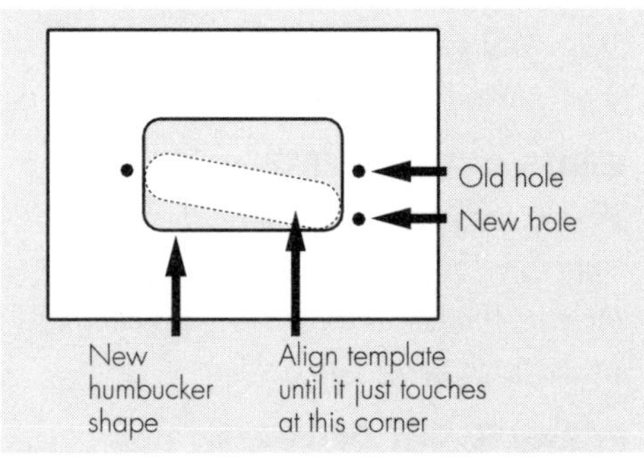

With most Strat-style guitars, the rear rout is slanted (above), and you can use the original mounting hole in the pickguard on the bass (low-*E*) side for mounting the humbucker. You'll have to drill a new hole on the treble side, though, leaving the original treble hole showing. These days most bridge-mount humbuckers are installed at right angles to the guitar's center line, and they're easy to lay out. The routing template has six holes drilled in it: The two center ones are for locating the height-adjustment screws, and the four corner ones locate the screw holes of a pickup mounting ring (as used on Les Pauls, 335s, and many others). If you plan on using a mounting ring over the pickguard, you can use the four corner screws to mount the template. If not, use double-stick tape, since you wouldn't want the holes to show in your pickguard. Note: Screwing down a template is the most solid and safest way to mount it; using double-stick tape works great, but you must be careful not to pull finish when removing the template. To avoid this, don't cover the entire template bottoms with tape. Experiment with routing and removing the template on a scrap of finished wood or on a junk guitar!

Place the template onto the pickguard with the bass-side holes for the height-adjustment screws lined up. Then align the template until its rear edge just touches the original single-coil cutout (as shown at left). Mark lightly on the pickguard in pencil, unfasten the pickups, toggle switch, and volume and tone controls, and remove the pickguard from the body. Now use the pencil marks to align the template as you stick it down to the pickguard with double-stick tape. You're ready to rout.

To do a perfect job, you should lay out and drill a 3/16" hole in each of the four inside corners of the area to be routed. This is because the smallest ball-bearing router bit is 3/8", which can't cut close enough to the four inside corners for the pickup cover to fit through the hole. The 3/8" bit will cut a proper size hole for a humbucker without a cover, however, since the corners don't need to be as tight. If you have trouble drilling the lower right corner because there's not enough plastic left from the original single-coil rout to hold the drill's tip, radius the corner with a small rat-tail file. You can do all the corners with a file, if you wish. Go ahead and rout. Routing templates are quite thin (3/16"), so be sure that the ball bearing is contacting the Plexiglas as you cut, and that the bearing can't slide up the shaft! If the bearing vibrates up the shaft, the router bit could cut an oversized hole. I use a length of ¼" Teflon tubing slid over the router bit shaft to hold the bearing in place. When the pickguard cutout is routed, replace the pickguard and use the new hole as a template to mark out the body rout.

Routing the body cavity is much the same as routing the pickguard, but you need a different template because the mounting bracket or "tabs" extend beyond the length of the pickup. The hole in the pickguard is smaller and just allows clearance for the upper part of the pickup or its cover. The hole in the body is slightly bigger to accommodate the pickup frame. Install the new pickup into the pickguard and measure its underside to find out how deep the body rout must be. Note: You don't need to make the whole rout as deep as the mounting brackets, as you'll see if you study the situation or look at a factory rout on a Gibson Les Paul. You only need to rout or drill an oversize hole at each end of the cavity for the brackets and height-adjusting screws to fit into; these holes are usually routed slightly oval in shape. For more information on pickup installation, read Mike Metz' article in the Jan./Feb. '90 issue of *String Instrument Craftsman.*

That's it for pickup installation. There's more to tell, but you'll find it for yourself if you look, and we've got lots more ground to cover. Now let's learn a little about safety in guitar electronics.

Safety measures

Shock protection should be of concern to anyone playing with an amplifier, especially when you're using lots of high-wattage equipment, playing in a sloppily wired building or in a wet environment, or your equipment is old and rundown or has been worked on by an amateur. Sometimes people are just unlucky. We've heard of players getting shocked, and sometimes killed, onstage. It's not the *guitar* that has the potential to kill; the danger lies in improper wiring and malfunctioning amps or PA gear. Follow these safety steps:

■ Modern electrical cords are equipped with three-prong plugs to ensure that the ground is always connected and to orient the plug so that the hot or "live" prong goes into the right slot in the outlet. *Caution: Never break off or remove the ground prong from your plugs.* This is really stupid! And if you use adapters that allow a three-prong grounded plug to be used in a two-prong outlet without a ground, remember that your amp isn't grounded.

■ For around $6.00 you can buy a circuit (outlet) checker at the hardware store. Keep it in your guitar case, and check every outlet that you plug into. This little device (right) indicates correct wiring, open ground, reversed polarity, open hot, open neutral, hot and ground reversed, and hot on neutral with hot open. You're looking for correct wiring—period!

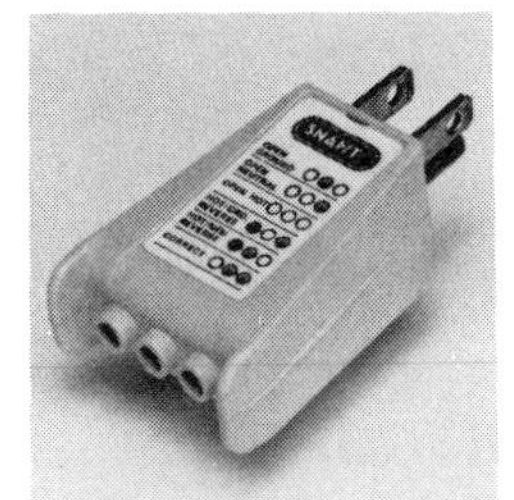

As far as your guitar and its wiring is concerned, here are some measures you can take to further protect yourself, but none of them are guaranteed:

■ A perfect shielding job allows you to disconnect or "float" the ground wire running from your strings to the ground; this usually runs from the tailpiece to the wiring harness. You could still get a shock from touching metal volume and tone knobs, the output jack, or a metal 1/4" input jack on your guitar cord, though. You'll have better luck shielding and removing the ground wire on humbucking pickups than single-coils. Try it, and see if you're happy.

■ Adrian Legg's *Customizing Your Electric Guitar* suggests adding a safety feature between the strings and the ground: Wire in parallel a 220k ohm resistor (colored bands are red, red and yellow, and silver or gold) and a .001 capacitor with a minimum voltage rating of 500 volts. Twist the wires together and solder them as seen at right. This can be done out of sight inside the control cavity, and it only lets about 40 volts through to your strings if a shock is headed your way. The normal string ground still functions, too. However, with this safety device you'll still get it if you touch metal knobs, jacks, or guitar cords.

■ You can be safe from volume or tone knob shock if your pots have nylon shafts, such as Fender used to use.

How piezo transducers work

Unless you're extremely sure of yourself, installing piezo pickups is definitely something you should leave to a pro.

Now that you're familiar with all the tools and techniques of guitar electronics, turning your acoustic guitar into an electric should be a "piezo cake." Here we'll look at the new generation of piezoelectric pickups that are available for do-it-yourself installation. Piezoelectric pickups are being produced by a number of manufacturers, most notably Fishman Transducers, Barcus-Berry, Shadow, Ovation, and L.R. Baggs. The technology developed by these makers is, in my opinion, largely responsible for the resurgence of acoustic popularity nationwide. Martin's Second Generation Thin-Line 332 (developed by Larry Fishman) and L.R. Baggs' LB-6 saddle replacement pickup are both great sounding.

Once a lowly and endangered species, acoustic players are now out of the bluegrass closet, playing on the same stages with drummers and electric guitarists. Moreover, they're actually being heard—without feedback, without rumble, and with a relatively true acoustic sound—all through the magic of piezo pickups. Lots of new guitars are available with factory-installed piezos, including Martin, Gibson, Yamaha, Takamine, Guild, Kramer's Ferrington line, Santa Cruz, Taylor, Larivee, Alvarez, Mossman, Seagull, and the entire Kaman family (including Ovation), as well as scores of custom builders such as James Goodall, Don Musser, and James Olsen. Our focus here, though, is on the various types of pickups available for installation. We'll look at how they work, and most important, how to install them. A piezo's installation isn't actually a piece of cake, but it's as important to the final sound as the transducer itself.

Under-the-saddle transducer pickups are all quite similar in construction, although different brands vary widely in sound. Basically, you've got six pressure-sensitive pieces of piezo ceramic that are linked by wire and held together in a strip by various bonding methods (encased in foil, silicone rubber, a brass channel, etc.). These elements transmit sounds by translating the pressure of the plucked strings on the saddle above them into electrical signals. The pickup's material makeup, size, thickness, and bonding method all contribute to each maker's individual sound. Larry Fishman explained this well to me when, upon hearing me praise his pickup, he modestly said, "We haven't invented any new technology at all. It's our 'recipe'—the blend of physical and electrical proportions—that's producing the sound that you like."

What this recipe talk means is that since each maker's pickup does sound so different, you have to do some research to find the right sound for you. Check with your dealer or local repairman for information. Perhaps you can find out which customers use which pickups, and then call those people to see if they'd mind giving you a quick demo. And many stores have new and used guitars with factory-installed piezos.

Over the years, I've known many guitarists who have experimented with piezo pickups, only to quickly give them up, complaining of a poppy, "Donald Ducky," crackling sound that's often joined by unruly overtones, feedback, excess body noise, and unbalanced string response. These discouraged, would-have-been acoustic players weren't aware that these problems could have been caused by impedance mismatch, lack of a preamp, or the wrong amplifier (they hadn't read L.R. Baggs' excellent article in the Oct. '87 issue of *Guitar Player* magazine, "Getting The Most From Your Piezo Pickup"). Last, but not least, is the possibility that the guitars they tried were equipped with incorrectly installed saddle pickups.

So before placing blame on the poor piezo, be sure that your saddle/pickup installation is correct, always keeping these four rules in mind:

1 The piezo strip must be located in the slot so that all six elements are under their respective strings.

2 The saddle must be made from the right material.

3 The saddle must be a slip—or "sliding"—fit, and in some cases split in two. Also, the piezo strip should be close to the same width as the saddle, and it should sit directly under the whole saddle.

4 The bottoms of the saddle and the saddle slot must be a perfect match.

Installing most under-the-saddle pickups is easy in theory and a little tricky in practice. And it requires certain specialized tools. If you're in doubt, leave the work to a pro; otherwise, here's straightforward advice for do-it-yourselfers.

LOCATION

The transducer must be located with its piezo elements directly under the strings, as shown below. First, the string spacing from

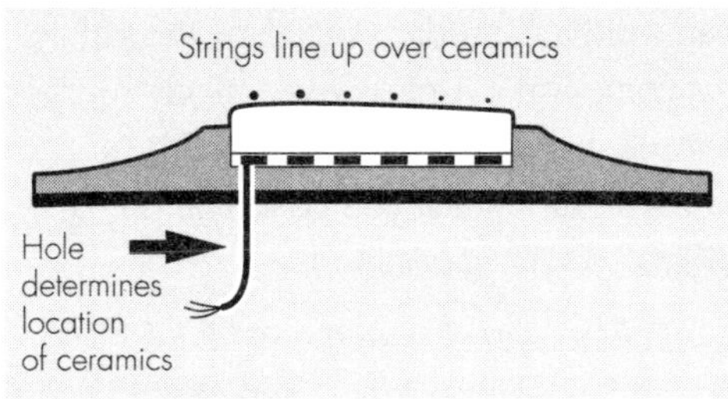

E to *E* must be taken into account. Martin guitars, for example, have a string spacing at the saddle, from center to center, measuring $2\frac{1}{8}$". Their pickup is made accordingly. Most conventional steel-string acoustics have string spacing similar to Martin's, and the various pickup brands are made to match. But if your guitar varies more than .050" from $2\frac{1}{8}$", you should check into having piezo elements custom-installed to match your spacing. Most of the manufacturers I spoke with do some custom work, although some welcome it more than others.

Actually, the location of the piezo relative to the string is really determined by where you drill the hole for the output wire. This hole is drilled in the bottom of the saddle slot, down through the bridge, top, and bridge plate on its way to the output jack that's usually installed in the end block for added strength. Each manufacturer's installation instructions will tell you the exact location of the clearance hole in the bridge, so just measure carefully. If the hole does get off towards one end or the other, you can enlarge it slightly to compensate.

MATERIAL

I often recommend bone or ivory for saddles, but Micarta, a synthetic, is the best material for transducer installation, since it's more even in texture throughout. It's also more flexible than bone, and it moves with the top, bridge, and piezo when a string is plucked. Bone or ivory may offer a stronger acoustic sound when the pickup is not being used, but it won't normally sound as good as the synthetic when you're plugged in.

THE FIT

To begin with, the piezo strip should be close to the width of the saddle slot, so that the whole saddle sits on it for even pressure. If it is too much narrower, it could end up close to the front or rear edge, or sitting at a cross-angle to the saddle (below). Any of these situations is less than optimum in terms of sound.

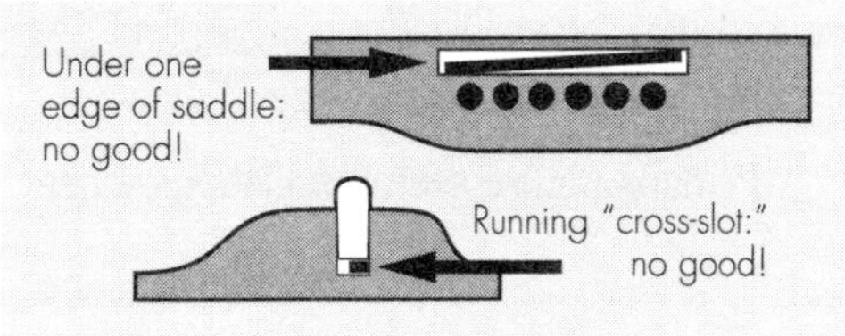

While most repairmen suggest that a saddle fit quite snugly, this is not true for piezo transducers. The saddle should slide or slip in without force. It shouldn't be loose, wiggly, or falling over, but it mustn't be tight.

Admittedly, this is a judgment call that's hard to describe on paper, but you'll get a feel for it after a couple of installations. A too-tight saddle won't exert the proper pressure down on the ceramic, and may cause the following problems: no sound at all, unbalanced string response (i.e., sound on some strings and not others, or some strings louder than others), unwanted overtones, lowering of the overall output, and 60-cycle hum.

In general, the saddle sides should fit the slot walls with a slip-fit tolerance of, say, .002" to .005". Some professionals recommend shaping a slight downward taper on a saddle to guarantee that it reaches the bottom (left). This is smart if you're unable to get a perfect slip-fit. The saddle bottom should mate with the slot bottom with the same accuracy as the sides. Often it's best to rout the slot bottom to get it flat, and then shape the saddle bottom flat to match. This technique, along with a jig you can make yourself for doing the job, will be explained shortly.

Slight taper toward bottom

INSTALLING PIEZO SADDLE PICKUPS

Now that you understand the basics of how the piezo pickups work, and you know a bit about the history of the various types available, let's begin the actual installation procedure. We'll list some of the important measurements you need to know for installation, and continue our work by learning which piezo saddles need to be split in half and which don't, how to use a router jig to flatten the saddle-slot bottom, and how to wire the output jack. Let's get right at it.

Perhaps you've seen installations where the saddle has been cut in half between the *D* and *G* strings (bottom, left). This is the proper method for some piezo saddle pickups, most notably the Barcus-Berry 1440 and the Shadow 1110. These systems utilize balanced phasing, which polarizes the pickup into two halves, like a humbucker. The *E*, *A*, and *D* strings face up (north), while the *G*, *B*, and high-*E* face down (south). If the saddle isn't cut, the *D* and *G* strings "read" each other's plucked string signal and cancel each other out. This can cause a lot of dead notes and bad sounds when the saddle is left in one piece on double-pole transducers.

The Martin Second Generation 332, the L.R. Baggs LB-6, and the Barcus-Berry 1440 SP do not require saddle splitting. The need for splitting the saddle should be considered before installation. Perhaps you simply don't want your saddle cut in two. It's also harder to make a perfect-fit split saddle, since you're sort of making two saddles—and one is hard enough! (Note: The L.R. Baggs Saddle Replacement Pickup comes with the Micarta saddle already bonded to the piezo bottom. In this case the routing and installation fit is the same as the others, except that rather than making a saddle, you shape the saddle that comes on it. Unless you're really sure of yourself, have this pickup installed by a professional, since if you go too far on the Micarta, you're in trouble.)

The bottom of both the saddle slot and the saddle itself must mate perfectly. I recommend that they be flat. Curved bottoms are okay when well matched, but it's easier to be sure of a fit if both are flat. Most so-called flat-top guitars actually have a

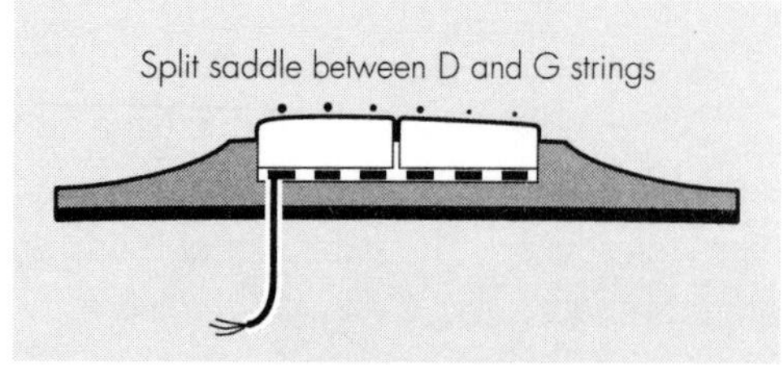

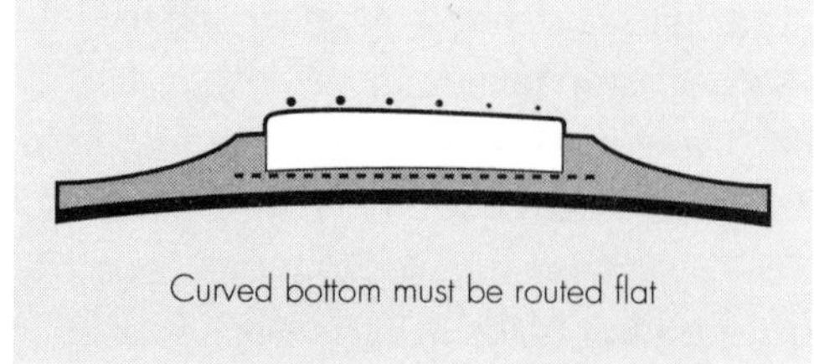

slight upward arch built into them. This effect increases over the years from string pull on the top, causing the guitar to visibly belly up. This is not necessarily bad; it's just a fact of guitar life. Realize that the bridge has slowly become curved to match the top, and therefore the bottom of its saddle slot is bent into the same slight curve. Even with the strings removed, the top and bridge remain somewhat curved, having taken a "set." It's best to re-rout the saddle slot to create a flat bottom within its curved shape (facing page, right). It won't take much, and in so doing, you might also find it necessary to widen the slot, as well, so that the transducer drops in without force.

Using a Dremel Moto-Tool and a $\frac{5}{64}$" bit, flatten the slot's bottom. Make a routing table cut from $\frac{3}{8}$" or thicker Plexiglas or plywood that sits taller than the bridge and gives the router a flat surface to ride over (below). The table is shimmed level where needed, and lightly taped to the guitar's face with duct tape so that it doesn't move. If you also don't move while routing, you'll get a flat bottom. Clean up any router marks, and square up the sides with a sharp chisel, following the saddle-making techniques described in Acoustic Adjustments.

If you're making the saddle slot a little wider than you started with, measure carefully and keep the walls parallel with each other. It's very tough to work on a saddle slot without widening it a little bit, so expect to replace the saddle with an over-sized blank that is filed down to fit. Micarta, bone, or ivory saddle blanks come in thicknesses ranging from $\frac{3}{32}$" to $\frac{1}{4}$",and they must be final-shaped by hand. The Martin Second Generation Thin-Line, Shadow's 1110, and the Barcus-Berry 1440 and 1440 SP fit into a $\frac{3}{32}$" slot, while the Fishman AG-125 and the L.R. Baggs require close to a $\frac{1}{8}$" slot. Ovation transducers require close to a $\frac{5}{16}$" saddle slot (their non-electric guitars, however, use a $\frac{1}{8}$" saddle slot, as do Guilds, Seagulls, and some others).

There are many repair situations where it's advisable or necessary to widen the saddle more than $\frac{3}{32}$" (compensation, warped slot, etc.). Some repairmen and builders prefer a wider saddle in general. The Fishman AG-l 25 and the Baggs LB-6 are well suited to these situations, and will be welcomed by repairmen. It's better not to install a thinner pickup ($\frac{3}{32}$") in a wider slot. Doing so might cause the piezo to become off-center or run at an angle to the bottom of the saddle.

If you've gotten this far, you definitely have enough information to help you make a wise pickup purchase, even if you don't feel like doing the installation yourself. As always, I remind you that my goal is to educate you, not talk you into doing tough jobs without experience. Installing these pickups is definitely something you should leave to a pro unless you're extremely sure of yourself. You still have to wire in the output jack.

The hardest part of installing the output jack is drilling the hole through the end block (you'll see some jacks mounted in the side of the lower bout, but this method isn't as strong without clever reinforcement).

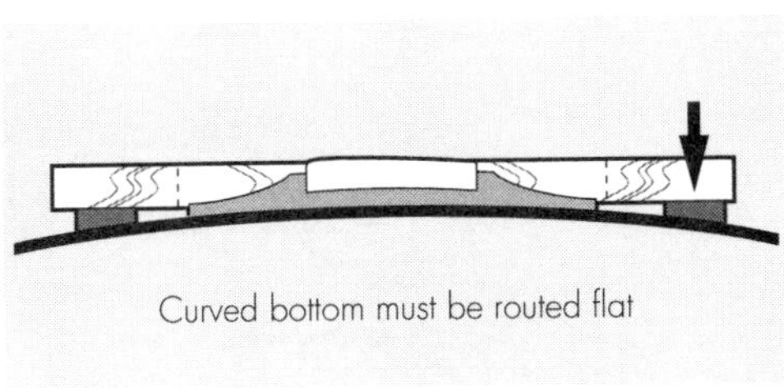

Curved bottom must be routed flat

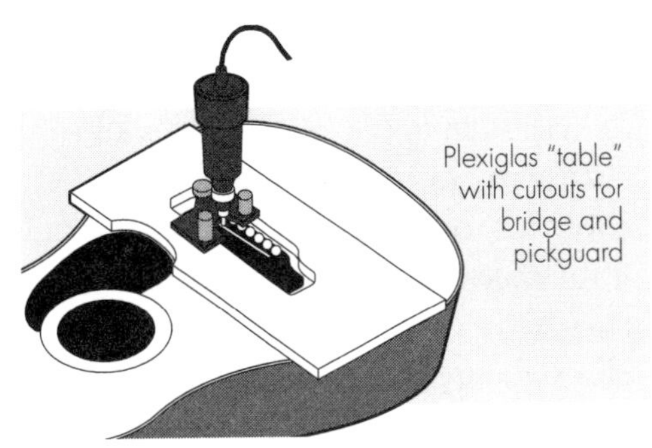

Plexiglas "table" with cutouts for bridge and pickguard

Most end blocks have a hole for the strap button. This hole must first be enlarged by reaming to accept a large drill bit (.469" to ½"), and then drilled at a perfect right angle through the block. I really recommend that you have this operation done at a professional shop. Go ahead and do your own wiring if you wish, but please, be careful with the drilling! If you must put the hole through your own block, a safer reaming method is explained in the next section.

Wiring the input jack is simple if you've been following since the beginning of the chapter, and the manufacturer's instructions tell you which wire goes where (but you *know* that—the hot wire goes to the prong tip, and the braided ground goes to the grounding lug of the ¼" female input jack). If you're unsure about soldering, let the shop that drills your end block install the jack at the same time. The only pointer that comes to mind is not to strip off any more of the wire shield than is absolutely necessary. If you remove too much shielding, the exposed section acts as an antenna. It then becomes a great source for picking up 60-cycle hum from fluorescent lights, dimmer switches, etc. When you've wired in the jack, find someone with a small enough arm to reach through the soundhole and tighten the lock nut against the inside of the end block; this is well illustrated in the next section.

There you have the basics. We haven't covered every aspect of bridge-saddle pickups and their installation, but we've covered a lot. If you don't want to take your guitar to a repair shop for some of the trickier drilling and reaming of the end block, or the wiring of the jack, read on.

PIEZO UPDATE

Here's an update on flat-top pickup installation from *Guitar Player*'s August '90 cover story on acoustic guitar amplification. It's an overview, and then some, of everything we've covered. There's also a really neat vacuum-chuck router installation jig for the serious-minded. I call this section "Piezin' In The Wind."

We've pretty much covered the installation of piezoelectric, under-the-bridge saddle transducer pickups in detail, but there's always more to tell. 1990 has brought about some new designs in non-transducer acoustic guitar pickups, like Ken Donnell's Mini-Flex microphone pickup and Acoustech's Dynamic Field Pickup, both of which require installation. So here's a review of acoustic guitar pickup installation, as well as a discussion of some of the latest tools and techniques.

Under-the-saddle transducers such as those offered by Barcus-Berry, Shadow, Lloyd Baggs, Martin, Takamine, Ovation, and Fishman are popular not only because they reproduce a guitar's natural sound, but also because they don't block the soundhole, aren't too expensive, and install with relatively minor modification of the instrument. Other transducers mount by means of a double-sided adhesive, while the Hot Dot style installs in holes drilled into the bridge body. However, the most popular versions are piezo transducer strips that rest under the saddle in the bridge saddle slot and are wired to a ¼" output jack (usually installed in the guitar's butt end at the same time).

The drawings below are repeated from the start of this section. They show a simple cross-section of a transducer strip: The black

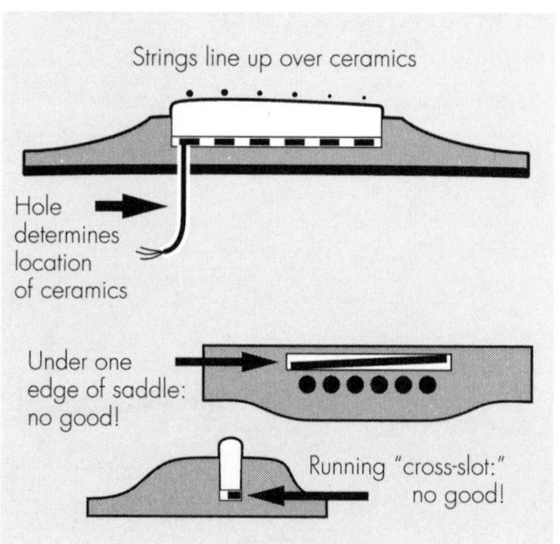

rectangles are six individual piezo elements imbedded in the plastic that holds them together. Each element sits directly under its own string—so element spacing is crucial—and the output wire runs out of the saddle slot's bottom, as described later in this article. Saddles made from Micarta, Corian, or other homogeneous material give the best tone and sound reproduction. Bone, generally recommended for acoustic saddles, is too inconsistent in density to perform well with piezos.

Installation of under-the-saddle transducers generally involves some light routing of the bridge saddle slot—sometimes widening it and often deepening it. Most important, the routing is done to ensure that the bottoms of the slot and saddle match perfectly. The transducer sits between the saddle and slot bottom and must contact both evenly, so shaping both flat is the easiest method for guaranteeing a good contact. It's best to use a transducer strip that's close to the same size as the saddle, so that it sits directly under the whole saddle—not cross-slot or under one edge. If you're unfamiliar with guitar repair, lack the proper tools, or don't feel confident about installing a piezo, have it done at a professional shop; the job is simple for repairmen who have the necessary experience and tools.

Speaking of tools: The serious transducer installer will be interested in the Vacu-Jig, manufactured by Guitar Systems (shown below). This tool uses the power of your Shop-Vac to suction onto a guitar top. Because it's adjustable, it aligns easily with any saddle slot, and then makes use of the Dremel Moto-Tool for pinpoint routing of the slot. The Vacu-Jig is a flat, stable surface for a Dremel router to ride over, which ensures a flat bottom for the saddle slot and eliminates the need for clamping a makeshift routing table around the bridge. The jig's adjustable fences entrap the router baseplate, guiding it in a straight line during the routing.

With under-saddle transducers, besides slightly routing the bridge saddle slot, you must also be willing to drill a small hole in the bottom of the slot (as well as down through the bridge, top, and bridge plate) for the pickup lead wire to run through. This isn't too serious a modification, but think twice about doing any such work on a vintage instrument. And, with either transducers or the new pickups offered by Ken Donnell and Acoustech, the end-pin (strap-button) hole in the guitar's end block must be enlarged to approximately ½" to accept a combination strap button and ¼" plug-in jack (unless you wish either to mount the jack in the guitar's side, which is thin and brittle, or let the wire and jack hang out of the soundhole, which is clumsy). In fact, the end-pin hole is the entire means of mounting the Ken Donnell Mini-Flex and Acoustech Dynamic Field pickups. Since this hole-enlarging operation is tricky, let's check it out.

When enlarging the end-pin hole, avoid chipping the wood around it, don't split the end block (usually mahogany, which splits easily), and keep the hole straight. A crooked hole leaves the input jack at an awkward angle, which looks bad and makes it hard to tighten the mounting hex nuts. A drill bit tends to grab into wood, especially when drilling into an existing hole. There are many ways of enlarging the hole with drilling tools (drill presses, hand-held electric drills, bit and brace, etc.), but they're all risky for the novice. The safest method is to use a hand-held ½" tapered reamer to enlarge the hole slowly.

If you want a built-in preamp, take your axe to the best repair shop you can find; it's a tricky job.

Most hardware-store reamers are about ½" at the widest end of the taper, and may be used straight from the shelf to do the job. They'll make the hole slightly larger than necessary, though, since the outside diameter (O.D.) of the thread on the end-pin jack measures .469"—that is, .031" (1/32") smaller than the .500" (½") hole that the reamer makes. If you want a snug-fitting jack, pay a machine shop a small fee to grind down the reamer's flutes (cutting edges) until they match the thread O.D. exactly. And while you're at it, have the shank ground to the same size, so that it's slim enough to allow the cutting edge to go entirely through the end block (left). Be careful as you work, since a reamer that's not held square can chip the wood or finish just like a drill bit. If your final fit is too snug, use a rat-tail file to finish the job.

Once the jack fits easily through the hole, you can go right to mounting the Mini-Flex or the Acoustech Dynamic Field, because they're prewired and need only to be fastened into the end-pin hole for a permanent mount. A piezo bridge-saddle pickup, however, must be wired to the jack before fastening it home in the end block, but that's simple: Solder the insulated (plastic-coated) lead wire to the prong-tip wiring lug, and solder the bare ground wire (or braided shield) to the casing. Be sure you slip the interior hex nut and washer over the wires—in that order—before you run them through the end-pin hole for soldering. I've soldered up more than one jack without remembering the nut and washer; it makes you feel kind of stupid. Here's a couple of tricks to help make the jack installation as easy as I say it is:

For pulling the wires through the hole, run an electric bass string through the hole and into the guitar. Then you can stick the loose wire ends into the large ball end, and use the length of bass string as a guide to pull the ball end and wires through the hole and out where you can solder them. An alligator-clip helping-hand soldering stand makes a good holder while you're soldering.

Probably the hardest part of installing the end-pin jack is getting the hex nut tight against the end block from the inside. I've popped blood vessels while trying to tighten this nut through the soundhole, and those of you with big arms haven't a prayer. I found a solution while visiting the C. F. Martin & Co. factory in Nazareth, Pennsylvania. Martin installs more piezo strips than any of us—in fact, they have a work area devoted solely to installing their Second Generation Thin-Line by Fishman. To hold the hex nut from the inside while tightening from the outside, they use a hollow-shaft, deep-socket 9/16" nut driver with a slot milled through one wall of the hex and into the hollow shaft. The slot allows the tool to slide onto the wires and follow along them, over the jack's soldering prongs and onto the hex nut, making it easy to hold the nut against the inside of the block while you tighten the outside nut home. It's a great tool; I'm already trying to figure out how to make one!

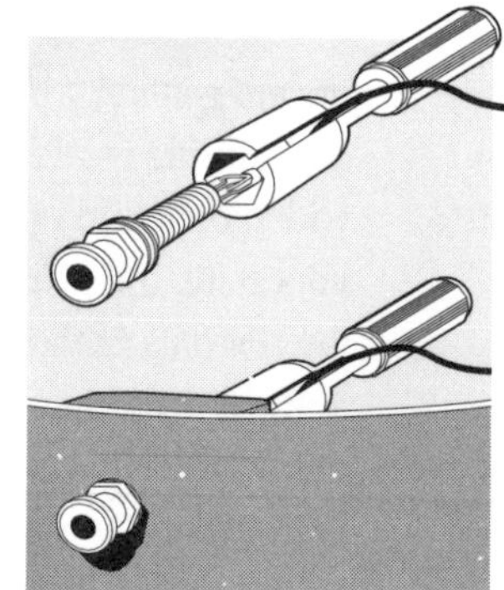

If I were to rate the degree of difficulty faced with installing any of the pickups mentioned so far, they would follow this order:

1 The Mini-Flex is easiest. Enlarge the end-pin hole, and the job's done. But to find the best sound, you still have to experiment with the flexible gooseneck that holds the microphone.

2 The Acoustech Dynamic Field rates second-easiest, although gluing the magnetic sensor to the bridge plate requires skill, intelligence, a mirror, and, in some situations, experience. The magnetic sensor gets glued to the bridge plate behind the bridge pins, and some guitars don't have a wide enough bridge plate to accept it. In that case, a piece of wood must be added to the plate or top as a gluing surface (below). And all fan-braced classicals without bridge plates need a slip of

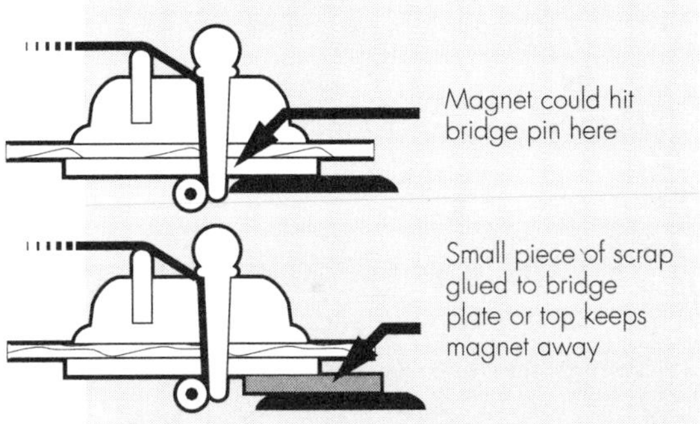

wood added to the top as a mounting ledge for the pickup. This kind of work is tricky, and of course you'd want to think twice before altering a vintage instrument.

3 The hardest installation has to be the under-the-saddle transducer because of the accurate routing involved, but the Dynamic Field isn't too much easier.

All of the manufacturers provide adequate instructions for installation, but none of the manuals are exceptional. Certain points are glossed over, probably to encourage novices to take the job to a professional, which may head off some customer-service problems. Before closing, I'd like to gloss over one point myself: Some manufacturers install a preamp with volume and tone controls in the side of the instrument near the neck block on the bass side. We're not discussing that installation, nor do I advise you to try it. If you want a built-in preamp, take your axe to the best repair shop you can find; it's a tricky job. Good luck, and if you have trouble—pieze on it!

Soap-bar pickups

You don't see many guitarists playing the old single-coil Gibson Les Pauls these days. Too bad! They're a great buy on the vintage market, and they have a killer sound. Here's some advice on caring for the pickups in those great old guitars, brought to mind by this letter from "C.B." in Bowling Green, Kentucky: "I own a '54 or '55 gold-top Les Paul, and I wish it had more output. Routing it for humbuckers would destroy its value on the vintage market (besides, the guitar belongs to my father). Are there high-output pickups that retrofit the same cavity as the original 'soap bar' pickups? Also, I've tried to remove these pickups to clean under them, but they fit tight. Probably glued in, right?"

If you choose to use replacement pickups, consider having the originals removed by a professional repair shop.

Even when new, the P-90 pickups in your guitar weren't as powerful or hum-free as most humbucking pickups. Still, there are many of us who prefer their unique sound to that of humbuckers. Replacement pickups with a higher output are available from DiMarzio, Seymour Duncan, and Bartolini. But before you order replacement pickups or remove the originals, consider the following information on old P-90s.

I like to keep things clean, too, and I'll never forget taking out my first soap-bar pickup to really get at the dirt. I removed the two screws that held it down, but like yours, it wouldn't budge. Imagine my surprise when, as I pried out the pickup of my '55 Les Paul, I found that several hundred feet of very thin copper wire unwound right along with it—all over my lap! I managed to scrounge up another pickup, but these days an authentic vintage replacement would be hard to come by.

Normally, Gibson P-90 soap-bar pickups come out fairly easily, but you'll find many that are really tight. If it's just the cleaning that you're worried about, I'd say leave the pickups alone and clean around them as best you can. If you choose to use replacement pickups, consider having the originals removed by a professional repair shop.

You may rest assured that your P-90 pickups aren't glued in. They're probably stuck because of all the beer that's been spilled onto them in some honky-tonk saloons, where many great guitars have paid their dues. Sometimes pickups stick to the lacquer upon which they sit, especially in humid weather. Perhaps the wood has swollen a bit. To loosen the pickups, raise the polepieces above the pickup surface (protect them with strips of wood as shown), and use Vise-Grips to gently pry or pull them out. Don't just grab the pickup by its cover and pull—this is what caused my catastrophe. Those pre-'55 P-90 coil forms were glued together rather than machined of solid stock like the post-'55 models, and when I pulled the pickup cover, the top plate of the bobbin stuck to it while the rest of the pickup remained snug in the cavity.

So, the pickup covers may or may not come free of the pickup easily, and in most cases there's no reason to ever take them off. Also, plastic covers shrink over the years and grip the pickup tightly. The plastic of both the covers and the pickup are probably brittle from age, and may be easily cracked or broken. Therefore, you should leave the covers on original P-90s, and if you get replacement pickups, buy a set of new replacement covers from your Gibson dealer (part number 13949 in black, and 13925 in cream).

Speaking of your Gibson dealer, I'd suggest that before you buy anyone else's replacement pickup, you might check out a set of new P-90s from Gibson. They have a higher output than the originals. It's also possible to "recharge" your old P-90s: Gibson R&D exec Tim Shaw points out that soap-bars made before 1968 had Alnico II magnets that demagnetize over time and lose power (we used to buy these magnets from Gibson and recharge our pickups with them, but they're no longer available). Tim suggests having your old magnets remagnetized at an automotive or bicycle shop that services speedometers. Ask them to saturate the magnets. This restores much of the original power and sound. If you remove the magnets, mark them so that you can replace them exactly as they came out. The great thing about remagnetizing is that you can increase your output without doing anything to damage the integrity of a fine vintage instrument—always the best solution!

Shrinking Strat pickguards

The UPS man brought me another guitar to fix, along with a note written by a fellow who probably thought he was alone in the world with this trouble. I thought I'd share his problem, along with a solution: "I have a '63 Strat that I dearly love. It's chipped and worn, and ugly to some, but it plays and sounds great. One thing worries me, though. The front pickup is almost touching the strings when I fret the high notes. I tried to lower it by loosening the two pickup height screws, but they move stiffly and the pickup goes nowhere. The pickup and screws seem to be stuck in the pickguard. Also, the pickup sort of leans at an angle. I'm afraid to take the pickguard off, but if I did, what difficulties might I run into?"

I've seen the problem you're describing, and some even worse. First of all, if you're unable to find professional help for your guitar or if you're afraid to mess with the pickguard, shim the neck slightly. This requires the consequent raising of the bridge inserts. The shimming moves the strings up and away from the pickups, and helps the fretted string clear the rhythm pickup's plastic cover. If your neck is already shimmed and the bridge inserts are as high as they'll go, or if you simply don't like the idea of a shim, you can fix the problem without too much trouble. You'll have to remove the pickguard, though.

Your best bet is to take your guitar to a good repair shop and let a pro do the work, even though it's not too hard. Face it, your vintage Strat could be worth a couple grand.

If you decide to tackle the problem yourself, the heart of the matter is the celluloid/nitrate material from which the pickguard is made. Nitrate has a tendency to shrink and warp, while the wood body and metal shielding plate remain their original size (a plastic less prone to shrinkage was substituted for nitrate by about 1965). The nitrate's shrinking may cause the following annoying problems, some of which are correctable:

1 A mismatch between the mounting-screw clearance holes in the pickguard and the metal shield. Pulled by the shrinking plastic, the mounting screws slant toward center, often becoming hard to take out or put in. I prefer to leave these as they are. To try to move or enlarge the holes in the pickguard could harm the guitar's value, and the slanting screws aren't really hurting anything, as long as they'll go in.

2 It sounds like your pickups have become squeezed by the surrounding plastic and are hard to move up or down, and that the height-adjustment screws are stuck in the metal shield clearance holes. These are off-center to the pickup height-adjustment holes, which have in turn shrunk and moved. To seat the pickups smoothly in their holes and make them adjustable again, you need to enlarge the holes in the metal plate as I'll describe shortly.

3 The pickups tilt out-of-square to the strings as a result of the combined warpage and shrinkage. I've never had any success straightening out the warp, and don't recommend trying it to a vintage pickguard. The tilting pickups, however, will straighten up if you get rid of the squeezing plastic and clear out the shield-plate holes as mentioned earlier.

Working on anything vintage these days takes nerve, even if it's your own guitar. You should have seen me when my wife Joan and daughters Kate and Meredith gave me a '56 Strat for Christmas '89. I wanted to take off the pickguard and verify it's date, but I was scared to death!

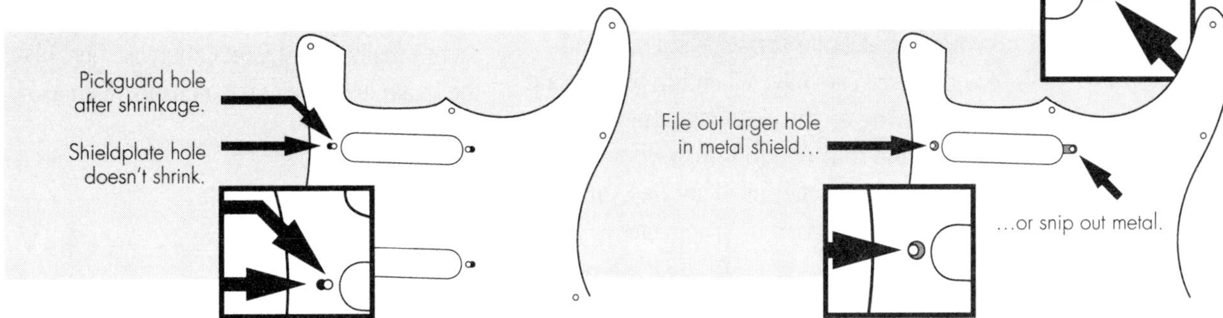

HERE'S WHAT YOU CAN DO:

You can remove the squeeze and relieve the tension. When the pickguard mounting screws are removed, lift the pickguard/shielding plate up gently, and turn it carefully over onto its face. Have a soft rag handy to place over the body cavity to protect both the finish and the pickguard face. The pickguard often sticks around the heel of the neck and at the bridge surround, so you may have to pry gently.

To make disassembly easier, the entire pickguard assembly can be removed by

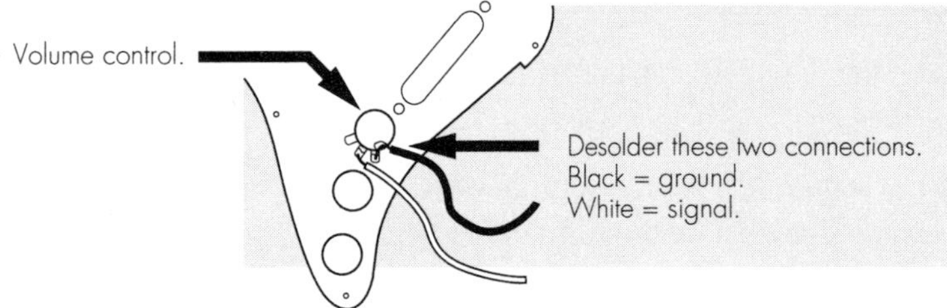

unsoldering the black (ground) and white (hot) wires at the volume pot (above). Or, if you're careful, you can work with the pickguard still attached, but it's tricky. (The reason I stress taking your guitar to a pro is that experience minimizes the chances of accidental damage to the delicate copper windings.) In order to do this work, you need to remove the pickups and the tone controls from the pickguard and shield.

With a sharp Phillips screwdriver, remove the pickup height-adjustment screws. They may be stiff, but firm pressure will get them out. Be gentle when pulling pickups (still in their cover) out of the pickguard. You may have to wiggle them out. Keep the pickups inside their covers to protect the delicate copper windings, and handle them carefully. When the pickups are out and lying on the clean rag, remove the volume and tone controls. Now your pickguard and metal shield are free, and can be cleaned and worked on separately.

To enlarge the holes in the metal shield: From the underside, look at the mounting screw holes in the metal shielding plate. Because of shrinkage, they probably are no longer lined up with the holes in the pickguard. Use a small, round needle file to file the holes slightly inward towards the pickup (previous page). Or, you could also simply snip out a section of metal with small wire snips or scissors.

To clean the plastic that surrounds the pickup: Next scrape or file the slightest bit off the sides of the pickup hole. You'll find that it's mostly caked-on dirt, perhaps mixed with a vintage spilled pop or beer. To clean or alter the cutout's round ends, use a 1/2" wood dowel wrapped with 120-grit sandpaper. Sand small amounts from the rounded ends of the mounting hole; once again, it's mostly grime. It won't take much filing and scraping to get the pickup moving through its hole again. It doesn't even have to move smoothly—just enough to raise or lower. Don't overdo it.

You may also have to enlarge the pickguard's height-adjustment holes ever so slightly by filing outward, away from the pickup. Remember that shrinkage has caused these holes to creep a little closer to the pickups than is desirable.

When you replace the pickups, be as cautious as you were during disassembly. If you've worked carefully, there should be no visible change when all is back together. The pickups will now adjust up or down and sit level, since the rubber grommet or compression spring is able to do its job (pushing the pickup down, eliminating the tilt, and allowing the polepieces to sit level with the strings). Once again, do this work only if there's really a problem. Otherwise, just play the guitar and don't take a chance with its vintage value.

Strat switch modification

Here's a guitar electronics question for you: How many luthiers does it take to change a light bulb? (Answer: Just one, but you've got to be willing to wait six months!) Thanks for letting me say that. Seriously, this letter from a *Guitar Player* reader will put your new-found knowledge to the test: "My Strat has a 5-way switch, which doesn't allow me to use three pickups at once, or the front and rear in combination. Do you have a

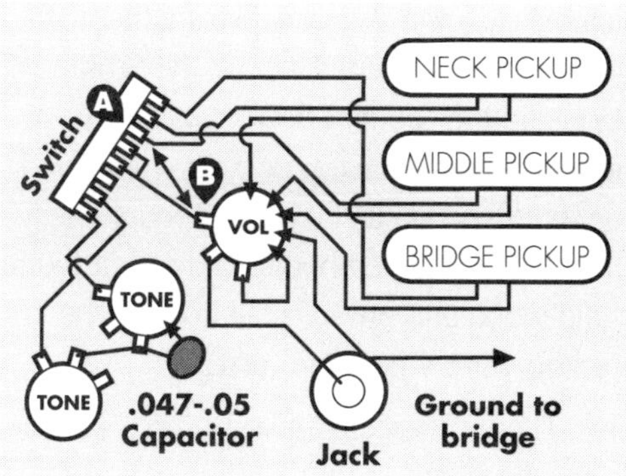

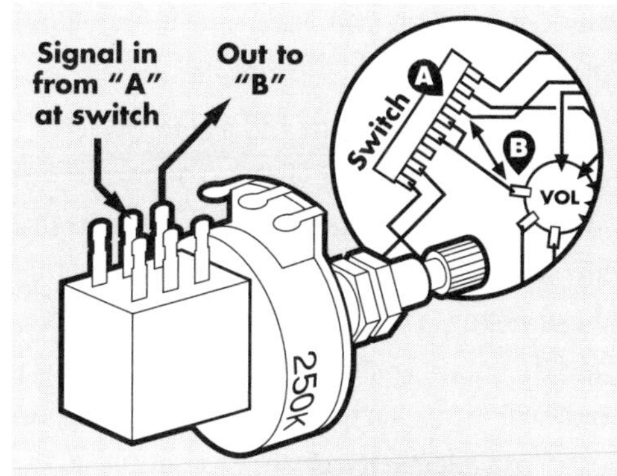

wiring diagram to modify it so that all seven pickup combinations can be used?"

Here are several ways of doing it that I learned from my friend and fellow repairman, Mike Koontz of Zoppi's Music in Ferndale, Michigan. Mike's an ace repairman at all levels and a whiz at guitar electronics, and he always seems to find an easier way.

A simple method for getting all possible pickup combinations is to install a single-pole/single-throw (SPST—two-terminal on/off) switch in between the neck pickup contact at the 5-way switch and the hot lug of the volume control. This way, the neck pickup is still controlled normally by the switch lever. But since it's also wired directly to the volume control through the on/off switch, you can cut it in or out at will. This allows you to use all three pickups at once, or the front and rear together. You can wire in the bridge (rear) pickup instead of the front and get the same combinations.

Shown above is a wiring diagram for a Stratocaster. Notice points "A" and "B"—you add the switch between these. But instead of drilling a hole in your pickguard and adding a switch, replace the rear most (middle pickup) tone control with a combination push/pull potentiometer. These pots are actually a regular potentiometer with a built-in double-pole/double-throw (DPDT) switch. The push/pull acts as both the normal tone control and as the new switch when activated by pulling up on the knob. The rear tone control is the easiest to wire, since you wire-in the new pot just like the one it replaces. Then run a wire from "A" at the 5-way switch into the new piggyback switch and out again to "B" of the volume pot (above). You only use one side (and two lugs) of the push/pull switch.

The 5-way switch illustrated here has all the contacts on one side. This is common with many of the totally enclosed replacement switches available. If your guitar has the Fender switch, the contacts alternate from side to side. With either switch, you must find the soldered contact where the neck (or bridge—your choice) pickup attaches, and go about the simple wiring mentioned above.

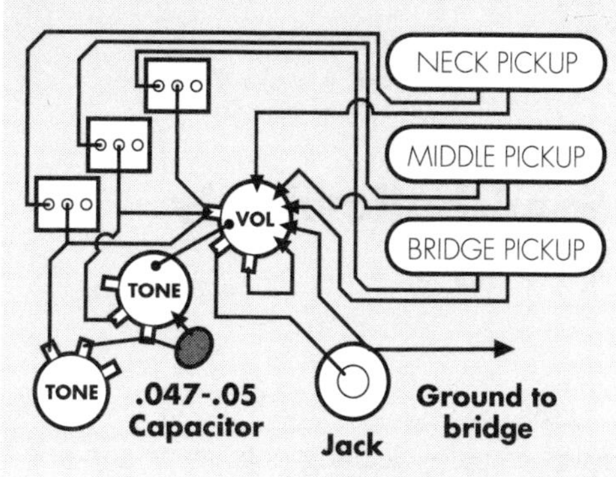

Another option that lots of builders and hot-rodders use eliminates the stock switch altogether by installing three mini switches—one for each pickup, as shown above. This involves drilling three holes in the pickguard. Better yet, have a pickguard custom-made with the standard switch slot eliminated and the holes right where you want them. Each switch controls one pickup, so you can have any combination you wish. You'll see many popular guitars with this set-up.

A third choice is to add a Starr Switch digital pickup selector (DPS). The Starr Model 4 has four touch-sensitive buttons that are somewhat like a calculator's. Three of these buttons control the pickup selection, and the fourth button can be used to control optional extras such as coil taps, phasing, or on-board effects. It can also act simply as a master on/off switch, or not be used at all. Switch selection is indicated with LEDs. The retrofit switch installs in the factory switch slot, and it's extremely quiet even at high volumes. A 9-volt battery is needed to power the unit, but there's plenty of room in the wiring cavity for that. Check with your local music store or mail-order supplier, or contact Starr Switch Co. Perhaps this switch talk, with its single poles, double throws, and ons and offs, is confusing—I hate to sound like a nag, but read Donald Brosnac's *Guitar Electronics For Musicians*. This book is the "bible" for guitar electronics. After studying the chapter on switches, you'll be able to shop for the parts to do any of the conversions mentioned here.

Semi-hollowbody wiring

As I said earlier, much of guitar electronics is simple—cleaning pots, switching capacitors, etc.—*if you can get at the work!* Here's advice for Gibson ES-335 owners faced with having to remove the electronics for cleaning or replacement. It's another of my favorite question-and-answer letters from *Guitar Player* magazine: "I own a 1968 Gibson 335. The controls are sticky and hard to turn, and one doesn't work at all. I can handle cleaning and/or replacing them, if I can only get at them. How do they come out? How did they go in? I doubt that they were installed before the top or back were glued on, but they couldn't have fit through the f-holes. I've removed both pickups, but found solid wood and only a small hole for the pickup wire! What's the secret?"

There's no secret. If you simply want to clean the pots, loosen their hex nuts and washers, let the pots fall down into the body, and spray them with a contact cleaner (most aerosol contact cleaners are equipped with small, flexible tube applicators for pinpoint spraying). If you're sure you need to remove the controls, I'd bet they went in through the f-holes, although they shouldn't have. Read on.

Gibson ES-335-style guitars have a solid wood block glued between the top and back, which runs lengthwise through the guitar's center (hence the name "semi-solidbody"). This block not only gives structural support, but considerably enhances the guitar's sustain. From the 335's inception in 1958 until 1961, the center block was truly solid, and the wiring harness was installed or removed through the f-holes. After 1961, the factory machined a good-sized notch in the block (the shaded area in the drawing at right) under the bridge pickup, which helped in the installation and removal of the electronics. A good picture of this type of construction is on page 143 of Tom Wheeler's book *American Guitars*.

Being of more recent vintage, your guitar should have the notched access for the electronics, but if it doesn't, perhaps the block was accidentally flipped over during gluing. This would put the notch on the bass side (look through the bass f-hole to see). You'll have to fish the controls through the f-hole as if it were a pre-'61 axe, de-soldering the pickup leads as the pots are pulled through the f-holes. As you can see in the drawing, the wood wall left by the notch isn't

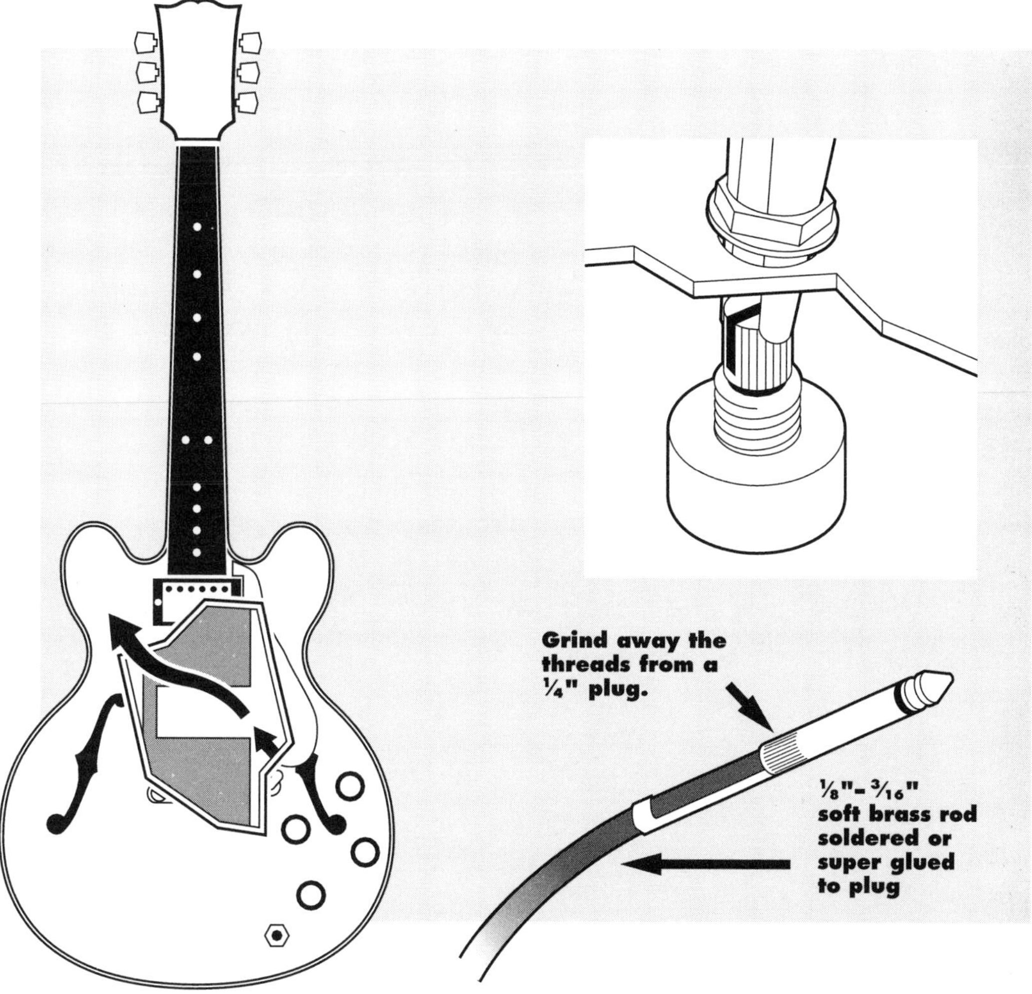

Some of the harder guitars to work on—some Gretsches especially—have all the wiring encased in spiral-wound, stainless steel, flexible cable for shielding. Besides being a wonderful ground and very high-class, the cable has great strength. But if it flips upside down when it's twisted, you have to back out and start over.

too thick (about ½"). A skilled worker could cut through the block on the treble side to give easier access for control removal.

Here are some other helpful tips for working on the electronics of any f-hole electric guitar:

Before removing the volume and tone controls, take off the knobs and mark the top of each shaft as an aid for later replacing them in the right order. Also, you'll have to remove the ground wire from the tailpiece in order to pull the parts out. Unscrew the tailpiece, and you'll find the wire—it may need unsoldering. For a stop-tailpiece 335, unsolder the ground wire as you remove the pots.

If you're replacing the whole harness after the guts have been removed, make a paper tracing of the empty control and toggle-switch holes on the guitar's face. Transfer these to stiff cardboard and drill them out. Flip the cardboard over to duplicate the holes as they'd be on the inside of the guitar, and do your wiring with the pots and switch held in this wiring jig. It makes a great holder for the parts and assures a perfect fit upon reinstallation.

Whether you have access through the rear pickup or the f-hole, you still need to slide your parts carefully—and in the right order—back into the body. Keep from twisting or crossing any wires that later might touch a bare contact and cause a short. I've found that a pair of curved or straight hemostats work great for reaching through a hole in the top and pulling a control shaft into place. Put the washer and hex nut on the hemostats before reaching through the hole (above) and tape them in place. Then you can drop them right onto the threaded shaft while holding it with the hemostats (I've always wished I had three hands when doing this).

Gibson R&D engineer Tim Shaw suggests making a tool for getting an output jack into the mounting hole in a guitar's face or side. This would be worth making for those who plan to do this job more than a few times. Solder or super glue a 12" length of 1/8" or 3/16" soft brass to a 1/4" plug (shown on previous page). Bend the tool gently, and run it through the jack hole and out the f-hole or rear pickup notch, and plug it into the jack. Now you can pull the jack into place, dragging the rest of the wiring harness roughly into place at the same time.

Tim Shaw also pointed out that when Gibson installed the electronics in those early ES-series semi-hollow guitars such as the 335, 345, and 355, they kept cans of touch-up lacquer of the proper shade (usually cherry or sunburst tones) right at the bench to touch up the f-holes afterwards. Don't be surprised if you can't get the pots in or out without some degree of scratching—a little masking tape in the right places would help. Good luck with your work.

Easy, right? Actually, it sounds easier here than it really is. Be patient, and you'll get the parts out and back in. You know one thing for sure: Those guitars weren't wired from *inside* the guitar! Someone had to do it.

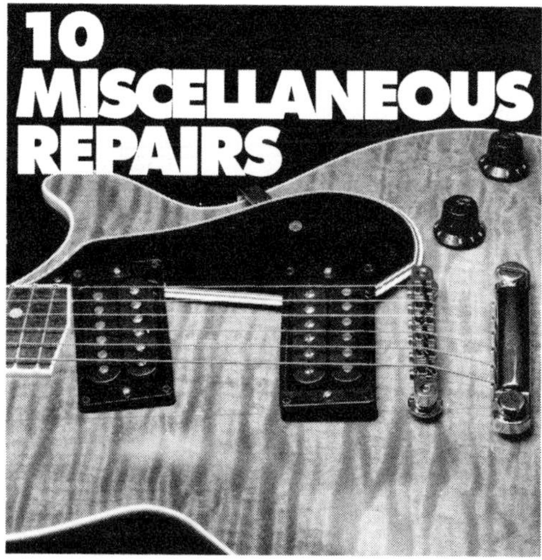

Super glue repairs and touch-ups

Super glues can be very versatile when applied to guitar repair. Since several varieties are available, here's a rundown on the different glues and accessories, as well as typical situations in which guitar players, builders, and repairmen can benefit from this glue's instant cure and super strength.

Hot Stuff Original Formula, in the red-label bottle: Its water-thin consistency allows it to "wick" (seep and penetrate) into cracks and hard-to-get areas that are untouchable by other glues. Hot Stuff's drying time is so fast (1-10 seconds) that parts must be pre-aligned, or they often freeze in place before being perfectly mated. Some typical uses for the red-label Hot Stuff are:

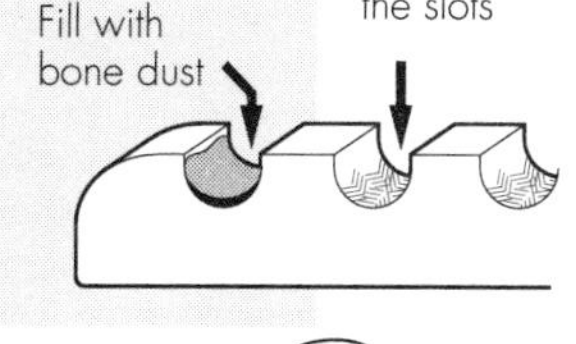

- Nut repair. Use with bone dust to build up worn slots.
- Gluing hairline splits in the top, back, sides, bridge cracks, etc.
- Fret work. Regluing fingerboard chips caused by fret removal, or fill chips with sawdust. (Notice the piece of plastic shoved into the fret slot as a dam to hold the fill.)

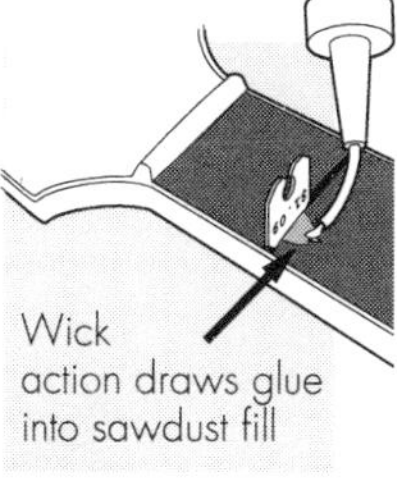

- Holding down loose fret ends.

Super T, in the yellow-label bottle, has the consistency of syrup and is a good gap-filler for ill-fitting parts. It cures more slowly than Hot Stuff original formula—usually 10 to 25 seconds, depending on the material. I use this most often in cases such as:

- Finish touch-ups. That is, drop filling chips or dents on acrylic or nitrocellulose lacquer, polyester, and polyurethane finishes. Lacquer fills tend to crater around a chip's edges, while super glue builds up evenly, and even crowns slightly.

- Gluing jigs and fixtures around the shop.
- Case repairs.
- Glue in frets during refretting.
- Mix with sawdust for filling dents on bare wood projects.

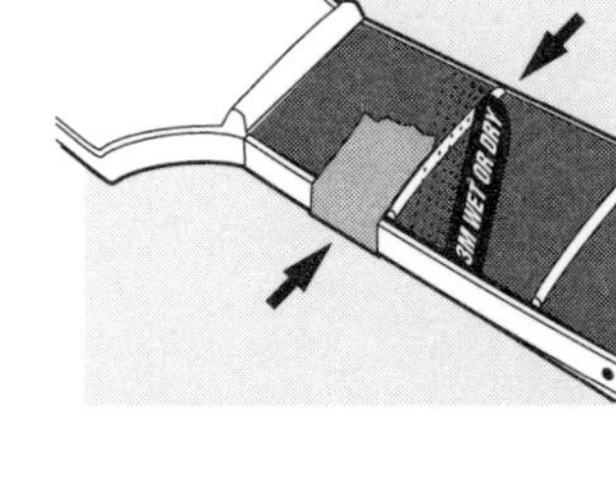

- Reglue loose bindings. Make a spatula of the desired shape from 1200-grit wet-or-dry sandpaper and use it to work the glue into the gap. Then tape the binding quickly, but gently, into place.
- Reinforce worn wood threads.
- Pearl inlaying.

Special T, in the green-label bottle, is an ultra gap-filler that's thick, like cold honey. It dries slower than Hot Stuff and Super T (usually 30 to 50 seconds, and sometimes up to a couple of minutes, depending on the application), so it allows more time for positioning and aligning parts after gluing. It can be used for many of the same applications as the yellow Super T, and therefore doesn't get used as much in my shop. However, occasionally its viscosity is perfect for filling certain gaps and cracks where the red- or yellow-label glues might run out.

Accessory products are available to complement the glues. Familiarize yourself with them if you wish to become a super gluer. These aren't gimmicks; each has a practical and valuable use.

Hot Shot and Kick-It are spray-on accelerators that speed the glue's cure time and can add to a glue joint's strength. Accelerator is sprayed on one part, while glue is applied to the other. I spray accelerator on drop fills before applying the glue to harden it from below, as well. Hot Shot is a basic accelerator, while Kick-It is even faster curing and has a longer on-part life (10 minutes vs. 5 minutes for Hot Shot).

Super Solvent is a must. It cuts the super-glue bond, and I've often used it to separate my thumb and forefinger. It ruins most finishes, so bear that in mind. Thoroughly wash your hands with soap and water after using it.

Teflon tubing is handy to insert in the bottle tip for dainty, accurate glue application and control.

Extra tips aren't expensive, and having them handy allows you to switch to a fresh one when the bottle tip becomes clogged and messy.

Pipettes are clear, 5¾" long, plastic micro-applicators with a squeeze bulb. They let you apply glue cleanly and accurately wherever you want it.

Super glue spears (pictured with pipettes, above) are pinpoint accurate, super-absorbent swabs developed for eye surgery. Use them for sucking up an overrun of super glue during a panic situation.

Most important of all, always wear eye protection and work in a well-ventilated area when using glues and finishes! Rubber gloves are a good idea, although some jobs simply can't be performed while wearing gloves—in that case, just be careful. Always practice on scrap before risking damage to a valued instrument. Follow the manufacturers' instructions, and good luck!

Albert King's Lucy

This column from the September '89 issue of Guitar Player *magazine has got to be my favorite. It really was a typical weekend repair—long hours, high pressure, lots of super glue, and no pay! (I'd never think of charging Albert King!) We did manage to keep our sense of humor, though, me and Lucy. Here it is:*

It was 10:00 on a rainy Sunday morning. I scratched at the 80-grit beard stubble on my middle-aged jowls, and sipped a cup of lukewarm coffee. It hit my gut like lacquer thinner. I had the guitar repair blues. I just couldn't face another routine fret job. Then the phone rang. Sounded like *Bb*. I picked it up, and a gravelly voice rumbled through the wire.

"Hello? Is Dan there?" There was no mistaking that voice. It was Albert King, one of the greatest bluesmen in the world.

About 18 months before, Albert's equipment trailer was hit by a tornado and ended up lying on its side in a creek. Most of its contents were replaceable, but Lucy, Albert's main squeeze, was in a world of hurt. The fingerboard and wood bindings came unglued, the neck was loose, and the finish was shot. Rick Hancock of Pyramid Guitars in Memphis did a miraculous restoration job, but over time Lucy continued to react to changes in wood stability and joinery caused by her swim. According to Albert, Lucy wouldn't stay in tune and was bottoming out. Albert told me he was sending her on the next Greyhound.

When she arrived late on Thursday, I found that her neck, which was glued from several pieces, had begun to delaminate. The fingerboard tongue was humped and rising, causing string buzz, and the finish had worn through along the fingerboard edges. Albert was flying to France the following Tuesday, so I was pressed for time. Here's a quick rundown of Lucy's condition and treatment.

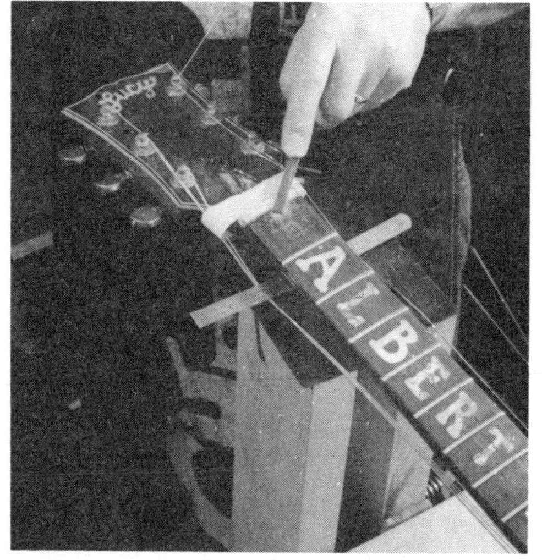

One of the highlights of my career came in 1972 when I built Lucy, a black walnut Flying V, for Albert King.

Lucy's tuning problem was caused by the nut. Too deep and no longer cleanly shaped, the string slots were pinching the string after a bend, so that the strings couldn't return to pitch. This problem was compounded by Lucy's fairly light strings—.009, .012, .024W, .028, .038, .050—and her low open tuning of, from low to high, *C F C F A D*. Solution: I filed and contoured the top of the nut to gain shallower string slots (one-half the diameter of the string, as we learned in Nut Work). I also reshaped the slot bottoms, polished them with 1500-grit Finesse wet-sanding paper, and finished up with a tiny drop of Magik Guitar Lube on each slot to lubricate the string.

Bottoming out describes a fretted string that won't sound a clean note, such as in fretting out, noting out, etc. Usually the problem is a high or low fret. In Albert's case, the fingerboard had a rising tongue, causing several high frets. Solution: With Lucy clamped into my bench-top neck jig, I removed the last six frets, planed out the rise in the fingerboard, and inserted new frets of a matching wire—a partial refret.

Later, when dressing the new frets into the old, the 16 original frets chirped as the

If you want to see my whole weekend with Lucy, get the *Super Glue Secrets* video from Stewart-MacDonald. Comes in a plain brown wrapper!

leveling file passed over them. This indicated loose frets, another cause of string buzz. I waxed the fingerboard on each side of the frets, and ran Hot Stuff red-label super glue under each one. They dried almost immediately and, once solid, could be dressed normally.

Gluing the neck laminates proved to be quite simple, and not as bad as I'd feared. Running red- and yellow-label Hot Stuff into the thin cracks "froze" them in place. Then slowly, in stages, I filled the cracks to the surface with super glue, water-sanding and buffing the glue line when it dried. The glue blended extremely well with the acrylic automotive lacquer that Rick had used on Lucy.

Albert's hard playing and the large ring on his fretting-hand pinky had worn through the finish on the fingerboard edges, allowing sweat and dirt to decay the wood; it was crumbly in places. With red- and yellow-label Hot Stuff, I saturated the fingerboard edge, building up a super-glue finish. The glue hardened the wood, hopefully making it impervious to Albert's assaults. Once again, the Hot Stuff melded beautifully with the surrounding finish.

Near the neck/body joint, the finish was well-worn on the corner of the cutaway (again, from Albert's ring shaking away on those high bends at the 15th and 17th frets). Here I tried something new: After carefully filling in chips and sealing the light-colored maple binding with thick, gap-filling super glue, I colored the worn corner of the walnut body with yellow-label Special T mixed with a tad of transparent brown sunbursting lacquer. It worked great! The finish was then built up with yellow-label super glue, sanded, and rubbed out.

Since the super glue repairs were completed on Friday, I was able to spend all day Saturday doing careful fret and nut work. This left Sunday for the final set-ups,

like replacing worn bridge saddles (above), restringing, and setting the intonation in a fairly relaxed manner (this is important, especially when setting up a guitar that's tuned low and played left-handed and upside down by a King of the blues).

Midnight on a rainy Monday night—blue Monday. Lucy's gone. I just can't face tomorrow's tremolo installation. I sip a cup of lukewarm coffee. It hits my gut like lacquer thinner...

Removing broken headstock screws

Everyone breaks off the head of a screw at one time or another—even pros. With guitars, it happens most often with tuner mounting screws installed into maple, since maple is hard and the screws are small—their heads twist off easily. If you follow the correct drilling technique for the screw thread and shoulder, you should never be faced with the problem, but don't never say never—I've snapped 'em off more than once when it seemed that everything was going right. Here's a clever trick for removing them, passed on to us by my good friend Paul Warmoth of Warmoth Guitar Products in Puyallup, Washington. It's a combination plug cutter/screw extractor.

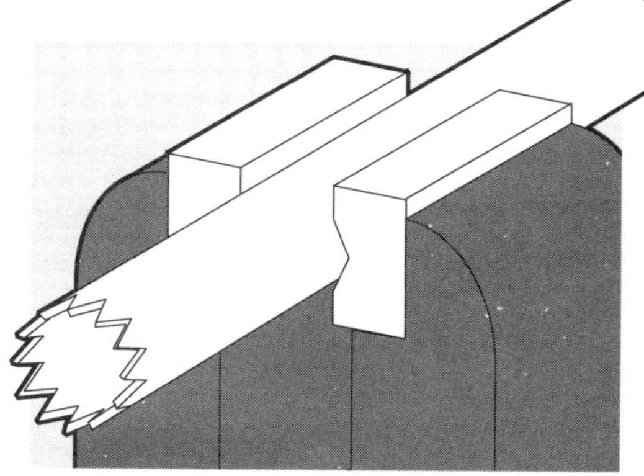

At the hobby store, buy a piece of hollow brass tubing large enough to completely surround the broken screw shank and some of the wood that it's embedded into. A 3/16" outside diameter tubing has a large enough inner diameter to straddle the screw because the tubing's walls are so thin. Clamp the tubing lightly into a vice and file small teeth into one end (above). I filed the teeth with a small feather-edge file that's used to sharpen the teeth of Japanese Dozuki and Ryobi hand saws, but any small, thin metal file will do. File the face and gullet of each tooth at slightly less than 90°, and the back or rake at any angle—you needn't be too specific—just so it angles back and away from the cutting edge to eliminate friction.

Chuck your new plug cutter into a hand drill, electric drill, or drill press, and drill slightly past the depth of the embedded screw. Then back out the cutter and wiggle the plug until it breaks off, which it will do quite easily (or use the cutter—gently, to avoid bending it—to "break" the plug out). The plug that pops out will have the broken screw in it! Now all you need to do is plug the hole with a piece of wooden dowel, and here's how you do that.

The hole you're going to fill is 3/16" in diameter, so whittle and file down a 7/32" or 1/4" dowel. When you get in the 3/16" ballpark, be very careful to keep the dowel round; you'll probably have to try several times, but dowel stick is cheap. If you have access to lots of drill bits, and preferably a drill press, there's a better way to size a wood dowel to keep it round and get a good fit.

Using a #9 drill bit, drill a hole through a 1/4" plate of steel or aluminum. The #9 bit measures .196", which is bigger by only *nine thousandths* than the 3/16" (.187") hole you wish to plug in the back of the headstock. File or sand a taper on the end of the whittled-down dowel (which is still slightly larger than 3/16"), and pound it through the hole drilled in the steel plate. The dowel compresses as it's forced through the sizing hole, allowing it to press-fit into the headstock hole when you tap it in. Then it will swell up tight if you glue it in with a water-base glue such as Franklin's Titebond or Elmer's Carpenter's Glue. Note: Whenever you drill steel, aluminum plate, or anything hard, clamp it down! Especially with steel or aluminum, and especially with a powerful tool such as an electric drill or drill press. When the metal binds to the drill bit—and it often does—it can go whipping around fast enough to cut your fingers off, at the very least! Speaking of drills and drill bits, here's some information you may be able to use:

A full set of drill bits (under a half-inch) is called a drill index, and has three types of bits: letter bits from A (.234") to Z (.413"), number bits from 1 (.228") to 80 (.013"), and fractional bits from 1/16" (.062") to 1/2" (.500"). These bits allow you to drill almost any size hole. Such a drill index was once out of reach for most of us, costing hundreds of dollars; we repairmen would buy just what we needed at a good hardware store. These days you can find the full set (of a lesser quality, but they're fine) for $49 in almost any mail-order tool catalog.

If you can get your hands on a full set of drill bits, try this old-time furniture maker's trick for sizing dowels: Drill a *series* of sizing holes. In our case, start at just under a 1/4", with perhaps a "D" or .246" bit, and drill holes at intervals of ten-thousandths until you get to the #10 (.193") size. The holes will actually *shave* the wood off as you drive the dowel

Whenever you drill steel, aluminum, or anything hard, clamp it down—especially with a powerful tool like an electric drill or drill press!

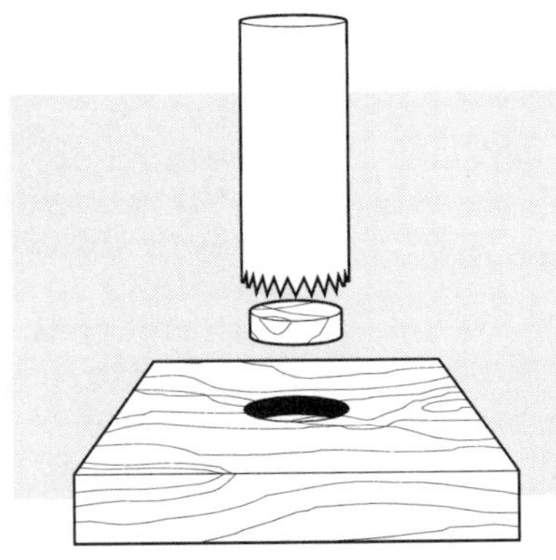

through the sizing plate, not just compress it!

There's a method here for everyone, so for the well-equipped do-it-yourselfer or the serious professional, here's *another* way to plug that hole in the headstock if you have access to a metal lathe.

Make two plug cutters: one to remove the screw and its surrounding wood, leaving a 3/16" hole in the headstock (.187"), and the other with a .196" (#9 bit) inner diameter to cut the plug that fills the hole. The smaller cutter is made from $\frac{3}{16}$" steel rod, and the larger one from 1/4" rod.

These measurements aren't set in stone. By going smaller on all the sizes, you can cut plugs that can be hidden by the housing of most tuners. I don't always use Tite-Bond glue, either; often it's Hot Stuff.

Chuck a $1\frac{1}{8}$" length of the $\frac{3}{16}$" rod into the lathe, face it off square, and bore a hole $\frac{5}{8}$" deep into the end, using a #25 (.150") bit. Remove the #25 bit, put a $\frac{3}{32}$ (.093") bit into the drill chuck, and bore a clearance hole completely through the length of the rod. This is so you can push the plug out later; we used the smaller bit for the clearance hole so the plug cutter would have some strength. File the teeth, and this is your extractor. It will cut a .150" plug around the screw and leave a $\frac{3}{16}$" hole in the headstock for you to fill.

Next chuck the $\frac{1}{4}$" rod and drill a .196" (#9) hole clear through it (a smaller clear-through hole isn't needed here, because the $\frac{1}{4}$" rod has quite a bit more strength). File the teeth, and this is your plug cutter—it will cut a *tight-fitting* .196" plug. The beauty of this method is that you can cut a plug out of *side* grain in any scrap of matching wood (maple, mahogany, whatever you have), and the match can be tremendous. Avoid burning your plug, especially in maple, by cutting slowly—these are somewhat crude, home-made bits (and they certainly aren't hard-ened)! And all this just from a little tool idea that Paul called me with one day.

Damage caused by over-oiled tuners

Something that's often overlooked when people are buying or caring for a used guitar is tuning gears that have been oiled too much. Most modern tuners are permanently sealed and lubricated, so they need no oil. However, I've seen hundreds of good guitars with tuners that have been oiled regularly, and this excessive oiling causes three common problems that can be expensive and aggravating.

The first problem is stripped mounting screw holes. The screws vibrate loose after years of playing, and when the owner tightens them, the soft, mushy wood no longer holds the screw's thread. Second, the finish lifts away around the tuners at the rear of the headstock or on the face of the headstock around the shaft hole. Finally, splits occur in the headstock wood itself. The oil seeps under the tuner, down the shaft hole, and into the wood's end grain. This eventually causes the wood to swell and sometimes split, or it may simply rot. Often these problems can be caught in time and aren't too serious. Before you attempt any repairs, the work area on the headstock needs a good cleaning and degreasing.

Begin by removing the strings and then the tuners themselves. The holes in the headstock—both the shaft holes and the mounting screw holes—are often swollen and mushy. You can remove much of the grease by packing the large shaft holes with Kleenex or cotton balls. Clean the screw holes with a pipe cleaner. An excellent absorber is the round, tightly-packed cotton wadding used by dentists. Soak up as much oil as you can, and then clean the larger holes with some lighter fluid applied with a rag, cotton, or Q-Tip; use a fresh pipe cleaner for the mounting holes. The lighter fluid helps degrease the problem areas. If you're not in a hurry, leave the holes exposed for an overnight dryout. Clean the tuner housings with lighter fluid also, so that they aren't reinstalled in their oily condition. Now that you've cleaned and degreased these, you can begin any necessary repairs.

The worn screw holes can be fixed quickly and easily with some baking soda and water-thin super glue. After you have cleaned and degreased the worn or stripped hole, fill the hole one-third full of baking soda, followed by a drop of super glue into the hole and onto the soda. The glue and soda harden immediately, usually with a puff of smoke. *Don't inhale the fumes or let them get into your eyes!* Fill the remaining two-thirds of the hole in the same manner, a third at a time, making sure that the glue saturates all the soda. When you've filled the hole flush to the surface, you can redrill it and know that the screw will hold.

It's important to use the proper size drill bit. It should match or be slightly larger than the screw's shaft, but it should not be as large as the outside measurement of the threads themselves (left). Some screws have a shoulder that is larger than the thread. You may need two drill bits in this case—one for the shaft thread, and one for the shoulder if it extends down through the tuner housing and into the headstock (right). Take the screw to a hardware store and pick out the appropriate bits. Look for number bits as well as standard fractional bits; number bits are available in a much larger selection, graduated in finer increments. Numbered drill bits ranging from #51 (small) to #44 (larger) are commonly used for tuner screws. Hold the screw against a background light and compare the bit to the screw shaft. You want to see thread on both sides of the drill bit without being able to see the screw's shaft. If the screw has a shoulder, choose a second bit that is slightly larger, to allow for clearance.

This super glue/baking soda technique works great on any stripped holes you are likely to come across, such as those for pickup mounting rings, truss rod cover plates, etc. When drilling a hole, wrap a piece of masking tape around the drill bit shaft as a depth guide as shown; this is to stop you from drilling too deep or even *through* the headstock.

To remedy the second common problem—finish that has lifted from the wood—let a small amount of lighter fluid seep under the finish where it has raised up. Allow it to evaporate and dry for at least several hours. Follow this with a drop of super glue. The glue will run under the finish as you touch the bottle's tip to the loose edge. Hot Stuff's thin, flexible applicator hose is perfect for this delicate work. Press the loose finish onto the wood, using any round, blunt object. If you wipe some wax onto this object, it will be less apt to stick to the finish or to any glue that squeezes out. Never use your finger! Don't use much super glue, and don't try to wipe off any excess. When the glue has dried—usually in a minute or two—you can remove the bead that may have squeezed out at the edges by carefully chipping it off with a sharp, pointed tool; a needle or pin will do. You may be wise to practice first on yardsale specials or a piece of old furniture.

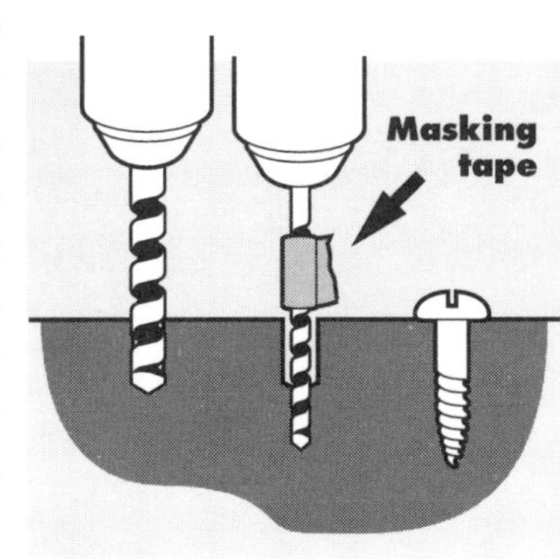

The final problem, splits in wood, should be dealt with by a qualified repairman. If you've noticed any serious split or separation of the wood at the headstock, get a pro's opinion. Regluing or filling a crack is usually inexpensive, and I'm advising you not to do this operation yourself.

To avoid these tuning-gear problems, use the proper lubricant. For the time when

If you use hide glue or Titebond, presoaking the dowel in water before installation guarantees a tight fit.

it *is* necessary to sparingly lubricate a stuck gear, use a powdered graphite or the new space-age lubricants such as Magik Guitar Lube, which have microscopic Teflon balls suspended in a solvent that evaporates quickly, leaving no oily film. A dab of Vaseline often works wonders. In most cases, the stuck tuner is an open-back, non-enclosed type. The gears are visible, so make sure that the parts aren't stripped or cross-threaded. If the gear looks worn or damaged, ask your local repairman for spare parts. Most repairmen save boxes of old gears and can match parts easily.

Broken headstocks

What's the scariest thing that can happen to your guitar? One look at the cover of this book tells you. I chose a broken headstock because it would get your attention. When your guitar's *head* breaks off, you feel like that's the end! But it isn't. Read on.

Leaving a small bandstand at the end of a performance can be tricky as you step over cords and cables, trying to snake around a ride cymbal while sidestepping a Fender Twin Reverb. Sooner or later, many guitarists watch with horror as their instrument springs from its stand and ends up on the dance floor with a broken headstock. The three most common breaks are hairline cracks, heads that are totally snapped off, or those that are cracked severely but still hanging on by the headstock veneer. You also occasionally find one that has been broken in the past and then repaired, with a new break on or near the old broken area.

In almost all cases, a broken headstock can be made like new again, but this repair is best left to a pro. (Always avoid the repairman who offers to squirt some glue in there for $20.00; this is seldom adequate.) Unless you have a great deal of woodworking experience, the best you can do with your damaged guitar is to tune down the strings immediately and place the instrument in its case—where it should have been in the first place. If the head is completely snapped off, clip the strings near the tuners and carefully wrap the head and severed neck end in newspaper; your repairman will want these slivers and fragments of wood to be as clean and untampered-with as possible.

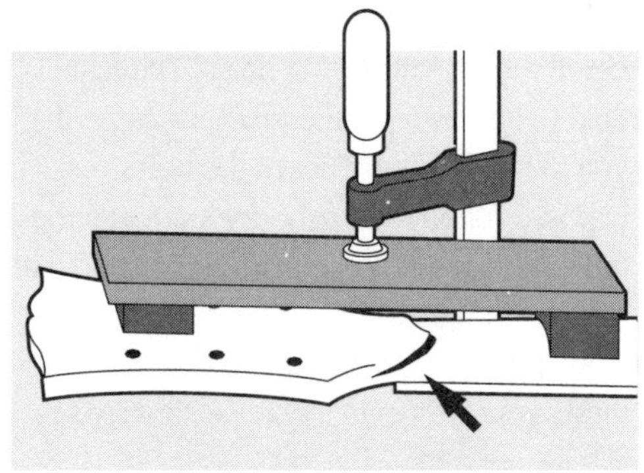

Here are some descriptions of common headstock breaks and how I think you should go about having them fixed. This information will help you in shopping for a repair job to make your guitar as good as new.

Many breaks are initially ignored because they are mistaken for simple cracks in the finish. Although these cracks are hard to open, the wood is usually broken. If the repair is not done soon, sweat, grease, and polish will find their ways into the joint, and the inevitable repair will be much more difficult and expensive. These breaks are carefully pressed open with a clamp, and cauls are used to protect the wood and finish (above). It is then easy to inject glue deep into the break. Ask your repairman if he intends to use this method.

Some headstocks snap off very cleanly, leaving a long, slanted wood surface showing. While these are easy to glue because of such a large surface area, they can be tricky to align because the two pieces

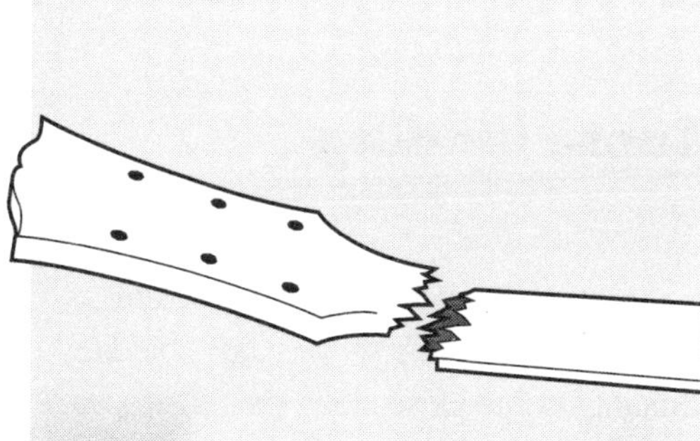

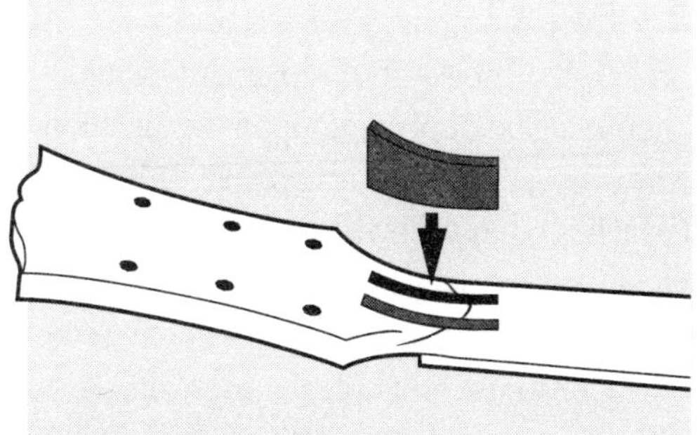

may want to slide once clamps are applied. These pieces need to be pinned temporarily during the gluing, thus ensuring proper alignment of the two surfaces. I have seen many headstocks that were glued on crooked; they seldom hold for long.

A headstock that is broken cleanly and hanging by the headstock veneer is easier to repair. Usually this case involves plastic veneer only, because wood veneer faces most often break when the headstock does. This plastic veneer is helpful in holding the two parts in alignment during clamping. However, I wouldn't advise that a novice even attempt this repair.

The most difficult repair is the clean snap with a very short break line (above). Here the two parts have fingers of wood that slide back together like a locking puzzle. Don't try to put the two parts together. Although it looks easy, you must very carefully remove even the tiniest piece of bent or loose wood. A repairman prefers to do this himself. After years of experience, I seldom even try mating the parts dry before applying glue. I can quickly judge which ones will mate. After applying the glue, I often drive the head home with a hammer tap.

The repairman must deal carefully with a new break around or on a previous fracture. Usually the re-break happens on an old glue line that wasn't repaired properly. All the old glue must be carefully scraped away down to bare wood, since new glue applied over old glue seldom holds.

Regardless of the type of break a headstock suffers, I believe that new wood (called a spline) should be inlaid through the break as a reinforcement. I generally use from two to four splines, and always run them well past the break into solid wood (from 1" to 2" on both sides of the break line). Over the years, I have repaired many headstocks by simply gluing them, and sometimes this method works. But if you're dealing with an instrument that you'd hate to

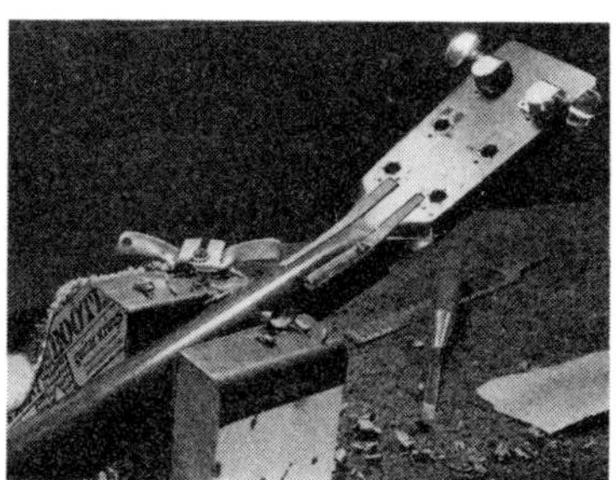

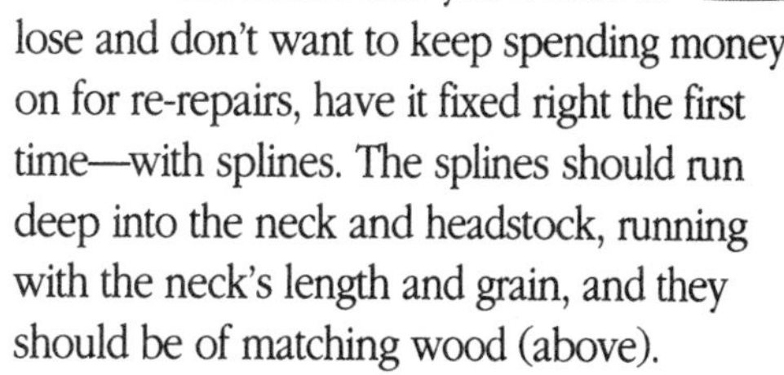

lose and don't want to keep spending money on for re-repairs, have it fixed right the first time—with splines. The splines should run deep into the neck and headstock, running with the neck's length and grain, and they should be of matching wood (above).

Sometimes, in addition to the splines, we'll put new headstock overlays on the headstock face, or cover the whole back of the headstock with a back strap (a veneer of wood that covers the back surface of the headstock and even runs out onto the neck—a common building technique for fancy banjos and certain higher-end guitars). By putting new wood on the front and back of the headstock, you can "sandwich" the broken area—right over the splines!

These techniques take an experienced touch and lots of practice. A repairman should be glad to discuss any technique with you beforehand—it's your guitar. Obviously, a fair amount of finish work has to be performed before the job is complete. Most headstocks can be artfully touched up so that few people would ever know that the job has been done. Once again, shop around. Not every repair shop can handle this job.

There is no *one* glue for repairing broken headstocks. The repairman should choose a glue depending upon the situation. Any of several glues is acceptable. White (which is often yellowish) or aliphatic-resin glues are especially effective when there is a clean, woody break. Sometimes epoxy is the only glue to use, but only the most skilled repairman can get away with applying it to a broken headstock, because it doesn't penetrate into the wood fibers as well as some others. Urea-resin glue comes in a dry powder form that mixes with water, and it has great penetration, strength, and gap-filling qualities. There are situations in which super glue is appropriate, but again this could only be used by a pro—too risky! Ask the repairman what type of glue he'll employ. If you find a repairman who's familiar with the techniques shown here, and you trust him, let him make the decisions.

If you're considering attempting the repair yourself, remember that to do the job right, you probably need to make the following investment in tools and supplies: clamps, $40.00; chisels, $20.00; files, $10.00; Plexiglas for gluing cauls, $4.00; glue, $2.00; wood spline material, $4.00; lacquer, thinner, stains, wood filler, $30.00; finishing equipment using Pre-Val aerosol spray units with extra jars, $20.00 (this is the least expensive finishing method). Total price: $130.00. I honestly don't think you can do a professional job without these supplies and a lot of practice, so use this article as an aid in finding someone willing to do the job right the first time. Better yet, keep your guitar in a case when it isn't in your hands. You can buy a lot of albums with $130.00.

Loose binding

One of the most common problems seen in a busy repair shop is loose binding. Bindings come loose along the fingerboard's edge, at the back or top edges where the sides join, on the headstock face, and around the soundhole ring of an acoustic. Most bindings come loose because the wood shrinks in one direction (across its width), while the binding shrinks in the opposite direction (lengthwise). This shrinking, combined with dry glue, climate factors, and in some cases improper glue application during construction, causes the bindings to come loose, which in turn will catch any loose shirt sleeve that passes by. While most modern guitars are bound with celluloid, you might own a guitar with wooden binding. These bindings require a bit more experience to repair or replace, and although many of my tips also apply to wood bindings, this section deals with the more common plastic ones, which can be reglued easily with few tools.

Plastic bindings generally are glued with an acetone-based, plastic-solvent glue. Often this glue melts the plastic into the wood. Usually melted bindings won't come loose in the first place, but if they do, a bit of wood may come with them. If you need this type of problem repaired, have it looked at by a professional. More often, however, the plastic pulls loose with a clean separation, although if the joint has been loose for years, there may be a fair amount of dirt wedged into the opening. This dirt should be removed before the regluing.

Cleaning the binding and the groove or channel it seats in can be easily done. When the section of binding is completely separated, gently remove any grease or dirt with a lint-free rag dipped in lighter fluid (I always wear disposable rubber gloves when I'm

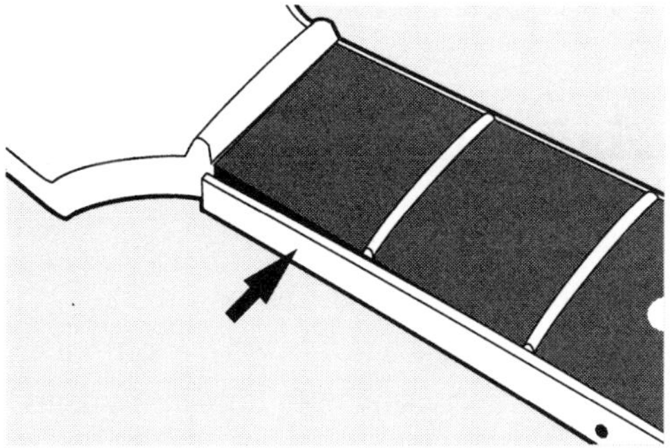

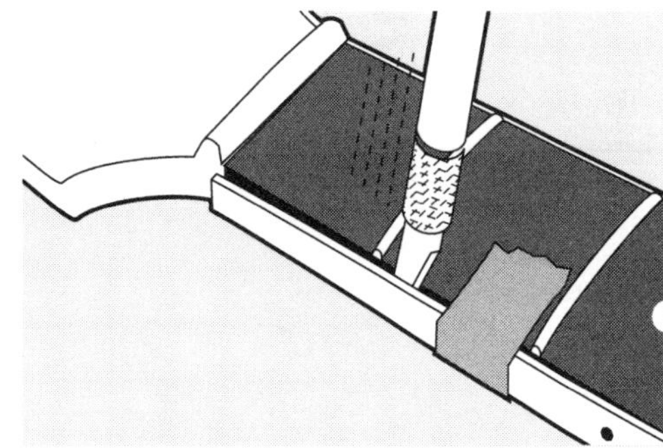

handling strong solvents). With a sharp X-acto knife, you can cut, chip, or gently scrape any hard, caked-on dirt. Using the back of this blade as a scraper is good for pulling dirt from a crevice or from binding that is only loose in a section while the main portion is still glued tight (above). The idea is to remove foreign matter and grease. In the case of a binding that's loose for only a small area—say, from the 1st to the 5th fret along the fingerboard's edge—stretch masking tape across the point where it's still glued. This way, you can gently peel the plastic away from its glue channel to clean it without further loosening the section that is holding well (above, right).

Binding at the guitar's waist or any area where a sharp curve has to be dealt with, such as a cutaway, is difficult to reglue. So is the fingerboard binding over the tongue. The binding at the waist can shrink and pull away from the body, and because it has shrunk so much, the piece cannot be forced back to its original position. Therefore, it must be cut and a patching piece fitted into the resulting gap. This patching-in requires some experience, as well as a supply of different binding pieces for a proper match. The fingerboard tongue is somewhat difficult to clamp and requires specialized tools. Don't work on these areas if you're just starting out—leave them to someone with experience. Most other areas are easy to glue, and all you'll need for pressure is a roll of masking tape.

Masking tape is the perfect clamp for headstock, fingerboard (though not over the tongue), and most body bindings. You can apply it near the loose areas on the guitar's side, top, back, headstock face, or back of the neck. For best results, stretch the tape as you go around the guitar's edge. The stretched tape tends to pull the binding into its channel. Caution: On old, checked, thin-finished vintage instruments, be careful not to pull off finish when removing the tape after the glue has dried. Repairs on vintage instruments are better left to a pro. In all cases, remove the masking tape slowly, pulling at a slight angle to the tape's length. Any job that can't be glued using tape for the clamp may also need the pro's touch. It's always good to practice a glue-up "dry"—using no glue—as a trial run.

Franklin's Titebond and Elmer's Carpenter's Glue are the best and safest for a beginner. When the loose area is properly cleaned, these glues do an adequate job of holding the plastic in place—if left to dry overnight. White glues are water-soluble and offer the advantage of neat, easy clean-up. They usually run into cracks easily, but if you have difficulty, spread the crack with your knife tip and push glue in with a finger. Note: I usually do plastic binding repair with Dupont Duco Cement or super glue, but these glues should not be used by the inexperienced. There are a few areas where these two glues are necessary, and when you've gained some experience and talked to a few repairmen and studied the subject, you will know when and how to use them.

It's important to think about *any* repair before you jump in and do something that can't be undone. Patience is hard to learn, and it usually comes the hard way.

Don't be alarmed if the binding is a little too short to fill the original gap. Remember that the plastic has shrunk from end to end. In order to stretch binding, you must use a Duco-type cement that actually softens the plastic on contact, allowing it to become somewhat flexible. However, this softening is the reason that I don't advise you to use this glue without experience. Don't try it on your old Les Paul or Martin D-28.

The usual problem with loose soundhole binding is that it pops up and out of its channel, often where two pieces butt together. While holding the piece up with your knife tip, work white glue in with a finger or by blowing it into the groove. Next, push the binding into place, wipe off the excess, and apply a small C-clamp for pressure. Use a piece of Plexiglas (lightly waxed so it won't stick) as a caul to hold it flat while drying (above). Protect the inside of the guitar from the clamp's jaw with a piece of wood or stiff cardboard. If you drill a few holes into the Plexiglas, the glue area will dry more easily. Leave the clamp on at least four hours. The proper-size clamp shouldn't cost more than $3.00 or $4.00.

Be sure to *study* the problems mentioned here before attempting any repairs, and certainly don't do anything if you aren't truly confident. If you're at all in doubt, take your guitar to a qualified repairman and pay the small fee that these jobs usually cost. Most repairmen enjoy having a customer to talk shop with—a customer who can appreciate the trade.

Fixing a guitar case

Repairmen would have less work—and I'd have much less to write about—if musicians conscientiously kept instruments in cases. It's sad enough to see a scratch, ding, or split on an inexpensive guitar, but the serious and sometimes total damage that I've seen inflicted on caseless vintage guitars would make even a hardened repairman wince. While almost any case is usually better than none at all, to ensure your instrument's safety and to avoid many of the problems I write about, consider several simple points that will keep your case as strong and safe as possible.

By far the most common problem with an older hardshell or softshell case is the normal loosening of the hinges that hold the top to the body. It may be necessary to remove and replace the rivets that hold a hinge to the case. Usually it's possible to clip off the head of the rivet from the case exterior using an end nipper, which is a common hardware store item (top right). Once the head is removed, use a sharp knife to cut the plush or leatherette lining, and simply peel it back inside the case to expose the remaining rivet (middle drawing). You can then remove the stretched, worn-out rivet and redrill, creating a slightly larger hole through the hinge and the side of the case. (The Tandy Leather Co. is a well-known supplier of tools and parts for this type of job.) The rivet can then be inserted through the new, enlarged hole. Then, holding a solid steel object inside as an anvil, use a hammer to pound the rivet into its seat from the outside.

If the cardboard is worn and spongy in the hinge area of an inexpensive chipboard case, glue an oversized piece of strong cardboard to the inside for reinforcement before drilling and riveting. If a hinge has torn loose and become lost, make your own from a scrap of leather or strong fabric that is wider than the torn area. Glue it on and install rivets for strength. The result doesn't look bad, and an otherwise useless case is salvaged.

Another common problem with cases is the eventual collapse of the accessories box. In a quality plywood (hardshell) case, the walls of the box are usually nailed to the side walls from the outside. These nails probably can be pried out, and then you can rebuild the accessories box by regluing the ends to the sides and inserting longer, stronger nails. If there is a plush lining, remove the parts carefully, but don't be afraid to cut the material in order to get at the problem. Usually, plush lining peels easily from the plywood and is reglued just as easily. To hide any new nails or rivets, put a dab of glue over each one, and then press down a tuft of the "fur" borrowed from a less conspicuous area of the case. This produces an invisible repair.

By carefully disassembling a wooden accessories box, you can reshape its cradle (the neck-support part), thus raising or lowering the neck's position in the case. I have done this often with cases that won't quite close because the neck is sitting too high on the support. I can generally re-cover it with the same material I peeled back before disassembly. A worn-out cardboard-type box can be easily removed and replaced with a new one constructed of a similar material, which is then glued to the case's sidewalls. A new lid can then be made and glued to the box, using a strip of cloth as a hinge (bottom drawing).

Repairing locks on a case is usually difficult, requiring specialized parts and tools. It is possible, however, to remove many locks and replace them entirely—if not with an exact match, at least with something that works. Locks are generally mounted with either rivets or metal tabs that are bent into the case walls as fasteners. If the lock clasp works properly but the lock is broken, you might consider leaving it as is and forget about trying to lock the case.

Hasps, clasps, and hinges usually cause trouble only when bent, and they are easily fixed by bending or hammering them back into the proper shape. A loose hasp can be re-installed using the rivet/hammer method. A broken case handle is often just as easy to fix, using the same rivet/hammer method. Sometimes, though, a replacement handle is the only solution. You can find suitable new handles in hardware stores, luggage shops, luthier suppliers, and many music stores. While you may not find a handle that duplicates the old one, perhaps you'll find one that you can adapt, using rivets to hold it on.

Many older plywood cases end up with the exterior leatherette worn away on the corners, and the wooden layers eventually separate. Reglue these plies by deeply injecting them with a slightly thinned mixture of white glue and water; I use veterinary syringes with large needles. Squeeze out any excess and clamp for a few hours. A little touch-up with a matching paint (not too glossy) looks good, especially if you stipple the paint in an attempt to match the case's grain.

The most common case repairs in my shop are rips, tears, and scratches in fairly new cases. I usually perform these repairs *gratis*, since they are quick and easy to do. A drop of super glue under a raised tear will hold it forever. As the glue sets, you can engrave grain lines into it for an extra touch. Accelerator causes the glue to harden almost instantly, and the reaction can cause it to mound up, looking somewhat like a bubble of leather. Using these techniques, you can get a lot more mileage from your case, and you may find the work is fun and easy to do.

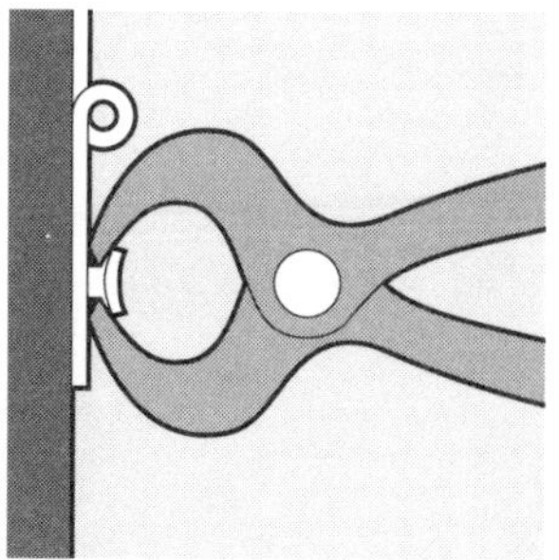

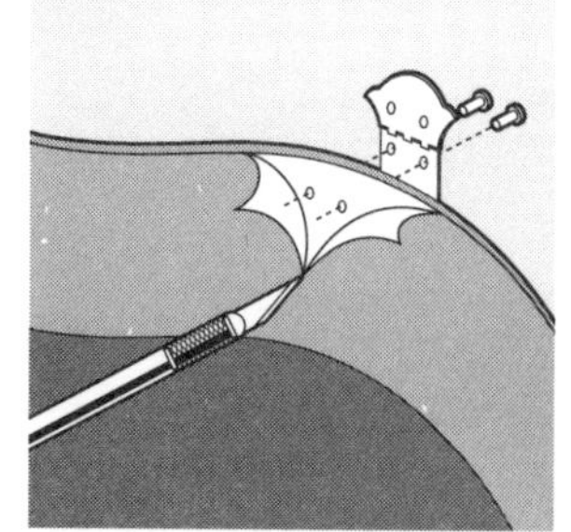

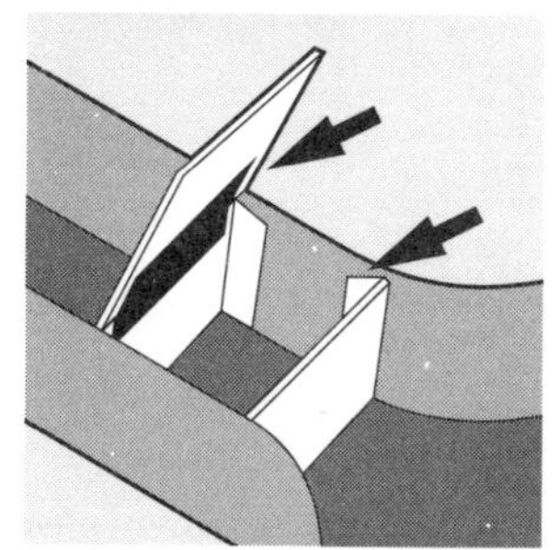

How to ship a guitar

Your '59 Sunburst has so many fret buzzes, it sounds like killer bees are swarming in your amp. Your prize prewar acoustic feels like it's strung with baling wire. Worse yet, your local "repair" shop's equipped with only two tools: a chainsaw and a really big hammer. Or maybe you're buying/selling an instrument, and just want to get it from here to there. What do you do?

Shape up and ship out! UPS does a great job of handling all kinds of fragile and expensive stuff. While recently packing a repaired guitar for its return trip, I decided to pass along some packing tips to those of you who find it necessary to ship a guitar now and then. If you pack 'em right, you won't *need* a repair book! (Just kidding.)

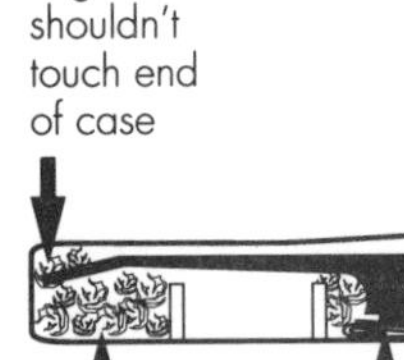

Good guitars should travel first-class in hardshell cases. If yours has a softshell case, buy a hard one or keep the guitar at home. The same commonsense principles apply to packing acoustic and electric guitars. First, pick up the heaviest guitar shipping box that you can find at your local music store; my favorites are those used by Martin, Gibson, Fender, and Guild. Then:

1 Remove any unnecessary items from the case's accessory box, and make sure that the lid can't open.

2 Tune down the strings until they're slack. During a fall, pressure from tuned-up strings can break a headstock.

3 Be sure that the tuners are tight and can't vibrate loose to rattle around inside the case.

4 Protect an electric guitar's fingerboard and pickups by sliding folded paper in between them. With an arch-top, pad all around the bridge with paper pushed under the strings and tailpiece, or remove the bridge entirely.

5 See that the neck rests in its support cradle. The headstock shouldn't touch the case, and it should be supported all around with crushed newspaper rolled into 2" to 3" balls (see drawing at left).

6 For acoustics, fold some paper and support the back of the guitar under the neck block area if there's a gap between it and the case.

7 The guitar shouldn't move inside when you shake the case. If it does, pad the waist and bout areas with paper.

8 Drop a layer of crushed newspaper balls into the bottom of your shipping box, and lower the case into it. Center the case in the box (below) and fill the box snugly on all sides with paper balls; use a stick to push them down where you can't reach.

9 If your shipping box still has the original cardboard fillers inside, use them and/or the crushed newspaper. Stiff cardboard placed in the right areas can really firm up a box.

10 Use gummed, fiber-reinforced tape (usually brown) to seal the box when it's full. Wet the gummed side with a damp rag.

11 Clearly print the shipping address on the box. I always print "Fragile, Please" on all four sides (adding the word "please" is important), and draw a picture of a broken long-stemmed wine glass—the international "fragile" symbol (below).

12 Insure the guitar for more than it's worth, pay the UPS person, say your prayers, and you're done. You'll be in good shape.

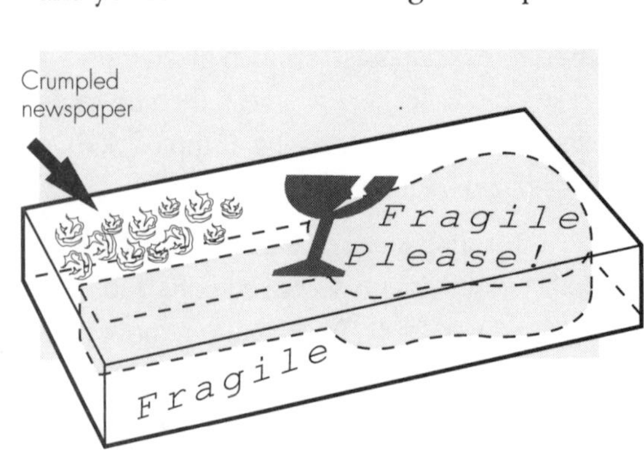

Tools, tools, tools...

The more you have, the more you want. All do-it-yourselfers have a love affair with tools. Before getting too involved with guitar repair tools, I'd like to give you the bare-bones details on sharpening two of our most important ones, chisels and scrapers. I gained much of my sharpening and woodworking knowledge from reading *Fine Woodworking* magazine (Taunton Press, 63 S. Main St., Box 5506, Newtown, CT 06470). If you're a woodworker, subscribe to this magazine! Most libraries have back issues, so read the chisel sharpening article in the July/August '81 issue. It tells all you need to know.

SHARPENING CHISELS

The Japanese are probably best at it. If you're buying your first good chisel, consider buying one of the Japanese versions—nothing sharpens quite as well. The English-made Marples are also a good choice. Woodcraft is a good source for these. I often use a capo on my guitar, and I use a "cheater" for chisel sharpening, too (right). The roller honing guide allows you to set your chisel at a preferred angle and keep it there as you make smooth strokes lengthwise on the stone. If you're not looking to go big-time into chisels and sharpening (buying lots of chisels and different-grit stones), make your first chisel a ½" one, and get a fine-grit synthetic/ceramic sharpening stone. These stones are easy to clean, don't wear out, and can be used without lubricant.

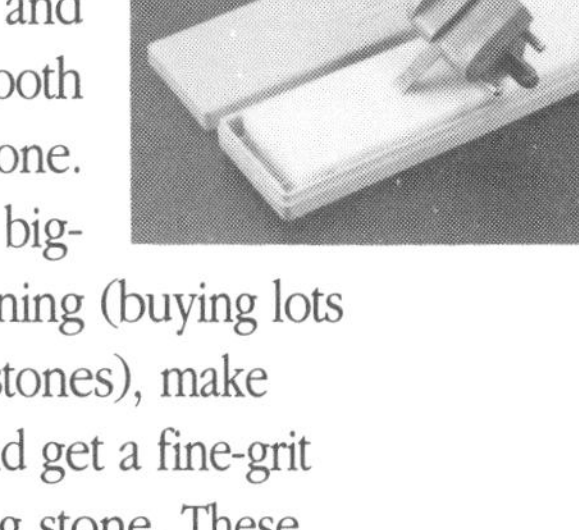

The most common angle for the bevel of a wood chisel is 35°. When worn-out and blunted, chisel bevels are renewed by first being ground on a bench grinder to the proper angle, and then honed smooth on the stone. (See the caution about grinder safety

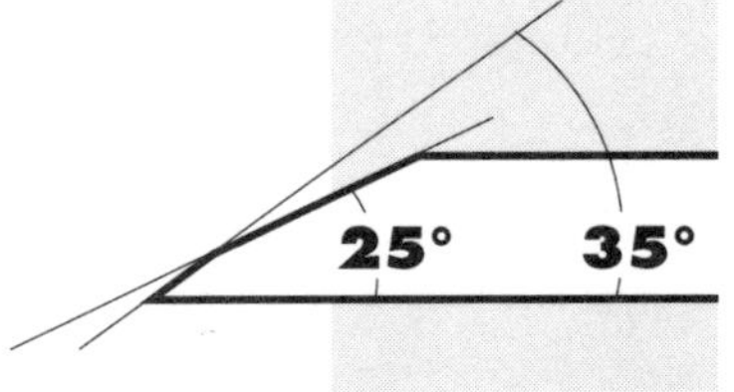

in "Making your own fret dressing files.") A good trick: If you first grind the initial bevel to a 25° angle, sharpening it to the required 35° bevel is quick and efficient.

SHARPENING SCRAPERS

This is an art, and everyone has his own way of doing it. Again, you'll find the facts in *Fine Woodworking* magazine, May/June '86. The idea is to clamp the scraper blade in a vise while you flatten and sharpen its thin edge, making it 90° to the sides. Do this with a smooth-mill metal file like the one used for fret leveling. Then hone the edge on your ceramic stone, holding it at 90° to the flat stone surface. Next lay the sharpened scraper on the edge of a firm surface and stroke the *flat* side of the scraper with a burnisher (a piece of steel that's harder than the scraper), holding it a few degrees off horizontal; this creates a burr on the thin edge. Now "turn" the burr by stroking the *thin* edge of the scraper with the burnisher, and you've got an edge that can cut shavings almost like a plane. A scraper is usually held at an angle to the grain of the wood, and is often bent or curved slightly by flexing it with both hands. If you're lazy or in a hurry, you can use a scraper immediately after the filing stage, skipping the other steps. It probably won't work as well, and it's not *proper*, but I do it all the time with good results! Every third or fourth time, I do it right, following every step for a great edge.

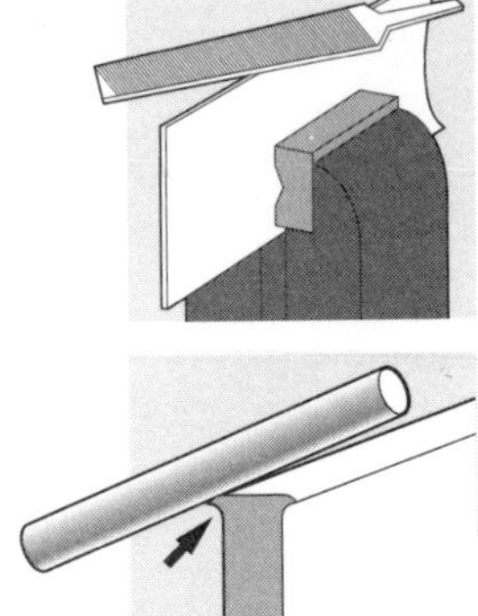

These are the two most important woodworking tools you'll use, along with a slim-handle X-acto knife and plenty of #11 blades. Never be without fresh X-acto blades; if you're in the middle of a job and the blade isn't doing its work, throw it out and grab a fresh one; professionals go through blades in a hurry. It's seldom worth sharpening them, since it's hard to get a factory edge.

Tools of the trade

Intonation getting weird? What about your action? Need a neck adjustment? More and more players are learning to maintain and adjust their own guitars, and it's common these days for them to invest in the simple tools needed for doing their own adjustments, set-ups, and minor repairs. These "case pocket" tools are the basis from which every full-fledged repair shop is built. Here we'll take a look at the tools that keep the guitar world running, from the common ones smart players use to keep their axes sharp to the specialized tools of guitar techs, builders, and repairmen—the tools of the trade.

PLAYER'S TOOL KIT

This should hold everything a well-adjusted guitarist needs to keep his or her guitar from going schizo. The list applies to players of acoustic and electric guitars and basses; if you play only one or the other, you may not need a certain tool, but get it anyway, since you may soon be setting up your friends' guitars, too.

- **Tuner.** An inexpensive reed-type A-440 tuner or pitch pipe, or a six-note pitch pipe (*E A D G B E*) will do. Make your first serious tuner investment an A-440 tuning fork; it will last a lifetime. Add an electronic tuner when you can afford a good one.
- **String cutter.** A pair of small end nippers or side cutters is a must. A needle-nose pliers/side cutter combo makes a versatile string cutter that can handle other jobs, too.
- **String winder.** Buy two—they're cheap. Keep one in your case and one in your tool-box. Get one with a bridge-pin puller on it.

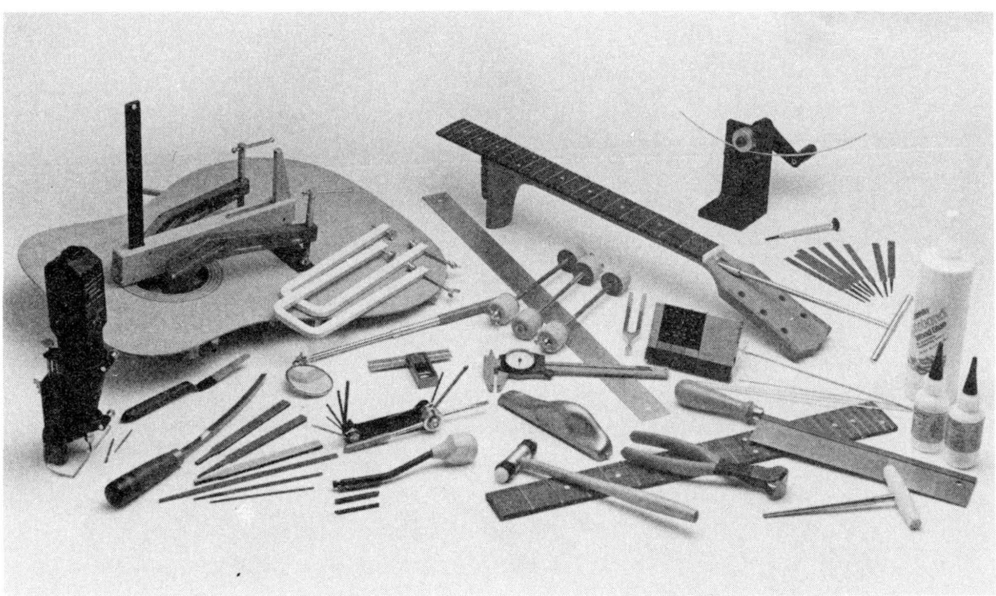

■ **Inspection mirror.** To check the insides of an acoustic guitar—a must if you're shopping for a flat-top.

■ **Screwdrivers.** Small-sized Phillips and flat-bladed screwdrivers for adjusting bridges and tightening parts on electrics or acoustics. Start with the small sizes and add the larger ones as they're needed for installing or removing strap buttons, tailpiece studs, etc.

■ **Allen wrenches.** You need these for hardware adjustments on most electrics. The most common small sizes for tremolos, locking nuts, and bridge saddles are .050", 1/16", 5/64", 3/32", 5/32", 7/64" (fractional), and 1.5mm, 2.5mm, 3.5mm (metric) for imported guitars. Many domestic and imported guitars have truss rod adjusting nuts in the larger 3/16" to 7mm size, too. The Guitool combines Allen wrenches, screwdrivers, and a string cutter all in one.

■ **Socket-head nut drivers.** These are needed for truss rod adjustments on many American guitars—most notably Gibson (5/16") and Guild (1/4"). Some are a bit too thick to get onto the truss rod nut and into the truss nut cavity at the same time. The long-shanked, "T"-handled, thin-wall wrenches styled after those used by Gibson are my favorites.

■ **Solvent cleaner.** This is helpful for cleaning dirty finishes and hardware. Naphtha (lighter fluid) is good for sticky or greasy spots on most finishes. A good polishing or cleaning is a must several times a year. For cleaning a really dirty guitar, use Meguiar's Mirror-Glaze #7. A light cleaning can be done with any of the creme-type guitar polishes.

■ **6" stainless-steel ruler.** For setting string height. General makes a good one that you'll find in almost every hardware store. It has fraction-to-decimal conversions on the back, which come in handy.

■ **Dial calipers.** A pair of these isn't a must, but it's a nice luxury—great for checking string gauges and action height. An inexpensive but accurate pair can be bought for about $30.00.

■ **A straightedge.** This is for neck adjustments. The two edges of a rafter square (a hardware store item) work for guitar or bass. The more expensive precision straightedges are even better, if you can afford one.

■ **Radius gauge.** Check the section on adjusting the bridge curve with a radius gauge as your guide. Stewart-MacDonald offers an inexpensive set of gauges, or make

your own after reading the Electric Adjustments chapter.

■ **Nut file.** Most players would benefit from owning a small, thin nut file for cleaning and reshaping nut slots and bridge saddle grooves. This is not a necessity, but nice. A thin X-acto razor-saw blade can serve as a substitute.

■ **Nail clippers.** Last but not least, this is an essential item for all guitarists. Don't leave home without one!

If you own all these tools and know when and where to use them, you can properly set up your instruments and keep them that way. You may need to visit a professional repair shop for fret work or a new nut, but you'll be relatively independent. If you also have the skills to troubleshoot and solve amplifier problems, set up and fine-tune effects, run a snake through a crowded stage while you're tuning six guitars and restringing a bass, and then have the stamina to pack it all into a semi at 4 AM, consider becoming a guitar technician—better known as a guitar tech.

Robert Cray's Greg Zaccaria (left) and John Hiatt's Andrew Burns—with a truckload of vintage guitars.

I've talked with many guitar techs, among them Steve Vai's Stan Schiller, the Georgia Satellites' Steve Winsted, Steve Parish with the Grateful Dead, Robert Cray's Greg Zaccaria, and John Hiatt's Andrew Burns. Their jobs involve a lot more than sitting around changing strings all day. They're responsible for setting up and maintaining anything to do with the guitarists' gear: all effects, wireless outfits, amplifier and speaker set-ups, and of course, the guitars. "Ultimately," says Stan Schiller, "I'm responsible for any sound Steve Vai makes onstage. I set the sweeps and delay time, and it's not uncommon for me to change settings on the [Bob] Bradshaw board two or three times in one song—maybe more!"

At a Grateful Dead concert, Steve Parish gave me a great backstage "tour de tools." Steve's operation is unusual in the sense that it has about three of every tech tool known to man, and then some. He travels with two tool chests. One's a large wooden one with drawers filled with guitar and bass strings, power cords, wire, outlets, light bulbs, vacuum tubes, capacitors, resistors, power supplies, ad infinitum—replacement parts for any occasion. It's more of a supply box. The other box, which holds his main tools, is a piggyback mechanic's tool chest. The lower drawers house a mini hardware store: crescent, box, open-end, and socket wrenches, vise-grips, hammers, hatchets, pipe wrenches, taps, dies, etc.—the large tools needed for tearing down amps and stage props, or for fixing the fuel pump on the band bus, for that matter. In the top drawers are the more specialized guitar tools.

For instance, there's a Dremel Moto-Tool, which, according to Steve, "is good for grinding on any kind of wood or metal. With the right bit or attachments, I can even cut the string groove in replacement metal bridge saddles. And I have screwdrivers of every description—drawers full of them. Miniature watchmaker's screwdrivers are handy for working on so many small electric gadgets. One of the main things most players should have is a good screwdriver set.

"Many of the tools I use are quite common but no less important, such as nut drivers, metric and standard Allen wrenches, scissors, files, drill bits, calipers, and a tape measure. Spray pot cleaner is a must—my favorite is Beaver Cleaner—as are glues such as epoxy, super glue, and Elmer's Glue-All or Titebond. I can't tell you how many times I've fixed something with Elmer's and matchsticks. [Author's Note: Matchsticks dipped in glue and shoved into a stripped hole will hold a screw's thread.] My volt-ohm meter [multi-meter] is important, because if Jerry Garcia's 9-volt battery drops just a little bit below voltage, he can hear it in his tone. So I'm constantly checking batteries. Bobby Weir uses a wireless set-up, so we can't go but one set without changing batteries—if you *push* it, you're pushing your whole deal. My meter's a Fluke SM 77. It's completely digital and extremely versatile—the high-price spread. You don't need one this good when you're starting out.

"With the Dead, each tech has his own station—keyboard station, drum station, like that—and each station has its own tools. One of the great things about the Dead has always been that when it comes to buying a tool, we can have anything we need, so I've got a great collection of them. My Paladin wire strippers are special—for $50.00 they should be! We also have a Porta-Sol soldering pencil that runs on butane, like a cigarette lighter. It gets hot fast, and I can use it anywhere. [Author's Note: Radio Shack has a similar soldering tool under its own name.]

"But most special of all is the little kit that I always keep in Jerry Garcia's case wherever he goes, even to sit in and jam at some club. This is in a leather holster, and it includes a Phillips and flat-blade screwdriver, wire cutters, and a string winder—your basic survival kit." Steve keeps a careful eye on all the playing aspects of the guitars, and he prefers to have fret work done by someone who specializes in it. In an emergency, he hires a local repairman: "There's more good repairmen around now than when I started, so it's easier to find help on the road. I used to carry frets on the road and would perform emergency surgery, but now I have spare guitars—it's much easier."

Most of the techs I interviewed don't play the guitar much, if at all. A technical understanding of how a guitar should play enables them to please their bosses. I learned, too, that there's a limit as to the type of guitar maintenance a tech is expected to do; in particular, I was curious as to who does any necessary work on frets and string nuts. While they all carry the specialized files for shaping the nut slots (see the "Repair shop tools" list) or dressing and recrowning frets in emergencies, as a rule these jobs are taken care of by a repair shop chosen by the tech when the band's off the road. An exception to the rule is Greg "Zak" Zaccaria of the Robert Cray Band.

Having interned with a repairman to pick up the necessary skills, Zak does the nut work, refretting, and fret dressing on Robert's guitars. He also plays guitar well, as does Andrew Burns, who's John Hiatt's tech. They've spent a lot of time together, since their bosses perform a lot of twin bills. Zak's the senior tech, and I got the impression that Andrew was glad to have the opportunity to work with him. I spent an afternoon watching the two of them set up for the evening show.

An electronics wiz who designs mixing consoles on the side, Zak is set-up as well as Steve Parish—a walking hardware/music store/Fender parts supply. He and Andrew travel with some 24 guitars and basses between them (13 for the Cray band, 11 for Hiatt's), all of which must be restrung, adjusted, and tuned for every show.

The guitarists in both bands change guitars often between songs, usually so quickly that the audience hardly notices it. The techs race across the rear of the stage in the dark, switch instruments, and then run back to the work table to replace a string or retune, all the while monitoring the levels of as many as three guitars at once. Robert Cray alternated between three different Strats during his hour-and-a-half show; he switched guitars at least a dozen times—once delivering the guitar to his tech by sliding it across the stage with his foot! Needless to say, the backs of some of Robert's instruments are a little worn.

Both techs operate on top of Zak's custom-made road chest, which folds open to expose drawers of tools and spare parts. The chest's top surface acts as a workbench, and it's equipped with miniature goose-neck lamps that allow quick repairs to be done in semi-darkness during songs. Robert Cray plays hard on heavy treble strings (.011, .013, .018, .028, .036, .046), and quickly wears grooves into the bridge saddles. Zak carries spare saddles, and replaces them often. Measuring between the bottom of the strings and the top of the last fret, Robert's guitars have a string height of 2mm (.079") for the first string, graduating to 2½mm (.098") for the sixth string.

All the techs agreed that investing in tools is a gradual process, and the consensus is that a good basic start could be made for several hundred dollars. Expect to invest from $1,000 to $2,000 by the time you're equipped as well as the professionals mentioned here. Such an investment may or may not include a significant amount of non-tool staples, such as cleaners, polishes, sandpaper, batteries, wire, solder, etc.

TECH TOOLS

Any way you look at it, there's a big tool gap between a well-adjusted player and the ready-for-all-emergencies guitar tech. Here's a list of tools that the serious tech carries on the road. I haven't included the player's tools mentioned at the beginning of the article, since a tech owns all of those, too.

- Several 6" and 12" bar clamps for general clamping and repairs—a "helping hand" when you're in need
- Tin snips (just because Steve Parish has some)
- Long and short needle-nose pliers for electrical work
- Vise-Grips (locking pliers)
- Multi-meter for testing circuits, batteries, voltage, etc.
- De-soldering tool (solder-sucker)
- Soldering pencil or gun
- Alligator clips, jumper cables (electrical connections for testing)
- Complete sets of small, large, Phillips, flat-blade, and watchmaker's screwdrivers
- Power screwdriver
- Dial caliper or micrometer
- Dremel Moto-Tool w/bits, grindstones, etc.

- Butane brazing torch (another luxury)
- Electronic tuner
- Complete sets of metric and standard Allen wrenches
- Wire strippers
- Tuner degreaser/cleaner
- WD-40 spray lubricant
- Fret-leveling file, appropriate sandpapers and steel wool
- Fret-rounding files
- Nut-slotting files
- Safety glasses
- $\frac{3}{8}$" electric drill (I love the cordless variety by Sears, Makita, Ryobi, Skil, etc.)
- Handsaws in several sizes
- Hand-held electric circular saw (Skil-saw)
- Electric jigsaw (sabre saw)
- Truss-rod wrenches
- Drill bits (fractional, by 64ths, from $\frac{1}{16}$" to $\frac{1}{2}$")
- Precision straightedges for checking neck straightness and fret height
- Tape measure
- Hammer
- Crowbar and flat-bar
- X-acto knife (the slim aluminum artist-type with the #11 blade)
- Hacksaw and replacement blades
- Vise for holding parts being worked on (a drill-press vise is quite handy)

REPAIR SHOP TOOLS

Let's add to the list by taking a look at the tools needed to operate a full-service guitar repair shop. Although most guitar repairmen haven't perfected the same electrical skills with amps and effects that a tech has, they use the same tools in repairing guitar electronics, so assume that a repair shop owns all the previously listed tools. I won't re-list them.

Repair shops are equipped similarly to shops that do only building, with the same basic power and woodworking tools, spray finishing equipment, and a lot more. In other words, a guitar repair shop is equipped to build almost anything, but not on a production basis. After speaking with scads of repairmen, I've come up with the following list of the tools necessary to operate a complete repair shop.

- Pliers for bending frets (both jaws ground to a basic fret shape for a good grip)
- Small brass hammer for fretting
- Flush-ground end nippers for removing frets and cutting them to size
- Dremel Moto-Tool, router base, and assorted bits
- Mid-sized electric drill
- Radius gauges ($7\frac{1}{4}$" to 20" radius templates for bridge saddle curvature and fret work)
- Taps and dies for retapping worn threads, tapping holes, all sorts of fabrication
- Drill index with fraction, letter, number bits
- Straight and curved hemostats for holding small parts during soldering
- Feeler gauge set for measuring action, fret height, string height at nut, etc.
- Thin palette knives and spatulas for mixing glues, separating wood joints, resetting necks, etc.
- Straight and curved wood scrapers for flattening and smoothing wood
- Vet's syringes and needles for glue injection in hard-to-get areas
- Infrared heat bulb to soften wood parts for removal (usually used with fingerboards)
- Pressure cooker for steaming necks out of their sockets
- Hot plate for heating pressure cooker, boiling water, steaming, cooking lunch, etc.
- Full set of chisels
- Full set of nut files
- Full set of woodworking files—rasps, rifflers, etc.
- Any fret-rounding files you can find
- 10" smooth mill file for fret leveling
- 6" triangle file for fret rounding
- X-acto knife (slim artist knife with #11 blades)

- Spray guns and air compressor
- Buffing and polishing pads
- Air brush
- Center punch
- Jeweler's saw and extra blades (for pearl cutting)
- Respirator
- Fret-slotting saw
- Fret nippers
- Fret bender
- Fret radius blocks for sanding, dressing, and prepping fingerboards
- Neck heater (for straightening necks)
- Tapered reamers (large $\frac{9}{16}$" and small $\frac{3}{8}$") for installing end pins and enlarging holes
- Ball-bearing router bits for template routing
- Routing templates for pickups, tremolos, etc.
- Precision straightedges—6", 12",18", 24", and 30", for testing fingerboard flatness, nut-to-bridge layout, etc. (I designed a set for Stew-Mac that has the works)
- Razor saws for cutting nut slots, fret slots, and all sorts of finely detailed work
- File cleaner to clean the teeth of clogged wood and metal
- Bending iron for curving wood, patching sides, etc.
- Scriber
- Inspection light
- Small brass spokeshaves for shaping wood (especially helpful for carving necks and bridges)
- Vise with padded jaws large enough to clamp a neck from side to side
- Workbenches—the more the merrier
- Glues of all types, stains, finishing materials, etc.

The following 13 varieties of clamps enable a shop to perform all sorts of repairs and building operations. They're used in neck resetting, as well as for gluing cracked sides, headstocks, bridges, and braces.

- Jorgensen pipe clamps for heavy gluing

8	6" Jorgensen bar clamps—the basic woodworking clamps for everything
4	12" Jorgensen bar clamps
8	4" C-clamps
12	2" C-clamps
4	6" Ibex cast-aluminum bridge clamps
6	7" Waverly or Herco bridge clamps
4	9" Waverly or Herco bridge clamps
4	5" Waverly soundhole/bridge clamps
4	$7\frac{1}{2}$" cam clamps
4	$4\frac{1}{2}$" cam clamps
18	small spool clamps
18	large spool clamps
18	small spring clamps

That's a good basic list of the tools a well-equipped shop should have. I'm sure I haven't listed everything—the most obvious omission being stationary power tools. Some shops have everything from thickness planers and sanders to vertical milling machines, and are equipped to manufacture almost anything. It isn't a must for a good repair shop to have that many power tools, but all of us dream of owning practically every tool there is. The three main stationary tools seen in most repair shops are a belt sander, a bandsaw, and a drill press. With those power tools and access to a local cabinet or millwork shop for an occasional wood-dimensioning task, any instrument can be built or repaired.

Some tools found in a repair shop are common ones that the average homeowner or hobbyist might own; others are extremely specialized, such as the fretting tools seen in the photo, which shows a Luthier's Mercantile fret-slotting jig, surrounded by a variety of fret tools from Stewart-MacDonald, including a Fret bender, brass-faced hammer, nippers, slotting saw, and an assortment of crowning files. Repairmen often customize existing tools, too, especially files (the Fret Work chapter covers making your own fret-dressing files from hardware store items).

For common hardware-type tools, it's hard to beat shopping through the *Sears Power And Hand Tool Catalog.* Specialty tools that you won't find at Sears or the corner hardware store are available from several woodworking and luthier supply firms. Here is a list of tools, wood, and parts suppliers that can help you set up and maintain a guitar shop, followed by a list of manufacturers that you may need to call on from time to time during the course of your work.

Lutherie suppliers

Allparts
Box 1318, Katy, TX 77492

Buck's Musical Instrument Products
40 Sand Rd., New Britain, PA 18901

Chandler Industries
5901 9th St., San Francisco, CA 94107

Euphonon Co.
Orford, NH 03777

Harbor Freight Salvage Co.
3491 Mission Oaks Blvd., Camarillo, CA 93011-6010

International Luthiers Supply
Box 580397, Tulsa, OK 74158

International Violin Co.
4026 W. Belvedere Ave., Baltimore, MD 21215

The Luthierie
2449 W. Saugerties Rd., Saugerties, NY 12477

Luthier's Mercantile
Box 774, 412 Moore Lane, Healdsburg, CA 95448

Stewart-MacDonald's Guitar Shop Supply
21 N. Shafer, Athens, OH 45701

Warmoth Guitar Products
6424 112th E., Puyallup, WA 98373

WD Music Products, Inc.
261-D Suburban Ave., Deer Park, NY 11729

Woodcraft Supply
210 Wood County Industrial Park, Box 1686, Parkersburg, WV 26102-1686

Woodworker's Dream
10 W. North St., Box 329, Nazareth, PA 18064

Manufacturers

Acoustech
1302 E. 19th, Lawrence, KS 66044

Alembic
45 Foley St., Santa Rosa, CA 95401

L.R. Baggs
1049 Saratoga Ave., Grover City, CA 93433

Barcus-Berry
5381 Production Dr., Huntington Beach, CA 92649

Bartolini
2133 Research Dr., #16, Livermore, CA 94550

B.B.E. Sound
5500 Bolsa Ave., Suite #245, Huntington Beach, CA 92649

Calliope & Co. (Michael Dresdner)
217 S. Fifth St., Perkasie, PA 18944

D'Addario
210 Rte. 109, Box J, East Farmingdale, NY 11735

DiMarzio
1388 Richmond Terr., Staten Island, NY 10310

Donnell Enterprises
624B Shasta St., Yuba City, CA 95991

Dunlop
Box 846, Benicia, CA 94510

Jeffrey R. Elliot / Luthier
2812 SE 37th Ave., Portland, OR 97202

Erlewine Guitars
3004 Guadalupe St., #7, Austin, TX 78705

Everly Guitars (Robert Steinegger)
Box 25334, Portland OR, 97225

Fender
1130 Columbia, Brea, CA 92621

Fishman Transducers
5 Green St., Woburn, MA 01801

Floyd Rose (c/o Kramer)
685 Neptune Blvd., Neptune, NJ 07753

Fred Gretsch Enterprises
Box 358, Ridgeland, SC 29936

Gibson
Box 100087, Nashville, TN 37210

Guild
2550 S. 17th St., New Berlin, WI 53159

Ibanez
Box 886, Bensalem, PA 19020

Jackson Guitars
4452 Airport Dr., Ontario, CA 91761

Kahler (APM)
Box 9305, Anaheim, CA 92802

Kamimoto String Instruments
836 St. Lucia Ct., San Jose, CA 95127

Ken Smith Basses
37 W. 20th St., Ste. 603, New York, NY 10011

Klein Custom Guitars
2560 Knob Hill Rd., Sonama, CA 95476

Kramer
685 Neptune Blvd., Neptune, NJ 07753

Lacey Guitars (Mark Lacey's Guitar Garage)
1507 N. Gardner St., Hollywood, CA 90046

Larrivee Guitars, Ltd.
267 E. 1st St., North Vancouver, British Columbia, Canada V7L1B4

Lost Mountain Editions, LTD (Richard Schneider—Classicals)
754 Lost Mountain Rd., Sequim, WA 98382

C.F. Martin & Co.
510 Sycamore St., Nazareth, PA 18064

Metal Tech Custom Guitar Hardware
422 W. Julian St., San Jose, CA 95110

Ontek
Box 14884, Minneapolis, MN 55414

Ovation
Box 507, Bloomfield, CT 06002

Peavey Electronics
711 A Street, Meridian, MS 39301

Pedulla Guitars
Box 226, Rockland, MA 02370

Pensa-Suhr Guitars
c/o Rudy's Music Shop
169 W. 48th St., New York, NY 10036

PRS Guitars
1812 Virginia Ave., Annapolis, MD 21401

Pyramid Guitars
1985 Madison Ave., Suite 3, Memphis, TN 38104

Rickenbacker
3895 S. Main, Santa Ana, CA 92707

Roger Sadowsky
1600 Broadway, #1000B, New York, NY 10019-7413

Santa Cruz Guitar Company
Box 242, Santa Cruz, CA 95061

Seymour Duncan
601 Pine Ave., Santa Barbara, CA 93117

Shadow Of America Electronics
Box 1083, Mountainside, NJ 07092

Sperzel Guitar Tuning
Machine Specialists
7810 Lake Ave., Cleveland, OH 44102

Starr Switch Co.
1717 Fifth Ave., San Diego, CA 92101

Stringfellow Studios (William Cumpiano)
31 Campus Plaza Rd., Hadley, MA 01035

Taylor Guitars
9353 Abraham Way, Santee, CA 92071

Tobias Guitars
3087 North California Street, Burbank, CA 91504

Trev Wilkinson Guitars
4531 E. La Palma, Anaheim, CA 92807

Turner, Rick, c/o Westwood Music
2301 Purdue Ave., West Los Angeles, CA 90064

Twelfth Fret
2402 S.E. Belmont, Portalnd OR 97214

Warmoth Guitar Products
6424 112th E., Puyallup, WA 98373

WD Music Products, Inc.
261-D Suburban Ave., Deer Park, NY 11729

Yamaha
6600 Orange Thorpe, Buena Park, CA 90622

Recommended reading

Here's a list of great books, all of which have been invaluable to me at one time or another. Remember, you only need to find one piece of information that helps make you look good in front of a customer or get the job done, and you've paid for the book several times over. For example, I've used Tom Wheeler's *American Guitars* hundreds of times to find facts about a guitar I'm repairing. I've looked up a vintage amp in R. Aspen Pittman's *The Tube Amp Book* while a customer eager to sell me an amp waited in the other room. Entries marked with an asterisk (*) indicate that the book deals *specifically* with the repair and building trades, and should be considered essential for the serious repairperson. It takes a long time to build a library, so don't be discouraged—just add to your collection as time goes by. If you can only buy *one* book, get Don Teeter's *Acoustic Guitar, Vol. 1.* I also highly recommend subscribing to *The String Instrument Craftsman*—better still, buy all the back issues and go from there!

BOOKS

Ken Achard, *The Fender Guitar*, Bold Strummer.

Ken Achard, *The History And Development Of The American Guitar*, Bold Strummer.

Sam Allen, *Wood Finisher's Handbook*, Sterling.

Craig Anderton, *Electronic Projects For Musicians*, Amsco.

H. Behlen, *Guide To Wood Finishing*, H. Behlen & Bros.

Ian C. Bishop, *The Gibson Guitar From 1950—Vol. I* and *Vol. II*, Bold Strummer.

Donald Brosnac, *Guitar Electronics For Musicians*, Amsco*.

Donald Brosnac, *The Amp Book*, Bold Strummer.

Donald Brosnac, *Scientific Guitar Design*, Bold Strummer.

John Bulli, *Guitar History Vol. II*, Bold Strummer.

Dave Crocker, John Brinkman, and Larry Briggs, *Guitars, Guitars, Guitars*, All American Music.

William Cumpiano and Jon Natelson, *Guitar Making: Tradition And Technology*, Rosewood Press*.

A. R. Duchossoir, *The Fender Stratocaster 1954-1984*, Hal Leonard*.

A. R. Duchossoir, *Guitar Identification*, Hal Leonard.

A. R. Duchossoir, *Gibson Electrics*, Hal Leonard.

Tom and Mary Anne Evans, *Guitars—Music, History, Construction, And Players*, Facts On File.

Pieter Fillet, *Do-It-Yourself Guitar Repair*, Amsco*.

Bill Foley, *Build Your Own Electric Guitar*, German Village Music Haus*.

Guitar History, Vol. I, Bold Strummer.

Melvyn Hiscock, *Make Your Own Electric Guitar*, Blandford Press*.

Bruce Hoadley, *Understanding Wood*, Taunton Press.

Franz Jahnel, *Manual Of Guitar Technology*, Verlag Das Musikinstrument.

Hideo Kamimoto, *Complete Guitar Repair*, Oak*.

Adrian Legg, *Customizing Your Electric Guitar*, Amsco*.

Mike Longworth, *Martin Guitars—A History*, 4 Maples Press*.

Tim Olsen and Cyndy Burton, *Lutherie Tools*, Guild Of American Luthiers*.

R. Aspen Pittman, *The Tube Amp Book*, Pittman.

Roger Siminoff, *Constructing A Solid-Body Guitar*, Hal Leonard.

Irving Sloane, *Guitar Repair*, Bold Strummer*.

Irving Sloane, *Classic Guitar Construction*, Bold Strummer.

Richard R. Smith, *The Complete History Of Rickenbacker Guitars*, Centerstream.

Patrick Spielman, *Router Jigs And Techniques*, Sterling.

Don Teeter, *The Acoustic Guitar, Vol. 1* and *Vol. 2*, Oklahoma Press*.

Akira Tsumura, *Guitars—The Tsumura Collection*, Kodansha International.

Adrian Walker, *The Encyclopedia Of Wood*, Facts On File.

Tom Wheeler, *American Guitars: An Illustrated History*, Harper & Row.

Tom Wheeler, *The Guitar Book: A Handbook for Electric and Acoustic Guitarists*, Harper & Row.

David Russell Young, *The Steel-String Guitar: Construction And Repair*, Bold Strummer*.

Ed Zwaan, *Animal Magnetism For Musicians*, Bold Strummer.

MAGAZINES

Acoustic Guitar, String Letter Corp., 412 Red Hill Avenue, #15, San Anselmo, CA 94960

Bass Player, Box 57324, Boulder, CO 80322-7324

Fine Woodworking, Taunton Press, Box 5506, Newtown, CT 06470-5506

Guitar For The Practicing Musician, Box 2078, Knoxville, IA 50198-7078

Guitar Player, Box 58590, Boulder, CO 80322-8590

Guitar World, 1115 Broadway, New York, NY 10010

The String Instrument Craftsman, Pen/Lens Press, 142 N. Milpitas Blvd., Suite 280, Milpitas, CA 95035

VIDEOS

I've produced 15 how-to videotapes for Stewart-MacDonald, covering everything from fret dressing and nut making to installing tremolos, pearl inlaying, and spraying a finish.

Organizations

I belong to both of these organizations, and I wouldn't trade the times I've had at our conventions for 10 NAMM shows, Leo Fender's autograph, or a jam with B. B. King. Both the GAL and ASIA are made up of people like us, so if you get seriously into guitar repair or building, join up!

Association of Stringed Instrument Artisans (ASIA)
14 S. Broad St., Nazareth, PA 18064 (publishes a quarterly journal and conducts Symposium, a semi-annual national convention).

Guild of American Luthiers (GAL)
8222 S. Park Ave., Tacoma, WA 98408 (publishes data sheets and a quarterly journal, and conducts the semi-annual national GAL convention).

Schools for guitar repair and building

Apprentice Shop
Box 267, Spring Hill, TN 37174

Bryan Galloup's Guitar Hospital
10495 Northland Dr., Big Rapids, MI 49307

Red Wing Area Vocational Technical Institute
Pioneer Rd. at Hwy. 58, Red Wing, MN 55066

Renton Vocational Technical Institute
3000 N.E. 4th St., Renton, WA 98056

Roberto-Venn School of Luthiery
4011 S. 16th St., Phoenix, AZ 85040

Timeless Instruments
Box 51, 341 Bison Street, Tugaske, Saskatchewan, Canada S0H 4B0

Lost Mountain Seminar for the Guitar (Richard Schneider)
Contact: Eric Hoeltzel, Box 44, Carlsborg, WA 98324

Vintage dealers

If you're into the vintage scene, I recommend three magazines: *Vintage Guitar*, Box 7301, Bismarck, ND 58502, *20th Century Guitar*, 135 Oser Ave., Hauppauge, NY 11788, and the *Guitar Digest*, Box 1252, Athens, OH 45701.

Here's a list of just *some* of the more well-known vintage dealers—I could never include them all! Many of the dealers operate professional repair services and are also factory-authorized warranty repairmen for major manufacturers. Matt Umanov advises:

"Stores with long-standing and well-respected repair departments on the premises are often a good bet, as they can back up the condition and authenticity of their merchandise with information derived from hands-on experience. They can also provide expert service when necessary." George Gruhn, another "old timer" in the vintage business, cautions: "As a vintage dealer, one of the greatest problems I encounter is bad repairs done by owners or amateur repair people. It's much easier to work on an instrument with warps or cracks or other such problems that have never been previously repaired than to try to undo poor work. In the case of vintage instruments, it is often important to know what not to do!"

Airline Vintage Guitars
5601 Airline Rd., Houston, TX 77076
(713) 694-8922

American Guitar Center
11264 Triangle Lane, Wheaton, MD 20902
(301) 946-3043

Angela Instruments
9584 Washington Blvd., Laurel, MD 20707
(301) 725-0451

Bernunzio Vintage Instruments
1738 Penfield Rd., Penfield, NY 14526
(716) 385-1800

Steve Brown
225 Stanford Ave., Schenectady, NY 12304
(518) 370-2164

Charley's Guitar Shop
11389 Harry Hines Blvd., Dallas, TX 75229
(214) 243-4187

Chris' Guitars
5116 Landershim Blvd., N. Hollywood, CA 91601 (818) 762-3026

City Lights
139 Easton Ave., New Brunswick, NJ 08901
(201) 846-3330

Dave's Guitar Shop
343 Causeway Blvd., La Crosse, WI 54603
(608) 785-7704

Herb David Guitar Studio
302 E. Liberty, Ann Arbor, MI 48104
(313) 665-8001

Dixie Guitars
560 Windy Hill Rd., Suite F, Smyrna, GA 30080 (404) 436-6642

Donel Music (David Stutzman)
4405 Ridge Rd. West, Rochester, NY 14626
(716) 352-3225

Elderly Instruments
1100 N. Washington, Lansing, MI 48901
(517) 372-7890

Erlewine Guitars
3004 Guadalupe St. #7, Austin, TX 78705
(512) 472-4859

Eugene's Guitars Plus
906 W. Jefferson, Dallas, TX 75208
(214) 942-7587

Fly By Nite Music
425 Fairground Rd., Neosho, MO 64850
(417) 451-5110

Fretted Instrument Workshop
49 S. Pleasant St., Amherst, MA 01002
(413) 256-6217

Fret & Fiddle
809 Pennsylvania Ave., St. Albans, WV 25177
(304) 722-5212

Fretware Guitars
4523 N. Miami St., Dayton, OH 45405
(513) 275-7771

Gordy's Music
23263 Woodward, Ferndale, MI 48220
(313) 546-SHIP

Gruhn Guitars
410 Broadway, Nashville, TN 37203
(615) 256-2033

Gryphon Stringed Instruments
211 Lambert Ave., Palo Alto, CA 94306
(415) 493-2131

Guitar Broker
3685 Davie Blvd., Ft. Lauderdale, FL 33312
(305)321-078

Guitar Hospital
10495 Northland Dr., Big Rapids, MI 49307
(616) 796-5611

Guitar Network
27 S. Market St., Frederick, MD 21701
(301) 694-3231

Guitar Emporium
1019 Bardstown Rd., Louisville, KY 40204
(502) 459-4153

Guitars, Etc.
1306 Old Leechburg Rd., Pittsburgh,
PA 15239 (412) 795-8668

Guitar Maniacs
1544 S. Fawcett, Tacoma, WA 98402
(206) 272-4741

Guitars West
10273 Canyon Dr., Escondido, CA 92026
(619) 489-8760

Honest Ron's Guitars
1129 N. May Ave., Oklahoma City, OK 73107
(405) 947-3683

Intermountain Guitar & Banjo
712 East 100 South, Salt Lake City, UT 84102
(801) 322-4682

Tim Kummer
51 Harbor Green Ct., Red Bank, NJ 07701
(201) 741-2843

Lark Street Music
227 Lark St., Albany, NY 12210
(518) 463-6033

Bernard E. Lehmann
34 Elton St., Rochester, NY 14607
(716) 471-2117

Lone Wolf Guitars
1017 S.W. 31st St. Oklahoma City,
OK 73019 (405) 634-2088

Jon Lundberg
2126 Dwight Way, Berkeley, CA 94710
(415) 848-6519

Mandolin Brothers
629 Forest Ave., Staten Island, NY 10310
(718) 981-8585

Midwest Guitar Exchange
505 Main St., Maple Park, IL 60151
(815) 827-3233

MusicMan
87 Tillinghaft Ave., W. Warwick, RI 02893
(401) 821-2865

Willie Moseley
1200 Woodbridge Dr., Suite D, Montgomery,
AL 36116-3520 (205) 284-1140

Music Emporium
2018 Mass Ave., Cambridge, MA 02140
(617) 661-2099

New York String Service (Steve Uhrik)
233 Butler St., Brooklyn, NY 11217
(800) 333-5589

Norm's Rare Guitars
6753 Tampa Blvd., Reseda, CA 91335
(818) 344-8300

Rainbow Music
Poughkeepsie Plaza Rt. 9, Poughkeepsie,
NY 12601 (914) 452-1900

Resophonic Guitars (Barbara Sinclair)
Box 2104, Costa Mesa, CA 92628
(714) 545-5172

Rockin' Robin Guitars
3619 Shepherd, Houston, TX 77098
(713) 529-5442

David Sheppard Instruments
1820 Spring Garden St., Greensboro,
NC 27403 (919) 274-2395

Marc Silber c/o The Musical Dunce
Box 9663, Berkeley, CA 94709
(415) 843-2883

Silver Strings
8427 Olive Blvd., St. Louis, MO 63132
(314) 997-1120

Soest Guitars
870 N. Eckhoff, Orange, CA 92668
(714) 538-0272

Somewhere In Iowa Guitars
1419 Daniels St. NE, Cedar Rapids, IA 52402
(319) 362-7600

Sound Southwest
2611 N. Belt Line Rd., Sunnyvale, TX 75182
(214) 226-3069

Southworth Guitars
4816 MacArthur Blvd., Washington
DC 20007 (202) 333-0124

Stringfellow Studios (William Cumpiano)
31 Campus Plaza Rd., Hadley, MA 01035
(413) 253-2286

Strings West
1305 S. Peoria, Tulsa, OK 74120
(918) 582-3535

Joe Summers
1705 N. Huron River Dr., Ypsilanti, MI 48197
(313) 482-1321

Third Eye Music
1904-A E. Meadowmere, Springfield,
MO 65804 (417) 862-5823

The Twelfth Fret
2402 S.E. Belmont, Portland, OR 97214
(503) 231-1912

Matt Umanov Guitars
273 Bleecker St., New York, NY 10014
(212) 675-2157

Tom Van Hoose
1509 Main St. #801, Dallas, TX 75201
(214) 760-8627

Vintage Fret Shop
20 Riverside Dr., Ashland, NH 03217
(603) 968-3346

Vintage Instruments (Fred Oster)
1529 Pine St., Philadelphia, PA 19102
(215) 545-1100

Voltage Guitars
1513 N. Gardner St., Hollywood, CA 90046
(213) 851-1406

Waco Vintage
Box 3413, Waco, TX 76707
(817) 772-1272

Waldo's Music
7406 Sunset Blvd., Hollywood, CA 90046
(213) 851-7129

Washington Street Music
Box 3231 Soquel, CA 95073
(408) 427-1429

Jim Werner
(collects Fender serial numbers)
R.R. 1, Letts, Iowa 52754

Harry & Jeanie West
3815 Tremont Drive, Durham, NC 27705
(919) 383-5750

Index